COMPUTING

P.M. Heathcote B.Sc. (Hons), M.Sc.

FIRST INDIAN EDITION 2003

Distributors:

MICRO BOOK CENTRE
2, City Centre, CG Road,
Near Swastic Char Rasta,
AHMEDABAD-380009 Phone: 6421611

COMPUTER BOOK CENTRE
12, Shrungar Shopping Centre, M.G. Road,
BANGALORE-560001 Phone: 5587923, 5584641

MICRO BOOKS
Shanti Niketan Building, 8, Camac Street,
KOLKATTA-700017 Phone: 2826518, 2826519

BUSINESS PROMOTION BUREAU
8/1, Ritchie Street, Mount Road,
CHENNAI-600002 Phone: 8534796, 8550491

DECCAN AGENCIES
4-3-329, Bank Street,
HYDERABAD-400001 Phone: 4756400, 4756967

MICRO MEDIA
Shop No. 5, Mahendra Chambers, 150 D.N. Road,
Next to Capital Cinema V.T. (C.S.T.) Station,
MUMBAI-400001 Ph.: 22078296, 22078297, 22002732

BPB PUBLICATIONS
B-14, Connaught Place, **NEW DELHI-110001**
Phone: 3325760, 3723393, 3737742

INFO TECH
G-2, Sidhartha Building, 96 Nehru Place,
NEW DELHI-110019
Phone: 6438245, 6415092, 6234208

INFO TECH
Shop No. 2, F-38, South Extension Part-1
NEW DELHI-110049
Phone: 4691288, 4641941

INFO TECH
B-11, Vardhman Plaza, Sector-16,
Electronics Nagar, **NOIDA-201301**
Phone: 914-512329, 515917, 515918

BPB BOOK CENTRE
376, Old Lajpat Rai Market,
DELHI-110006 PHONE: 3861747

Original ISBN - 1-903112-21-4
Copyright © 2002 Payne-Gallway Publishing
First Edition

    All rights reserved. No part of this book shall be reproduced, stored in a retrieval system, or transmitted by any means, electronic, mechanical, photocopying, recording, or otherwise, without written permission from the publisher except fo rthe inclusion of brief quotation in a review.

    All terms mentioned in this book that are known to be trademarks or service marks have been appropriately capitalized. Payne-Gallway Publishing/BPB cannot attest to the accuracy of this information. Use of a term in this book should not be regarded as affecting the validity of any trademark or service mark.

This edition is Authorized for sale in **INDIAN SUBCONTINENT ONLY**.

Printed in India by arrangement with
Payne-Gallway Publishing, U.K.

Price : Rs. 150/-

ISBN 81-7656-696-9
Published by Manish Jain for BPB Publications, B-14, Connaught Place
New Delhi-110 001 and Printed by him at Pressworks, Delhi.

Preface

The aim of this book is to provide a comprehensive yet concise textbook covering all the topics studied for an Advanced Level course in Computing.

The book is divided into 5 sections covering all the material for each paper in a modular scheme such as that offered by the Assessment and Qualifications Alliance (AQA). Within a section, each chapter covers material that can comfortably be taught in one or two lessons, and the chapters are sequenced in such a way that practical sessions can be based around the theory covered in the classroom.

Sections 1 to 3 cover all the requirements of the AQA AS specification, with the remaining sections being studied in the second year.

Each chapter contains exercises and questions from past examination papers, so that the student can gain plenty of experience in 'exam technique'.

For Teachers only

Answers to all the questions are available, to teachers only, in a separate Teacher's Supplement which can be downloaded from our web site www.payne-gallway.co.uk

Contents

Module 1
Computer Systems, Programming and Network Concepts   1

Module 2
Principles of Hardware, Software and Applications   95

Module 3
Practical Systems Development   173

Module 4
Processing and Programming Techniques   191

Module 5
Advanced Systems Development   281

Appendix A   359

Index   377

Table of Contents

MODULE 1
Computer Systems, Programming and Network Concepts — 1

Chapter 1 – Computer Hardware — 2
- Introduction — 2
- Computer systems — 2
- The components of a computer — 2
- Types of computer — 3
- The processor — 3
- Main memory — 3
- RAM and ROM — 4
- Cache memory — 4
- Disk storage — 4
- Input and output devices — 6
- Embedded computers and special-purpose computers — 6

Chapter 2 – Classification of Software — 8
- Categorising software — 8
- Systems software — 8
- Applications software — 9
- General purpose software — 9
- Integrated packages and software suites — 9
- Generic and special purpose software — 10
- Bespoke or off-the-shelf? — 10

Chapter 3 – Bits and Bytes — 12
- The binary system — 12
- Bits and bytes — 12
- The ASCII code — 12
- Representing numbers — 13
- Memory addressing — 14

Chapter 4 – Introduction to Programming — 16
- The earliest computers — 16
- Generations of programming language — 16
- Why use assembly code? — 18
- Types of program translator — 18
- Assembler — 18
- Compiler — 18
- Interpreter — 18
- Relative advantages of compilers and interpreters — 19

Chapter 5 – Introducing Pascal — 20
- Learning to program — 20
- A Pascal program — 20
- The parts of a program — 20
- Comments — 21
- Variable declaration — 21
- The statement part of the program — 21
- Formatting the output — 22

Chapter 6 – Variables, Assignments, Reading and Writing — 23
- Types of data — 23
- Rules for identifiers — 24
- Assignment statements — 24
- Reading in data from a keyboard — 25
- Displaying data on the screen — 25
- Formatting output — 26
- Compound statements and punctuation — 26
- Clearing the screen and positioning the cursor — 26
- Improving the readability of a program — 26
- Using Turbo Pascal's trace and debugging facilities — 27

Chapter 7 – Iteration & Selection — 28
- Looping (also called iteration or repetition) — 28
- The WHILE..DO statement in Pascal — 29
- An introduction to procedures — 29
- Program to calculate the average of a set of marks — 30
- Selection (IF..THEN..ELSE) — 31
- Trace tables — 31
- Program constants — 32

Chapter 8 – Program Design and Maintenance — 35
- Program design aims — 35
- Top-down design — 35
- Jackson structure diagrams — 35
- The building blocks of a structured program — 36
- Representation of a loop — 36
- Representation of selection — 36
- Modular programming — 39
- Advantages of modular programming — 39

Chapter 9 – More on Selection and Iteration — 41
- The CASE statement — 41
- The REPEAT..UNTIL statement — 42
- The FOR statement — 42
- Pseudocode — 42
- Generating random numbers — 44

Chapter 10 – Arrays and Data Types — 46
- Introduction — 46
- Declaring data types — 46
- The Boolean function eoln — 47
- Looking up tables of values — 47
- Multi-dimensional arrays — 48

Chapter 11 – Procedures and Functions — 50
- Program structure — 50
- Procedure and function structure — 50
- Global and local identifiers — 50

Block structure	51
A sample program outline	51
Scope of identifiers	51
Parameters	52
A further example of parameter passing	53
Standard functions	56
User-written functions	56

Chapter 12 – Sequential File Processing   59
Introduction	59
Record declaration	59
Assigning an external name to a file	59
Input and output	60
Accessing fields in a record	60
Writing to the printer	60
A sample program	60

Chapter 13 – Random Access File Processing   63
Introduction	63
The Pascal 'seek' procedure	63
Initialising a random access file	63

Chapter 14 – Queues and Stacks   67
Introduction to data structures	67
Queues	67
Stacks	68
Implementation of a stack	68
Applications of stacks	68
Using stacks to store return addresses	69
Using a stack to reverse the elements of a queue	70
Overflow and Underflow	70

Chapter 15 – Binary Trees   71
Constructing an ordered binary tree	71
Traversing a binary tree	72
Preorder traversal	72
Inorder traversal	72
Postorder traversal	73

Chapter 16 – Data Representation   74
Input-process-output	74
Sources of data	74
Character coding schemes	74
The binary number system	75
Binary Coded Decimal (BCD)	75
Advantages and disadvantages of BCD	76
Boolean values	76
Digitised sound	76
Bit-mapped graphics	77

Chapter 17 – Inside the Computer   79
Introduction	79
Memory and the stored program concept	80
The Processor	80
Buses	80
Control bus	81
Data bus	82
Address bus	82
Word size	82
I/O Controllers	82

Chapter 18 – Communication Methods   84
Principle of electronic data communication	84
Serial and parallel data communication	84
Transmission rate	84
Parity	85
Synchronous and asynchronous transmission	85
Handshaking	86
Modems	86
ISDN lines	86
Data compression	86
Protocol	86
Factors affecting rate of data transmission	87

Chapter 19 – Network Environments   88
Communications networks	88
Advantages and disadvantages of networks	88
Network topologies	88
Star network	88
Advantages of a star network	89
Disadvantage of star network	89
Bus network	89
Ring network	90

Chapter 20 – Wide Area Networks   91
Wide Area Network (WAN)	91
Communications media	91
Communications links	91
The Internet	92
Uniform Resource Locator (URL)	93
Domain names	93
IP addresses	94
Intranets	94

MODULE 2
Principles of Hardware, Software and Applications   95

Chapter 21 – Information Processing Applications   96
Computing – a look backwards	96
Computers and employment	96
The changing nature of employment	96
Teleworking	97
Benefits of teleworking	97
The problems of teleworking	98
Case study: Socket to 'em now	98
Changing locations of work	98
Consequences of computer failure	99

Chapter 22 – Computer Crime and the Law — 101
- Computer crime and abuse — 101
- Hacking — 101
- Theft of data — 101
- Viruses — 102
- 'Logic bombs' — 102
- Digital crime and the law — 102
- The Computer Misuse Act of 1990 — 103
- Case study 1 — 103
- Software copyright laws — 103
- Case study 2 — 105
- Using computers to combat crime — 105

Chapter 23 – Privacy and Data Protection Legislation — 106
- Personal privacy — 106
- Case study: James Wiggins – a true story — 106
- The Data Protection Act — 106
- The Data Protection Principles — 106
- Useful definitions from the 1984 Act — 107
- Data Subjects — 107
- The Data Protection Commissioner — 107
- A data user's Register entry — 108
- Exemptions from the Act — 108
- The rights of data subjects — 109
- Encryption technology — 109
- E-mails and privacy issues — 109

Chapter 24 – Health and Safety — 111
- Computers and health — 111
- Stress — 111
- Case study: Information overload — 112
- Repetitive strain injury (RSI) — 112
- Case study: Bank staff 'driven to injury' — 113
- Eyestrain — 113
- Extremely low frequency (ELF) radiation — 114
- Computers, Health and the law — 114
- The ergonomic environment — 115
- Software can be hazardous to your health — 115

Chapter 25 – General Purpose Packages — 116
- Word processing software — 116
- Desktop publishing — 116
- Spreadsheets — 118
- Spreadsheet features — 118
- Electronic mail (e-mail) — 119
- Presentation graphics software — 120
- Integrated packages — 121
- Databases — 121

Chapter 26 – Records and Files — 123
- Hierarchy of data — 123
- Text and non-text files — 124
- Primary key — 124
- Secondary key — 124
- Fixed and variable length records — 124
- Advantages and disadvantages of variable length records — 125
- Estimating file size — 125

Chapter 27 – File Organisation — 126
- Master and transaction files — 126
- File organisation — 126
- Types of file organisation — 126
- Serial file organisation — 127
- Sequential file organisation — 127
- Adding and deleting records on a serial file — 127
- Adding and deleting records on a sequential file — 128
- Merging two sequential files — 128
- Random files — 129
- Synonyms — 129
- Properties of a good hashing algorithm — 130
- Adding and deleting records from a random file — 130
- Indexed sequential files — 130

Chapter 28 – File Processing — 131
- The role of various files in a computer system — 131
- Operations on files — 131
- Interrogating or referencing files — 131
- Updating files — 132
- Updating by overlay — 133
- File maintenance — 133
- File access methods — 133
- Criteria for use of sequential and direct access files — 134
- Hit rate — 134
- Use of serial files — 134
- Use of sequential files — 134
- Use of indexed sequential files — 134
- Use of random files — 135

Chapter 29 – File Security Methods — 136
- Threats to information systems — 136
- Data security — 136
- Keeping data secure from fraudulent use or malicious damage — 136
- Password protection — 137
- User IDs and passwords — 137
- Communications security — 137
- Data encryption — 137
- Access rights — 138
- Biometric security measures — 139
- Case study: Iris recognition technology — 139
- Disaster planning — 139
- Periodic backups — 139
- Recovery procedures — 139

Chapter 30 – Data Processing Integrity Methods — 141
- Data integrity — 141
- Standard clerical procedures — 141

Data entry methods	141
Types of input error	142
Batch processing	143
Validation checks	143
Check digits	144
Verification	144
Detecting transmission errors	144
Protection against viruses	145
Write-protecting disks	145

Chapter 31 – Entity-Relationship Modelling 146
The conceptual data model	146
Types of relationship	146
Entity-relationship diagrams	146

Chapter 32 – Database Concepts 149
Traditional file approach	149
The database approach	149
Validation of input data	149
Relational database design	150
Primary and secondary keys	150
Indexing	150
Linking database tables	151
Querying a database	151

Chapter 33 – Operating Systems 153
What is an operating system?	153
Functions of an operating system	153
Multi-programming	153
Provision of a virtual machine	154
Batch	154
Interactive	154
Real-Time	155
Network	155
File Management	155
Drives, folders and files	155
Pathnames	156
Access rights and other attributes	156
Backing up and archiving	157

Chapter 34 – Input Devices 159
Keyboard data entry	159
Voice data entry	159
Scanners and OCR	159
Case study: Automating college enrolment	160
Key-to-disk systems	160
Mouse, joystick, light pen, touch screen	161
Magnetic Ink Character Recognition (MICR)	161
Magnetic stripe	161
Smart cards	161
Optical Mark Recognition (OMR)	162
Bar code reader or scanner	162
Hand-held input devices	163
Digitiser (Graphics tablet)	163

Chapter 35 – Output Devices 165
Printers	165
Dot matrix printer	165
Ink jet printers	166
Laser printers	166
Plotters	167
Visual display unit (VDU)	167

Chapter 36 – Storage Devices 169
Primary and secondary storage	169
File processing concepts	169
Floppy disks	170
How data is stored	170
Hard disks for microcomputers	170
Hard disks for minis and mainframes	170
Magnetic tape	171
Uses of magnetic tape	171
CD-ROM	172
WORM disks	172
Magneto-optical disks	172

MODULE 3
System Development 173

Chapter 37 – The Classical Systems Life-Cycle 174
Overview of the systems life cycle	174
The waterfall model	175
What prompts a new system?	176
Feasibility study	176
Analysis/Requirements analysis	177
Data flow diagram (DFD)	177

Chapter 38 – From Design to Evaluation 180
System design	180
System specification	180
Program design methods	180
Prototyping	180
Choosing a software solution	181
Testing strategies	181
Test plan and test data	181
Technical documentation	181
Contents of a documented system	182
Implementation	182
Evaluation	182
System maintenance	182

Chapter 39 – Human Computer Interface 184
Introduction	184
The importance of good interface design	184
Designing usable systems	184
Interface styles	185
Command-line interface	185
Menus	185
Natural language	186
Advantages and disadvantages of natural language dialogue	186

Forms and dialogue boxes	187
The WIMP interface	188
Advantages of a common user interface	188
Speech input (voice recognition)	188
Speech/sound output	189

MODULE 4
Processing and Programming Techniques — 191

Chapter 40 – Structure and Role of the Processor — 192
Inside the CPU	192
The steps in the fetch-execute cycle	193
How the CPU registers are used	194
The stack pointer	194
Recap: the accumulator and general purpose registers	195
Interrupts	195
Types of interrupt	195
Interrupt priorities	195
The interrupt handler	196
The vectored interrupt mechanism	196
Processor performance	196
Clock speed	197
Word size	197
Bus size	197

Chapter 41 – Number Bases and Representation — 199
The denary number system	199
The binary and hexadecimal number systems	199
Denary to binary and hexadecimal	200
Translating back to denary	200
Representation of negative numbers using twos complement	201
Converting a negative denary number to binary	201
Binary subtraction	202

Chapter 42 – Floating Point Numbers — 203
Fixed point binary numbers	203
Floating point binary	204
Normalisation	204
Negative floating point numbers	205

Chapter 43 – Assembly Language Instructions — 206
The instruction set	206
Data transfer instructions	206
Arithmetic instructions	206
Carry and overflow	207
Shift instructions	208
Logical instructions	208
Conditional branches	209
Unconditional branches	210

Chapter 44 – Instruction Formats and Addressing Modes — 211
Instruction format for an 8-bit microprocessor	211
Zero address instructions	211
One address instructions	211
Two address instructions	211
A 16-bit instruction format	212
Addressing modes	212

Chapter 45 – High Level Languages — 215
High and low level languages	215
Typical high level language facilities	215
Procedural (imperative) languages	216
Object-oriented languages	216
Declarative languages	216
Languages for real-time embedded systems	217
Criteria for selecting a programming language	217

Chapter 46 – Object-Oriented Programming — 218
Windows applications	218
Objects and classes	218
Objects in Windows	219
Encapsulation	219
Inheritance	220
Polymorphism	221
Containment	222

Chapter 47 – Prolog Programming (1) — 223
Procedural and declarative languages	223
Prolog	223
A Prolog program	224
Practical Prolog	225
Using facts in Prolog	226
Entering items in a Prolog database	226
Entering rules	227
Creating a permanent Prolog database	228

Chapter 48 – Prolog programming (2) — 229
Listing a Prolog program	231

Chapter 49 – Recursion — 235
Recursive procedures and stacks	235
Another example of recursion	236
Advantages and disadvantages of recursion	237

Chapter 50 – Lists — 239
Definition of a list in Prolog	239
Manipulating lists	239
Writing out a list	240
Operations on a list	240
A recursive procedure to print a list	241
Implementation of a list using an array	241
Retrieving and deleting an item from a list	242

Chapter 51 – Linked Lists — 244
- Definition — 244
- Operations on linked lists — 244
- Management of free space — 246
- Inserting an item — 246
- Deleting an item — 248
- Pseudocode for deleting an item from a linked list — 250
- Printing out all the names in a linked list — 250
- Use of free memory, heap and pointers — 250
- Pointer variables — 251
- Getting and returning memory locations dynamically — 251

Chapter 52 – Queues and Stacks — 253
- Definition of a queue — 253
- Procedures to implement a circular queue — 253
- Implementing a queue as a linked list — 254
- Uses of Queues — 254
- Stacks — 255
- Uses of Stacks — 255

Chapter 53 – Trees — 257
- Definition — 257
- Implementation of trees using arrays — 258
- A recursive algorithm for an inorder tree traversal — 258
- Preorder tree traversal — 259
- Postorder tree traversal — 259
- Recursion — 259
- Summary — 259

Chapter 54 – Searching and Sorting — 262
- Linear search — 262
- Binary search — 262
- Bubble sort — 263
- Quicksort — 263
- Insertion sort — 264
- Choice of sorting method — 264

Chapter 55 – Operating System Classification — 267
- The operating system — 267
- Loading an operating system — 267
- Modes of operation — 267
- Single-user single-process — 267
- Multi-programming — 267
- Multi-user — 268
- Multi-tasking — 268
- Batch — 268
- Multi-user and batch — 268
- Real-Time — 268
- Client-server system — 269
- Distributed computer systems — 269

Chapter 56 – Operating System Concepts — 270
- Command line interface — 270
- Job control language — 270
- Graphical user interface — 271
- Operating system functions — 272
- Process states — 272
- The process control block (or process descriptor) — 273
- Interrupt handling — 273
- Types of interrupt — 273
- How the interrupt mechanism works — 274
- Allocating job priorities — 274
- Scheduling objectives — 275
- Round robin scheduling — 275

Chapter 57 – Memory, File and I/O Management — 277
- Virtual memory and paging — 277
- Dynamically linked libraries — 278
- File management — 278
- Blocks and buffers — 279
- Input/Output management — 279
- Device drivers — 279

MODULE 5
Advanced Systems Development — 281

Chapter 58 – Database Concepts — 282
- Traditional file approach — 282
- The database approach — 282
- The Database Management System (DBMS) — 283
- Entity-relationship modelling — 283

Chapter 59 – Database Design and Normalisation — 284
- What is a relational database? — 284
- Linking database tables — 284
- Normalisation — 285
- First normal form — 285
- Second normal form - Partial key dependence test — 287
- Dealing with a Many-to-Many relationship — 288
- Third normal form - Non-key dependence test — 288
- Foreign keys — 288
- Comparing a flat-file system with a relational database — 288

Chapter 60 – Querying a Database — 290
- SQL — 290
- tblSoftware — 290
- SELECT .. FROM .. WHERE — 290
- Conditions — 292
- Specifying a sort order — 293
- GROUP BY — 293
- Extracting data from several tables — 294

Chapter 61 – Database Management and Manipulation — 295
- The three-level architecture of a DBMS — 295
- Data Definition Language (DDL) — 295
- Data Manipulation Language (DML) — 295
- Open systems and ODBC (Open Database Connectivity) — 295
- The Database Management System (DBMS) — 296
- The data dictionary — 296
- The multi-access database — 297
- Ensuring the integrity of a shared database — 297
- Locking — 297
- Deadlock... or 'Deadly embrace' — 298
- Software protection techniques — 298
- Client-server database — 298
- Object-oriented databases — 299

Chapter 62 – Analysing a System — 300
- Systems investigation — 300
- Methods of fact finding — 300
- Reporting techniques — 300
- Data Flow Diagrams — 301
- Levelled DFDs — 301
- Entity Attribute Modelling (EAR) — 303
- Data dictionary — 303
- Volumetrics — 304

Chapter 63 – Systems Design, Development and Testing — 305
- Prototyping — 305
- Systems flowcharts — 305
- Systems flowchart symbols — 306
- User Interface — 307
- User Interface — 308
- Program design — 309
- Development — 309
- Testing strategies — 309
- Program testing — 309

Chapter 64 – Implementation, Evaluation and Maintenance — 311
- Implementation — 311
- Methods of conversion — 311
- Software testing — 312
- Alpha testing — 313
- Beta testing — 313
- Post implementation review (evaluation) — 313
- Software maintenance — 313
- Factors affecting maintainability — 314

Chapter 65 – Training and Documentation — 316
- Introduction — 316
- Installation manual — 316
- Operations manual — 316
- User manual — 316
- Training in the use of information technology — 317
- Training for users — 317

Chapter 66 – Input and Output Methods — 318
- Input and output devices — 318
- How a scanner works — 318
- Touch screens — 318
- Choice of input method — 319

Chapter 67 – Networking — 321
- Wide area networks — 321
- Communications links — 321
- Cabling systems — 321
- Synchronous data transmission — 322
- Time-division multiplexing — 322
- Circuit switching — 322
- Packet switching — 322
- Virtual circuits — 323
- Advantages of packet switching — 323
- Asynchronous Transfer Mode (ATM) — 323
- Standard protocols — 324

Chapter 68 – Local Area Networks — 325
- Network topology — 325
- Bus — 325
- Ring — 326
- Star — 326
- Ethernet — 327
- Segmentation — 327
- Server-based vs peer-to-peer networks — 328

Chapter 69 – Wide Area Networks — 330
- Wide area network (WAN) — 330
- Value-added networks — 330
- Electronic data interchange (EDI) — 330
- Connecting to a wide area network — 331
- Internetworking — 332
- Routers and Gateways — 332

Chapter 70 – The Internet — 334
- Structure of the Internet — 334
- The World Wide Web — 335
- On-line Service Providers — 335
- Usenet newsgroups — 335
- Internet Relay Chat (IRC) — 336
- Videoconferencing — 337
- E-mail — 337
- Advantages of e-mail — 338
- Disadvantages of e-mail — 338

Chapter 71 – The World Wide Web — 339
- The World Wide Web — 339
- Web browsers — 339
- Internet Search Engines — 340
- Java applets — 341
- HTML — 342
- HTML structure — 342
- A sample HTML program — 343

Chapter 72 – On-line Shopping and Banking 345
E-commerce 345
On-line banking 345
Shopping on the Internet 346
Doing business on the Web 346
Advantages to business 347
Advantages to the customers 347
Doing the weekly shopping on-line 348
Registering a domain name 348
Cybersquatting 348

Chapter 73 – Internet Security and Other Issues 350
Internet-based fraud 350
Digital certificates 350
Encryption 351
Strong and weak encryption 351
Factoring 352
Firewall 352
Virus spread and detection 352
Security and the Law 352
Social and cultural issues 353

Chapter 74 – Artificial Intelligence and Expert Systems 354
Definition of artificial intelligence 354
Expert systems 354
Programming the knowledge base 354
Case study: ELSIE the expert system 356
Expert system shells 356
Uses of expert systems 356

Case study: Protecting endangered species 357
And finally… applications of computers 357

Appendix A
Book List 359

AQA Specification Summary 362

Module 1

Computer Systems, Programming and Network Concepts

In this section:

Chapter 1 -	*Computer Hardware*
Chapter 2 -	*Classification of Software*
Chapter 3 -	*Bits and Bytes*
Chapter 4 -	*Introduction to Programming*
Chapter 5 -	*Introducing Pascal*
Chapter 6 -	*Variables, Assignments, Reading and Writing*
Chapter 7 -	*Iteration & Selection*
Chapter 8 -	*Program Design and Maintenance*
Chapter 9 -	*More on Selection and Iteration*
Chapter 10 -	*Arrays and Data Types*
Chapter 11 -	*Procedures and Functions*
Chapter 12 -	*Sequential File Processing*
Chapter 13 -	*Random Access File Processing*
Chapter 14 -	*Queues and Stacks*
Chapter 15 -	*Binary Trees*
Chapter 16 -	*Data Representation*
Chapter 17 -	*Inside the Computer*
Chapter 18 -	*Communication Methods*
Chapter 19 -	*Network Environments*
Chapter 20 -	*Wide Area Networks*

Chapter 1 – Computer Hardware

Introduction

On this course you will be learning about the internal structure of computers, how they operate and how they are used in solving problems. You will also learn the fundamentals of computer programming, and build on your existing knowledge of software packages.

In addition, you will need to develop an awareness of the wider implications for individuals and for society of the increasing use of computers. This is best done by keeping your eyes and ears open, noticing new uses of computers, reading newspapers and magazines which contain computer-related articles, and watching appropriate and relevant television programmes.

This course, with its emphasis on the more technical aspects of computing, including operating systems and programming, is suitable for students who intend to go on to study Computing or Software Engineering at University, or make their career in computing.

Computer systems

A *computer system* consists of *hardware* and *software*. Hardware is the physical machinery – the components that make up the computer. Software consists of the computer programs (sequences of instructions) that tell the computer what to do in response to a command or some event. In this chapter we'll take an introductory look at hardware.

The components of a computer

All computers, whatever their size or function, have certain basic components. They have input devices for reading data into main memory, a central processing unit (CPU) for processing the data, output devices for printing, displaying or outputting information, and auxiliary storage devices for permanent storage of programs and data.

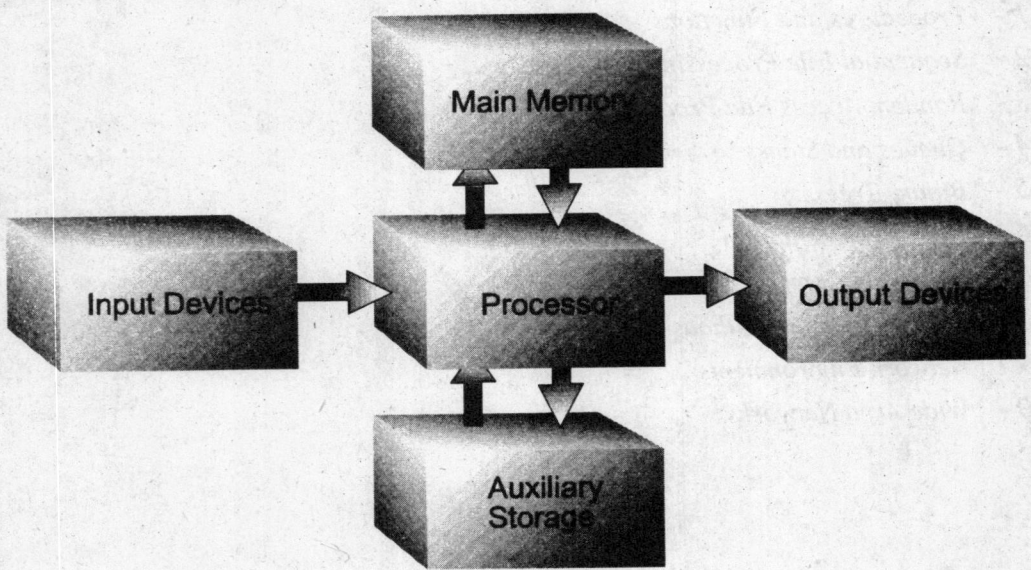

Figure 1.1: Block diagram of a computer system

Types of computer

We are so used to seeing PCs on desktops at home, school, businesses and other organizations that it is easy to forget that there are other types of computer.

Mainframe computers are used by large organisations such as banks, building societies, insurance companies, airlines and government departments. A mainframe may have thousands of terminals attached to it at geographically remote locations, and occupy an entire site with hundreds of disk drives and other hardware units. Frequently, the actual siting of a mainframe computer is kept secret to lessen the danger of a terrorist attack that could cause chaos to an organisation.

Supercomputers are the largest category of computer, costing millions of pounds. They are mostly used by scientific and industrial research departments, government agencies such as NASA, the Weather Centre, Stock Exchanges and by very large commercial organisations.

The processor

The processor has the following functions:
- it controls the transmission of data from input devices to memory;
- it processes the data held in main memory;
- it controls the transmission of information from main memory to output devices.

Most computers use integrated circuits, or chips, for their processors and main memory. A chip is about 1cm square and can hold millions of electronic components such as transistors and resistors. The CPU of a microcomputer is called a **microprocessor**. The processor and main memory of a PC are commonly held on a single board called a mother board.

In 1965 Gordon Moore predicted that the capacity of a computer chip would double every year. He looked at the price/performance ratio of computer chips (the amount of performance available per dollar) over the previous three years and simply projected it forwards. He didn't really believe the rate of improvement would last for long, but in fact to this day chip capacity is still doubling every 18 months or so.

Main memory

Instructions and data are held in main memory, which is divided into millions of individually addressable storage units called **bytes**. One byte can hold one character, or it can be used to hold a code representing, for example, a tiny part of a picture, a sound, or part of a computer program instruction. The total number of bytes in main memory is referred to as the computer's memory size. Computer memory sizes are measured as follows:

1 Kilobyte (Kb)	=	1000 bytes (or to be exact, 1024 bytes)
1 Megabyte (Mb)	=	1,000,000 bytes (more accurately 1,048,576 bytes)
1 Gigabyte (Gb)	=	1,000,000,000 (1 billion) bytes
1 Terabyte (Tb)	=	1,000,000,000,000 (1 trillion) bytes

As with processing power, the amount of memory that comes with a standard PC has increased exponentially over the past 20 years. In about 1980, BBC microcomputers with 32K of memory were bought in their thousands for home and school use. In 1981, Bill Gates of Microsoft made his famous remark "640K ought to be enough for anybody". In 2000, a PC with 64Mb or 128Mb of memory is standard, costing around £1,000 including bundled software.

RAM and ROM

There are basically two kinds of memory; **Random Access Memory (RAM)** which is the ordinary kind of memory referred to above, used for storing programs which are currently running and data which is being processed. This type of memory is **volatile** which means that it loses all its contents as soon as the machine is switched off.

Read Only Memory (ROM) is the other type of memory, and this is non-volatile, with its contents permanently etched into the memory chip at the manufacturing stage. It is used for example to hold the **bootstrap loader**, the program which runs as soon as the computer is switched on and instructs it to load the operating system from disk into memory. In special purpose computers used in video recorders, washing machines and cars, the program instructions are stored in ROM.

Cache memory

Cache memory is a type of very fast memory that is used to improve the speed of a computer, doubling it in some cases. It acts as an intermediate store between the CPU and main memory, and works by storing the most frequently or recently used instructions and data so that it will be very fast to retrieve them again. Thus when an item of data is required, a whole block of data will be read into cache in the expectation that the next piece of data required is likely to be in the same block. The amount of cache memory is generally between 1Kb and 512Kb.

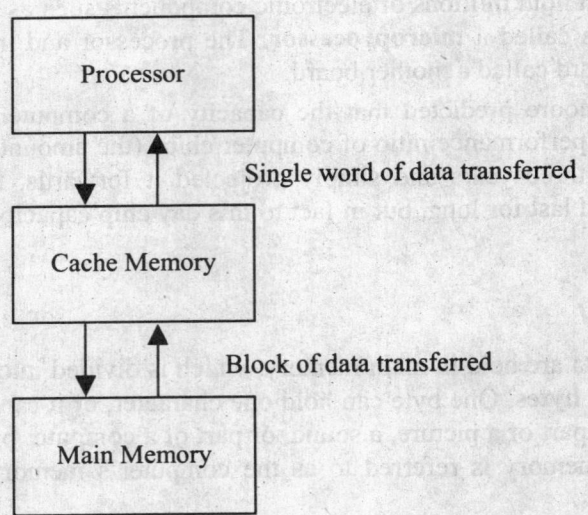

Figure 1.2: How cache memory operates

Disk storage

The most common form of auxiliary storage (also known as **external** or **secondary memory** or **backing store**) is disk. All standalone PCs come equipped with an in-built hard disk, the capacity of which is also measured in bytes. A typical hard disk for a PC stores several gigabytes, and is used for storing software including the operating system, other systems software, application programs and data.

Floppy disks consist of a thin sheet of mylar plastic encased in a hard 3½" casing. The standard type of disk in use today has a capacity of 1.44Mb.

Chapter 1 – Computer Hardware

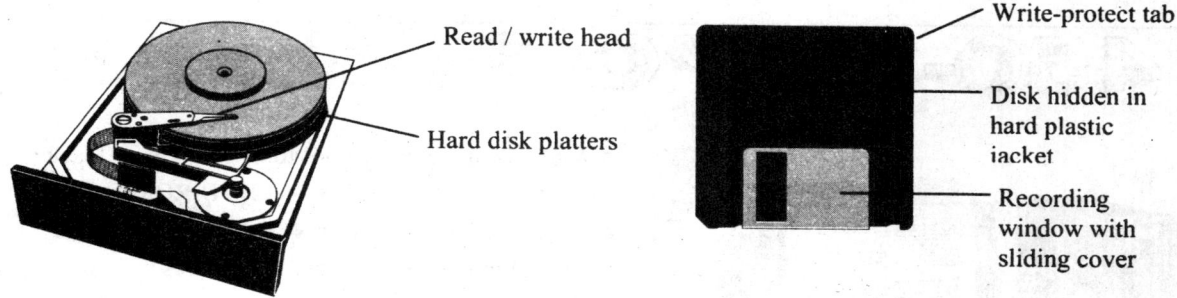

Figure 1.3: Hard disk and floppy disk

By 2005, Hitachi and a team at Cambridge University hope to make the hard drive obsolete. They are developing a new kind of chip that will be able to download a full-length movie in just a few seconds.

> Q1: Two advertisements for computers are shown below. What do the various terms and abbreviations mean? Note how the price has fallen and the specification has increased in less than two years. Is Moore's Law still holding?

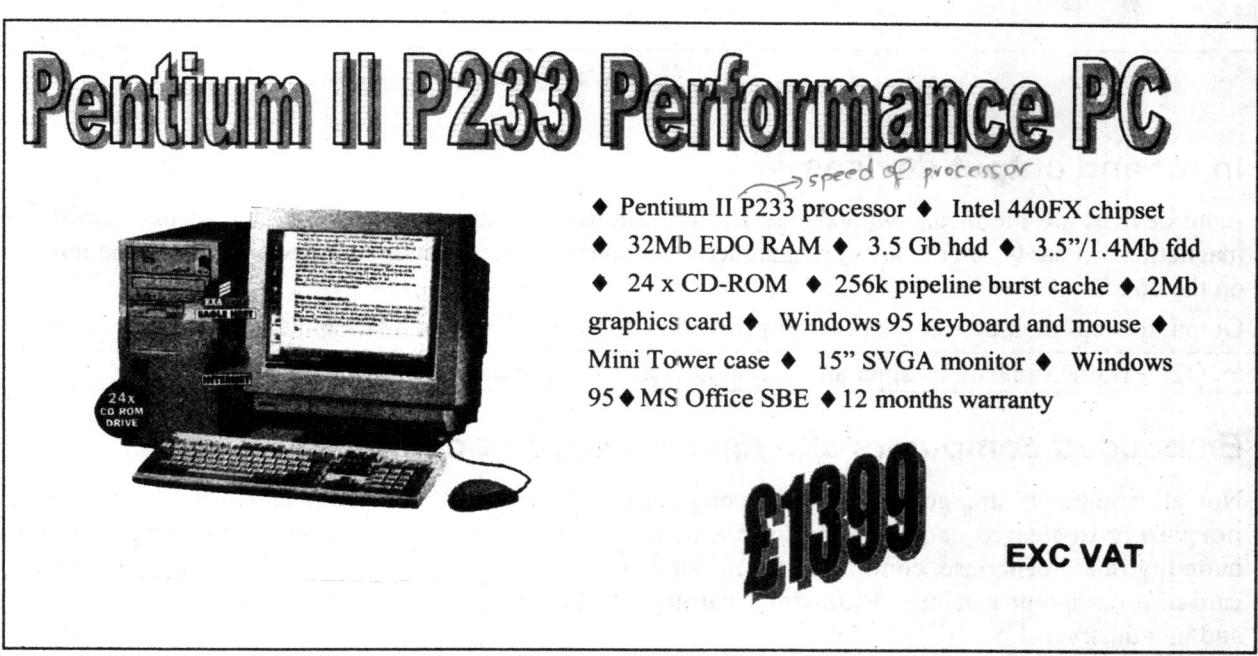

Figure 1.4: A high specification PC advertised in September 1997

Module 1 Computer Systems, Programming and Network Concepts

Figure 1.5: A high specification PC advertised in May 1999

Input and output devices

Input devices are the means whereby computers can accept data or instructions, and include keyboards, magnetic strip cards, smart cards and magnetic ink character recognition devices for reading the numbers on the bottom of cheques.

Output devices include various types of printer, VDU (Visual Display Unit) and speakers.

> Q2: Name some other input and output devices and their uses.

Embedded computers and special-purpose computers

Not all computers are general-purpose computers with a screen, keyboard and disk drive. **Special-purpose** or **dedicated** computers perform a wide variety of tasks from controlling the temperature and humidity in a greenhouse, controlling traffic lights to smooth the flow of traffic or enabling you to use a card at a cashpoint machine. **Embedded computers** are widely used in household goods, automobiles and in industry.

Special purpose computers have the same basic components of input, output, processor and memory, as general purpose computers, but typically the programs that they run are etched permanently into memory so that they cannot be altered. These programs are sometimes known as **firmware** – a combination of hardware and software.

Exercises

1. A typical business microcomputer stores all its software and data files on hard disk. It also has a floppy disk drive. Outline **two** different reasons why the floppy disk drive may still be needed.

2. In the context of a typical computer system, state the purpose of
   (a) internal memory
   (b) external memory. [backing store]

Module 1 Computer Systems, Programming and Network Concepts

Chapter 2 – Classification of Software

Categorising software

Software is the general term used to describe all the programs which run on a computer. There are three general categories of software: systems software, applications software and general-purpose software. This categorisation is not rigid, however, and some people would say that general-purpose software and applications software can be grouped together. You will soon discover that very little in computing is black and white; whatever you read, someone will soon come up with an apparently contradictory statement on most topics, leaving you to choose your own truth!

Systems software

Systems software includes the following types:

1. **Operating system.** Every computer needs an operating system to act as an interface between the user and the computer hardware. An operating system is a set of programs that allows the user to perform tasks without having to know how they are done. For example, a user can give a command to save a file on disk without having to know where the file will be stored or how it will be retrieved again. When a command is given to print a document, the user does not have to be concerned with the details of how the printer works – a program called a device driver takes care of the details.

   Application programs are usually written to work with a particular operating system, so that a word processor which works with Windows will not work on an Apple Mac, which has a different operating system.

2. **Library programs.** A library program is available to all users of a multi-user computer system, typically to carry out common tasks required by everyone. For example a routine that searches for lost files or restores corrupted files may be stored in a library. Many of these programs fall into the general category of **utility programs** (see below.)

3. **Utility programs.** These are programs designed to make life easier for computer users. Utility programs perform common tasks that thousands of computer users need to do at one time or another, such as search for lost files, sort files of data into a particular sequence, copy disk files to magnetic tape for backup purposes and so on.

   One common utility is compression software such as PKZip, that 'zips' files so that they occupy less space. This is very useful if you want to transmit a graphic or long data file over the Internet, as the transmission time will be much reduced.

> Q1: Have you used any utility programs? Where did you get them and what are they used for?

4. **Programming language compilers, interpreters and assemblers.** Compilers and interpreters are different types of program used to translate the statements in a programming language such as Pascal, Visual Basic or C into a form that the computer can understand. An assembler performs a similar function, translating the statements of a low-level programming language (assembly code) into machine code.

Applications software

Applications software is written to perform specific tasks such as order entry, payroll, stock control or hospital appointments. The software may be designed specifically for one particular company, (**bespoke software**) and written especially for them using a programming language or software such as a database management system. Alternatively, the software may be purchased 'off the shelf'.

General purpose software

All common application packages such as word processing, desktop publishing, spreadsheet, database, computer-aided design (CAD) and presentation graphics packages fall into this category. Most general purpose software is sold as a package, including a CD containing the software and manuals to help you get started and to be used as a reference.

Figure 2.1: General purpose software

Integrated packages and software suites

The main productivity tools used by organisations include word processing, spreadsheets, databases, presentation graphics and communications software to enable users to communicate with each other either locally or across the world in an international company.

Integrated packages which combine features from all five of these products were once very popular, because they offered capabilities from all these packages in a single product at a relatively low price, and data could be transferred between applications. However, a single integrated package (e.g. Microsoft Works) has fewer and less sophisticated features than are found in separately purchased packages.

Today, complete **software suites** such as Microsoft Office or Lotus SmartSuite offer four or more software products packaged together at a much lower price than buying the packages separately. Microsoft Office, for example, includes Word, Excel, Access, a multimedia presentation graphics package called PowerPoint and Microsoft Outlook.

Terminology in the computer world soon becomes fuzzy and MS Office is sometimes referred to as an integrated suite. The advantage of buying such a suite of programs is that the individual applications are completely compatible so that there is no difficulty importing or exporting data from one package to another, if for example you wish to put a spreadsheet in a word processed report. Also, the packages all have the same look and feel, with the same shortcut keys used for various operations (such as F7 for checking spelling) and this makes learning new software an easier task.

Generic and special purpose software

Note that software such as word processing, spreadsheet and database software is sometimes referred to as **generic** software. This simply implies that any of the dozens of spreadsheet packages, for example, can be made to do many different tasks, and is not designed specifically for one type of application. The other type of application software such as a payroll or stock control system mentioned above, or a software package such as a program to help fill in an income tax return, is in contrast **special purpose** because it is designed to do one particular task.

Bespoke or off-the-shelf?

When an organisation decides to computerise an area of its business, a decision has to be made whether to buy an off-the-shelf package or have software specially written. The advantages of buying an off-the-shelf package include the following:

- it is generally a less expensive solution;
- it may be possible to speak to other users of the package for their evaluation before spending money;
- the software can be bought and installed straight away;
- the software is tried and tested and likely to contain fewer bugs than newly written software;
- the software is usually well documented;
- training may be available in common software packages.

Conversely, there are also advantages in buying tailor-made (**'bespoke'**) software:

- the software is designed to do exactly what the user wants;
- the software can be written to run on specified hardware;
- the software can be integrated with existing software;
- there may not be a suitable software package on the market.

Exercises

1. Computer systems require both *application software* and *system software*.
   (i) Distinguish between these two types of software.
   (ii) Give **one** example of each.

2. Give three points a user should consider before deciding to purchase a software package.

3. Describe three housekeeping utilities normally provided with the operating system for a single-user personal computer. Your description should include a typical task for which each utility is used.

4. There is a trend for general purpose packages to include additional features normally found in different classes of package. A word processing package with a graphics capability is an example of this trend.
   (a) Give **two** reasons for this trend.
   (b) What are the implications of this trend for:

   the users of the package;

   the hardware required to run the package;

   data compatibility?

5. Distinguish clearly between an Integrated Package and integration between packages.

6. A typical computer operating system resides in
   (a) External memory
   (b) ROM
   (c) RAM

   Explain why **each** type of memory is used by the operating system.

Chapter 3 – Bits and Bytes

The binary system

All digital computers use the **binary** system for representing data of all types – numbers, characters, sound, pictures and so on. A binary system uses just 2 symbols to represent all information. The symbols could be anything like + and -, or 0 and 1. The great advantage of the binary system is that the digits 1 and 0 can be represented by electrical circuits that can exist in one of two states – current is either flowing or not flowing, and a circuit is either closed or open, on or off.

Figure 3.1: Electrical circuits can represent 1 or 0

Bits and bytes

A binary digit (1 or 0) is known as a '**bit**', short for **BI**nary digi**T**. In most computers today, bits are grouped together in 8-bit **bytes**. A byte can hold 2^8 different combinations of 0s and 1s, which means that, for example, 256 different characters can be represented.

One byte holds one character.

The ASCII code

Over the years, different computer designers have used different sets of codes for representing characters, which has led to great difficulty in transferring information from one computer to another. Most personal computers (PCs) nowadays use the ASCII code (American Standard Code for Information Interchange), but many mainframe computers use a code called EBCDIC (Extended Binary Coded Decimal Interchange Code – pronounced EB-SUH-DICK or EB-SEE-DICK according to taste).

ASCII originally used a 7-bit code. The 128 different combinations that can be represented in 7 bits is plenty to allow for all the letters, numbers and special symbols. Later, the eighth bit was also used, which allowed an extra 128 characters to be represented. The extra 128 combinations are used for symbols such as Ç, è, ü, ©, ®, Œ, etc.

> **Q1:** About how many different combinations of 0s and 1s are required to represent all the keys on a keyboard? (Remember to include uppercase and lowercase letters).

The first 32 ASCII codes are used for simple communications protocols, not characters. For example ACK stands for 'acknowledge' and would be sent by a device to acknowledge receipt of data or communication signal.

The ASCII codes are shown below.

Character	ASCII	Char	ASCII	Char	ASCII	Char	ASCII
NULL	0000000	space	0100000	@	1000000	`	1100000
SOH	0000001	!	0100001	A	1000001	a	1100001
STX	0000010	"	0100010	B	1000010	b	1100010
ETX	0000011	£	0100011	C	1000011	c	1100011
EOT	0000100	$	0100100	D	1000100	d	1100100
ENQ	0000101	%	0100101	E	1000101	e	1100101
ACK	0000110	&	0100110	F	1000110	f	1100110
BEL	0000111	'	0100111	G	1000111	g	1100111
BS	0001000	(	0101000	H	1001000	h	1101000
HT	0001001	)	0101001	I	1001001	i	1101001
LF	0001010	*	0101010	J	1001010	j	1101010
VT	0001011	+	0101011	K	1001011	k	1101011
SF	0001100	,	0101100	L	1001100	l	1101100
CR	0001101	-	0101101	M	1001101	m	1101101
SO	0001110	.	0101110	N	1001110	n	1101110
SI	0001111	/	0101111	O	1001111	o	1101111
DLE	0010000	0	0110000	P	1010000	p	1110000
DC1	0010001	1	0110001	Q	1010001	q	1110001
DC2	0010010	2	0110010	R	1010010	r	1110010
DC3	0010011	3	0110011	S	1010011	s	1110011
DC4	0010100	4	0110100	T	1010100	t	1110100
NAK	0010101	5	0110101	U	1010101	u	1110101
SYN	0010110	6	0110110	V	1010110	v	1110110
ETB	0010111	7	0110111	W	1010111	w	1110111
CAN	0011000	8	0111000	X	1011000	x	1111000
EM	0011001	9	0111001	Y	1011001	y	1111001
SUB	0011010	:	0111010	Z	1011010	z	1111010
ESC	0011011	;	0111011	[	1011011	{	1111011
FS	0011100	<	0111100	\	1011100	|	1111100
GS	0011101	=	0111101	]	1011101	}	1111101
RS	0011110	>	0111110	^	1011110	~	1111110
US	0011111	?	0111111	_	1011111	del	1111111

Figure 3.2: ASCII codes

Representing numbers

Using ASCII, each character has a corresponding code, so that if for example the 'A' key on the keyboard is pressed, the code '01000001' will be sent to the CPU. If the key '1' is pressed, the code '00110001' will be sent to the CPU. To print the number '123', the codes for 1, 2 and 3 would be sent to the printer.

This is fine for input and output, but useless for arithmetic. There is no easy way of adding two numbers held in this way, and furthermore they occupy a great deal of space. Numbers which are to be used in calculations are therefore held in a different format, as **binary numbers**.

Before we look at the binary system, it is helpful to examine how our ordinary decimal or **denary** number system works. Consider for example the number '134'. These three digits represent one hundred, three tens and four ones.

i.e.

100	10	1
1	3	4

This represents 100 + 30 + 4 = 134

As we move from right to left each digit is worth ten times as much as the previous one. We probably use a **base 10** number system because we have ten fingers, but essentially there is no reason why some other base such as 8 or 16 could not be used.

In the binary system, as we move from right to left each digit is worth twice as much as the previous one. Thus the binary number 10000110 can be set out under column headings as follows:

128	64	32	16	8	4	2	1
1	0	0	0	0	1	1	0

This represents 128 + 4 + 2 = 134

> Q2: Convert the following binary numbers to decimal:
> 0011   0110   1010   01000001   01000101
>
> Q3: Convert the following numbers to binary:
> 5   7   1   26   68   137
>
> Q4: What is the largest binary number that can be held in
>
> (i) 8 bits?   (ii) 16 bits?   (iii) 24 bits?   (iv) 32 bits?

Obviously, using only one byte (8 bits) to hold a number places a severe restriction on the size of number the computer can hold. Therefore two or four consecutive bytes are commonly used to store numbers.

Memory addressing

The memory of a computer can be thought of as a series of boxes, each containing 8 bits (1 byte), and each with its own unique address, counting from zero upwards. The memory capacity of a computer is measured in thousand-byte units called kilobytes, megabytes or gigabytes.

These measures can be abbreviated to Kb, Mb and Gb. These are all powers of 2; thus although 1Kb is often thought of as being 1,000 bytes, it is actually 1024 bytes.

You will find it useful to memorise certain powers of 2.

2^{10} bytes = 1024 = 1Kb

2^{20} bytes = 1024 x 1024 = 1Mb

2^{30} bytes = 1024 x 1024 x 1024 = 1Gb

Exercises

1. (a) Show how the denary (decimal) numbers 13 and 32 would be represented as 8-bit binary integers.
   (b) Given that the ASCII code for the character 1 is 00110001, show how the text string 1332 would be held in a 4-byte word in a computer's memory.

2. (i) What will be the highest address in a computer with
   (a) 1K of memory?
   (b) 16K of memory?
   (ii) How many Mb is 2^{24} bytes?
   (iii) How many Gb is 2^{32} bytes?

Module 1 Computer Systems, Programming and Network Concepts

Chapter 4 – Introduction to Programming

The earliest computers

It is an astonishing fact that as we enter the 21st century, computers have been around for less than 60 years. Many of those who worked on the earliest computers are still alive to tell us of their experiences. If you ever get a chance to watch a series of programs made for television called 'The Codebreakers', do not miss it – it is a fascinating account of the breaking of the Enigma code (used by the Germans to code all their most secret messages), with the aid of the first programmable computer, named Colossus, built for this purpose in 1943.

Generations of programming language

Machine language – the first generation

Programming languages are often characterised by 'generation'. The first generation of computer language, known as machine code, executes directly without translation. Machine code is the actual pattern of 0s and 1s used in a computer's memory. The programming of Colossus and other early computers was laboriously done with toggle switches representing a pattern of binary codes for each instruction.

Machine language, however it is entered into a computer, is time-consuming, laborious and error-prone. Few programmers code in it today. A language suited to the particular application would be used instead.

Assembly code – the second generation

In the 1950s when computers were first used commercially, machine code gave way to **assembly code**, which allowed programmers to use mnemonics (abbreviations that represent the instructions in a more memorable way) and denary numbers (i.e. 0–9) instead of 0s and 1s. Thus ADD or ADX might be an instruction to add two numbers, SUB or SBX an instruction to subtract.

Programs written in assembly languages have to be translated into machine code before they can be executed, using a program called an **assembler**. There is more or less a one-to-one correspondence between each assembly code statement and its equivalent machine code statement, which means that programs can be written in the most efficient way possible, occupying as little space as possible and executing as fast as possible. For this reason assembly code is still used for applications where timing or storage space is critical. Assembly languages are called **low level** languages because they are close to machine code and the detail of the computer architecture.

Since different types of computer have different instruction sets which depend on how the machine carries out the instructions, both machine code and assembly code are machine-dependent – each type of computer will have its own assembly language.

```
                LOAD    A, #0              \Load register A with 0
                LOAD    X, #8              \Load index register with 8
        LOOP:   SUB     X, #1              \Subtract 1 from index register
                STORE   X, (&50000), A     \Store contents of A in location
                                           \50000 indexed by contents of X
                BNE     X, LOOP            \Branch if not zero to LOOP
                HALT                       \Stop execution
```

Figure 4.1: Part of an assembly code program

Imperative high level languages – the third generation

As computer use increased dramatically in the 1950s, the need grew to make it easier and faster to write error-free programs. Computer manufacturers and user groups started to develop so-called **high-level languages** such as Algol (standing for ALGOrithmic Language) and Fortran (standing for FORmula TRANslation). In the 1950s most of the people actually writing programs were scientists and engineers and so both these languages were created to be used in mathematical applications.

COBOL (COmmon Business Oriented Language) was invented by the redoubtable Admiral Grace Hopper in 1960 specifically for writing commercial and business, rather than scientific programs. Whilst serving in the US Navy in 1947, Grace Hopper was investigating why one of the earliest computers was not working, and discovered a small dead moth in the machine. After removing it (and taping it in her logbook) the machine worked fine, and from then on computer errors were known as 'bugs'.

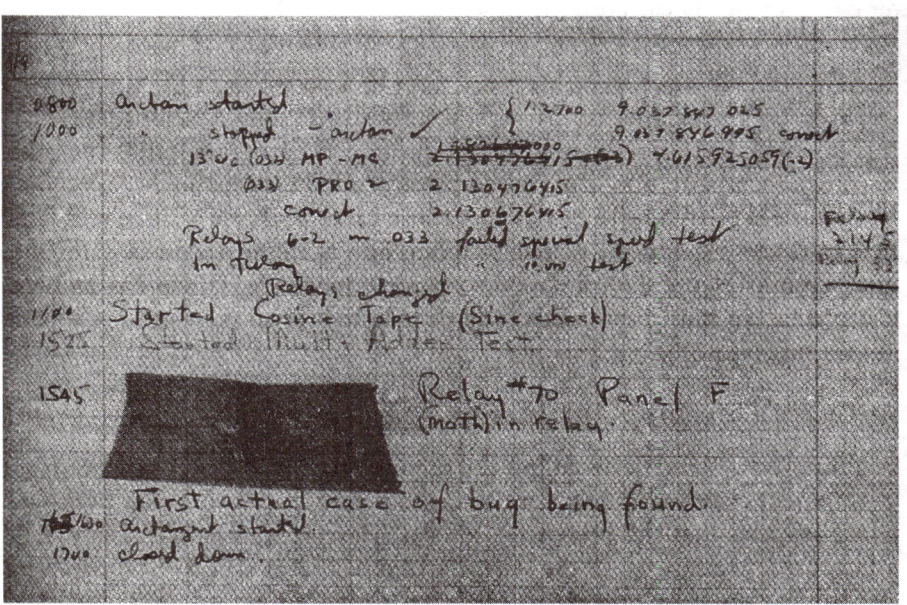

Figure 4.2: Admiral Grace Hopper and the first computer 'bug'

Other third generation languages followed: **BASIC** was created in the 1960s as a language for students to learn programming. Early versions of the language however did not contain the facilities to write well-structured programs that were easy to maintain and debug, although the language has since developed. In 1971 Nicklaus Wirth designed **Pascal** (named after the seventeenth century French mathematician) to teach structured programming to students.

High level languages are so-called because they are independent of the architecture of any particular computer; one statement written in a high level language is translated into several machine code

Module 1 Computer Systems, Programming and Network Concepts

instructions before it can be executed. The term **imperative** high level language refers to languages such as Pascal, BASIC, COBOL and Fortran. Programs written in these languages consist of a number of instructions which the computer follows in a particular programmer-defined sequence – in contrast with **object-oriented** and **declarative** languages which you will learn about in the second year of this course.

> ➤ **Q1:** Do you know the names of any other high-level languages? Why do you suppose there are so many of them?

Why use assembly code?

Assembly language, although it is laborious to write and hard to debug, is still used in some circumstances:

- there is a need for the program to execute as fast as possible;
- the program must occupy as little space as possible;

Parts of an operating system, and device drivers that control the operation of devices such as a printer, mouse or CD-ROM may be written in assembly code. Programs in embedded systems like satellite decoders, encryption and decryption software, and routines that are called frequently from high-level programs may also be written in assembly code.

Types of program translator

There are three types of program used for translating the code that a programmer writes into a form (i.e. machine code) that the computer can execute. These are:

- assembler;
- compiler;
- interpreter.

Assembler

An assembler is a program which translates an assembly code program into machine code ready for the computer to execute it. Since each type of computer has its own assembly language, it also has its own assembler. The assembler itself could be written in assembly code or in a high level language such as C which has special facilities useful for this type of programming.

Compiler

A compiler is a program which translates a high level language into machine code. The Turbo Pascal compiler, for example, translates a program written in Turbo Pascal on a PC into machine code which can be run on a PC. The code written by the programmer is known as the **source code**, and the compiled code is known as the **object code**.

A compiler is a complex program which takes the source code and scans through it several times, each time performing different checks and building up tables of information needed to produce the final object code. When you write a short program, this process appears to happen almost instantaneously, but a long program of several thousand lines can take several minutes to compile.

Interpreter

An interpreter is also a program which translates high-level source code into object code. However the crucial difference between a compiler and an interpreter is **that an interpreter translates one line at a time and then executes it**; no object code is produced, and so the program has to be interpreted each time it is to be run. If the program performs a section of code 10,000 times, then that section of code is translated into machine code 10,000 times as each line is interpreted and then executed.

Relative advantages of compilers and interpreters

A compiler has many advantages over an interpreter:

- the object code can be saved on disk and run whenever required without the need to recompile. However, if an error is discovered in the program, the whole program has to be recompiled.
- the object code executes faster than interpreted code.
- the object code produced by a compiler can be distributed or executed without having to have the compiler present.
- the object code is more secure, as it cannot be read without a great deal of 'reverse engineering'.

An interpreter has some advantages over a compiler:

- it is useful for program development as there is no need for lengthy recompilation each time an error is discovered.
- it is easier to partially test and debug programs.

Exercises

1. (a) *Compilers* and *interpreters* are both items of software concerned with the translation of source programs into machine code. Distinguish between them.
   (b) Give one advantage of using a compiler to translate a program rather than an interpreter.

2. Give an example of a first generation, second generation and third generation programming language. Explain two differences between second and third generation languages.

3. (i) What is meant by a *high-level programming language*?
   (ii) There is a large number of high-level languages: FORTRAN, COBOL, BASIC ...etc. Why are there so many?

Module 1 Computer Systems, Programming and Network Concepts

Chapter 5 – Introducing Pascal

Learning to program

If you have chosen to do Computing rather than Information Technology, you will probably find learning to program is one of the most enjoyable parts of the course. The choice of programming language will be a matter for individual schools and colleges, and to some extent it does not matter which imperative high-level language you study. C, Basic and Pascal all have similar statements and structures.

Pascal was invented in the 1970s by Niklaus Wirth to teach structured programming. It is a good language to start with and you will find it easy to learn, say, Delphi (which is based on Pascal) or Visual Basic if you have studied Pascal.

The examples in this book were all written in **Turbo Pascal**.

A Pascal program

As a first example, consider a program that calculates an electricity bill. The standing charge is £7.41 per quarter, and the unit rate is 6.5 pence per unit. The number of units used this quarter is 1200.

```pascal
program elec;
{a program to calculate electricity bills}

var
    standing_charge     :real; {the fixed quarterly charge}
    unit_rate           :real;
    units_used          :integer;
    total_bill          :real;

begin
    standing_charge:=7.41;
    unit_rate:=0.065;   {converted to £}
    units_used:=1200;
    total_bill:=standing_charge+(unit_rate*units_used);
    writeln('Total amount payable',total_bill)
end.
```

The parts of a program

The Pascal program shown above consists of three parts:

1. the **program heading**, consisting of the word **program** and a program name of our choice;
2. a **declaration** of each item of data to be used by the program;
3. a sequence of actions (statements) enclosed between the words **begin** and **end**.

Certain words in the program have been written in boldface type to show that these are **reserved words**, or **keywords**. They are part of the Pascal language and can only be used for the purpose defined by the rules of the language. A complete list of reserved words can be found in the Pascal manual for your version of Pascal.

Comments

The second line of the program is a **comment**; a comment may occur anywhere in the program and is enclosed in curly brackets { }, or alternatively (* *) may be used. Comments are ignored by the compiler but provide essential documentation for anyone who wants to know such things as:

- who wrote the program, and when it was written;
- what the program does;
- how parts of it work;
- what certain variables are used for, and so on.

Variable declaration

This section of the program is headed **var** which stands for **variable**. All the data items used, read in or calculated by the program must be declared in this section. Each data item has a name called an **identifier**; for example, **standing_charge**, **unit_rate**, etc., and this should be chosen by the programmer to be self-explanatory wherever possible. **Standing_charge** is a better name than **sc** even if it takes longer to type in!

Some of the items are defined as **real**, meaning that they will hold numbers with a decimal point such as 123.45, -23.0, or 0.15. **Integer** values are whole numbers such as -7 or 1990.

A real number has to have a number preceding the decimal point in Pascal; you will get an error message if you write a statement such as

```
rate := .5
```

> **Q1:** What should you write instead, if you want to assign the value .5 to a real variable called rate?

The statement part of the program

The part of the program where the actual work is done is enclosed between the key words **begin** and **end**. The punctuation is important and will be explained in due course.

> **Q2:** Type in and run the program elec.
> Would it be permitted to write the following?
> ```
> var
>     standing_charge,unit_rate,total_bill:real;
>     units_used:integer;
> ```

There is one way to find out; try it! You will find that it is quite permissible to declare more than one variable on a line. However, some people prefer to write only one variable per line, and line up all the semi-colons by using the tab key, which makes the program look neat, and it also makes it easier to spot where variables have been declared, and to check that a variable declaration has not been omitted by mistake.

> **Q3:** Change the **writeln** statement to
>   **writeln** ('Total amount payable',total_bill:8:2);
> What can you deduce about the 8:2?
> Try changing it to 8:3, 12:2, 4:2 and running the program each time.

Formatting the output

If you have tried out the suggestions in the question above, you will have deduced that writing

```
total_bill:8:2
```

causes the number to be displayed to 2 decimal places. The number 8 is the **total field width**; for example the number 123.45 has a total field width of 6 (including the decimal point). Writing it with the format 8:2 will mean that it will be padded out with 2 spaces on the left hand side.

Exercises

1. Using **elec** as a model, write a program which defines the bills received in each quarter of the year as £35.00, £37.78, £22.53 and £43.85 respectively and calculates and outputs the total bill for the year.

2. Complete the following program, which calculates the number of rolls of wallpaper required to cover a wall of any dimensions.

```
program wallpaper(input,output);
{written by:                                          }

var
    length:real;
    (missing statements here)
    height : real;
    price : real;
    paper_width, paper_length    :real;
    wall_area, no_of_rolls       :real;
    const cost
begin
    {enter dimensions of wall and wallpaper roll}
    write('Enter the length of the wall: ');
    readln(length);
    write('Enter the height of the wall: ');
    (missing statement here)
    readln (height);
    write('Enter the width of the roll: ');
    (missing statements here)
    readln (paper_width);
    {calculate number of rolls required}
    wall_area:=length*height;
    roll_area:=(complete this statement) paper_width * paper_length
    no_of_rolls:=wall_area/roll_area;
    no_of_rolls:=1.10*no_of_rolls;        {add 10% for matching pattern}
    writeln('You will need ',no_of_rolls:6:1,' rolls of wallpaper')
end.  total_cost :=
```

(handwritten margin note: Enter the length of the roll / read (paper_length))

3. Amend the program to accept the price per roll and display the total cost of wallpaper. Write down some test data and check that your program is giving the expected answers.

4. Write a program to enable a student to calculate how much money will be needed per week to buy a meal and two drinks each weekday. The program should ask how much a meal costs, and how much a drink costs, and then calculate and display the total weekly cost.

5. Amend the above program to calculate and display the total cost for a 13-week term, assuming that the student also has to buy books and stationery costing an average of £x per month. (User to enter a value for x).

Chapter 6 – Variables, Assignments, Reading and Writing

Types of data

There are four primitive built-in data types defined in the Pascal language. These are
- integer (whole numbers);
- real (numbers with a decimal point);
- character (any ASCII character such as a letter, number or 'special character' like @, or #);
- boolean (a variable which can only hold the value **true** or **false**).

Note: Turbo Pascal defines 5 different integer types, which are listed below:

type	Range	Format
shortint	-128 .. 127	signed 8-bit
integer	-32768 .. 32767	signed 16-bit
longint	-2147483648 .. 2147483647	signed 32-bit
byte	0 .. 255	unsigned 8-bit
word	0 .. 65535	unsigned 16-bit

Each of these is stored in a different way in the computer's memory. Therefore before we attempt to store any data in memory, either by reading it in or by the use of an **assignment** statement, we must tell the compiler what type of data we intend to store in any particular variable. This is done using the **var** declaration. For example:

```
var
    grade:char;
    mark1:integer;
    mark2:integer;
    average:real;
```

If a variable has been declared as an integer, for example, we cannot store a character or a real number in it.

In addition, we need some way of storing a **string** of characters such as a student's name, and most versions of Pascal allow a string to be defined as, for example,

```
student_name:string;
```

which in Turbo Pascal allows up to 255 characters to be stored in student_name, using a statement such as

```
student_name:='Mary Jones';
```

Note that the string has to be enclosed in single quote marks.

Module 1 Computer Systems, Programming and Network Concepts

Rules for identifiers

The program name and the variable names are all called **identifiers**, and the following rules apply:
- they must always start with a letter;
- they can consist of letters, digits and the underscore character;
- uppercase and lowercase letters are treated as identical.

> **Q1:** Which of the following are valid identifiers?
> (i) Prog-1   (iii) student mark   (v) K.O'R.
> (ii) TaxProgram   (iv) 1st_grade   (vi) program1.pas

Assignment statements

In Pascal a value or expression is **assigned** to a variable using the symbol ':='. Here is an example of an assignment statement:-

```
daily_cost := cost_of_lunch + 2 * cost_of_drink;
```

The following mathematical symbols are used in constructing expressions:

Operator	Operation	Operand types	Result type
+	addition	integer type real type	integer type real type
-	subtraction	integer type real type	integer type real type
*	multiplication	integer type real type	integer type real type
/	division	integer type real type	real type real type
div	integer division	integer type	integer type
mod	remainder	integer type	integer type

In addition, brackets ( ) are used wherever necessary, or to clarify the meaning of the expression. The same rules of precedence apply as in ordinary arithmetic; multiplication and division are performed before addition and subtraction, and expressions in brackets are evaluated first.

Example: x := 31 div 6   puts 5 in x since 6 goes 5 times into 31
              x := 31 mod 6   puts 1 in x since 1 is the remainder when 31 is divided by 6.

> **Q2:** Evaluate x in the following expressions: (assume x is an **integer** variable)
> (i)   x:=5*7+3*4   (iv)   x:=27 div 4
> (ii)   x:=5*(7+3)*4   (v)   x:=27 mod 4
> (iii) x:=5*(7+3*4)   (vi)   x:=24/4
>
> **Q3:** Find the errors in the following program (you should find about ten!):
> ```
> program error;
> var
>    student-name:string;
>    mark1,mark2,mark3;integer;
>    total,average:integer;
> ```

```
begin
  student_name:='Jo';
  mark_1:=50;
  mark_2:=52;
  mark_3:=68;
  total_mark:=mark_1+mark_2+mark_3
  average:=total_mark*3;
  writeln('Average mark=';AVERAGE:8:2)
end
```

Notice that there are two types of error in the above program; **syntax** errors – errors in the way the Pascal language has been used – and a **logic** error. The compiler will detect all the syntax errors but it cannot detect the logic error.

Reading in data from a keyboard

Data is read into a Pascal program using either a **read** or a **readln** statement. We could read in three student marks from the keyboard with the statement

```
read(mark_1,mark_2,mark_3);
```
or
```
read(mark_1);
read(mark_2);
read(mark_3);
```

where mark_1, mark_2 and mark_3 are integer values all typed on one line, separated by at least one space.

readln has the effect of skipping to a new line after reading the variable.

```
read(mark_1);
readln;
```
has the same effect as
```
readln(mark_1);
```

Displaying data on the screen

The **write** and **writeln** statements are used to display data. As with **readln**, **writeln** causes a skip to a new line after writing the data. Thus

```
write('Average=');
writeln(average);
```
has the same effect as
```
writeln('Average=',average);
```

> **Q4:** What will be output when the following lines of code are executed?
> ```
> write ('Beam me up ');
> write ('please ');
> writeln ('Scotty. ');
> writeln ('Fast!');
> ```

Formatting output

It is convenient to be able to control the number of spaces used by the computer to print integers, and to be able to specify the number of decimal places to be displayed in the case of a real number. This is done by specifying the total field width and number of places after the decimal point, separated by colons. Thus if the value of **average** is say 74.0,

```
writeln('Average=',average:5:1);
```

will print

```
Average = 74.0
```
(leaving one space after the = sign, for a total field width of 5).

Compound statements and punctuation

All the statements between **begin** and **end** can be regarded as a single compound statement, with the semi-colon acting as a **separator** between statements. (The significance of a **compound statement** will become clearer later on when looping and branching are covered). All statements between **begin** and **end** need to be separated from each other, but there is no need to put a semi-colon after the final statement before **end**. However it will not cause an error if you do so. Notice also that the last statement of the program, **end**, has to be followed by a full-stop.

Clearing the screen and positioning the cursor

The screen can be cleared with the statement

```
clrscr;
```

The cursor can be positioned at row x, column y with the statement

```
gotoxy(x,y);
```

These are **built-in procedures** – part of Turbo Pascal's library of useful routines, and to access them, you need to include an instruction at the top of the program, just under the program header, to look in the library unit **crt** for the **clrscr** and **gotoxy** procedures. e.g.

```
program Test;
{This program demonstrates the use of the built-in procedures
clrscr and gotoxy}

{Notice that the desired x and y coordinates 35,10 are passed to the
procedure by putting them in brackets after the procedure name. They
are called PARAMETERS}

uses crt; {you may need uses wincrt depending on the version of Pascal
           you are using}
begin
    clrscr;
    gotoxy (35,10);
    writeln('Hello!);
    readln
end.
```

Improving the readability of a program

You will find your programs are easier to understand and debug if they are clearly laid out. You should:
- be generous with your comments;
- use tabs to indent sections of code. For example, indent all the code between **begin** and **end**.
- use meaningful variable names;
- leave blank lines between chunks of code to make it more readable.

Using Turbo Pascal's trace and debugging facilities

Turbo Pascal provides what is known as an 'integrated development environment', meaning that once you have loaded up the package, you can type in your program, compile it, run it, edit it, save it and so on. Turbo Pascal also provides you with many invaluable debugging facilities and you should get to grips with them as soon as possible. Try stepping through your program one line at a time, using the function key F7. Alternatively, position the cursor where you would like execution to proceed to before stepping begins, and press F4. Then step through using F7.

Try adding watches to your program using the appropriate debug option from the menu.

Look at the Window option and see the effect of 'tiling' Windows.

Learn what other key combinations are used for; Alt-F5 to switch to the 'user screen', F2 to save, F9 to compile and so on. Don't be afraid to experiment! The sooner you become an expert, the easier you will find it to debug more complicated programs.

Exercises

1. Write a program which allows a user to input a student's name and 3 marks, then calculates the average and displays the result in the following format:

   Student name: xxxxxxxxxxxxxxxxxxxx
   Marks: 99   99   99
   Average: 99.9

2. Imagine that you and a friend are planning to set up a hamburger stand. The initial setting up cost will be £200.00 for the stand. Write a program which will input the cost price and proposed selling price of a hamburger, and the estimated number of hamburgers that you will sell in a day, and calculate how long it will take to recoup the cost of the stand.

   What other software could you use for this type of problem instead of writing a Pascal program? What are the relative advantages of each method of solution?

3. On a screen layout chart, a coding sheet or a piece of squared paper, draw up the layout for the till receipt in exercise 4. (Do not draw the box around the receipt; this represents the screen.)

4. Write a program to display a receipt for a customer who has purchased a single item. The program should display the blank receipt, accept the item description, quantity and price, calculate the value and display it. Then input the amount tendered and display the change due.

```
                    TAYLOR GROUP PLC

                              UNIT
       ITEM           QTY     PRICE      VALUE
       xxxxxxxxxxxxx  99      999.99     99999.99

       amount tendered                   99999.99
                                         ------------
       change due                        99999.99

              PLEASE RETAIN YOUR RECEIPT
              THANK YOU FOR YOUR CUSTOM
```

Chapter 7 – Iteration & Selection

Looping (also called iteration or repetition)

In the last chapter we looked at a program for calculating the average of 3 marks. The method used could be summarised as

```
Read in the marks
Add them up
calculate the average
output the result
```

This worked well enough for three numbers but would be quite impractical for 30 or 300!

We will consider a slightly different problem: the program is to input the marks for any number of students, calculate the average mark and display the number of students and the average mark.

What we need to do is to keep a running total; keep reading in the next mark and adding it to the total until there are no more marks to enter. The number of marks entered must be counted too, so that the average can be calculated.

The outline solution is, then, as follows:

```
Set total_mark, no_of_marks to 0

while there is another mark to enter
    read a mark
    add it to total_mark
    add 1 to no_of_marks
endwhile

calculate the average mark
display no_of_marks and average
```

How will the program know when there are no more marks to enter? There are three ways of handling this.

1. The program asks before reading each mark: "Are there any more marks to enter?" and waits for the user to answer Yes or No.

2. As soon as a mark is entered, the program tests to see if a special value such as -1 or 999 which would not normally occur as a data item, has been entered. This value is called a **sentinel** or **dummy** value, or sometimes a **rogue** value, and can be recognised by the program as a signal that all of the actual data items have been processed.

> ➢ Q1: Can you think of the third way?
> ➢ Q2: Which of the three methods do you prefer? Why?

The WHILE..DO statement in Pascal

The syntax of the **while..do** statement is shown by the following **syntax diagram:**

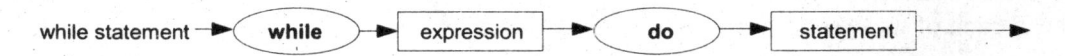

while statement → (while) → [expression] → (do) → [statement] →

The expression controlling the repetition must be of type *boolean;* that is, one which evaluates to *true* or *false*.

The following operators may be used in making comparisons:

```
=       equal to
>       greater than
<       less than
>=      greater than or equal
<=      less than or equal
<>      not equal
in      member of      (eg while num in [70..100] )
```

Note that when using the 'in' operator, the values in the square brackets must be integers or characters, not real numbers or strings.

For example:

```
write('Please enter the first mark; enter -1 to end');
readln(student_mark);
while student_mark <> -1 do
    begin
        total_mark:=total_mark+student_mark;
        no_of_marks:=no_of_marks+1;
        write('Please enter the next mark; enter -1 to end');
        readln(student_mark)
    end; {endwhile}
```

Notice the **compound** statement which includes the **begin** and **end** and all the statements in between. If there was only one action to be performed, the **begin** and **end** would not be necessary.

The program will continue to execute the compound statement until a mark of -1 is entered.

Note that the condition 'student_mark <> -1' is tested **before** entering the loop.

> ➢ Q3: Why not put the write and readln statements at the beginning of the loop?
> ➢ Q4: What happens if the first mark entered is -1?
> ➢ Q5: Write statements to perform the following:
>   (i) Add up the numbers from 1 to 100 and display the result
>   (ii) Read in a number between 1 and 75 and then print that number of asterisks in a line.

An introduction to procedures

Three main tasks can be identified in the program to calculate the average of a set of marks:

```
Initialise
Input and process marks
Output results
```

This could be called the **top-level** solution to the problem; recognising the major steps that are to be performed without specifying in any detail how they are to be achieved.

The program can thus be broken down into **modules**; and the preferred way of writing a program is to code each of these tasks as a separate **procedure**. The main program will then reflect the top-level solution, and call each of these procedures in turn. Note that:

- each procedure is given a name, and has the same structure as a program;
- the procedure is **called** from the main procedure simply by writing its name;
- any procedure that is called must be written **before** it is called; that is, it must be placed physically above the statements in the main program.

Program to calculate the average of a set of marks

A complete program to input a set of student marks and calculate the average is shown below.

Notice that '**input_and_process**' is **one** procedure; you should **not** try to write separate procedures for '**input**' and '**process**', which complicates things unnecessarily.

```
Program mark_avg(input,output);
{program to calculate average of a set of students' marks}
var
    student_mark, total_mark, no_of_marks:integer;
    average:real;

Procedure initialise;
begin
    no_of_marks:=0;
    total_mark:=0;
end; {end of procedure}

Procedure input_and_process;
begin
    write('Please enter the first mark, -1 to end: ');
    readln(student_mark);
    while student_mark<>-1 do
    begin
        total_mark:=total_mark+student_mark;
        no_of_marks:=no_of_marks+1;
        write('Please enter the next mark, -1 to end: ');
        readln(student_mark)
    end; {endwhile}
end;     {end of procedure}

Procedure output_result;
begin
    average:=total_mark/no_of_marks;
    writeln('Average mark is ',average:5:2);
    writeln('Total number of students: ',no_of_marks:3)
end; {end of procedure}

{******   MAIN PROGRAM - EXECUTION STARTS HERE   *******}
begin
    initialise;
    input_and_process;
    output_result
end.
```

(Exercises 1, 2, 3 and 5 may be done before covering Selection)

Selection (IF..THEN..ELSE)

It is often necessary to take different routes through a program depending on some condition. This can be achieved in Pascal by the **if..then..else** statement, the syntax of which is shown below:

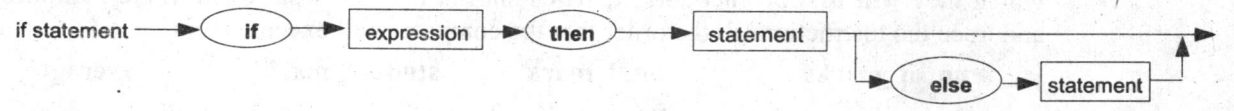

```
if statement ──▶( if )──▶[ expression ]──▶( then )──▶[ statement ]──┬────────▶
                                                                     │
                                                                     └──▶( else )──▶[ statement ]──▶
```

The expression must produce a result of type *boolean* (*true* or *false*).

Example:
```
if mark>=70 then
    writeln('Merit')
else
    if mark>=50 then
        writeln('Pass')
    else
        writeln('Fail');
{endif}
```
The above is an example of a 'nested if' statement.

> **Q6:** Amend the above statement so that if the mark is 70 or above the program prints 'Well Done' on the line beneath the grade; and if the mark is less than 50 the program prints 'You are required to resit this assignment' on the line beneath the grade.

Compound conditions can be constructed using **and**, **or**, and **not**. For example:
```
if (status='m') and (salary<2400) then tax:=0;
```
or
```
if (hours>40) and (hours<48) then
    begin
        overtime_rate:=1.5*normal_rate;
        calculate_pay
    end
else
    double_time;
```

Note the brackets round the conditions, and note that you **cannot** write
```
If hours>40 and <48 then      etc etc
```

Example: Write a Pascal statement to mean "if reply not equal to 'Y' call a procedure no_more"

Answer: `if not (reply ='Y') then no_more;`
or alternatively `if (reply <>'Y') then no_more;`

Trace tables

When a program is not working correctly (perhaps producing a wrong answer, or getting into an infinite loop), it is useful to trace through the program manually, writing down the values of the variables as they change. The variable names can be written as column headings and their values underneath the headings to form a trace table. Being able to trace manually through the steps of a program is an essential skill in program debugging.

Module 1 Computer Systems, Programming and Network Concepts

Example: Use a trace table to show the values of the variables **student_mark**, **total_mark**, **no_of_marks** and **average** when the program **mark_avg** is run (see two pages back). You may assume that the user enters the marks 7, 5, 9, -1.

Answer: Take a look at the program and write down the variable names across the page. The order is not particularly important; in the example below, they have been written in the order in which they will first be encountered. Then start at the first instruction in the main program and trace the instructions in the order that the computer will execute them.

no_of_marks	total_mark	student_mark	average
0	0	7	?
1	7	5	
2	12	9	
3	21	-1	7

> **Q7:** The following extract from a program is intended to calculate the sum of the squares of a series of numbers entered by the user. The end of data entry is signalled by the dummy value -1. Use a trace table to find out why the program is not giving the right answer when the user enters the values 2, 5, 3, 1, -1. The first couple of lines of the trace table have been filled in for you; notice that a column has been allocated for the condition n <> -1, and this can only take the values True or False.
>
> What output would you expect the program to produce if it was working correctly?
>
> ```
> n:=0;
> total:=0;
> while n<>-1 do
> begin
>     write ('Please enter a number');
>     readln(n);
>     total:=total+n*n;
> end; {while}
> writeln('Total=',n:8:2);
> ```
>
> | n | n*n | total | n<>-1 |
> |---|---|---|---|
> | 0 | 0 | 0 | True |
> | 2 | 4 | 4 | True |

Remember: a programming environment such as Turbo Pascal has facilities for stepping through a program one instruction at a time, setting breakpoints in a program, showing the values of selected variables as you step through, and many more useful programming aids. You should make sure you find out all you can about how to use such features, which can save hours of debugging time.

Program constants

Every program that we have encountered has had a **variable declaration**, starting with the reserved word **var**. In addition to variable identifiers, some programs use **constant** values which never change throughout the program. For example, in the program which prints a triangle of asterisks (exercise 3 below), you could define a constant identifier called, say, *symbol*, to hold the character '*'. To do this, insert above the **var** declaration, a **const** declaration as follows:

```
program triangle;
const
    symbol='*';   {note the syntax carefully; = and not := is used here}
var etc
```

Although it is perfectly possible to write any program without a **const** declaration, it sometimes is convenient to use constants. The advantage is that it is easy to modify the program; for example by changing the constant declaration in the above example you could make the program print out a tree of X's or any other symbol instead of an asterisk. As an added bonus the program will run a nanosecond or two faster because the compiler will replace all references to a constant by its actual value at compile time.

Exercises

1. Use a **trace table** to show the values of var1, n and the condition **n < 5** when the following statements are executed:

    ```
    var1 := 3;
    n := 0;
    while n < 5 do
        begin
            var1 := var1 + n;
            n := n + 1
        end;
    ```

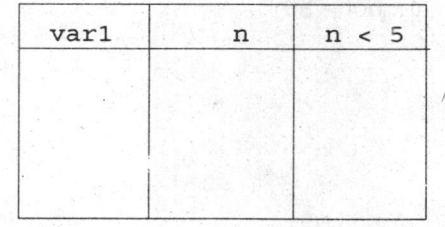

var1	n	n < 5

*For each of the programs below write a **top-level** solution in ordinary English, breaking down the problem into its major components, then code the program using procedures.*

2. Write a program which calculates a simplified payroll. For each employee the user enters name, hourly rate and number of hours worked. The program calculates gross pay, deducts tax at 25% of gross, and prints out the employee name, hours, rate, gross pay, tax and net pay. At the end of the program the total gross, total tax and total net pay for all employees is to be printed out together with the number of employees.

3. Write a program to print out a triangle of stars, with 41 stars in the last row:

    ```
            *
           ***
          *****
         *******
           etc
    ```

    (n.b. Do not use 41 writeln statements! The statement part of the main program should consist of two procedure calls: **Initialise** and **Print_stars**.)

4. Write a program which allows the user to input a date, eg March 1, followed by the noon temperature on that day for the last several years, from meteorological records. The program has to calculate the maximum, minimum and average temperature and display the results.

Module 1 Computer Systems, Programming and Network Concepts

5. A computer language has variable names which must conform to the syntax shown below.

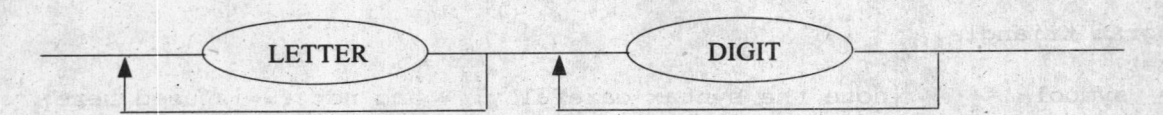

```
─────▲────( LETTER )────▲────( DIGIT )─────
     │_____│    │_____│
```

State which of the following are legal variable names. For each incorrect variable name, explain why it is incorrect.

(a) 5thyear   (b) class6a   (c) st561

6. Which of the following are valid Boolean conditions in Pascal?

(a) value => 100.0   {value is a real variable}
(b) (max>37.5) and (max<42.0)   {max is a real variable}
(c) day in ['Mon','Tue','Wed','Thu','Fri']   {day is a string variable}
(d) (mark not > 80)   {mark is an integer variable}

Chapter 8 – Program Design and Maintenance

Program design aims

Effort put into good program design can often save costly maintenance and debugging costs later on. The aims of program design may be summarised as:

- reliability; the program must always do what it is supposed to do;
- maintainability; the program must be easy to change or modify if this becomes necessary;
- readability; the program must be easy for another programmer to read and understand;
- performance; the program must do its job fast and efficiently;
- storage saving; the program ideally must occupy as little memory as possible, especially if it is a very large program.

Top-down design

Top-down design is the technique of breaking down a problem into the major tasks to be performed; each of these tasks is then further broken down into separate subtasks, and so on until each subtask is sufficiently simple to be written as a self-contained **module** or procedure. The program then consists of a series of calls to these modules, which may themselves call other modules.

Jackson structure diagrams

It is useful to have some way of representing the **structure** of a program – how the modules all relate to form the whole solution – and a Jackson structure diagram is one way of doing this. When a program is large and complex, it becomes especially important to plan out the solution before doing any coding, and a structure diagram also serves a useful purpose as documentation when the program is complete.

The diagram resembles a family tree, with the main program modules written **across** the top line.

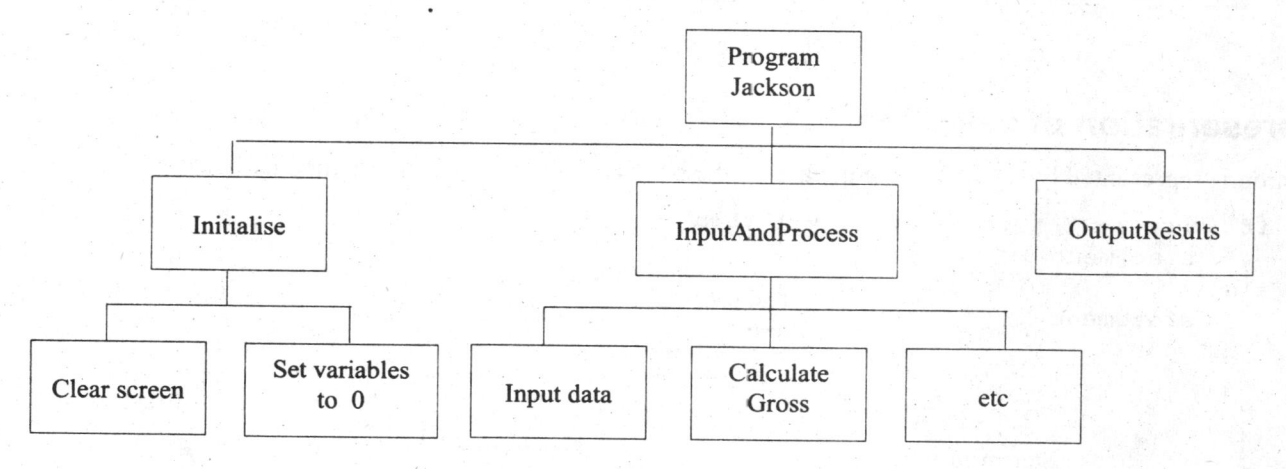

Figure 8.1: A Jackson Structure diagram

The building blocks of a structured program

Only three different 'building blocks' or **program constructs** are needed to write a structured program. These are

- **sequence** – in which one statement follows another and the program executes them in the sequence given
- **selection** – 'if..then..else' is an example of selection, where the next statement to be executed depends on the value of an expression
- **iteration** – a section of the program is repeated many times, as for example in the 'while..do' statement.

Notice the absence of the GO TO statement! Experience has shown that programs which are written without using GO TO statements are easier to follow, easier to debug and easier to maintain.

Programs that are written using **top-down** techniques, and using only the three constructs described, are called **structured programs**.

Representation of a loop

An asterisk in a box, with the condition written outside the box and the statements or modules within the loop written on the next level down, is used to indicate a section of code to be repeated.

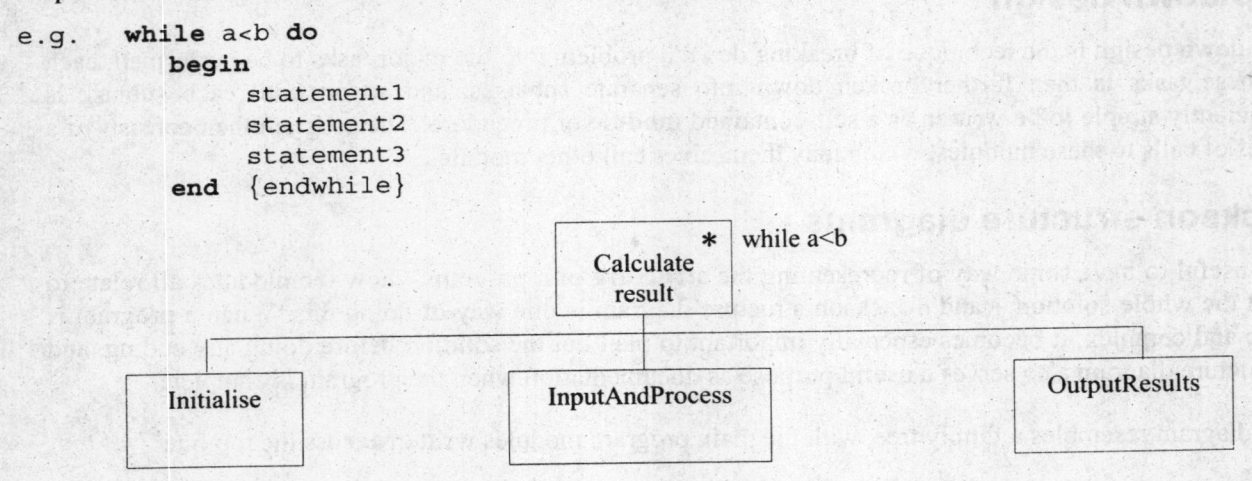

```
e.g.   while a<b do
          begin
              statement1
              statement2
              statement3
          end  {endwhile}
```

Figure 8.2: Iteration

Representation of selection

Selection is represented by a small circle in each of the boxes representing the alternative paths:

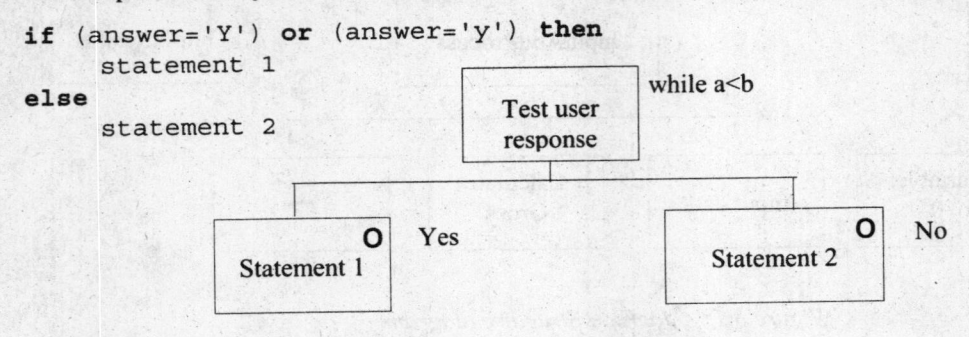

```
if (answer='Y') or (answer='y') then
    statement 1
else
    statement 2
```

Figure 8.3: Selection

Chapter 8 – Program Design and Maintenance

Example: Draw a structure diagram and code a program to input a number of sales transaction records each of which contains a salesperson's number (between 1 and 3) and a sales amount in £. Accumulate the total sales for each salesperson and the total overall sales, and output these figures at the end of the program.

The structure diagram can be drawn as follows:

```
                          ┌──────────────┐
                          │   Program    │
                          │    Sales     │
                          └──────┬───────┘
            ┌────────────────────┼────────────────────┐
     ┌──────┴──────┐      ┌──────┴──────┐      ┌──────┴──────┐
     │  Initialise │      │ ProcessData │      │ OutputTotals│
     └──────┬──────┘      └──────┬──────┘      └──────┬──────┘
     ┌─────┴──────┐              │              ┌─────┴──────┐
     │Set totals  │         *  Until no         │  Display   │
     │   to 0     │            more data        │   Totals   │
     └────────────┘              │              └────────────┘
                    ┌────────────┼────────────┐
              ┌─────┴─────┐ ┌────┴─────┐ ┌────┴─────┐
              │Input data │ │  Add to  │ │  Add to  │
              │           │ │correct   │ │Grand Total│
              │           │ │  total   │ │          │
              └───────────┘ └────┬─────┘ └──────────┘
           Salesman=1       Salesman=2       Salesman=3
     ┌──────┴──────┐   ┌──────┴──────┐   ┌──────┴──────┐
     │ Add to   O  │   │ Add to   O  │   │ Add to   O  │
     │ Total1      │   │ Total2      │   │ Total3      │
     └─────────────┘   └─────────────┘   └─────────────┘
```

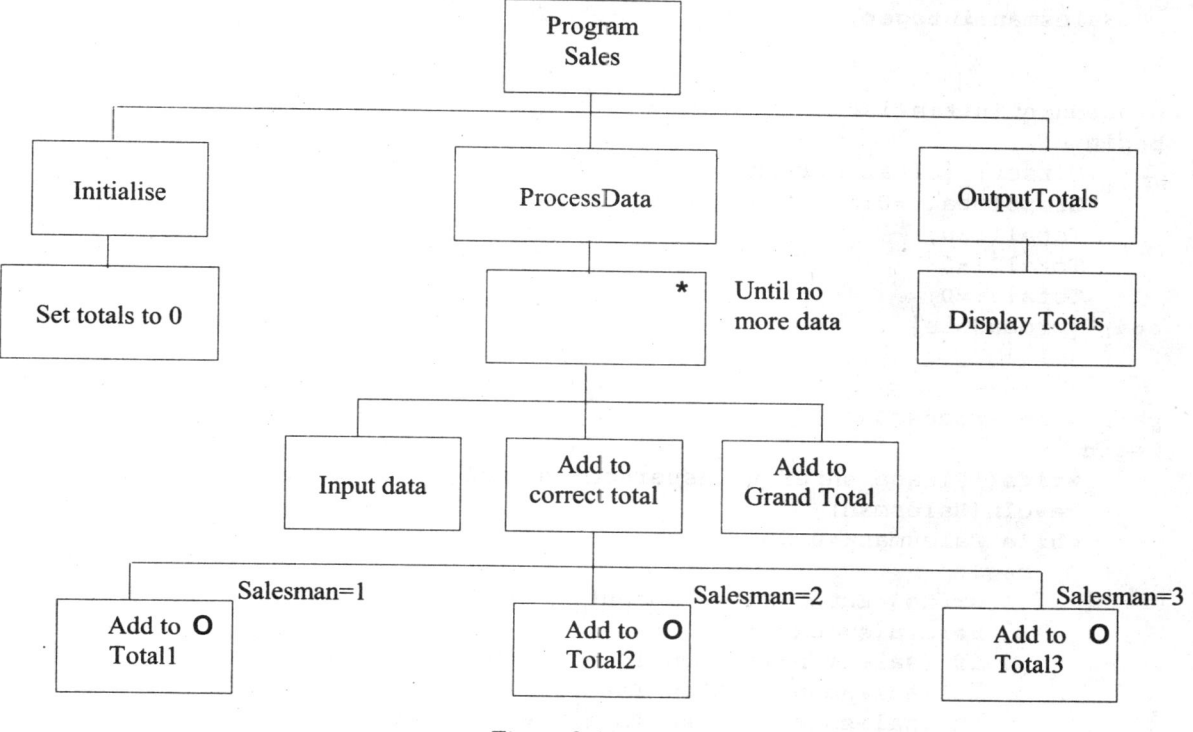

Figure 8.4

A guideline for drawing Jackson structure diagrams is that you should not put boxes representing loops (ie boxes containing asterisks) on the same level as other types of boxes. This is why in the diagram above, the box containing the asterisk appears **below** the 'ProcessData' box.

The same guideline applies to boxes containing circles representing selection; **all** the boxes on the same level must be 'selection' boxes if any of them are.

> ➢ **Q1:** Compare the structure diagram above with the coding on the next page. What details of the procedure **ProcessData** have been omitted from the structure diagram? Do you think the omissions matter?

```pascal
program Sales;
{program to accumulate sales totals for three salesmen}

uses crt;    {calls in Turbo Pascal's library routines}

var
    GrandTotal, Total1, Total2, Total3, Amount:real;
    Salesman:integer;


procedure initialise;
begin
    Clrscr; {clear screen}
    GrandTotal:=0;
    Total1:=0;
    Total2:=0;
    Total3:=0;
end; {procedure}


procedure ProcessData;
begin
    write('Please enter salesperson''s number (0 to finish): ');
    readln(Salesman);
    while Salesman<>0 do
        begin
            write('Enter sales amount: ');
            readln(Amount);
            if (salesman=1) then Total1:=Total1+amount;
            if (salesman=2) then Total2:=Total2+amount;
            if (salesman=3) then Total3:=Total3+amount;
          GrandTotal:=GrandTotal + Amount;
            write('Please enter next salesperson''s number (0 to finish): ');
            readln(Salesman)
        end
    {endwhile}
end; {procedure}


procedure OutputTotals;
begin
    writeln;
    writeln('Total for salesperson 1: ',Total1:8:2);
    writeln('Total for salesperson 2: ',Total2:8:2);
    writeln('Total for salesperson 3: ',Total3:8:2);
    writeln('Grand Total of all sales: ',GrandTotal:8:2)
end; {procedure}

{***** MAIN PROGRAM ******}

begin
    Initialise;
    ProcessData;
    OutputTotals
end.
```

Modular programming

Any programs that you write for this course are likely to be relatively short; however, in industry and commerce most problems will require thousands, if not tens of thousands, of lines of code to solve. Windows 2000, at 35 million lines of code, is the biggest program ever written. The importance of splitting up the problem into a series of self-contained **modules** then becomes obvious. A module should not exceed 100 or so lines, and preferably be short enough to fit on a single page; some modules may be only a few lines.

Advantages of modular programming

1. Some modules will be standard procedures used again and again in different programs or parts of the same program; for example, a routine to display a standard opening screen. *code re-use*

2. A module is small enough to be understandable as a unit of code. It is therefore easier to understand and debug, especially if its purpose is clearly defined and documented.

3. Program **maintenance** becomes easier because the affected modules can be quickly identified and changed.

4. In a very large project, several programmers may be working on a single program. Using a modular approach, each programmer can be given a specific set of modules to work on. This enables the whole program to be finished sooner. *team work*

5. More experienced programmers can be given the more complex modules to write, and the junior programmers can work on the simpler modules. *team work*

6. Modules can be tested independently, thereby shortening the time taken to get the whole program working.

7. If a programmer leaves part way through a project, it is easier for someone else to take over a set of self contained modules.

8. A large project becomes easier to monitor and control.

Exercises

1. Draw a structure diagram for a program which calculates and prints staff mileage allowances. Allowances are paid at the rate of 28p per mile if the purpose of the trip is to visit one or more students, and 22p per mile for any other type of journey. The program should clear the screen and display a heading with today's date, then continue to input data and calculate and print mileage allowances until the user indicates that there is no more data. Include statements to check that a valid journey type is entered.

2. Code and test the above program.

3. Draw a structure diagram and write a program which allows a user to input a sentence terminated by a full-stop. The program is to count and display the number of words in the sentence, and also count and display the number of words over 3 letters.

4. Consider the following algorithm where all the variables are integers. (The operator **div** gives the whole part of the answer, and **mod** gives the remainder, when one integer is divided by another. Thus **9 div 4** is **2** and **9 mod 4** is **1**.)

```
start  input n
       if n < 1000    goto error
       if n > 9999    goto error
       a = n div 100
       b = n mod 100
       c = a div 10
       d = a mod 10
       e = b div 10
       f = b mod 10
       g = c + d*10 + e*100 + f*1000
       output g
       end
error  display "Error in value" message
       goto start
```

(a) Perform a trace of the algorithm showing the values of each of the variables **a** to **g** if the input value is **1234**.

(b) Explain what will happen if the input to the algorithm is the value **123**.

(c) The algorithm is poorly structured. Rewrite the algorithm as a structured algorithm which does not contain any jumps.

Chapter 9 – More on Selection and Iteration

The CASE statement

We have already seen one type of conditional statement; the **if..then..else** construct. The **case** statement is useful when a choice has to be made between several alternatives. The syntax diagram is as follows:

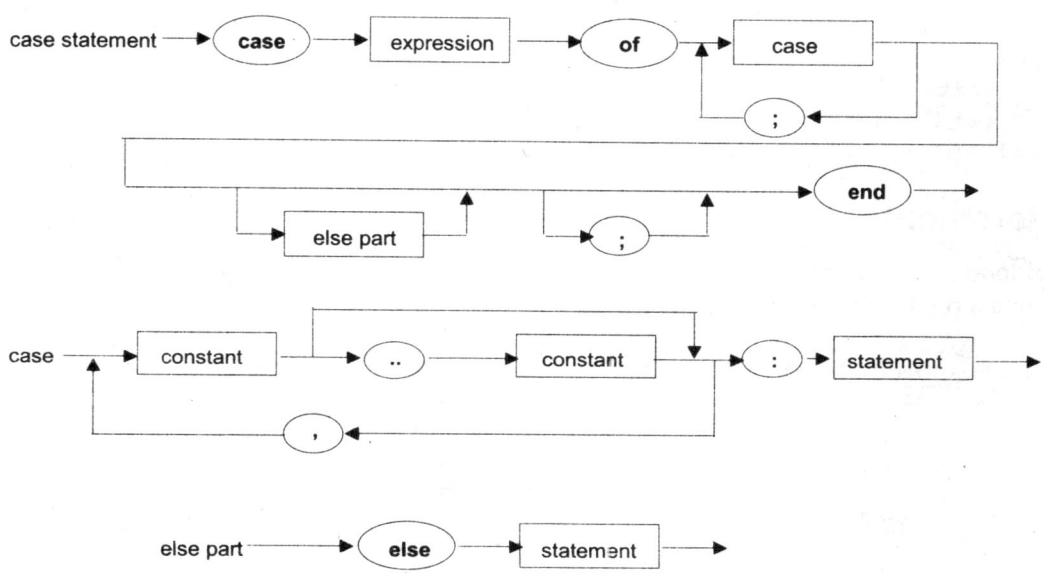

> **Q1:** Are the two examples below valid **case** statements?
>
> (i)
> ```
> case choice of
>     0,2,4,6,8: writeln('This is an even digit');
>     1,3,5,7,9: writeln('This is an odd digit');
>     10..100  : writeln('This is a number between 10 and 100');
> else
>     writeln('Negative or >100');
> end; {case}
> ```
>
> (ii)
> ```
> case month of
>     'Jan','Mar','May','Jul','Aug','Oct','Dec' :no_of_days:=31;
>     'Apr','Jun','Sep','Nov'                   :no_of_days:=30;
>     'Feb' : if year mod 4=0 then
>                 no_of_days:=29
>             else
>                 no_of_days:=28;
>            {endif}
> end; {case}
> ```
>
> **Q2:** Write a **case** statement instead of a nested **if** statement for the problem posed in **Q6** in Chapter 7. (Set grade to 'Merit' for a mark of 70 or over, etc)

The REPEAT..UNTIL statement

The **repeat..until** statement is rather similar to the **while..do** statement, except that the expression controlling the loop is tested **after** the execution of each sequence, so that the loop is always performed at least once.

The syntax is as follows:

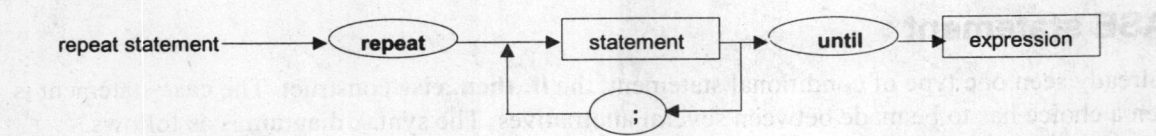

repeat statement → (repeat) → [statement] → (until) → [expression]
                                    ↑   ↓
                                    (;)

Example:
```
repeat
    write('Do you wish to continue? Answer Y or N');
    readln (answer);
until answer in ['Y','y','N','n'];
```

The FOR statement

The third type of loop is a **for** loop, which causes a statement (which may be a compound statement) to be repeatedly executed a predetermined number of times.

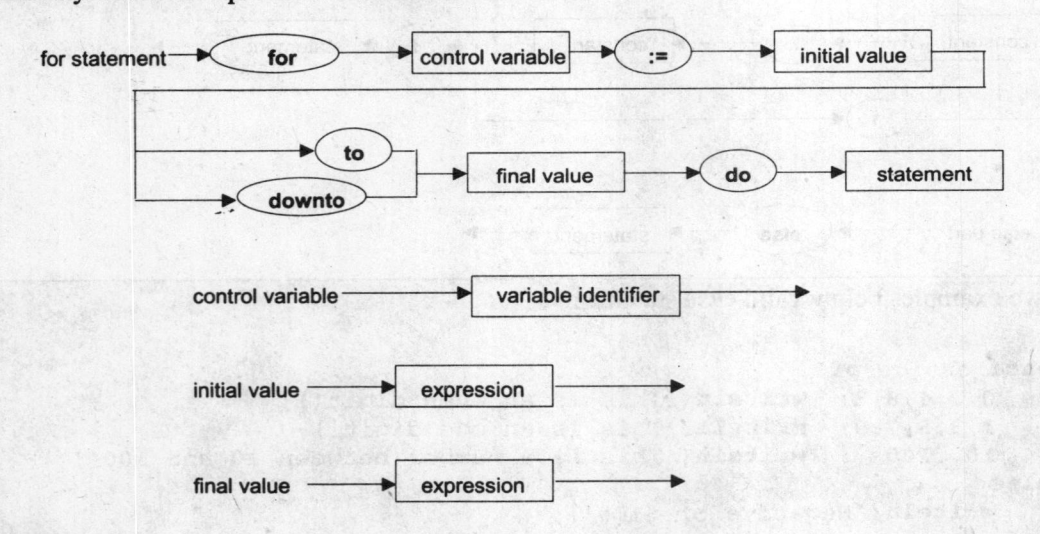

for statement → (for) → [control variable] → (:=) → [initial value]
    → (to / downto) → [final value] → (do) → [statement]

control variable → [variable identifier] →

initial value → [expression] →

final value → [expression] →

Example:
```
total:=0;
for day:=1 to 7 do
    begin
        readln(sales);
        total:=total + sales
    end;
```

Pseudocode

In the last chapter we looked at structure diagrams as a way of developing a solution to a problem, and saw how useful they are in implementing a top-down approach. If, however, we try to write down all the details of every module in a structure diagram, it becomes unwieldy. It is most useful in specifying the structure of a program down to the module level.

Pseudocode provides a means of expressing algorithms without worrying about the syntax of a particular language. (An **algorithm** is a sequence of instructions for solving a problem.)

Typical pseudocode constructs include the following:

```
If .. Then .. Else .. EndIf
Case .. Of .. EndCase
For .. To .. EndFor
Repeat ... Until ..
While .. Do .. EndWhile
Procedure ...EndProc
Function ... EndFun
```

There are no hard and fast rules as to how pseudocode statements should be written; an assignment statement to assign the value 10 to X, for example, could be written in any of the following ways:

```
Assign 10 to X
X← 10
X:=10;
Put 10 in X
```

Example: Write pseudocode for an algorithm to find the maximum, minimum and average of a set of marks.

```
Procedure FindMaxMark
begin
    set max no. of marks and total to zero
    set min to 100
    read the first mark
    while not end of data
        if mark > max then set max = mark
        endif
        if mark < min then set min = mark
        endif
        add mark to total
        add 1 to no. of marks
        read the next mark
    endwhile
    calculate average
    print results
end procedure
```

Note that
- keywords such as **begin, end, while, endwhile, if,** and **endif** mark the limits of procedures, loops and conditional statements;
- the actual statements of the algorithm can be written in ordinary English;
- the indentation is important – it gives a visual picture of the extent of loops and conditional statements.

As stated above, there are no absolute rules for writing pseudocode; for example both versions of the **repeat** construct shown below would be quite acceptable:

```
    repeat until end of data
        statements
        .....
        .....
        .....
    end repeat

    repeat
        statements
        .....
        .....
        .....
    until end of data
```

Generating random numbers

In many types of problem it is useful to be able to generate a series of random numbers in a given range. Different versions of Pascal have different functions for doing this, but all work on the same principle. A 'seed' is supplied either by the user or automatically by the system, using the system clock, to generate the first random number, which will be in the range 0 <= random number < 1. Subsequent numbers are all generated from the previous one in the series. If you wish to repeat the same sequence of numbers then you provide the 'seed', otherwise you leave it to the computer.

Example: In Turbo Pascal, a random number between 2 and 12 can be generated by first initializing the random number generator with a call to **randomize,** or by assigning a specific integer value to the predefined identifier **randseed,** and then calling the function **random**. **Random(n)** returns a random number of type **word** within the range 0 <= x < n. If no argument is supplied, it returns a random argument of type **real** in the range 0 <= x < 1.

i.e.
```
    begin
    ......
    randomize;
    {or randseed := 5; (or any other integer) to generate the same
    sequence of random numbers each time}
    repeat
        ......
        test_num := random(11) + 2;{to get an integer between 2 and 12}
        etc

    until ....
```

The random number generator's seed (which is obtained from the system clock) is stored in a predeclared integer variable called **randseed**. By assigning a specific value to **randseed**, a specific sequence of random numbers can be generated over and over. This is particularly useful in data encryption and simulation.

Exercises

1. Draw a structure diagram for a program used to help young students learn multiplication tables. The program should:

    (a) accept entry of student's name and use the name in any interaction between computer and student.

Chapter 9 – More on Selection and Iteration

(b) ask the student what table they wish to be tested on.

(c) ask 5 random questions from the table, by calling a standard random number generator such as **random** in Turbo Pascal, giving the correct answer if the student gets it wrong.

(d) on completion, give the score out of 5, make a suitable remark, and offer the student another go.

(e) when the student decides to end, make a suitable closing remark and end the program.

2. Devise suitable test data for this program. Can you be absolutely sure that the program is working correctly?

3. What improvements can you suggest could be incorporated in your program?

4. Write a program for a game in which the user guesses what random number between 1 and 1000 the computer has "thought of", until he or she has found the correct number. The computer should tell the user for each guess whether it was too high, too low or spot on! How many carefully chosen guesses should the user need before getting the right answer?

5. Write a program to let the computer guess what number YOU have thought of, within a specified range.

6. In a typical high level programming language the simplest program construct consists of a sequence of statements. Describe **two** other program constructs, illustrating your answer with an example in each case.

7. The following algorithm is intended to check two dates (each in the form of three integers – day month year) and to print the message "Dates in chronological order" or "Dates not in chronological order" as appropriate.

```
begin module
   input day1 month1 year1
   input day2 month2 year2
   if year1 < year2
   then output "Dates in chronological order"
   else output "Dates not in chronological order"
   endif
   if (year1 = year2) and (month1 < month2)
   then output "Dates in chronological order"
   else output "Dates not in chronological order"
   endif
   if (year1 = year2) and (month1 = month2) and (day1 < day2)
   then output "Dates in chronological order"
   else output "Dates not in chronological order"
   endif
end module
```

The algorithm does not work correctly. Explain the reason why and correct the algorithm.

Module 1 Computer Systems, Programming and Network Concepts

Chapter 10 – Arrays and Data Types

Introduction

In Chapter 8 there is a sample structure diagram (Figure 8.4) and program for accumulating total sales for each of three salespersons. Now clearly if there were, say, 150 salespeople, the method used would be quite impractical. We need some way of defining all 150 totals in one statement, and this is where **arrays** come in. The statement

```
var
     total:array[1..150] of real;
```

defines 150 real variables, which will be referred to as total[1], total[2], ...total[150]. The number in brackets is called the **index** or **subscript** of the array. In this example it can be an integer, or an integer variable, or an integer expression; for example total[i+1] , where i is an integer variable. Of course we must be careful that the value of i+1 lies between 1 and 150 or a run-time error will occur, and a message 'subscript out of range' or something similar will be displayed.

An array is a way of **organising** data in memory, and is an example of a **data structure**.

> Q1: Add a line of code to initialise all 150 elements of the array **total** to zero.
>   for I := 1 to 150 do

> Q2: Define an array of integers called **temp** whose index varies between -10 and +50.

An array may also be used to hold strings of characters. For example we could define an array to hold the names of the months:

```
var
     month_name:array[1..12] of string[9];
```

The array could be initialised with a procedure containing 12 statements of the form

```
month_name[1]:='January  ';
month_name[2]:='February ';
etc
```

> Q3: Write statements to input a month number between 1 and 12 , together with a sales amount, and display 'The sales figure for xxxxxxxxx is 9999.99' (where xxxxxxxxx represents the month name, and 9999.99 the sales amount. You may assume the existence of a procedure to initialise the month names, as given above).

Declaring data types

Pascal allows the programmer to define data types other than the simple types **real, integer**, etc. If for example we wish to access individual characters in a string, the string has to be defined as an **array of char**. We can define a **type** consisting of an array of characters as follows:

```
type
    input_string=array[1..6] of char;
var
    number:input_string;
```

The Boolean function eoln

The built-in Pascal function **eoln** is used to detect the **end of line** when data is being read in from a keyboard character by character. It is set to **true** when the *next* character to be entered is a **<Return>** character. You may wonder how the computer can perform this mind-reading feat – the answer is that as the characters are typed, they are placed in a **line buffer** and none of them is processed until **<Return>** is pressed. The computer therefore has all the characters in the line of input available to it and can scan ahead to check the next character.

Example: Write a procedure which allows the user to enter up to **max** digits, terminated by <Return>, and checks that each character entered is a valid digit between 0 and 9. If any invalid character is encountered a 'flag' **error_detected** is set to **true**. (This type of routine is useful for validating input, so as to ensure that a program will not crash when a user enters a non-numeric character when a numeric character is expected. Instead, the program could print out an error message and ask the user to re-enter a numeric value.)

```
procedure validate_integer;
    {assume all variables have been declared in the main program}

begin
    count:=0;
    error_detected:=false;

    while not eoln do
      begin
        count:=count+1;
        if count > max then error_detected:=true {too many digits}
        else
            begin
                read(number[count]);
                if not(number[count]in['0'..'9'])then
                    error_detected:=true;
                {endif}
            end {endif}
     end;
    {endwhile}
    readln {this is needed to go to the next line}
end; {procedure}
```

Looking up tables of values

Arrays are frequently used to store tables of values. For example, suppose we have 3 arrays, one containing the names of the 12 countries in the Common Market, and the other two containing the name of each country's currency and the current exchange rate. Given a particular country's name, we can look it up in the appropriate array and then, having determined the array subscript, print the corresponding currency name and exchange rate.

Module 1 Computer Systems, Programming and Network Concepts

> **Q4:** Assuming the existence of three arrays **country_name**, **currency**, and **exchange_rate**, and assuming each element of all the arrays has been initialised with an appropriate value, write statements to input the name of a country, look it up in the array **country_name**, and display the name of the country together with the corresponding currency name and exchange rate. You should allow for the possibility that the country name is not in the array, in which case the message 'Country not known' should be displayed.
>
> ```
> {arrays defined as follows}
> var
>     country_name      :array[1..12] of string[15];
>     currency          :array[1..12] of string[15];
>     exchange_rate     :array[1..12] of real;
>     country           :string[15];
>     ....
>     ....
> begin
>
>     {first two lines are as follows:}
>     write('Please input the name of the country: ');
>     readln(country);
> ```

Multi-dimensional arrays

An array can have more than one dimension; for example, a two-dimensional array could be declared as follows:

```
total:array[1..150,1..5] of real;
```

The first index could represent a particular salesperson, and the second index a particular department in a store.

> **Q5:** Suppose that input consists of a salesperson number between 1 and 150, a department number between 1 and 5 and a sales amount. Write statements to input **salesman_no**, **dept**, and **amount** and add the sales amount to the correct element of **total**.

Exercises

1. Draw a structure diagram or write pseudocode for the following program, and then code and test it:

    (a) input a number of sales transactions, each consisting of a salesperson's number (between 1 and 150), a Department number (between 1 and 5) and a sales amount.

    (b) accumulate and print out the total sales for each employee with non-zero sales, and the total sales for each Department together with the name of the Department. (Departments are as follows:

    1=Electrical, 2=Household goods, 3=Toys and Games, 4=Menswear, 5=Ladies' Fashion).

2. Write a program to simulate throwing a die a number of times, and display the number of times each face appears. Your program should allow the user to specify how many 'throws' he wants to make.

3. The following section of pseudo-code illustrates the process of converting a positive integer value into a character string for output.

DIGITS is a one dimensional array; I, K, X and Y are integer variables. Each element of DIGITS can be used to store an integer equivalent to the code of a single ASCII character. The value to be processed is initially stored in X.

Initialise I = 0
Repeat Add 1 to I
    Assign the whole number part of X/10 to Y
    calculate X − 10*Y and Assign result to K
    calculate K + 48 *(the ASCII code for the digit held in K)*
        and Assign to element I of DIGITS
    Assign X = Y
Until X = 0

(a) Copy and complete the following dry-run table for this algorithm given that the initial value of X is 7046.

X	I	Y	K	Elements of DIGITS					
				1	2	3	4	5	6

(b) Write down what would be printed if the following algorithm is now used to output the contents of DIGITS, given that I now equals 4.

Initialise K = 1
While K less than I
    Print element K of DIGITS
    Newline
    Add 1 to K
Endwhile
    (4)

(c) Rewrite the pseudo-code given in part (b) so that the original integer given in X is printed correctly.

Module 1 Computer Systems, Programming and Network Concepts

Chapter 11 – Procedures and Functions

Program structure

In standard Pascal, all programs have to conform to a particular format given below:

```
program heading;
label
    labels;
const
    constant declarations;
type
    data type definitions;
var
    variable declarations;
procedures and functions;
begin
    main program
end.
```

Procedure and function structure

Procedures have an almost identical structure:

```
procedure procname(formal parameters);
label
    labels;
const
    constant declarations;
type
    data type definitions;
var
    variable declarations;

procedures and functions;

begin
    main body of procedure;
end;
```

Functions have exactly the same structure as procedures except that a function starts with a function header:

```
function funcname(formal parameters):data type;
```

Global and local identifiers

Any procedure or function can include the declaration of constants and variables using **const** and **var** statements. Identifiers declared within a subprogram (that is, a procedure or function) are **local** identifiers and exist only during a call to the subprogram. Identifiers which are declared in the **main** program are called **global** variables and can be used throughout the program and all subprograms.

Block structure

Pascal is said to be a **block structured** language. A **block** consists of a **declaration** part, which includes constant, variable, label and type definitions and procedure and function declarations, and a **statement** part.

A sample program outline

```
program MainProg;
var  var1:real;
     var2,xxx:integer;

     procedure FirstProc;
     var a,b,c:real;

         function Func1;
             begin {Func1}
             .
             .
             end; {Func1}

         begin {FirstProc}
         .
         .
         end; {FirstProc}

     procedure SecondProc;
     var d,e,xxx,n,m:real;










begin {Mainprog}
.
.
end. {Mainprog}
```

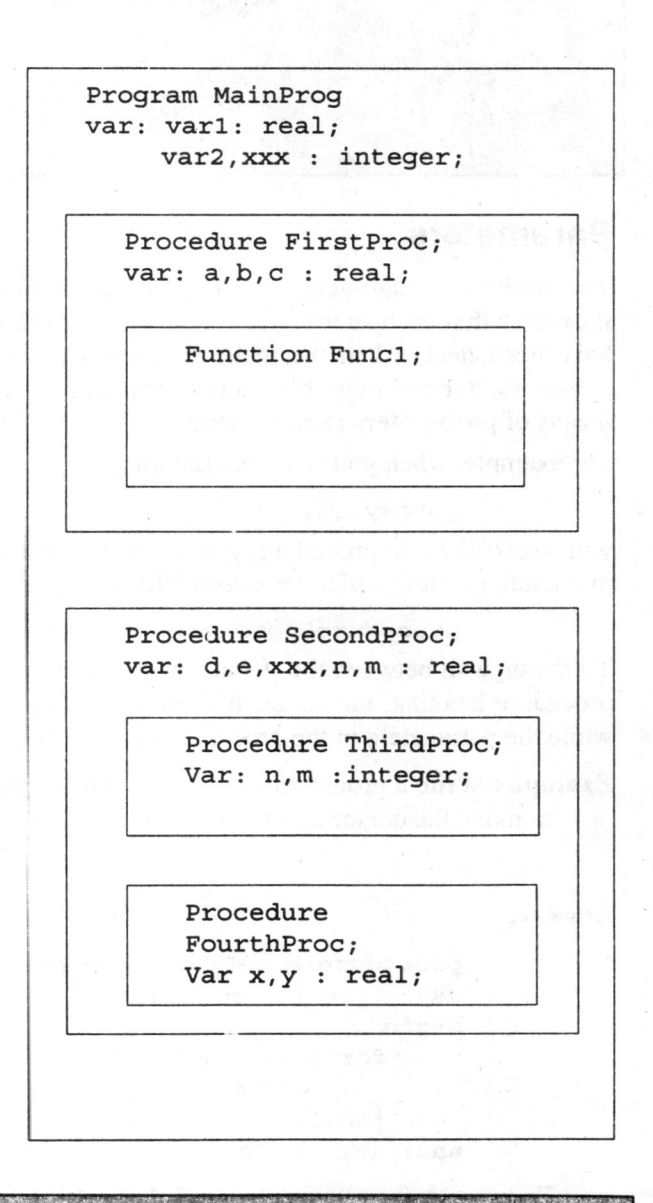

```
Program MainProg
var: var1: real;
     var2,xxx : integer;

    ┌─────────────────────────────────┐
    │ Procedure FirstProc;            │
    │ var: a,b,c : real;              │
    │                                 │
    │   ┌─────────────────────────┐   │
    │   │ Function Func1;         │   │
    │   │                         │   │
    │   │                         │   │
    │   └─────────────────────────┘   │
    │                                 │
    └─────────────────────────────────┘

    ┌─────────────────────────────────┐
    │ Procedure SecondProc;           │
    │ var: d,e,xxx,n,m : real;        │
    │                                 │
    │   ┌─────────────────────────┐   │
    │   │ Procedure ThirdProc;    │   │
    │   │ Var: n,m :integer;      │   │
    │   └─────────────────────────┘   │
    │                                 │
    │   ┌─────────────────────────┐   │
    │   │ Procedure               │   │
    │   │ FourthProc;             │   │
    │   │ Var x,y : real;         │   │
    │   └─────────────────────────┘   │
    └─────────────────────────────────┘
```

> **Q1:** Complete the outline program, according to the diagram on the right hand side showing the 'blocks' that make up the program.

Scope of identifiers

All identifiers have to be declared before they can be used, and the **scope** of an identifier includes the block (program or subprogram) in which it is declared, and all blocks included within it.

An exception to this rule occurs when an identifier has the same name as one in a block which calls it, as for example the variable **xxx** in the outline program above.

> Q2: Complete the following table:

Identifier	Scope
var1,var2	MainProg, FirstProc, SecondProc, ThirdProc, FourthProc, Func1
xxx	MainProg, FirstProc, Func1. Once SecondProc is called, the **local** variable takes precedence. Its scope is SecondProc, ThirdProc and FourthProc.
a,b,c	
d,e	
n,m	

Parameters

The ability to declare local variables within subprograms is very useful in modular programming because it ensures that each subprogram is completely self-contained and independent of any global variables that have been declared in the main program. However, there has to be some way of passing information between outer and inner blocks (e.g. between the main program and its subprograms) and this is done by means of **parameters** (also sometimes referred to as the **arguments** of the subprogram).

For example, when you write the statement

```
gotoxy(35,10);
```

you are calling a procedure gotoxy with **parameters** 35 and 10. The procedure itself will have a procedure heading which looks something like the following:

```
procedure gotoxy(x,y:integer);
```

To distinguish between the parameters used when calling the routine and those which are declared in the procedure heading, the values that are passed (35 and 10 in the example) are called **actual parameters**, while the parameters in the procedure heading (x and y in the example) are called **formal parameters**.

Example: Write a procedure to move the cursor down the screen n lines, and show how you would use it to move the cursor down the screen   (a) 5 lines

(b) m lines.

Answer:

```
procedure MoveDown(n:integer);
var line_number : integer;
begin
    for line_number = 1 to n do
        writeln
    {endfor}
end; {MoveDown}
```

To move down 5 lines, the procedure will be called with the statement

```
MoveDown(5);
```

To move down m lines the procedure will be called with the statement

```
MoveDown(m);
```

The formal parameter n in the above example does not change value in the procedure. It is called a **value parameter**, and the actual value 5, or the value of m in the second call, is passed to the memory location n from the calling procedure (or main program). This is called **passing parameters by value**.

In the next example, the procedure performs a calculation and passes the answer back to the calling procedure or main program.

Example: Write a procedure which accepts a number of seconds and converts this number to hours, minutes and seconds, passing the answer back to the calling routine.

Answer:
```
procedure TimeConversion(TotalSeconds:integer;
                         var hours, minutes, seconds :integer);
begin
    hours := TotalSeconds div 3600;
    minutes := (TotalSeconds mod 3600) div 60;
    seconds := (TotalSeconds mod 3600) mod 60
end; {TimeConversion}
```

> **Q3:** How will you use this procedure to convert 4000 seconds to hours, minutes and seconds, storing the result in h, m, and s?

Hours, minutes and seconds in the above example are **variable parameters**, and must be preceded by the word **var** in the procedure heading. They are passed **by reference**; the **addresses,** not the **values,** of h, m and s are passed to the procedure.

A further example of parameter passing

On the following page is a program which allows the user to enter an integer of up to 9 digits, and then calculates a modulus-11 check digit and prints out the whole code number, incorporating the calculated check digit. The top-level solution to this problem could be expressed as

```
repeat until no more integers
    input the digits
    calculate the check digit
    output the code number
end repeat
```

The procedure **calc_checkdigit** is called with the following statement:

```
calc_checkdigit(raw_number, no_of_digits, check_digit);
```

The identifiers in brackets are the so-called **actual parameters;** they represent the actual values that will be passed to the subroutine or passed back from the subroutine. In this example, **raw_number** and **no_of_digits** are passed to the subprogram, which calculates and returns the value **checkdigit.**

The **declaration** of the procedure **calc_checkdigit** is as follows:

```
procedure calc_checkdigit(y:array_n; n:integer; var checkdigit:char);
```

The identifiers in brackets are the so-called **formal** parameters. Important points to note are summarised below:

- The **order** in which the parameters are declared is crucial; it must correspond to the **actual parameter list** in the calling statement.
- Any identifier whose value will be **changed** in the subprogram (e.g. **checkdigit**) must be declared as a **variable** using the **var** statement. These are called **variable** parameters (or sometimes **output** parameters), and they provide two-way communication. Parameters whose values do **not** change in the subprogram are called **value** parameters (or sometimes **input** parameters).
- Each identifier must have its type declared.
- The types that are allowed in a parameter list are the simple data types such as real, integer, char, boolean, or any declared type. This means that whenever a parameter is a structured type such as an

Module 1 Computer Systems, Programming and Network Concepts

array, the type must be defined by the programmer and the type identifier used in the procedure heading. The type array_n has for this reason been declared in the main program.

```
program check_dig; {program to calculate check digits}

type array_n = array[1..9] of char;

var    answer,check_digit  : char;
       raw_number   : array_n;
       no_of_digits : integer;


procedure input_integer(var x:array_n; var count:integer);
{Accepts entry of the integer digit by digit and validates each digit}
var  entry_valid : boolean;
     next_digit  : char;

begin
  repeat
     count := 0;
     writeln('Enter an integer of up to 9 digits, followed by <Enter>');
     while not eoln do
        begin
           count := count + 1;
           read(next_digit);
           x[count] := next_digit;
           if not (next_digit in ['0'..'9']) then
              begin
                 writeln('Error - please redo from start');
                 entry_valid := false;
                 readln;
              end
           else
              entry_valid := true;
           {endif}
        end;
     {endwhile}
  until entry_valid;   {end repeat}
  readln;
end; {input_integer}

procedure calc_checkdigit(y:array_n; n:integer; var checkdigit:char);
const  x = 'x';
       zero = '0';
var    count,weight,weighted_value,remainder,sum  :integer;
begin
  weight :=2;
  sum := 0;
  for count := n downto 1 do
     begin
        weighted_value := (ord(y[count])-48) * weight;
        sum := sum + weighted_value;
        weight := weight + 1;
     end;
  {endfor}
```

54

```
      remainder := sum mod 11;
      case remainder of
      0          : checkdigit := zero;
      1          : checkdigit := x;
      2..10      : checkdigit := chr(48 + 11 - remainder);
      end; {case}
   end; {calculate checkdigit}

   procedure output_code(x:array_n; n:integer; checkdigit:char);
   var  counter : integer;

   begin
      write('The code number is ');
      for counter := 1 to n do
         write (x[counter]);
      {endfor}
      write (checkdigit);
      writeln;
   end;

{***** MAIN PROGRAM ******}
begin
   repeat
      input_integer(raw_number,no_of_digits);
      calc_checkdigit(raw_number,no_of_digits,check_digit);
      output_code(raw_number,no_of_digits,check_digit);
      writeln;
      writeln('Another? (Y or N): ');
      readln(answer);
   until answer in ['n','N'];
end.
```

> **Q4:** In the program above which calculates and outputs check digits:
>   (i) Identify 4 global variables.
>   (ii) Identify two variables which are local to the procedure input_integer.
>   (iii) Identify two parameters which are passed by value to the procedure calc_checkdigit.
>   (iv) Identify one parameter which is passed by reference to the procedure calc_checkdigit. Explain the difference between passing parameters by value and passing them by reference.

> **Q5:** Which of the following procedure headings is valid?
>   (i) **procedure** proc1 (a b, c; **var** d, e: **integer**);
>   (ii) **procedure** proc2 (**var** m, n : **char**; **var** s, t : **real** ; v : **real**);
>   (iii) **procedure** proc3 (x : **array**[1..10] of **integer**; **var** z : **char**);
>   (iv) **procedure** proc4;
>   (v) **procedure** proc5 (d, e : **real**;   f, g : **integer**;   **var**   p : **char**; q, r, s : **real**);

> **Q6:** The last procedure above is called with the statement
>   proc5 (j, k, l, m, n, x, y, z);
>   Which are **value** parameters and which are **variable** parameters? Explain the difference.

Standard functions

Pascal has many built-in functions, some of which such as **ord** and **char** we have already come across. A summary of some of the most frequently used functions is given below. There are many others, which will be listed in your Pascal manual.

Chr   returns a character of a specified ordinal number eg chr(69) = 'E'
Ord   returns the ordinal number of an ordinal-type value eg ord('A') = 65
Round   rounds a type real value to an integer value eg round(3.6) = 4
Trunc   truncates a type real value to an integer value eg trunc(5.8) = 5
Sqr   returns the square of the argument
Sqrt   returns the square root of the argument
Length   returns the dynamic length of a string
Random   returns a random number.

For convenience, the ASCII codes for the common characters and numbers are given below:

ASCII	Char	ASCII	Char	ASCII	Char	ASCII	Char
32	space	56	8	80	P	104	h
33	!	57	9	81	Q	105	i
34	"	58	:	82	R	106	j
35	£	59	;	83	S	107	k
36	$	60	<	84	T	108	l
37	%	61	=	85	U	109	m
38	&	62	>	86	V	110	n
39	'	63	?	87	W	111	o
40	(	64	@	88	X	112	p
41	)	65	A	89	Y	113	q
42	*	66	B	90	Z	114	r
43	+	67	C	91	[	115	s
44	,	68	D	92	\	116	t
45	-	69	E	93	]	117	u
46	.	70	F	94	^	118	v
47	/	71	G	95	_	119	w
48	0	72	H	96	`	120	x
49	1	73	I	97	a	121	y
50	2	74	J	98	b	122	z
51	3	75	K	99	c	123	{
52	4	76	L	100	d	124	|
53	5	77	M	101	e	125	}
54	6	78	N	102	f	126	~
55	7	79	O	103	g	127	del

User-written functions

We can also write our own functions, and everything that has been said about procedures also applies to functions; the only difference between them lies in the way they are declared and called. The example below, which returns the largest of two integers, illustrates this.

```
function max(a,b:integer):integer;
  begin
    max:=a;
    if b>a then max:=b
  end;
```

This function would be called with the statement (for example)

```
MaxValue := max(x,y);
```

Note that

- the function has to contain an assignment statement to give it its value;
- the function **type** (**real, integer** etc) has to be specified;
- a function is not normally used when more than one value is to be passed back, this value being passed back in the actual function name, e.g. **max** in the above example.

Exercises

1. Write a procedure which positions the cursor at a given point on the screen and then writes a character string. (Use the Turbo Pascal GOTOXY procedure or equivalent).

2. Write a program to simulate storing 80 records with 4-digit keys in a random file of between 80 and 160 spaces, as specified by the user. For each 'record', the program should generate a random 4-digit integer to represent a record key, and then calculate the record address using the algorithm

    address := record_key **mod** filesize

    The key should then be stored in the corresponding element of an array (which represents the file). If there is already a key at the address, the new key is to be stored in the next available free element, and a variable counting the number of 'collisions' should be incremented by 1.

    Print out after each 10 keys have been stored, the number of collisions which have occurred.

    From this simulation, how much space would you recommend allowing for a random file if 80 records have to be stored? Is there any other information which could usefully be obtained if appropriate enhancements were made to the program?

3. Write a function called Power which has integer arguments x, n and returns x^n.

4. Write a program which allows the user to input a sentence of up to 60 characters at the keyboard (terminated by a full-stop), and then calls a procedure which encrypts the sentence as follows:

    Generate a random number between 1 and 6. Then, for each character in turn, find its ASCII code, add to it the random number, and convert it back to a character.

    Print out the encrypted sentence, and then call another procedure which 'decrypts' it and print out the decrypted version.

5. Explain how **each** of the following can contribute to the production of good quality software:

    (a) Procedures

    (b) Local variables

    (c) Parameters.

6. The following is a fragment of a computer program.

   integer n_records
   .
   .
   .

   procedure display_record(n)
   integer linenum
   .
   .
   .
   if (n>n_records) **then**
       display_error_message_box()
   endif
   .
   .
   .
   endproc

   (a) For the fragment above, identify the following:
       (i) the local variable
       (ii) the global variable
       (iii) the parameter

   (b) Describe briefly what is meant by
       (i) local variables
       (ii) global variables
       (iv) Parameters

   (c) What is the benefit of using parameters with a procedure?

Chapter 12 – Sequential File Processing

Introduction

This chapter is concerned with writing data to disk files and reading data from disk files for further processing or producing reports. In serial and sequential file organisation, records are written to a file one after the other in the order in which they are input.

Record declaration

A data file will consist of a number of **records**, each of which is divided into a number of **fields**. For example, a stock file could consist of records having the following fields:

```
field name              type
item_no                 string[6]
description             string[20]
selling_price           real
qty_in_stock            integer
```

Pascal uses a built-in composite data type **record** to define the fields in the record as follows:

```
type stock_rec_type = record
         item_no        :string[6];
         description    :string[20];
         selling_price  :real;
         qty_in_stock   :integer
     end;
```

The data type for the **file** of records now has to be declared as follows:

```
stock_file_type = file of stock_rec_type;
```

and finally the variables of type **file_of_stock** and **stock_rec** are declared:

```
var
    stock_file      :stock_file_type;
    stock_item      :stock_rec_type;
```

Note that item_no and description have been given a fixed length of 6 and 20 respectively. In the sample program later in this unit, character strings will be defined as arrays of characters, which makes input easier for the user because the input routine can be written to 'pad out' each field with spaces if necessary.

> **Q1:** Imagine you are to create a file of stock transaction records, each consisting of a 6-character item number and a quantity sold. Write the type and var declarations to declare the file and associated record structure.

Assigning an external name to a file

Before a file variable can be used, it must be associated with an external file. In Turbo Pascal, this is achieved by means of the **assign** statement; for example

```
assign(stock_file,'a:\data\stock.dat');
```

In other versions of Pascal, the filename must appear in the parameter list of the program heading, and this name will then be used as the external file name:

```
program stock(input,output,stock_file);
```

Input and output

A file must be 'opened' before it can be read from or written to. An existing file can be opened for reading with the **reset** procedure, and a new file can be created and opened with the **rewrite** procedure.

When a file is processed sequentially, it may be read from or written to with the standard procedures **read** and **write**; for example

```
read(stock_file,stock_item);
```

In Turbo Pascal (but not in standard Pascal) a file should be closed when processing is completed, using the standard procedure **close**.

```
close(stock_file);
```

The standard boolean function **eof** detects the end of a file when reading records sequentially. It will return **true** when the last record in a file has been read, and **false** otherwise.

Accessing fields in a record

In order to refer to a field of a record, the **dot notation** is used. For example, to refer to item_no in the field stock_item, we write

```
stock_item.item_no
```

> **Q2:** If we have also defined a record called **trans_rec** which has a field **item_no**, how will this be referred to?

The dot notation can become rather cumbersome and Pascal provides a more convenient way of referring to fields within a record, namely, the **with** statement.

with statement ──→ (with) ──→ [record identifier] ──→ (do) ──→ statement ──→

e.g.
```
with stock_rec do
begin
     write('Enter item number');
     readln(item_no);

end; {with}
```

Writing to the printer

To write to the printer in Turbo Pascal, include **printer** in the program's **uses** clause just beneath the program header at the start of the program (e.g. **uses crt, printer**) and use

```
writeln(Lst,data)
```

A sample program

The following program demonstrates both writing to disk, and reading from disk. Stock records are accepted at the terminal and written to disk, and then when all records are written, the file is closed and reopened for input and the records are read and displayed on the screen.

```pascal
program s_create;

{Program to accept data from the keyboard and write to stock master
file.}

uses crt;
const max = 20;

type
   string_max = array[1..max] of char;
   stock_rec_type = record
   item_no        : integer;
   description    : string_max;
   selling_price  : real;
   qty_in_stock   : integer
end;

stock_file_type = file of stock_rec_type;

var
   stock_file   : stock_file_type;
   stock_item   : stock_rec_type;
   filename     : string[20];


procedure read_text_string (no_of_chars:integer;
                                        var text_string : string_max);
const space = ' ';
var counter:integer;

begin
   for counter := 1 to no_of_chars do
      if eoln then text_string[counter]:=space
      else read(text_string[counter]);
      {endif}
   {endfor}
   readln
end; {procedure}

Procedure initialise;
begin
   clrscr;
   writeln('Please enter the name of the file, including pathname
   (eg a:\stockmas.dat);' );
   readln(filename);
   assign(stock_file,filename);
   rewrite(stock_file);
   write('Enter item number; 999 to finish: ');
   readln(stock_item.item_no)
end; {procedure}

Procedure write_recs;
begin
   with stock_item do
```

Module 1 Computer Systems, Programming and Network Concepts

```pascal
      begin
        while item_no <>999 do
        begin
          write('Enter description: ');
          read_text_string(20,description);
          write('Selling price   : ');
          readln(selling_price);
          write('Quantity in stock: ');
          readln(qty_in_stock);
          { **** write the record to the file ****}
          write(stock_file,stock_item);
          write('Enter item number; 999 to finish: ');
          readln(item_no)
        end; {while}
      end {with}
    close(stock_file);
  end; {procedure}


  Procedure read_recs;
  begin
    reset(stock_file);
    with stock_item do
      begin
        while not eof(stock_file) do
        begin
          read(stock_file,stock_item);
          writeln(item_no:7, description:22, selling_price:8:2,
          qty_in_stock:5)
        end {while}
      end; {with}
    close(stock_file)
  end; {procedure}


  {***** MAIN PROGRAM *****}

  begin
  initialise;
  write_recs;
  read_recs
  end.
```

Exercises

1. Write a program which accepts stock transactions from the keyboard giving item number and quantity sold, and writes them to a transaction file on disk. (n.b. Input the transactions in item number sequence, to avoid having to sort them before testing the update program in Exercise 2).

2. Write a program which performs a sequential file update of the stock master file, using as input the old stock master file and the transaction file, and creating a new stock master file.

Chapter 13 – Random Access File Processing

Introduction

A random access file may be used in an application which requires direct access to any particular record in the file. For example in a stock control system, it may be desirable to look up any stock item to check its price or the quantity in stock, and to update the record when an item is sold.

In the simplest type of random file organisation, the record address is given by the key field of each record. That is stock item number 168 is held at address 168, stock item 2746 is held at address 2746 and so on. This means that each record has to have a numeric key field which lies within a given range, say 1 to 2000 for a file which can hold up to 2000 records.

If the records do not have numeric keys, or have keys which are too widely spread to be used as record addresses, then a **hashing algorithm** has to be used to convert the key to an address. The programming then becomes more complex but the principle is unchanged; in either case, we are using the record key to calculate an address.

The Pascal 'seek' procedure

The **seek** procedure moves a pointer from its current position in the file to a specified record number represented by a long integer. The syntax is as follows:

    seek (Filename, RecordAddress)

Suppose you want to read record number 3 from a file named BookFile, into a record buffer named BookRec.

    seek (BookFile, 3);
    read (BookFile, BookRec);

The pointer is moved along automatically when the record is read, as shown below:

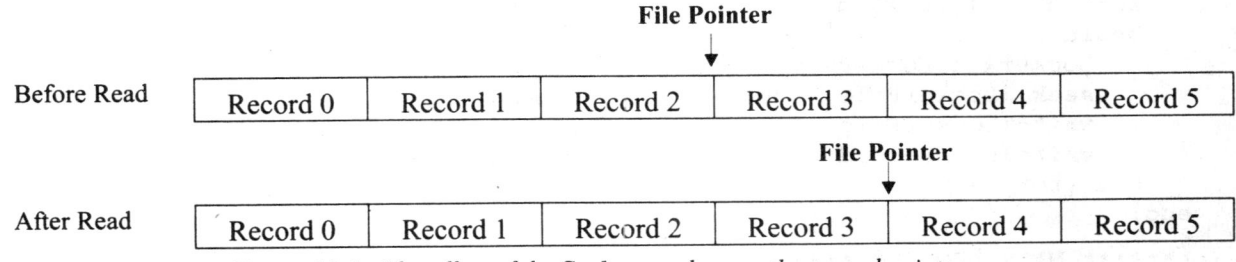

	Record 0	Record 1	Record 2	Record 3	Record 4	Record 5
Before Read (File Pointer at Record 2)						
After Read (File Pointer at Record 3)						

*Figure 13.1 - The effect of the **Seek** procedure on the record pointer*

Therefore, if you want to update BookRec and then write it back to the file, you must call the **seek** procedure again before the **write** statement.

Initialising a random access file

It is common practice to set up a file of blank records ready for use. If the file will eventually hold 100 records, then 100 blank records are written to a new file, with each record containing as well as blank data fields, an extra field which indicates an empty record. When data is written to a particular record, this field is changed to show that the record now contains data.

Module 1 Computer Systems, Programming and Network Concepts

The sample program below sets up 20 blank records which will be used to hold details of which students have been allocated each of 20 lockers numbered 1 to 20.

```pascal
program CreateRandom;
{stored as Ch13Rnd1}
{Locker File Creation program}
uses crt;

type LockerType= record
    LockerNumber  : integer;
    Name          : string;
    Year          : integer;
    Status        : char
end;

var
    LockerFile    : file of lockertype;
    LockerRec     : LockerType;

procedure A1_Init;
begin
    clrscr;
    writeln ('Locker File Creation');
    writeln;
    assign (LockerFile, 'a:\lockerf.dat');
    rewrite(LockerFile)   {open a new file or overwrite an existing one}
end;

procedure A2_FillRecord;
begin
    LockerRec.Name:='Empty';
    LockerRec.Year:=0;
    LockerRec.Status:='E'  {indicates an empty locker}
end;

procedure A3_Output;
var Sub  : integer;
begin
    for Sub:= 1 to 20 do
    begin
        LockerRec.LockerNumber:=sub;
        seek (LockerFile, sub);
        write(LockerFile, LockerRec);
        writeln ('Record ',sub, ' written')
    end {for}
end;

{****** MAIN PROGRAM *******}
Begin
    A1_Init;
    A2_FillRecord;
    A3_Output;
    close (LockerFile)
    readln;
end.
```

The next program allows the user to find, add, and list records in the random file. The two procedures for deleting a record and editing a record have been left incomplete for you to write.

Chapter 13 – Random Access File Processing

```pascal
program LockerMaint;
{stored as Ch13Maint}
{program to look up, add, delete, edit and list locker records}
uses crt;
type LockerType= record
    LockerNumber  : integer;
    Name          : string;
    Year          : integer;
    Status        : char;
end;
var
    LockerFile    : file of lockertype;
    LockerRec     : LockerType;
    LockerInUse   : boolean;
    LockerNum     : integer;

procedure OpenFile;
begin
    assign (LockerFile, 'a:\lockerf.dat');
    reset(LockerFile);
end;

procedure GetLocker(var InUse:Boolean);
begin
    clrscr;
    writeln('Please enter the locker number');
    readln(LockerNum);
    seek(LockerFile, LockerNum);
    read(LockerFile, LockerRec);
    if (LockerRec.Status='E') then LockerInUse := False
    else LockerInUse:=True;
end; {GetLocker}

procedure FindRec;
begin
    GetLocker(LockerInUse);
    if LockerInUse then
        writeln ('Locker ',LockerNum, ' ',LockerRec.Name, ' ',LockerRec.Year)
    else writeln ('Locker ',LockerNum, ' empty');
    readln;
end; {FindRec}

procedure AddRec;
begin
    GetLocker(LockerInUse);
    If LockerInUse then
        begin
            writeln ('This locker is already in use');
            readln;
        end
    else
    begin
        write ('Enter student name: ');
        readln(LockerRec.Name);
        write ('Enter student''s year: ');
```

```pascal
      readln(LockerRec.Year);
      LockerRec.Status:= 'F';
      seek(LockerFile,LockerNum);
      write(LockerFile,LockerRec);
    end;{if}
end;{AddRec}

procedure DeleteRec;
begin
end; {DeleteRec}

procedure EditRec;
begin
end; {EditRec}

procedure ListRec;
var sub : integer;
begin
  for sub:=1 to 20 do
  begin
     seek(LockerFile,sub);
     read(LockerFile,LockerRec);
     writeln('Record',sub, ' :',LockerRec.LockerNumber,
                    LockerRec.Name, ' 'LockerRec.Year)
  end;{for}
  readln
end; {ListRec}

procedure DisplayMenu;
var choice : char;
begin
   repeat
     clrscr;
     gotoxy(26,4);   write('LOCKER FILE MAINTENANCE');
     gotoxy(26,6);   write('1. Look up locker details');
     gotoxy(26,8);   write('2. Add student name to file');
     gotoxy(26,10);  write('3. Delete student name');
     gotoxy(26,12);  write('4. Edit locker details');
     gotoxy(26,14);  write('5. List all lockers');
     gotoxy(26,16);  write('6. Quit');
     gotoxy(26,18);  write('Please enter choice: ');
     readln (choice);
     case choice of
       '1' : FindRec;
       '2' : AddRec;
       '3' : DeleteRec;
       '4' : EditRec;
       '5' : ListRec;
       '6' : exit
     end;{case}
   until choice='6'
end; {DisplayMenu}

{****** MAIN PROGRAM *******}
begin
   OpenFile;
   DisplayMenu;
   close (LockerFile)
end.
```

Chapter 14 – Queues and Stacks

Introduction to data structures

All data processing on a computer involves the manipulation of data. This data can be organised in the computer's memory in different ways according to how it is to be processed, and the different methods of organising data are known as **data structures**.

Computer languages such as Pascal have built-in **elementary data types** (such as *integer*, *real*, *Boolean* and *char*) and some built-in **structured** or **composite** data types (data structures) such as *record*, *array* and *string*. These composite data types are made up of a number of elements of a specified type such as *integer* or *real*.

Some data structures such as queues, stacks and binary trees are not built into the language and have to be constructed by the programmer. In this module it is only necessary to recognize the different data structures and use them in simple ways. In the second year of the course you will learn how to implement them.

Queues

A queue is a First In First Out (FIFO) data structure. New elements may only be added to the end of a queue, and elements may only be retrieved from the front of a queue. The sequence of data items in a queue is determined, therefore, by the order in which they are inserted. The size of the queue depends on the number of items in it, just like a queue at the cinema or supermarket checkout.

Queues are used in a variety of applications.

- Output waiting to be printed is commonly stored in a queue on disk. In a room full of networked computers, several people may send work to be printed at more or less the same time. By putting the output into a queue on disk, the output is printed on a first come, first served basis as soon as the printer is free.

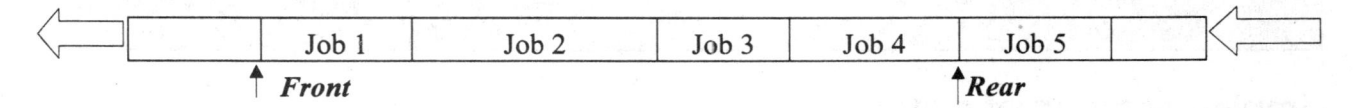

⇐ | Job 1 | Job 2 | Job 3 | Job 4 | Job 5 | | ⇐
    ↑*Front*   ↑*Rear*

Pointers mark the front and rear of the queue.

> **Q1:** What will the queue look like when 4 jobs have been printed and 2 new jobs, Job 6 and Job 7, have joined the queue? Remember to mark in the pointers **Front** and **Rear**.

- Characters typed at a keyboard are held in a queue in a keyboard buffer.
- Jobs waiting to be run by the computer may be held in a queue.
- Queues are also useful in simulation problems. A simulation program is one which attempts to model a real-life situation so as to learn something about it. An example is a program which simulates customers arriving at random times at the check-outs in a supermarket store, and taking random times to pass through the checkout. With the aid of a simulation program, the optimum number of check-out counters can be established.

Stacks

A stack is a particular kind of sequence which may only be accessed at one end, known as the top of the stack (like plates on a pile in a cafeteria).

Only two operations can be carried out on a stack. **Adding** a new item involves placing it on top of the stack (**pushing** or stacking the item). **Removing** an item involves the removal of the item that was most recently added (**popping** the stack). The stack is a **LIFO** structure – Last In, First Out.

Note that items do not move up and down as the stack is pushed and popped. Instead, the position of the top of the stack changes. A pointer called a stack pointer indicates the position of the top of the stack:

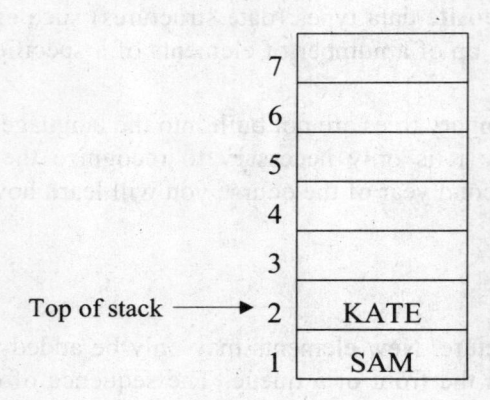

7	
6	
5	
4	
3	
2	KATE	← Top of stack
1	SAM

> **Q2:** Show the state of the stack and stack pointer after each of the following operations:
> (i) Initialise the stack
> (ii) Add ELAINE
> (iii) Add HOWARD
> (iv) Remove one item
> (v) Add MICHAEL
> (vi) Add TAMARA

Implementation of a stack

A stack can be represented in memory by an array and two additional integer variables, one holding the size of the array (i.e. the maximum size of the stack) and one holding the pointer to the top of the stack (**Top**). **Top** will initially be set to 0, representing an empty stack.

Applications of stacks

Stacks are very important data structures in computing. They are used in calculations, translating from one computer language to another, and transferring control from one part of a program to another.

Chapter 14 – Queues and Stacks

Using stacks to store return addresses

Stacks are used to store the return address when a subroutine is called. The principle is shown below:

Instruction Address	Instruction
1	**subroutine** suba
2	....
3	....
4	**return**
5	**begin** { *** MAIN PROGRAM *** EXECUTION STARTS HERE}
6	**call** suba
7	....
8	**end**

The return address (7) will be placed on a stack when SUBA is called and popped when the RETURN statement is encountered.

> **Q3:** Show the contents of the stack as addresses are pushed and popped during the execution of the following simplified program outline.

Instruction Address	Instruction
1	**subroutine** suba
2	....
3	....
4	**return**
5	**subroutine** subb
6	....
7	....
8	**return**
9	**subroutine** sub1
10	....
11	....
12	**call** suba
13	**call** subb
14	**return**
15	**subroutine** sub2
16	....
17	**call** suba
18	....
19	....
20	....
21	**return**
22	**begin**{*** MAIN PROGRAM *** EXECUTION STARTS HERE}
23	**call** sub1
24	**call** sub2
25	**end**

Using a stack to reverse the elements of a queue

The elements of a queue can be reversed by pushing them one by one on to the stack, and then popping them one by one and replacing them in the queue. For example:

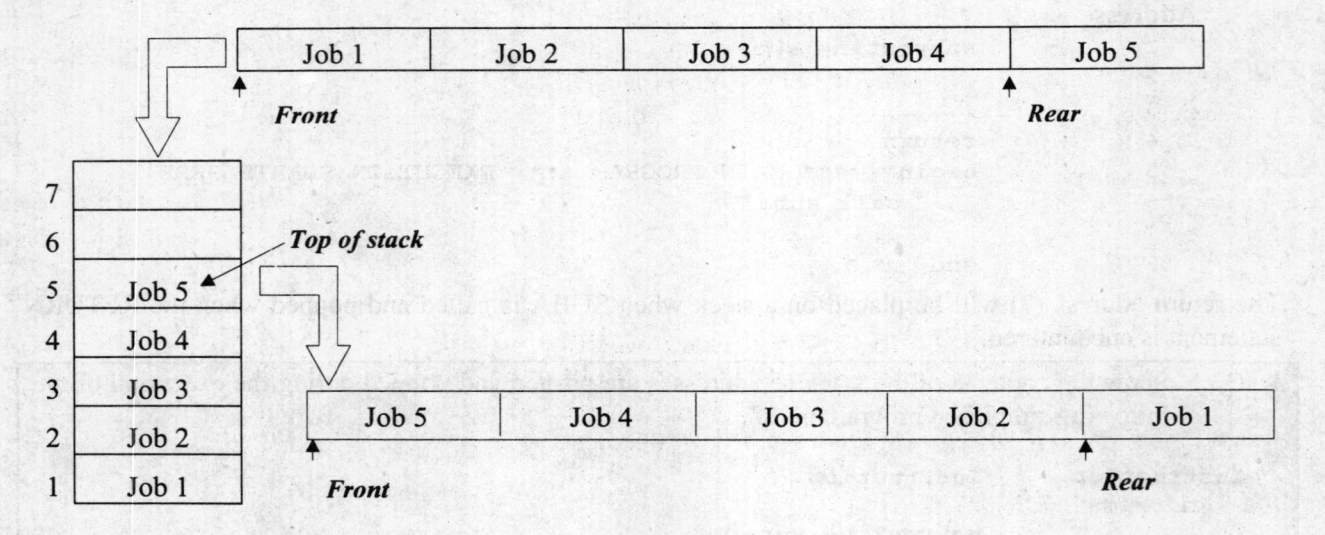

	Job 1	Job 2	Job 3	Job 4	Job 5

Front ... *Rear*

```
7 |      |
6 |      |  ← Top of stack
5 | Job 5|
4 | Job 4|
3 | Job 3|
2 | Job 2|
1 | Job 1|
```

Job 5	Job 4	Job 3	Job 2	Job 1

Front ... *Rear*

Overflow and Underflow

A queue or a stack may have a maximum size. An attempt to add a new element to a queue or stack which is already full will result in an **overflow** error. An attempt to remove an item from an empty queue or stack will result in an **underflow** error.

Exercises

1. With the aid of a clearly labelled diagram which includes a stack pointer, describe how a previously empty stack would hold these names arriving in the given sequence:

   Shane, Eithne, Greta, Petroc, Abdul

   Show what the stack would then contain if three of these names were popped (retrieved) from it, and two more names (**Simon** and **Jasmine**) were pushed (added).

2. With the aid of a clearly labelled diagram which includes front and rear pointers, describe how a previously empty queue would hold these names arriving in the given sequence:

   Phil, Trevor, Anna, Laura, Gary

   Show what the queue would then contain if two of these names were retrieved from it, and one more name (**Sue**) was added.

3. Describe the data structure known as a queue and explain what is meant by underflow and overflow in relation to a queue.

Chapter 15 – Binary Trees

Introduction

A binary tree is a data structure consisting of a root node and zero, one or two subtrees as shown in the diagram below.

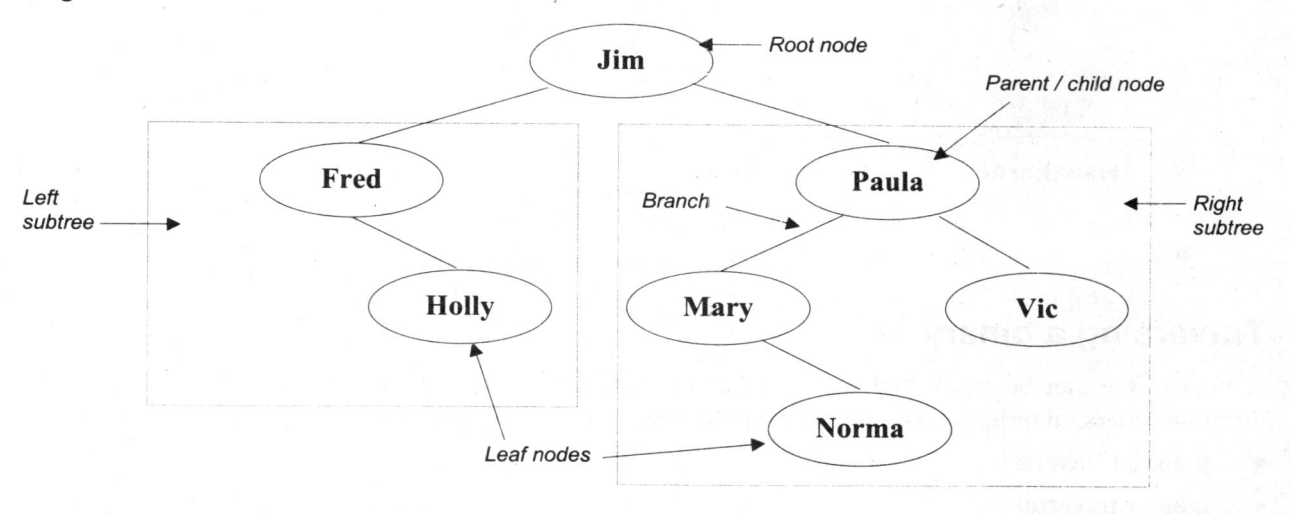

Figure 15.1: A binary tree

Note that:

- Lines connecting the nodes are called **branches** and every node except the root is joined to just one node at the higher level (its parent).
- Nodes that have no children are called **leaf nodes**.
- Some nodes may be both **parent** and **child** nodes. For example Paula is the child of Jim and the parent of **Mary** and **Vic**.

Constructing an ordered binary tree

A **search tree** is a particular application of a binary tree, such that a list of items held in the tree can be searched easily and quickly, new items easily added, and the whole tree printed out in sequence (alphabetic or numeric).

Constructing a binary tree

We could, for example, store a list of names (and, say, telephone numbers or other data as required) in a binary tree. Take the following list of names:

Legg, Charlesworth, Illman, Hawthorne, Todd, Youngman, Jones, Ravage.

In order to create a binary tree that can be quickly searched for a given name, we follow the rules:

- Place the first item in the root.
- Take each subsequent item in turn.
- Start at the root each time. If the item is less than the root, branch to the left and if it is greater than the root, branch to the right.
- Apply the rule at each node encountered.

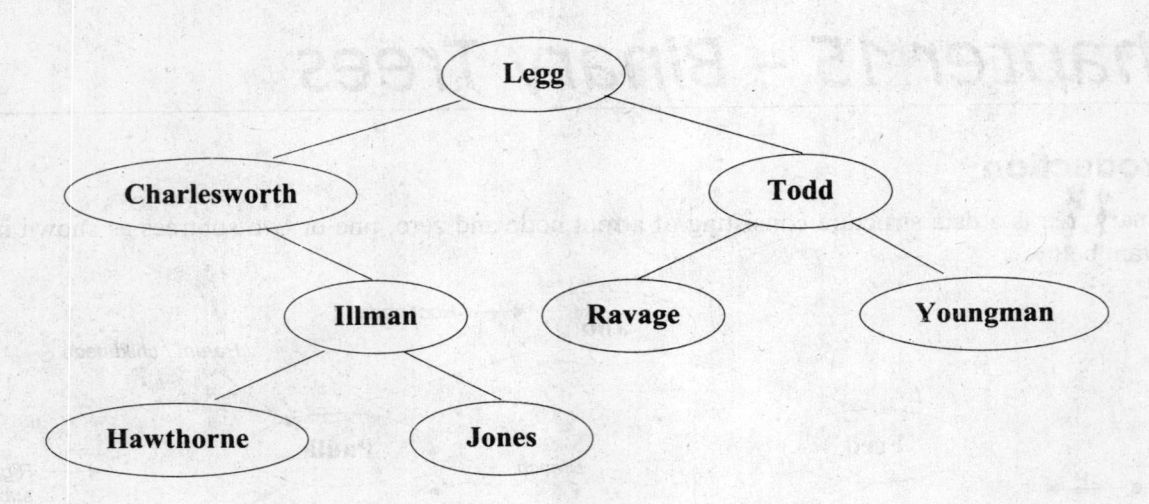

Module 1 Computer Systems, Programming and Network Concepts

```
                    Legg
                   /    \
          Charlesworth   Todd
                  \      /   \
                Illman Ravage Youngman
                /    \
          Hawthorne  Jones
```

Figure 15.2: Items in an ordered binary tree

Traversing a binary tree

A binary tree can be **traversed** in a number of different ways; that is, the nodes may be visited in different orders, in order to extract data from the tree. The methods are known as

- preorder traversal
- inorder traversal
- postorder traversal

In each case, the algorithms for traversal are **recursive**, that is, they call themselves. The names **preorder**, **inorder** and **postorder** refer to the stage at which the node is visited.

Preorder traversal

1. Start at the root node
2. Traverse the lefthand subtree
3. Traverse the righthand subtree.

The nodes of the tree below would be visited in the following order: D B A C F E G.

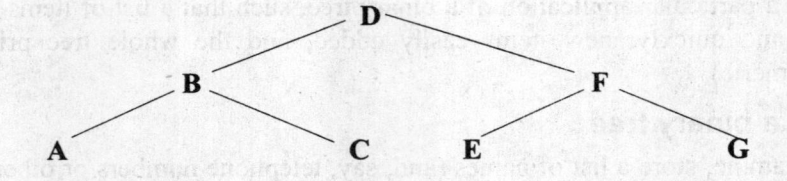

```
           D
          / \
         B   F
        / \ / \
       A  C E  G
```

Figure 15.3

Inorder traversal

1. Traverse the lefthand subtree
2. Visit the root node
3. Traverse the righthand subtree.

The nodes are visited in the order: A B C D E F G

Postorder traversal

1. Traverse the lefthand subtree
2. Traverse the righthand subtree
3. Return to the root node.

The nodes are visited in the order: A C B E G F D

> **Q1:** Referring to the tree in Figure 15.2 (Legg, Charlesworth etc.), write down the order in which the data will be listed using:
> a) preorder traversal
> b) inorder traversal
> c) postorder traversal.
>
> **Q2:** In which order should the tree be traversed in order to obtain a list in alphabetical sequence?

Exercises

1. The following numbers are to be entered in order to be stored in a binary tree for subsequent processing.

    14, 25, 31, 45, 19, 4, 16, 2, 8, 26

    Show, with the aid of a diagram, how this data structure will store these values.

2. The figure below shows a binary tree.

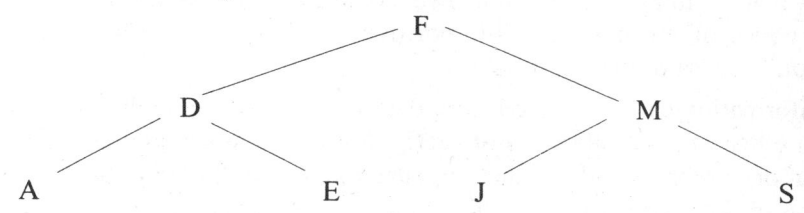

```
              F
           /     \
          D       M
         / \     / \
        A   E   J   S
```

The letter at each node is printed as the tree is traversed. What will be printed when the traversal is

(a) in-order?

(b) pre-order?

(c) post-order?

Chapter 16 – Data Representation

Input-process-output

The main purpose of using computers is to process data as quickly and efficiently as possible to produce useful information.

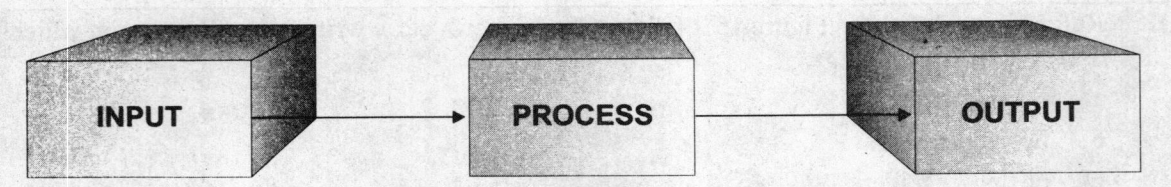

```
INPUT → PROCESS → OUTPUT
```

Computers read incoming data called **input**, process or operate on it and display or print information called **output**.

Data can be defined as the raw material which a computer accepts as input and then processes to produce useful information. A stream of data such as 44, 45, 66, 82, 77, 67 has no meaning until it is processed by the appropriate program and information produced. The numbers could represent the marks of 6 students, the number of computers sold by a manufacturer in the past 6 months (in thousands), the weekly hours of sunshine in the past 6 weeks.

Sources of data

Data can be collected from many sources, either directly or indirectly. Data which is collected for a specific purpose is said to be collected **directly**. For example, the times at which an employee clocks in and out may be collected by punching a time card, and this data is used in the calculation of the weekly pay packet. Similarly, when a library book is borrowed, data about the book and the borrower is collected by scanning the bar codes of the book and the borrower's library card. This data is used directly to produce information on where a particular book is.

On the other hand, information can be derived from data which was originally collected for a completely different purpose – in other words, collected **indirectly**. For example a credit card company collects data about each transaction or purchase made so that the customer can be billed at the end of the month. This is the **direct** collection of data. At a later date, the data may be used to build a profile of the customer – perhaps how often they use their credit card for holiday travel, for example. The company could sell a list of all well-travelled customers to a travel company who would use it in a direct mail advertising campaign. This is the **indirect** collection of data – use of the data for a purpose other than the one for which it was originally collected.

> ➢ Q1: Think of several examples of data which is originally collected for one purpose, and then used for additional purposes.

Character coding schemes

In Chapter 3 the ACSII coding scheme was described. This is a 7- or 8-bit code for representing characters and is used by almost all PCs.

Unicode is an international 16-bit coding scheme which can represent 65536 different characters. This is sufficient to represent all the characters in any language or script from ancient Egyptian hieroglyphics to Chinese, Russian, Greek, Japanese or Urdu, to name but a few.

Chapter 16 – Data Representation

The binary number system

You met binary numbers briefly in Chapter 3, so this is by way of a little recap.

A number such as 1, 25, 378 etc. can be represented in a computer in many different ways. It can be held as a number of characters so that, for example, the number 25 is coded in ASCII as 0011 0010 0011 0101 (refer to Figure 3.2 in Chapter 3). Alternatively, it can be held as a **pure binary number**.

To translate 25 from decimal to binary, you can draw a table of powers of 2. Then find the largest power of 2 that is less than or equal to 25 (16 in this case). Subtract 16 from 25 and repeat. You end up with

128	64	32	16	8	4	2	1
0	0	0	1	1	0	0	1

16+8+1 = 25

To translate from binary to decimal, perform the process backwards. Put each binary digit under the correct heading in the table. For example, to translate 01000101 into decimal, arrange the digits in the table as follows:

128	64	32	16	8	4	2	1
0	1	0	0	0	1	0	1

64+4+1 = 69

The representation of negative numbers, numbers with decimal points and binary arithmetic will be covered in Section 4.

> **Q2:** (i) Translate the number 227 into binary.
> (ii) Translate the binary number 1011 0111 into denary (i.e. a decimal number).

Binary Coded Decimal (BCD)

In the BCD system each decimal digit is represented by its own 4-bit binary code.

Decimal	Binary
0	0000
1	0001
2	0010
3	0011
4	0100
5	0101
6	0110
7	0111
8	1000
9	1001

The number 3765 is coded as 0011 0111 0110 0101.

> **Q3:** (i) Write down the BCD representation of 2906.
> (ii) Translate the BCD number 0110 0111 1001 0011 into denary (i.e. a decimal number).

Advantages and disadvantages of BCD

The advantage of the BCD representation is the ease of conversion from BCD to decimal and vice versa. For example, when binary numbers have to be electronically decoded for a pocket calculator display, a number held in BCD format simply has to be split into groups of four bits and each group converted directly to the corresponding decimal digit.

A further advantage of the BCD representation is that since each decimal digit is encoded separately, using as many bits as necessary to represent the complete number exactly, no 'rounding' of numbers occurs. Hence BCD arithmetic is used in business applications where every significant digit has to be retained in a result.

The disadvantage of BCD is that calculations with such numbers are more complex than with pure binary numbers. For example, try adding the BCD representations of 1 and 19:

```
We get    0000 0001
          0001 1001
          ---------
          0001 1010   The first digit, 1, is wrong and 1010 is an invalid code!
```

The problem arises because only the first ten out of sixteen combinations of four digits are used to encode the decimal symbols '0' to '9'. Therefore, whenever the sum of two binary digits is greater than 9, 6 has to be added to the result in order to skip over the six unused codes. Adding the binary representation for 6 to 1010:

```
          0001 1010
               0110
          ---------
          0010 0000   i.e. 20 in BCD which is the correct answer.
```

Boolean values

So far we have seen how a given binary pattern could represent an ASCII character, a binary integer, or a number held in BCD. A Boolean variable (named after the English mathematician George Boole) is one which can only have one of two values, **true** or **false**, represented by 1 and 0. There are many occasions when it is useful to use one binary digit to show whether something is true or false. For example, a particular bit in memory can be set to show whether a disk drive is connected, another can be set if the 'Break' key is pressed, and yet another set if overflow occurs during an arithmetic operation. Single bits used in this way are called **flags**.

Digitised sound

Sound such as music or speech can be input via a microphone, CD or electronic keyboard with MIDI (Musical Instrument Digital Interface) to be processed by a computer. Since sound waves are continuously variable or **analogue** in nature, an **analogue to digital converter** is needed to transform the analogue input to a **digital** form, i.e. a binary pattern, so that it can be stored and processed. Undesirable sounds such as wrong notes or scratches on an old recording can be edited out before a new digital version is produced.

Sound in analogue form may be represented by wave forms. The height of these wave forms may be sampled at regularly spaced time intervals, with the height being represented by, say, a 16-bit code. The more frequently the samples are taken, the more faithfully the sound will be represented. (See Figure 16.1.)

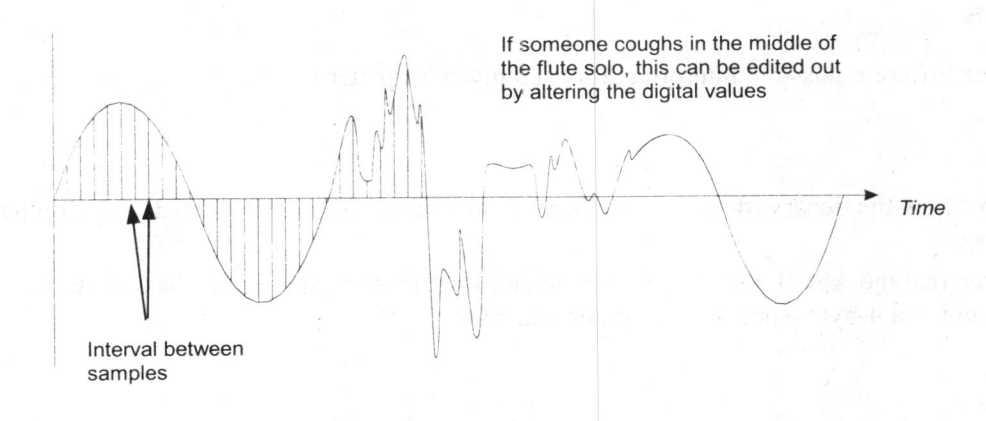

Figure 16.1: Converting sound from analogue to digital form

Bit-mapped graphics

Binary patterns are also used to store graphics. In a **bit-mapped** system for displaying text and graphics on a VDU, the screen is divided up into a grid, and each square on the grid is called a **pixel** (picture element). A low resolution screen may have 320 by 240 pixels, and a high resolution screen may have 1280 by 1024 pixels or more. A monochrome screen will need just one bit in memory to represent each pixel; if the bit is 1, the pixel is on, and if it is 0, the pixel is off. On a colour screen, each pixel may correspond to one byte in memory, giving a possible 256 colours for each pixel. Two bytes per pixel gives a possible 64K different colours. The memory used is additional to the RAM used for programs and data; it is supplied on a graphics 'card' specific to the type of screen.

If the screen was magnified you would be able to see the individual pixels. The more pixels to the square inch, the higher the resolution and the smoother the image.

Figure 16.2: An image on the screen is composed of thousands of pixels

Module 1 Computer Systems, Programming and Network Concepts

Exercises

1. State **four** different possible interpretations of a given bit pattern in a computer's memory.

2. (a) Show how the denary (decimal) numbers 13 and 32 would be represented as 8-bit binary integers.

   (b) Given that the ASCII code for the character 1 is 00110001, show how the text string 1332 would be held in a 4-byte word in a computer's memory.

3. Music is often recorded digitally. Describe briefly **two** advantages of this method of representing sound.

4. A PC may be described as having a 1Mb graphics card, meaning that 1Mb of memory is available to represent a full screen image. If a screen resolution of 1024 x 1024 is selected by the user via the 'Control Panel', how many bytes would be available to represent each pixel on the screen? How many different colours could be represented?

   If more colours are wanted, should the screen resolution be increased or decreased?

Chapter 17 – Inside the Computer

Introduction

A computer system is composed of both internal and external components. In this chapter we'll look in more detail at the computer's **internal components** and how programs and data are stored.

The internal components are contained in the **Central Processing Unit** (CPU). The terminology here is vague and often ambiguous: the term CPU is sometimes used to mean the actual processor unit which carries out the fetching, decoding and executing of instructions. Other times it is used in a broader sense as the unit which houses the processor, or processing unit, plus memory and controllers (see Figure 17.1 below).

- The processor;
- Main memory;
- I/O controllers, some of which may be input only, some output only, some both input and output;
- Buses.

The **external components** are also known as **peripherals** and include input, output and storage devices such as keyboard, mouse, printer and disk drives. The processor receives and transmits data from and to the processor through a part of an I/O controller called an **I/O port**.

The components of a simple computer system are shown in the diagram below:

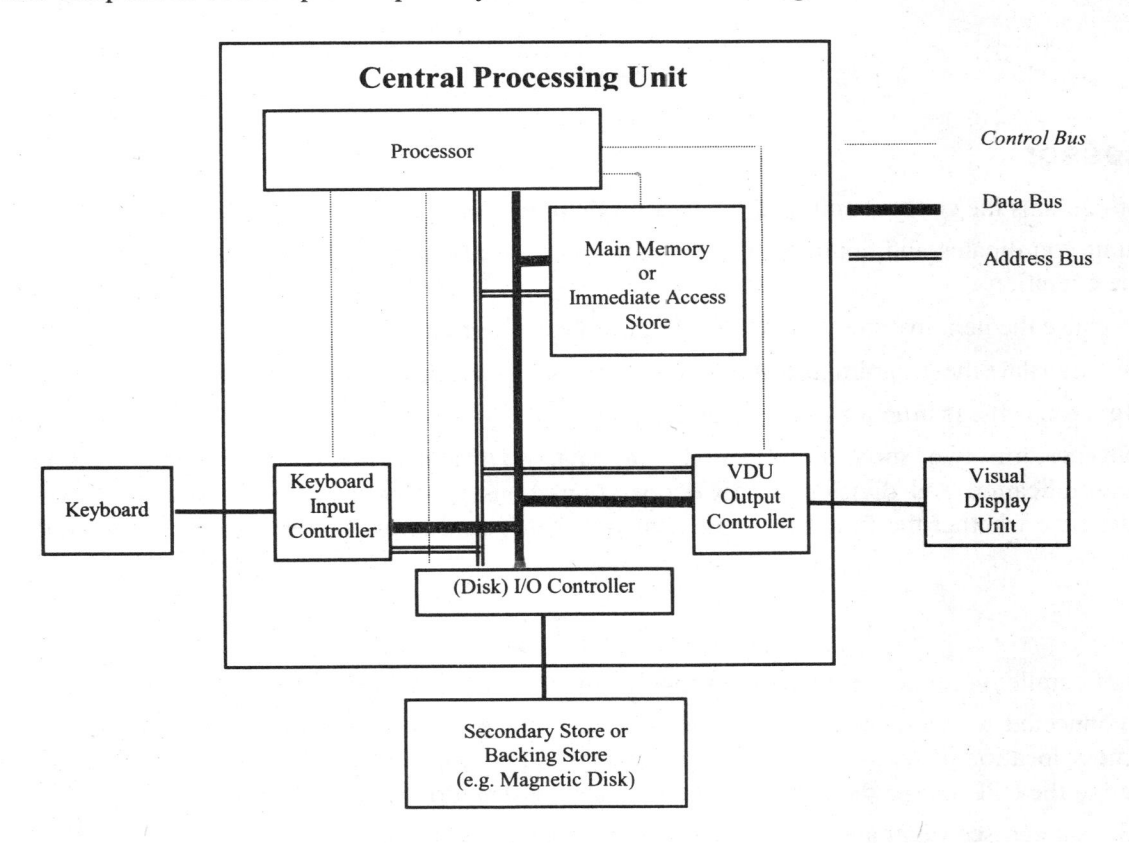

Figure 17.1: The internal and external components of a computer

Memory and the stored program concept

Computers as we know them were first built in the 1940s, and two of the early pioneers were Alan Turing and John von Neumann. Each of them separately came up with the concept of a machine that would hold in a single store (main memory) both the instructions (program) and the data on which the instructions were to be carried out. Virtually all computers today are built on this principle, and so the general structure as shown in Figure 17.2 is sometimes referred to as the **von Neumann machine**.

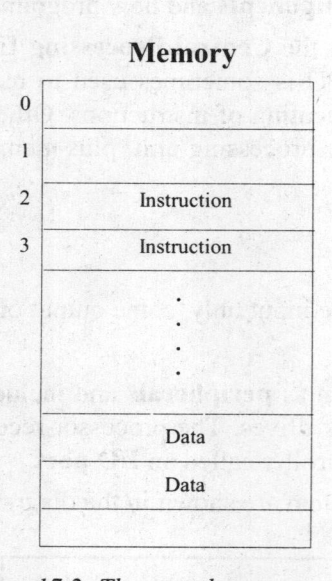

Memory

0	
1	
2	Instruction
3	Instruction
⋮	⋮
	Data
	Data

Figure 17.2: The stored program concept

The Processor

The processor contains the **control unit** and the **arithmetic/logic unit (ALU)**.

The control unit coordinates and controls all the operations carried out by the computer. It operates by repeating three operations:

- **Fetch** – cause the next instruction to be fetched from main memory;
- **Decode** – translate the program instruction into commands that the computer can process;
- **Execute** – cause the instruction to be executed;

The ALU can perform two sorts of operations on data. **Arithmetic** operations include addition, subtraction, multiplication and division. **Logical** operations consist of comparing one data item with another to determine whether the first data item is smaller than, equal to or greater than the second data item.

Buses

A **bus** is a set of parallel wires connecting two or more components of the computer.

The CPU is connected to main memory by three separate **buses**. When the CPU wishes to access a particular memory location, it sends this address to memory on the **address bus**. The data in that location is then returned to the CPU on the **data bus**. Control signals are sent along the **control bus**.

In Figure 17.3, you can see that data, address and control buses connect the processor, memory and I/O controllers. These are all **system buses**. Each bus is a shared transmission medium, so that only one device can transmit along a bus at any one time.

Data and control signals travel in both directions between the processor, memory and I/O controllers. Addresses, on the other hand, travel only one way along the address bus: the processor sends the address of an instruction, or of data to be stored or retrieved, **to** memory or **to** an I/O controller (see figure below.)

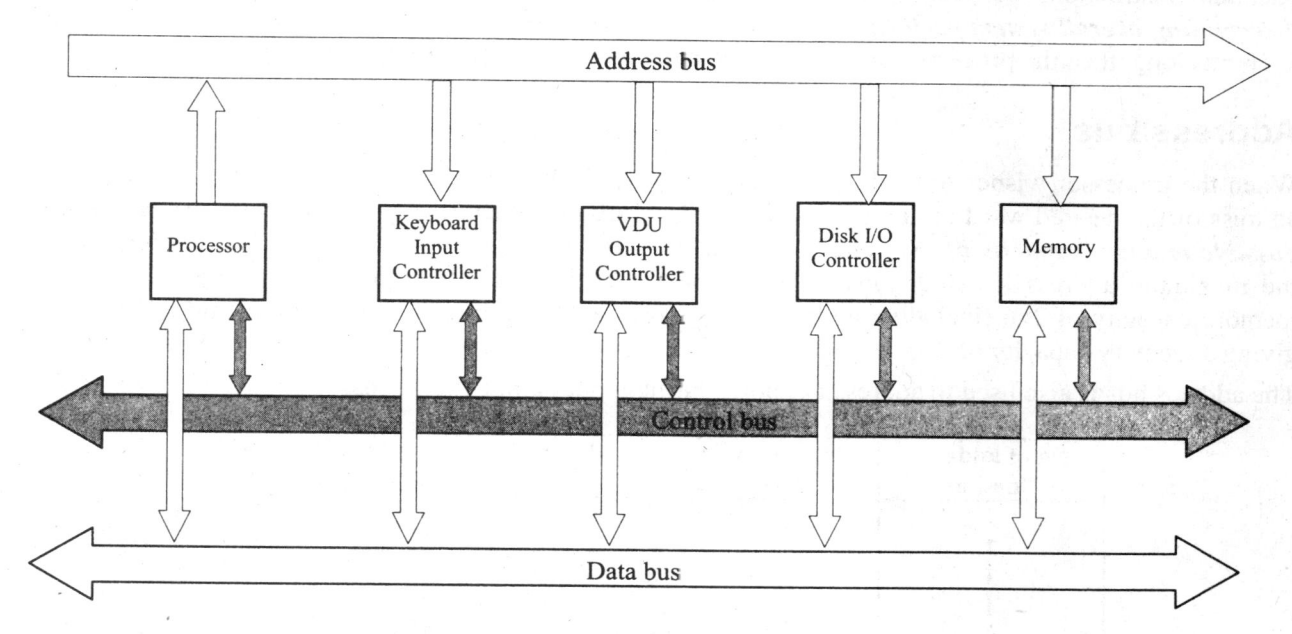

Figure 17.3: Direction of transmission along the buses

Control bus

The control bus is a bi-directional bus meaning that signals can be carried in both directions. The data and address buses are **shared** by all components of the system. Control lines must therefore be provided to ensure that **access to and use of the data and address buses** by the different components of the system does not lead to conflict. The purpose of the control bus is to transmit command, timing and specific status information between system components. Timing signals indicate the validity of data and address information. Command signals specify operations to be performed. Specific status signals indicate the state of a data transfer request, or the status of a request by a component to gain control of the system bus.

Typical control lines include:

- *Memory Write*: causes data on the data bus to be written into the addressed location.
- *Memory Read*: causes data from the addressed location to be placed on the data bus.
- *I/O Write*: causes data on the data bus to be output to the addressed I/O port.
- *I/O Read*: causes data from the addressed I/O port to be placed on the data bus.
- *Transfer ACK*: indicates that data have been accepted from or placed on the data bus.
- *Bus Request*: indicates that a component needs to gain control of the system bus.
- *Bus Grant*: indicates that a requesting component has been granted control of the system bus.
- *Interrupt request*: indicates that an interrupt is pending.
- *Interrupt ACK*: acknowledges that the pending interrupt has been recognised.
- *Clock*: used to synchronise operations.
- *Reset*: initialises all components.

Data bus

The data bus, typically consisting of 8, 16, or 32 separate lines provides a bi-directional path for moving data and instructions between system components. *The width of the data bus is a key factor in determining overall system performance.* For example, if the data bus is 8 bits wide, and each instruction is 16 bits long, then the processor must access the main memory twice during each instruction cycle.

Address bus

When the processor wishes to read a word (say 8, 16 or 32 bits) of data from memory, it first puts the address of the desired word on the address bus. *The width of the address bus determines the maximum possible memory capacity of the system.* For example, if the address bus consisted of only 8 lines, then the maximum address it could transmit would be (in binary) 11111111 or 255 - giving a maximum memory capacity of 256 (including address 0). A more realistic minimum bus width would be 20 lines, giving a memory capacity of 2^{20}, i.e. 1Mb.

The address bus is also used to address I/O ports during input/output operations.

No of address lines, m	Maximum no of addressable cells	Maximum no of addressable cells expressed as a power of two, 2^m
1	2	2^1
2	4	2^2
3	8	2^3
4	16	2^4
8	256	2^8
16	65536	2^{16}
20	1048576	2^{20}
24	16777216	2^{24}

Table 17.4: Relationship between number of address lines m and maximum number of addressable memory cells

Word size

The **word size** of a computer is the number of bits that the CPU can process simultaneously, as opposed to the bus size which determines how many bits are transmitted together. Processors can have 8-, 16-, 32- or 64-bit word sizes (or even larger), and the word size will be one of the factors which determines the speed of the computer. The faster, more powerful PCs have 32-bit processors, and most mainframes have 32-bit words. Supercomputers may use a 64-bit or 128-bit word size.

I/O Controllers

Peripheral devices cannot be connected directly to the processor. Each peripheral operates in a different way and it would not be sensible to design processors to directly control every possible peripheral. Otherwise, the invention of a new type of peripheral would require the processor to be redesigned. Instead, the processor controls and communicates with a peripheral device through an **I/O or device controller**. I/O controllers are available which can operate both input and output transfers of bits, e.g. floppy disk controller. Other controllers operate in one direction only, either as an input controller, e.g. keyboard controller or as output controller, e.g. vdu controller.

The controller is an electronic circuit board consisting of three parts:

- an interface that allows connection of the controller to the system or I/O bus;
- a set of data, command and status registers;
- an interface that enables connection of the controller to the cable connecting the device to the computer.

An interface is a standardised form of connection defining such things as signals, number of connecting pins/sockets and voltage levels that appear at the interface. An example is an RS232 interface which enables serial transmission of data between a computer and a serially connected printer. The printer also contains an RS232 interface so that both ends of the connection are compatible with each other.

Exercises

1. What is meant by each of the following terms?
   - (i) bit
   - (ii) byte
   - (iii) word

2. A microprocessor *data bus* has 16 lines and its address bus has 24 lines. What is the maximum memory capacity that can be connected to the microprocessor?

3. (a) What is meant by the term **bus** in the context of computer hardware?
   (b) There are three types of external bus connecting the processor to main memory. Briefly describe a purpose of each.

4. (a) Briefly describe the roles of the data bus and the address bus within the Central Processing Unit (CPU).
   (b) (i) State **one** benefit of increasing the width of the data bus.
       (ii) State **one** benefit of increasing the width of the address bus.

5. A memory location in a certain microcomputer contains 8 bits.
   - (i) How many different data patterns can be stored in one memory location?
   - (ii) What is meant by the term "word" in this context?

6. Briefly describe **two** factors in a computer's architecture which will influence the structure of its internal buses.

Chapter 18 – Communication Methods

Principle of electronic data communication

Data communication involves sending and receiving data from one computer or data processing device to another. Applications using for example e-mail, supermarket EPOS (electronic point of sale) terminals, cash dispensers, facsimile, and video conferencing are all examples of this.

Data communication also takes place between the CPU and its peripheral devices; for example, data to be printed has to be sent to the printer, or in the case of a computer controlling a robot, signals have to be sent to tell the robot what to do.

Serial and parallel data communication

Data can be sent in one of two ways: serial or parallel. In **serial data transmission**, bits are sent via an interface one bit at a time over a single wire from the source to the destination. Very high data transfer rates can be achieved – for example using fibre-optic cable data transfer rates of 1000 Mbits per second can be achieved, which is much faster than parallel transmission in some systems.

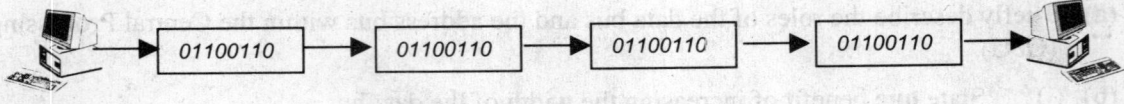

Figure 18.1: Serial transmission

Parallel data transmission is used inside the computer (using the various computer **buses**) and for very short distances of up to a few metres. A parallel port, for example, can send 8, 16 or 32 bits simultaneously down separate lines. A printer is often connected to a PC via a parallel port if the printer is sitting right next to the computer.

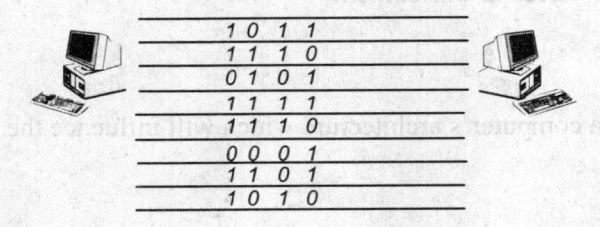

Figure 18.2: Parallel transmission

Transmission rate

The speed at which data is transmitted serially is known as the **baud rate**. Generally, one baud is one bit per second, but there is no simple relationship between the baud rate and the rate of data transfer between devices. This is because additional 'framing' bits have to be transmitted with each character to provide start and stop bits, error detection and other communications controls. Thus a baud rate of 56K does not mean that 7000 characters per second will be transmitted – the actual figure will be much lower.

Parity

Computers use either **even** or **odd** parity. In an even parity machine, the total number of 'on' bits in every byte (including the parity bit) must be an even number. When data is transmitted, the parity bits are checked at both the sending and receiving end, and if they are different or the wrong number of bits are 'on', an error message is displayed. In the diagram below the parity bit is the most significant bit (MSB).

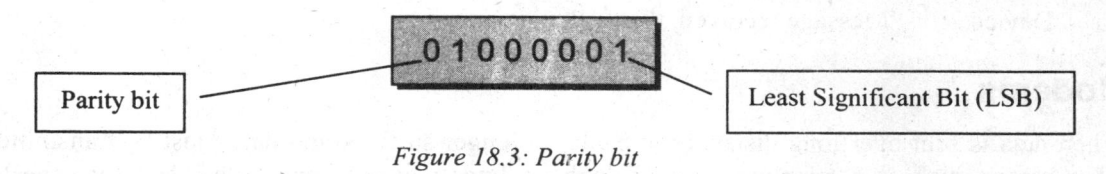

```
        01000001
Parity bit              Least Significant Bit (LSB)
```

Figure 18.3: Parity bit

> **Q1:** The ASCII codes for P and Q are 1010000 and 1010001 respectively. In an even parity transmission system, what will be the value of the parity bit for the characters P and Q?

Synchronous and asynchronous transmission

With **asynchronous** transmission, one character at a time is sent, with each character being preceded by a start bit and followed by a stop bit. The start bit alerts the receiving device and synchronises the clock inside the receiver ready to receive the character. The baud rate at the receiving end has to be set up to be the same as the sender's baud rate or the signal will not be received correctly.

A parity bit is also usually included as a check against incorrect transmission. Thus for each character being sent, a total of 10 bits is transmitted, including the parity bit, a start bit and a stop bit. A series of electrical pulses is sent down the line as illustrated below:

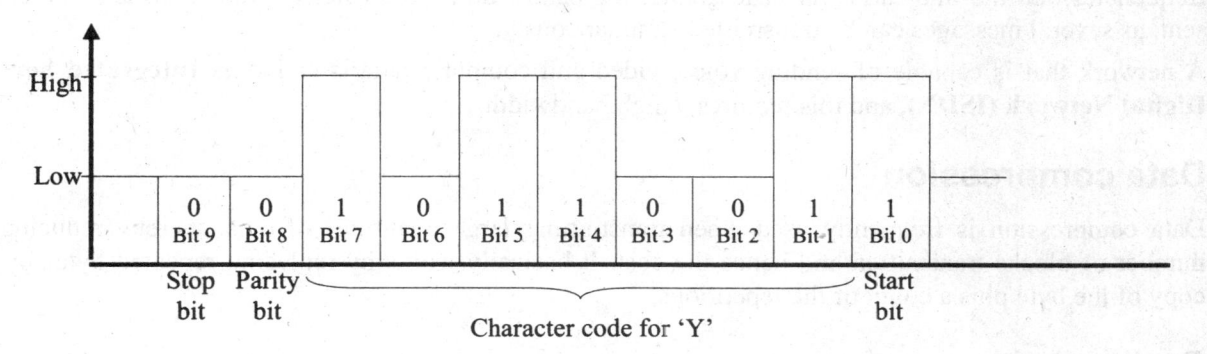

```
High
Low
     0     0     1     0     1     1     0     0     1     1
    Bit 9 Bit 8 Bit 7 Bit 6 Bit 5 Bit 4 Bit 3 Bit 2 Bit 1 Bit 0
    Stop  Parity                                          Start
    bit   bit                                             bit
               Character code for 'Y'
```

Figure 18.4: Asynchronous transmission

This type of transmission is usually used by PCs, and is fast and economical for relatively small amounts of data.

In **synchronous** transmission mode, timing signals (usually the computer's internal clock) control the rate of transmission and there is no need for start and stop bits to accompany each character. Mainframe computers usually use synchronous transmission. It is less error-prone than asynchronous transmission.

Handshaking

Handshaking is the exchange of signals between devices to establish their readiness to send or receive data, for example between a computer and printer. It is one method of ensuring that both the sender and receiver are ready before transmission begins. The 'conversation' between two devices is along the lines of the following:

    Device 1:   "Are you ready to receive some data?"
    Device 2:   "Yes, go ahead."
    Device 1:   *(sends data)*
    Device 2:   "Message received, thanks!"

Modems

When data is sent over long distances, a cable no longer suffices and data must be transmitted by some other means such as a telephone line. Telephone lines were originally designed for speech, which is transmitted in analogue or wave form. In order for digital data to be sent over a telephone line, it must first be converted to analogue form and then converted back to digital at the other end. This is achieved by means of a modem (MOdulator DEModulator) at either end of the line.

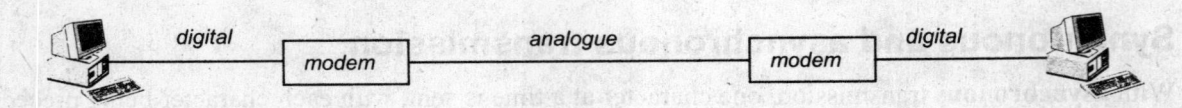

Figure 18.5: A modem converts digital signals to analogue and vice versa.

ISDN lines

The amount of data that can be sent over a line depends partly on the **bandwidth**, which is the range of frequencies that the line can carry. The greater the bandwidth, the greater the rate at which data can be sent, as several messages can be transmitted simultaneously.

A network that is capable of sending voice, video and computer data is called an **Integrated Services Digital Network (ISDN)**, and this requires a high bandwidth.

Data compression

Data compression is frequently used when transmitting large quantities of data, thereby reducing the number of blocks transmitted and hence the cost. It basically works by replacing repeated bytes by one copy of the byte plus a count of the repetitions.

Protocol

In order to allow equipment from different suppliers to be networked, a strict set of rules (**protocols**) has been devised covering standards for physical connections, cabling, mode of transmission, speed, data format, error detection and correction. Any equipment which uses the same communication protocol can be linked together.

It is also possible to link equipment using a special translation device called a protocol converter to link, for example, a PC to a mainframe. This overcomes problems of incompatibility such as

- different types of transmission – the PC may use asynchronous transmission, and the mainframe synchronous transmission;

- different character representations – PCs commonly use ASCII to represent characters, whereas many mainframes use a different code such as EBCDIC (Extended Binary Coded Decimal Interchange Code);
- different error detection and correction methods (such as extra check bits that are calculated and added to each block of data, to be checked on receipt).

Factors affecting rate of data transmission

- The speed of the modem. Different modems provide different data transmission rates, varying typically between 9K bps (bits per second) to 56K bps.
- The nature of the transmission line. A digital line such as an ISDN line has a much higher transmission speed than an analogue line.
- The type of cable used. Twisted pair cable has a transfer rate of about 10Mbps, whereas fibre optic cable is about 10 times as fast.
- The type of transmission, synchronous or asynchronous.

Exercises

1. A user wishing to access the Internet may use a modem or an ISDN connection.
   (a) What is the purpose of a modem?
   (b) Explain why using an ISDN connection to the Internet eliminates the need for a modem.
   (c) State three forms of communication that can be transmitted by ISDN.

2. A parity system enables you to deduce that a data transmission error has occurred but does not enable you to guarantee that an error has not occurred during transmission.
   (a) An odd parity system is being used to transmit the seven bits 0100111. What actual byte of data would be transmitted if the parity bit is the Most Significant Bit?
   (b) Assuming that data is being transmitted using an odd parity system, what can you deduce if each of the following bytes was received?
       (i) 10100101
       (ii) 10111001

3. In the context of data communication, distinguish between synchronous and asynchronous data transmission.

4. A small computer and printer use *handshaking* as they communicate with each other. Explain the term *handshaking* and give an example of the type of communication that could take place between a computer and a printer.

5. Explain the difference between serial and parallel data transmission. Under what circumstances would it be appropriate to use parallel transmission?

Module 1 Computer Systems, Programming and Network Concepts

Chapter 19 – Network Environments

Communications networks

A Local Area Network (LAN) is a collection of computers and peripherals confined to one building or site, connected together by a common electrical connection. A LAN can be connected to other LANs, or to a Wide Area Network (WAN).

Advantages and disadvantages of networks

A network has several advantages over a collection of stand-alone microcomputers:

- It allows the sharing of resources such as disk storage, printers, image scanners, modems and central servers;
- It allows sharing of information held on disk drives accessible by all users;
- It is easier to store application programs on one computer and make them available to all users rather than having copies individually installed on each computer;
- It allows electronic mail to be sent between users;
- It is easier to set up new users and equipment;
- It allows the connection of different types of computer which can communicate with each other.

The main **disadvantages** of networks are:

- Users become dependent on them; if for example the network file server develops a fault, then many users will be unable to run application programs. (On many sites, a back-up file server can be switched into action if the main server fails).
- If the network stops operating then it may not be possible to access various hardware and software resources.
- The efficiency of a network is very dependent on the skill of the system manager. A badly managed network may operate less efficiently than stand-alone machines.
- It is difficult to make the system secure from hackers, novices or industrial espionage.
- As traffic increases on the network the performance degrades unless it is properly designed.

Network topologies

The **topology** of a network is its physical layout – the way in which the computers and other units (commonly referred to as **nodes**) are connected. Common topologies include **star**, **bus** and **ring**, discussed below.

Star network

Each node in a star network is connected to a central **host computer** which controls the network. This is a common topology for a wide area network in large companies which have a mainframe computer at the Head Office, and computer facilities (perhaps linked together in a LAN) at each branch. It has the advantage that each node is independent of the others so a fault at one branch will not affect the other branches. On the other hand if the main computer goes down, all users are affected.

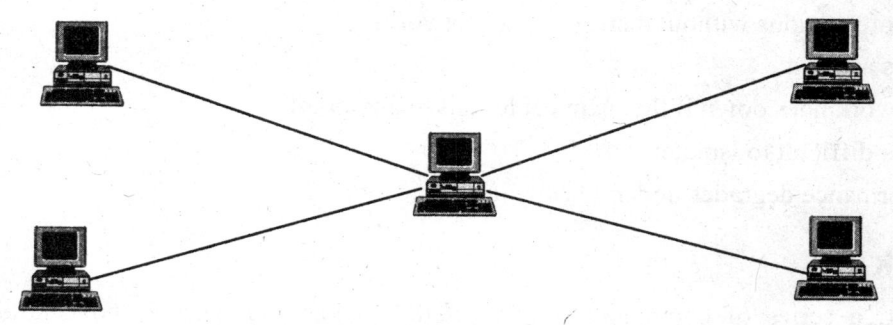

Figure 19.1: A star network

Advantages of a star network

- If one cable fails, the other stations are not affected.
- Consistent performance even when the network is being heavily used.
- Reliable, market-proven system.
- No problems with 'collisions' of data since each station has its own cable to the server.
- Easy to add new stations without disrupting the network.

Disadvantage of star network

- May be costly to install because of the length of cable required. The cabling can be a substantial part of the overall cost of installing a network.

A variation of the star topology is the **distributed star** topology. A number of stations are linked to connection boxes which are then linked together to form a 'string of stars'.

Bus network

This is a typical topology for a LAN, with all the devices on the network sharing a single cable. Information can be transmitted in either direction from any PC to any other. This system works well if the channels are not too heavily loaded. On the other hand if sixteen students sit down at sixteen computers all at once and all try to load software from the network's hard disk, the whole system more or less grinds to a halt!

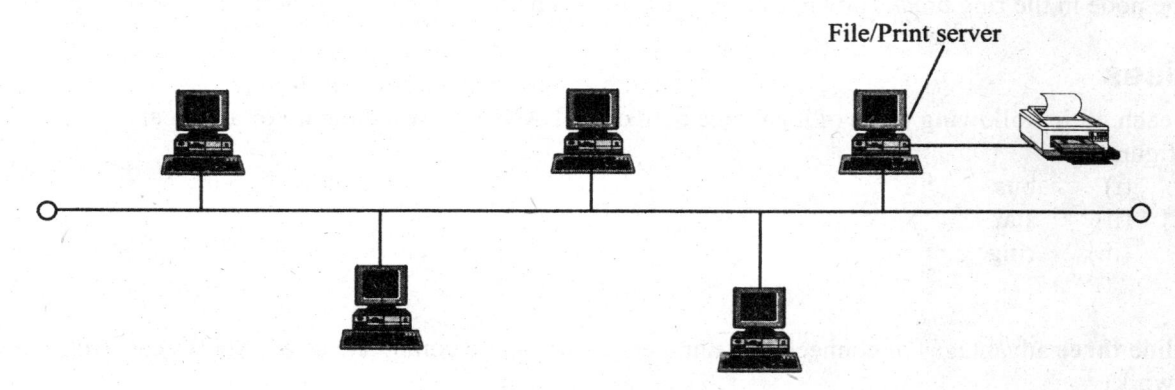

Figure 19.2: A bus network

Module 1 Computer Systems, Programming and Network Concepts

The **advantages** of a bus system are that it is:
- easy and inexpensive to install as it requires the least amount of cable;
- easy to add more stations without disrupting the network.

The **disadvantages** are that:
- the whole network goes down if the main cable fails at any point;
- cable failure is difficult to isolate;
- network performance degrades under a heavy load.

Ring network

In a ring network, a series of computers is connected together and there is no central controlling computer. Each computer may communicate with any other computer in the ring, with messages being specifically addressed to the destination computer.

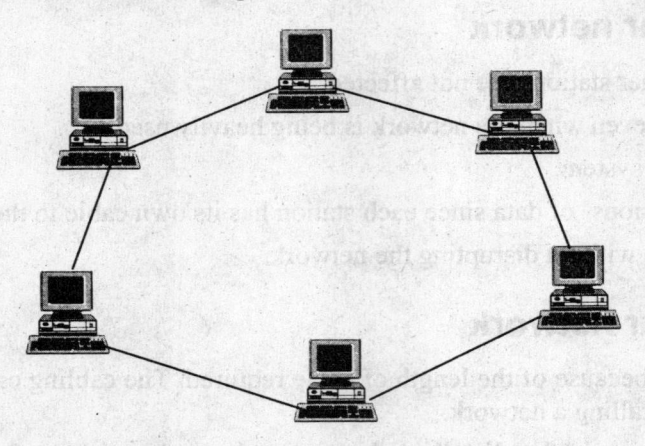

Figure 19.3: A ring network

The **advantages** of a ring system are:
- there is no dependence on a central computer or file server, and each node controls transmission to and from itself
- transmission of messages around the ring is relatively simple, with messages travelling in one direction only
- very high transmission rates are possible.

The **disadvantage** is:
- if one node in the ring breaks down, transmission between any of the devices in the ring is disrupted.

Exercises

1. For each of the following types of local area networks (LANs), draw a diagram of a typical configuration:
   - (i) bus
   - (ii) star
   - (iii) ring

2. Outline **three** advantages of connecting a number of standalone computers as a LAN (Local Area Network).

Chapter 20 – Wide Area Networks

Wide Area Network (WAN)

A WAN connects computers or networks over a wide geographical area; for example different sites, towns or continents. The connection between computers in a WAN may be any of several alternatives, described below.

Communications media

Communication may take place over a combination of different media:
- Twisted pair (copper cable), used in much of the telephone network;
- Coaxial cable - high quality, well insulated cable that can transmit data at higher speeds;
- Fibre optic cable through which pulses of light, rather than electricity, are sent in digital form;
- Microwave - similar to radio waves. Microwave stations cannot be much more than 30 miles apart because of the earth's curvature as microwaves travel in straight lines. Mobile telephones use microwave radio links.
- Communications satellite, using one of the hundreds of satellites now in geosynchronous orbit about 22,000 miles above the earth. (Geosynchronous orbit means that they are rotating at the same speed as the Earth, and are therefore stationary relative to Earth.)

Communications links

In the UK, British Telecom, Mercury and other telecom operators provide services and data links. Telephone lines may be either:
- Public lines, on which the cost of sending data depends on the length of time taken. This is known as dial-up networking.
- Private or leased lines, for which there is a fixed annual fee and the line can be used as often as needed for no extra cost.

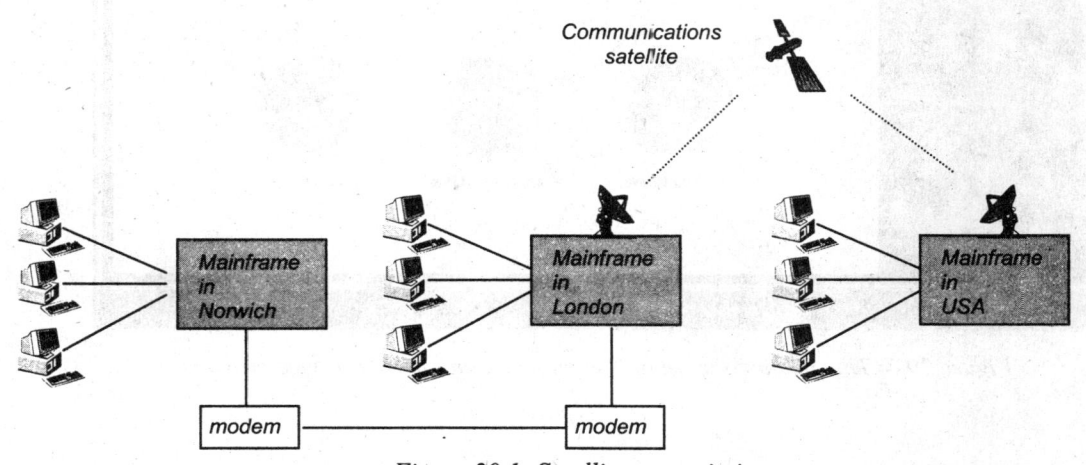

Figure 20.1: Satellite transmission

Module 1 Computer Systems, Programming and Network Concepts

The Internet

The Internet is the largest wide area network in the world. In fact it is not a single network, but a collection of thousands of computer networks throughout the world. These linked networks are of two types:

- LAN (Local Area Network), covering an office block or University campus, for example;
- WAN (Wide Area Network), connecting computers over a wide geographical area, even over several countries.

All LANs and some WANs are owned by individual organisations. Some WANs act as **service providers**, and members of the public or businesses can join these networks in return for a monthly charge.

There is no central authority or governing body running the Internet: it started with an initial 4 computers in 1969 and grew over the next ten years to connect 200 computers in military and research establishments in the US Today there are more than 4 million host computers, any of which could be holding the information you are looking for, and as many as 50 million people connected, any of whom could be future customers, friends or problem-solvers.

Figure 20.2: The opening screen of CompuServe, an Internet service provider

Uniform Resource Locator (URL)

A URL is the standard address used to find a page, Web server or other device on the Web or the Internet. A typical address or URL is

http://www.payne-gallway.co.uk

The first part of the address specifies the protocol used for connection to the server. *http* stands for Hypertext Transfer Protocol, which is used for Web sites. Other kinds of addresses include:

https:// 'Hypertext Transfer Protocol, secure' or a Web site with security features. Credit card numbers should be safer here.

ftp:// 'File Transfer Protocol' – an FTP site.

Localhost:// Information from a local Web server – typically on a user's own computer.

Domain names

The next part of the URL specifies the name of the server on which the Web resource is held. This name, called the domain name, is a string of identifiers separated by full-stops (called 'dot' when you are reading out an address). The domain names of servers identify the type of organisation and often the country in which the server is located.

International codes include:

.ac   an academic institution

.co   a company that trades in a single country

.com   a commercial organisation that trades internationally

.edu   an educational establishment

.gov   a government department or other related facility

.nato   a NATO installation

.net   an organisation or company that provides Internet access

.org   a non-commercial organisation, such as a charity

.tm   a trade-marked business name

UK-specific codes include

.ltd   a UK Limited company

.sch   a school

A 2-character country code may follow – there are hundreds of these including

au   Australia

es   Spain

sg   Singapore

uk   UK

> Q1: Suppose you wanted to log on to the IBM Web site but did not know the address. What would you try first?
>
> Q2: What address would you try for the AQA (Assessment and Qualifications Alliance?)

IP addresses

Every Web site has a 'Home Page' with a unique address known as its IP address. These addresses consist of a set of four 3-digit numbers separated by full-stops, like 177.234.143.186 for example. However, as nobody can remember or work out addresses like these, the domain name system maps the domain names onto the IP addresses.

Intranets

An Intranet is a company-wide network run along the lines of the World Wide Web, making it possible to share documents, databases and applications. Many schools have Intranets, and selected information is downloaded from the Internet for students to access. This saves wasting time browsing aimlessly through thousands of files and also enables unsuitable material to be screened out.

Exercises

1. (a) What is meant by a *wide area network*?
   (b) Explain the term *protocol* in the context of transmission over a wide area network.
   (c) Why is a protocol needed for a wide area network?

2. What is an Intranet? Give 2 advantages to a company of setting up an Intranet.

3. You have been asked to look up two Web addresses http://www.stjohns.sch.uk and http://www.experts.co.au
   What can you deduce about each of the Web sites?

4. Explain briefly the terms Uniform Resource Locator (URL), Domain name and IP address.

Module 2

Principles of Hardware, Software and Applications

In this section:

Chapter 21 -   *Information Processing Applications*
Chapter 22 -   *Computer Crime and the Law*
Chapter 23 -   *Privacy and Data Protection Legislation*
Chapter 24 -   *Health and Safety*
Chapter 25 -   *General Purpose Packages*
Chapter 26 -   *Records and Files*
Chapter 27 -   *File Organisation*
Chapter 28 -   *File Processing*
Chapter 29 -   *File Security Methods*
Chapter 30 -   *Data Processing Integrity Methods*
Chapter 31 -   *Entity-Relationship Modelling*
Chapter 32 -   *Database Concepts*
Chapter 33 -   *Operating Systems*
Chapter 34 -   *Input Devices*
Chapter 35 -   *Output Devices*
Chapter 36 -   *Storage Devices*

Module 2 Principles of Hardware, Software and Applications

Chapter 21 – Information Processing Applications

Computing – a look backwards

Within half a century, computers and information technology have changed the world and affected millions of lives in ways that no one could have foreseen. Here are some of the things that people have said about computers:

"I think there's a world market for maybe five computers." *(Thomas Watson, the chairman of IBM, in 1940)*

"I have travelled the length and breadth of this country and talked with the best people, and I can assure you that data processing is a fad that won't last out the year." *(The editor in charge of business books for Prentice Hall, in 1957)*

"There is no reason why anyone would want to have a computer in their home." *(President of Digital Equipment Corporation, in 1977)*

Contrary to these predictions, computers are transforming the ways in which we learn, communicate, do business, enjoy our leisure and live our everyday lives. Whatever career you pursue in the future, a knowledge of computer skills and concepts is likely to be beneficial or even essential. This course aims to make you competent and confident in the use of computers and to give you an understanding of the uses and impact of computers in society today.

In this chapter we'll look at some of the ways that information and communications technology has changed patterns of work. We'll also examine how dependent we have become on computer systems, and what the consequences might be when these systems fail.

Computers and employment

Ever since the industrial revolution, people have feared that machinery will displace workers, and information technology is no exception.

In spite of dire predictions, however, there is no evidence that the introduction of computers has led to mass unemployment – in fact, overall more jobs have been created by computers than have been displaced by them. Nevertheless, in some areas computers have substantially replaced the workforce. In the 1980s, thousands of factory workers were made redundant by the introduction of robots on the factory floor making everything from biscuits to cars. In the 1990s, thousands of clerical and white-collar workers have seen their jobs disappear with the introduction of company databases, desktop publishing, computerised accounting systems and increased automation in banks, building societies and organisations of all kinds, large and small.

The changing nature of employment

Today, most people no longer work in farms or factories but are found instead in sales, education, health care, banks, insurance firms and law firms. They provide services such as catering, writing computer software, or advertising and delivering goods. These jobs primarily involve working with, creating or distributing new knowledge or information. Knowledge and information work account for about 70% of the labour force in Britain and the US.

Computers have taken over many of the tedious tasks that humans once performed. Consider that only a generation or so ago:

- taking cash out from your bank account involved queuing at the bank's counter, having the cashier give you the money and manually note the transaction in a book;
- putting a newspaper together involved picking up individual letters made out of lead and placing them manually in position, with correct spacing achieved by placing a strip of lead ('leading') between lines;
- all long distance calls had to go through an operator who manually made the connection.

The introduction of computers has in many instances led to a change in the types of job available. Many publishing firms feared that desktop publishing would result in fewer jobs in the publishing and printing industries. In fact thousands of new publishing and printing companies have been created in the last decade – a quick flip through the yellow pages under 'Printing' will verify this!

In many cases, workers displaced by computers are retrained to perform computer-related jobs that may be more satisfying than their original jobs.

- A secretary may find it more satisfying to use a word processor to produce high quality output which can be saved and amended, rather than having to retype whole pages because a minor error was made.
- An engineer or draughtsman may find it more satisfying to create designs using a computer-aided design system with complete accuracy, than drawing by hand.
- An accounts clerk may prefer to use an Accounts software package rather than to do the accounts manually.

> Q1: Computerisation often leads to a change in the tasks that a worker has to perform. In some cases the new tasks may be more satisfying, and in other cases, less satisfying. Think of some examples where computerisation has one of these two outcomes.

Teleworking

Teleworking involves carrying out work away from the office and communicating with the employer through the use of computer and telecommunications equipment. Often teleworkers are based at home, but they can also work from telecentres, satellite offices or even on the move. Although a study done in 1995 at Newcastle University found that less than 1 worker in 100 was a teleworker (spending at least half of their working week at home using a computer), organisations are becoming increasingly interested in various forms of teleworking, which has benefits both for the employer and the employee. According to research done by Henley Business School in 1997, there are already 4 million teleworkers in the UK.

Benefits of teleworking

- It may be easier to concentrate on work in a quiet environment at home than in a noisy office.
- Workers save on commuting time and costs, with the associated environmental benefits of keeping cars off the roads.
- Workers enjoy greater flexibility, and can arrange their working hours around other commitments such as picking children up from school.
- Employers save on the costs of office space and overheads such as heat and light.
- People in different locations can work in a team.

- People can be recruited from a much wider geographical area.
- People who are not able to take employment in standard office hours can be recruited.

The problems of teleworking

- Management may fear difficulties in controlling a workforce that is not in the office.
- There is a problem in ensuring that remote staff understand corporate goals and retain a sense of loyalty to the organisation.
- Employees may feel isolated and miss the social environment of an office full of colleagues.
- Employees may find it difficult to work in teams, or to get help when they need it.
- Some teleworkers may find it difficult to separate home from work, and find work encroaching on their leisure or family time. Conversely, it may be difficult to concentrate on work with children making demands on a parent's time.

Case study: Socket to 'em now

A survey of 200 companies published last summer by consultant Small World Connections suggests as many as three-quarters of employers have some form of teleworking, and 85% say they expect to be using teleworkers at some point in the future.

The advantages to employees of being able to work from home are obvious, but there is a business case for their employers, too. Employers can reduce their office costs, enabling them to replace permanent workstations with a smaller number of 'hot' desks.

It means they can increase their employees' productivity – one hour less commuting means one hour more work, theoretically. Supporters of teleworking say companies who use homeworkers also find it easier to recruit and retain staff, and it opens the door for companies to attract other sources of labour such as the disabled or women returners.

BT has more than 1,500 staff who telework on a full-time basis and another 15,000 who work from home occasionally. Teleworking has also been embraced by companies in sectors such as retailing, banking and the legal profession. Davis & Co, a firm of City solicitors, allows 30 of its lawyers to enjoy the benefits of teleworking. The firm offers clients 24-hour, seven-day-a-week access to home-working solicitors who use a combination of e-mail, audio-conferencing, faxes and voice mail to keep in touch.

On the down side, teleworking could deal a body blow to the unions, which find it easier to recruit and organise members who are clustered together, not scattered throughout the country. Without effective union representation, teleworkers could be open to exploitation. Research is needed on how well workers are able to cope with long periods of isolation from the office and how this impacts on their motivation, job satisfaction or promotion prospects.

Source: Ian Wylie, The Guardian 1 November 1997

Changing locations of work

Not only are the type of jobs we do changing, the location of work is changing too. When Britain changed in the 19th century from an agricultural to an industrial society, more and more workers were forced to move from farm work into towns and large industrial centres. The advent of communications technology is now starting to reverse this trend. There is no need for much of the work of an organisation to be done at a Head Office in a city; it is often more economical for it to be done in a more remote area where office rates and housing are cheaper, and employees can be paid less. Results of data processing can be transferred to wherever they are needed via a telecommunications line.

In fact, many large companies such as some airlines and the London Underground have their daily data processing carried out in countries like India where labour is cheap and plentiful.

Consequences of computer failure

Individuals, organisations and society in general are totally dependent on computer systems for everything from withdrawing £10 at the local cashpoint to transferring millions of pounds' worth of shares every day of the week on the Stock Exchange. Computers play a crucial role in thousands of everyday tasks such as figuring out how many pineapples need to be imported from Kenya to meet demand in Sainsbury's next week, or recording £10 million worth of lottery ticket sales every week.

The consequences of computer failure, however, can be anything from inconvenient to catastrophic. When the bank's computer goes down you may be unable to withdraw cash or pay your bills. When a hospital computer monitoring a patient's vital signs fails, it may be life-threatening.

Exercises

1. Individuals and organisations have become so dependent upon I.T. systems that the consequences of their failure could be catastrophic to the individual or the organisation.

    Give **two** different examples of types of I.T. system for which failure would be catastrophic. In each case explain why the failure could prove to be catastrophic.

2. Replacing a manual system by a computerised system can have certain unwelcome consequences. Suggest three different examples of these unwelcome consequences at least one of which should be social and at least one economic.

3. With the aid of examples, explain how computer technology has changed people's home environment.

4. Many businesses now expect their employees to work at home and go to the office only occasionally.
    (a) Explain how Information Technology can help with this mode of working.
    (b) Explain **one** advantage and **one** disadvantage of this mode of working for
        (i) the individual,
        (ii) the company,
        (iii) society

5. Point of sale (POS) terminals are now used in most supermarkets.
    (a) Suggest **two** advantages to the customer of POS terminals connected to a central computer.
    (b) Suggest **two** advantages to the management of the supermarket of these POS terminals. (Your four advantages must all be different.)

Module 2 Principles of Hardware, Software and Applications

6. Over the next few weeks, write a case study of one major information application of computing. You should consider:
   - the purpose of the application;
   - the application as an information system in the context chosen;
   - specific user-interface needs;
   - the communication requirements of the application;
   - the extent to which the given system satisfies both the organisation's and user's needs;
   - the economic, social, legal and ethical consequences of the application.

Chapter 22 – Computer Crime and the Law

Computer crime and abuse

New technologies generally create new opportunities for crime; as soon as one avenue is blocked to the criminal, another one is discovered. As information technology has spread, so too have computer crime and abuse. The Internet, for example, is used not only by innocent members of the public but also by fraudulent traders, paedophiles, software pirates, hackers and terrorists. Their activities include planting computer viruses, software bootlegging, storing pornographic images and perpetrating all sorts of criminal activities from credit card fraud to the most complex multinational money laundering schemes. **Computer abuse** refers to acts that are legal but unethical.

Hacking

Hacking is defined as unauthorised access to data held on a computer system. The extent of hacking is extremely difficult to establish as it is usually only discovered by accident, with only about two percent of security breaches discovered as a result of positive action on the part of security staff. (*Digital Crime* by Neil Barrett, page 40.)

Hacking is often perpetrated by employees of a company who have acquired inside knowledge of particular user Ids and passwords. The ability of such hackers to carry out illegal actions without being detected is often hampered by the audit and monitoring software that all computer operating systems supply.

The motive behind hacking can often be mischievous rather than anything more sinister: computing students who are learning about operating systems may take delight in penetrating a university's security system to prove that it can be done, or to gain access to exam questions and answers.

In November 1997 Mathew Bevan, a 23 year-old computer technician obsessed with the X-Files and the search for alien spacecraft, and Pryce, a teenager working independently, walked free after a 3 year-long case against them collapsed. They had quite separately penetrated US Air Force computers, Mathew partly motivated by a belief that a captured alien spacecraft was being held secretly at a remote Nevada airbase, and Pryce by an interest in Artificial Intelligence. They were traced not by infowar techniques but by traditional police methods, when Pryce boasted to an undercover informant of his activities on an Internet chat line and gave him his London phone number. They were charged with three offences under the Computer Misuse Act 1990, but eventually it was decided that they in fact presented no threat to national security and they were acquitted after the prosecution offered 'No Evidence'.

Mathew Bevan is now forging a career in Information Security and has a web site www.bogus.net/kuji full of interesting information which you might like to look at.

Theft of data

Data can be stolen by illegally accessing it, or by stealing the computer on which the data is stored. In December 1990 Wing Commander Farquhar's notebook computer was stolen from his car when he left it unattended for a few minutes. It contained the preliminary Allied invasion plan for the impending Gulf war, and could have had potentially disastrous consequences.

Viruses

Viruses are generally developed with a definite intention to cause damage to computer files or, at the very least, cause inconvenience and annoyance to computer users. The first virus appeared at the University of Delaware in 1987, and the number of viruses escalated to over 9000 different variations in 1997. The virus usually occupies the first few instructions of a particular program on an 'infected' disk and relies on a user choosing to execute that program. When an infected program is executed, the virus is the first series of instructions to be performed. In most cases the virus's first action is to copy itself from the diskette onto the PC and 'hide' within obscure files, the operating system code or within unused disk blocks which are then marked as being 'bad' and unavailable for reuse. The virus can then proceed to perform any of a number tasks ranging from the irritating to the catastrophic such as reformatting the hard disk.

Some viruses lie dormant, waiting to be triggered by a particular event or date – the 'Friday 13th' virus being a well-known one. The virus then infects other diskettes, perhaps by modifying operating system programs responsible for copying programs. From there, the next PC to use the diskette will be infected.

ORIGINATION
A programmer writes a program - the virus - to cause mischief or destruction. The virus is capable of reproducing itself

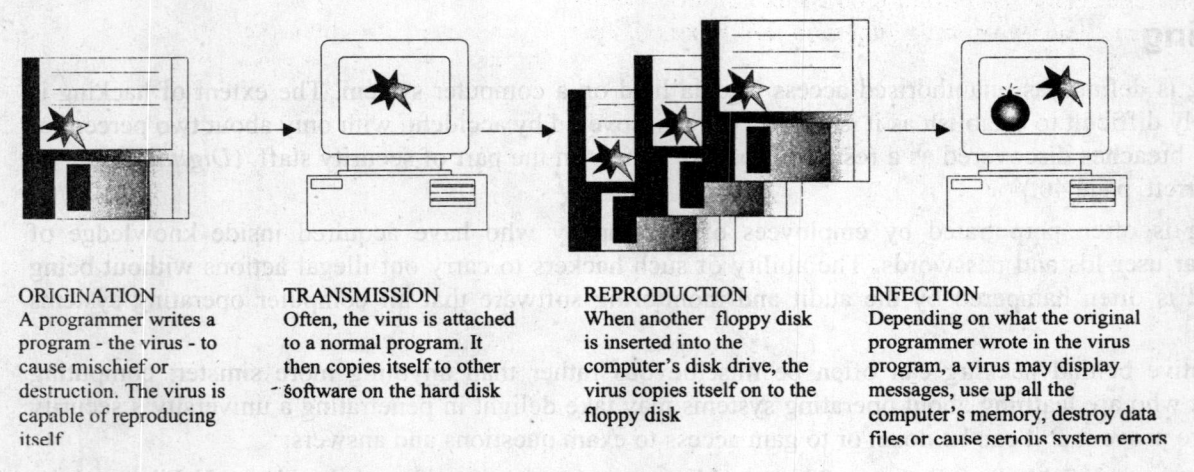

TRANSMISSION
Often, the virus is attached to a normal program. It then copies itself to other software on the hard disk

REPRODUCTION
When another floppy disk is inserted into the computer's disk drive, the virus copies itself on to the floppy disk

INFECTION
Depending on what the original programmer wrote in the virus program, a virus may display messages, use up all the computer's memory, destroy data files or cause serious system errors

Figure 22.1: How a virus works

'Logic bombs'

A 'logic bomb' is similar to a virus and is sometimes delivered by means of a virus. The 'bomb' can be written to destroy or, worse, subtly change the contents of an organisation's computer systems. However, it does not begin this activity until signalled to do so by the hacker or extortionist, or it may be activated if a cancelling signal fails to arrive. In many cases the bomb itself is not actually planted; a warning message alerting the organisation to the placing of a bomb is usually sufficient to persuade vulnerable institutions to hand over huge sums of money. Estimates suggest that at much as £500 million has been handed to extortionists threatening attacks on computer installations between January 1993 and June 1996.

Digital crime and the law

The rapid progress of computer technology has led to the need for new laws to be introduced so that all perpetrators of computer crime can be prosecuted. Laws in the US impact on computer users in this country, since the majority of systems and Internet content is American. A general approach to a common standard for Internet-related laws throughout the European Union formed part of a proposed European Commission directive discussed by member states in October 1996.

Chapter 22 – Computer Crime and the Law

The Computer Misuse Act of 1990

In the early 1980s in the UK, hacking was not illegal. Some universities stipulated that hacking, especially where damage was done to data files, was a disciplinary offence, but there was no legislative framework within which a criminal prosecution could be brought. This situation was rectified by the Computer Misuse Act of 1990 which defined three specific criminal offences to deal with the problems of hacking, viruses and other nuisances. The offences are:

- unauthorised access to computer programs or data;
- unauthorised access with a further criminal intent;
- unauthorised modification of computer material (i.e. programs or data).

To date there have been relatively few prosecutions under this law – probably because most organisations are reluctant to admit that their system security procedures have been breached, which might lead to a loss of confidence on the part of their clients.

Case study 1

A Sunday Times investigation in 1996 established that British and American agencies were investigating more than 40 'attacks' on financial institutions in New York, London and other European banking centres since 1993. Victims have paid up to £13m a time after the blackmailers demonstrated their ability to bring trading to a halt using advanced 'information warfare' techniques learnt from the military.

Criminals have penetrated computer systems using 'logic bombs', electromagnetic pulses and 'high emission radio frequency guns' which blow a devastating electronic 'wind' through a computer system. They have also left encrypted threats at the highest security levels, reading: "Now do you believe we can destroy your computers?"

In most cases victim banks have given in to blackmail rather than risk a collapse of confidence in their security systems.

> Q1: Under which clause of which act could a hacker leaving a threatening message as described above, be prosecuted?

Software copyright laws

Computer software is now covered by the Copyright Designs and Patents Act of 1988, which covers a wide range of intellectual property such as music, literature and software. Provisions of the Act make it illegal to:

- copy software;
- run pirated software;
- transmit software over a telecommunications line, thereby creating a copy.

Software can easily be copied and bootlegged (sold illegally). In addition, the programming *ideas* and *methods* can be stolen by a competitor. Microsoft was sued (unsuccessfully) many years ago by Apple Computers for copying the 'look and feel' of their graphical user interface. It is possible for an expert programmer to 'reverse engineer' machine code to establish the specific algorithms used, so that they can be copied. Some software manufacturers put 'fingerprints' into the code – little oddities which do not affect the way the program runs – so that if the same code is found in a competitor's program, they can prove that it was illegally copied.

The Business Software Alliance in 1998 targeted some 20,000 small- and medium-sized companies to ensure that all software being used is correctly licensed. Offences include using 'pirate' copies of software and using software on more machines than is permitted under the terms of the licence.

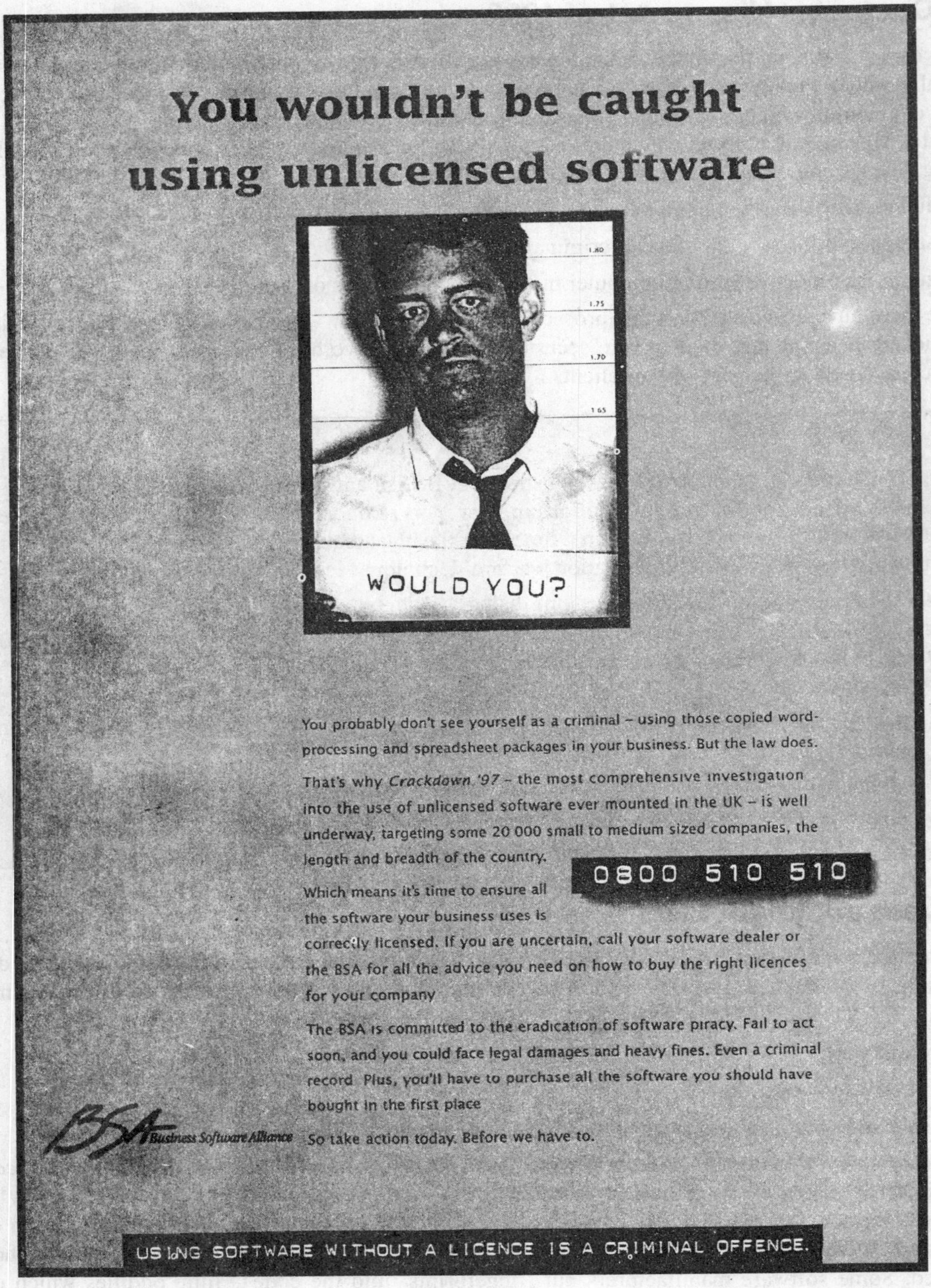

Module 2 *Principles of Hardware, Software and Applications*

Figure 22.2: BSA Advertisement 1997

Chapter 22 – Computer Crime and the Law

> **Case study 2**
>
> Bill Gates's empire is being jeopardised by Russian software pirates. Microsoft Office '97 is being sold for £3 on the Russian black market, a minute fraction of the normal retail price of £315. In 1996, 91% of software programs being used in Russia were pirate copies.
>
> Gates recently travelled to Moscow in an attempt to persuade those trading in pirated copies of software programs to refrain from doing so. The overall cost of this illegal activity to the software industry is around £300 million each year. However, it is unlikely that this personal appeal will succeed while fines for being caught in possession of pirated materials are insignificant in comparison with the revenue generated from the pirate industry itself, set at over £500,000 per month. As one stallholder reportedly said: "Mr Gates has gone home and we are trading happily – he makes about £18 million a month, so we do not feel too bad about selling these copies to people who cannot afford to buy it."
>
> *(Computer Consultant October 1997)*
>
> ➢ Q2: Who are the stakeholders (the people affected) in this story? Who are the victims? Is the stallholder acting ethically?

Using computers to combat crime

Although computers are often involved in criminal activities, there is a more positive aspect to computers in crime; they can prove invaluable in the detection and prevention of crime. Detection is very often about collecting and collating huge amounts of information until a key piece of evidence emerges. In the search for Peter Sutcliffe, the 'Yorkshire Ripper', literally millions of hand- or type-written cards were stored in a mass of filing cabinets while investigators pored over them and tried to pull together threads from the often conflicting evidence. Sutcliffe himself was interviewed several times but overlooked before the key evidence against him emerged from the mass of data. This case acted as the impetus for the implementation of 'HOLMES' (Home Office Large Major Enquiry System).

Databases of fingerprints, stolen vehicles and criminal records are all essential tools in today's fight against crime. Data matching exercises which match, for example, a 'modus operandi' ('style' of crime) with possible suspects can narrow the search field. Analysis of tax returns against the average profits for a particular type of business in a particular area can highlight possible tax fraud.

Exercises

1. The Computer Misuse Act defines three types of offence. With the aid of examples, describe each of these **three** types of offence.

2. A bank uses computers connected by large networks to hold information about customers as well as its own business activities.
   (a) Explain how this type of system may be open to computer crime.
   (b) Suggest methods which may be used to reduce such crime.

3. Computer software houses are concerned about the illegal use of their software products. Briefly outline *two* techniques which are employed to discourage illegal use of software.

4. Many people, often called "hackers", gain unauthorised access into computer networks.
   (i) Describe two ways in which a hacker might benefit from such activities.
   (ii) Describe three ways in which hacking into a network can be made as difficult as possible.

Chapter 23 – Privacy and Data Protection Legislation

Personal privacy

The **right to privacy** is a fundamental human right and one that we take for granted. Most of us, for instance, would not want our medical records freely circulated, and many people are sensitive about revealing their age, religious beliefs, family circumstances or academic qualifications. In the UK even the use of name and address files for mail shots is often felt to be an invasion of privacy.

With the advent of large computerised databases it became quite feasible for sensitive personal information to be stored without the individual's knowledge and accessed by, say, a prospective employer, credit card company or insurance company to assess somebody's suitability for employment, credit or insurance.

> ### Case study: James Wiggins – a true story
>
> In the US, James Russell Wiggins applied for and got a $70,000 post with a company in Washington. A routine pre-employment background check, however, revealed that he had been convicted of possessing cocaine, and he was fired the next day, not only because he had a criminal record but because he had concealed this fact when applying for the job. Wiggins was shocked – he had never had a criminal record, and it turned out that the credit bureau hired to make the investigation had retrieved the record for a James Ray Wiggins by mistake, even though they had different birthdates, addresses, middle names and social security numbers. Even after this was discovered, however, Wiggins didn't get his job back.
>
> **If the pre-employment check had been made *before* Wiggins was offered the job, he would not have been offered it and no reason would have been given. The information would have remained on his file, virtually ensuring that he would never get a decent job – without ever knowing the reason why.**

The Data Protection Act

The Data Protection Act 1984 grew out of public concern about personal privacy in the face of rapidly developing computer technology. It provides rights for individuals and demands good information handling practice.

The Act covers 'personal data' which are 'automatically processed'. It works in two ways, giving individuals certain rights whilst requiring those who record and use personal information on computer to be open about that use and to follow proper practices.

The Data Protection Act 1998 was passed in order to implement a European Data Protection Directive. This Directive sets a standard for data protection throughout all the countries in the European Union, and the new Act was brought into force in March 2000. Some manual records fall within the scope of the Act and there will also be extended rights for data subjects.

The Data Protection Principles

The Data Protection Act became law on 12th July 1984 and was updated in 1998.

Once registered, data users must comply with the eight Data Protection principles of good information handling practice contained in the Act. Broadly these state that personal data must be:

1. fairly and lawfully processed;

2. processed for limited purposes;
3. adequate, relevant and not excessive;
4. accurate;
5. not kept longer than necessary;
6. processed in accordance with the data subject's rights;
7. secure;
8. not transferred to countries without adequate protection.

Useful definitions from the 1984 Act

'PERSONAL DATA' — information about living, identifiable individuals. Personal data do not have to be particularly sensitive information, and can be as little as a name and address.

'AUTOMATICALLY PROCESSED' — processed by computer or other technology such as document image-processing systems. The Act doesn't currently cover information which is held on manual records, e.g. in ordinary paper files.

'DATA USERS' — those who control the contents and use of a collection of personal data. They can be any type of company or organisation, large or small, within the public or private sector. A data user can also be a sole trader, partnership, or an individual. A data user need not necessarily own a computer.

'DATA SUBJECTS' — the individuals to whom the personal data relate.

(The Schedules of the Act may be downloaded from the web site www.hmso.gov.uk and following links for Legislation, United Kingdom, Acts of the UK Parliament. This site contains a lot of information on this topic.)

Data Subjects

We are all 'data subjects'. All types of companies and organisations ('data users') have details about us on their computers. This growth of computerised information has many benefits but also potential dangers. If the information is entered wrongly, is out of date or is confused with someone else's, it can cause problems. You could be unfairly refused jobs, housing, benefits, credit or a place at college. You could be overcharged for goods or services. You could even find yourself arrested in error, just because there is a mistake in the computerised information.

The Data Protection Commissioner

The Commissioner is an independent supervisory authority and has an international role as well as a national one.

In the UK the Commissioner has a range of duties including the promotion of good information handling and the encouragement of codes of practice for data controllers, that is, anyone who decides how and why personal data, (information about identifiable, living individuals) are processed.

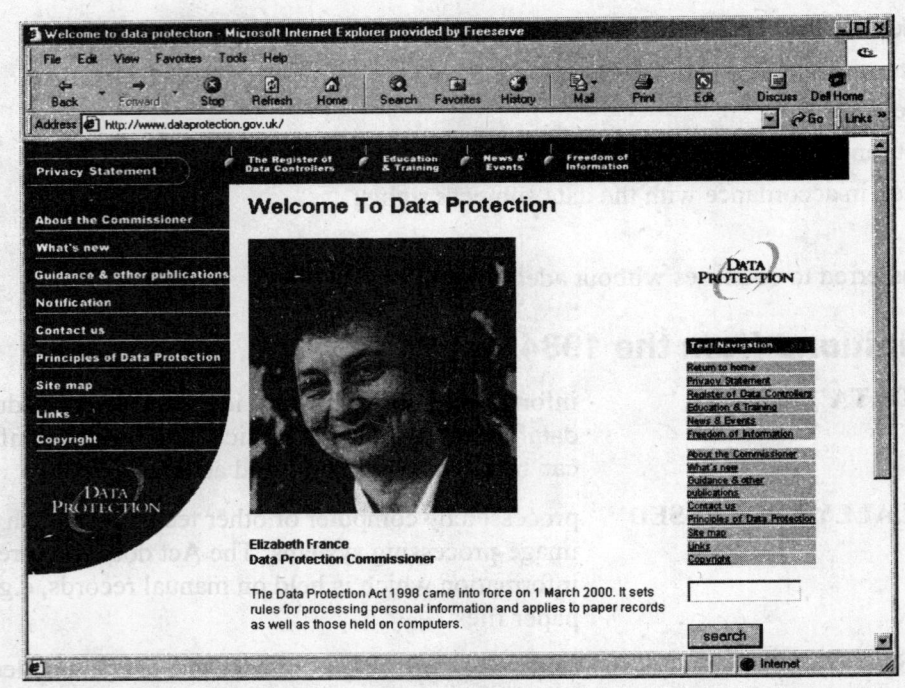

Module 2 Principles of Hardware, Software and Applications

Figure 23.1: The Data Protection Commissioner's Home Page

A data user's Register entry

With few exceptions, all data users have to register, giving their name and address together with broad descriptions of:

- those about whom personal data are held;
- the items of data held;
- the purposes for which the data are used;
- the sources from which the information may be obtained;
- the types of organisations to whom the information may be disclosed i.e. shown or passed on to;
- any overseas countries or territories to which the data may be transferred.

Exemptions from the Act

- The Act does not apply to payroll, pensions and accounts data, nor to names and addresses held for distribution purposes.
- Registration may not be necessary when the data are for personal, family, household or recreational use.
- Subjects do not have a right to access data if the sole aim of collecting it is for statistical or research purposes, or where it is simply for backup.
- Data can be disclosed to the data subject's agent (e.g. lawyer or accountant), to persons working for the data user, and in response to urgent need to prevent injury or damage to health.

Additionally, there are exemptions for special categories, including data held:

- in connection with national security;
- for prevention of crime;
- for the collection of tax or duty.

The rights of data subjects

The Data Protection Act allows individuals to have access to information held about themselves on computer and, where appropriate, to have it corrected or deleted.

As an individual you are entitled, on making a written request to a data user, to be supplied with a copy of any personal data held about yourself. The data user may charge a fee of up to £10 for each register entry for supplying this information but in some cases it is supplied free.

Usually the request must be responded to within 40 days. If not, you are entitled to complain to the Registrar or apply to the courts for correction or deletion of the data.

Apart from the right to complain to the Registrar, data subjects also have a range of rights which they may exercise in the civil courts. These are:

- right to compensation for unauthorised disclosure of data;
- right to compensation for inaccurate data;
- right of access to data and to apply for rectification or erasure where data are inaccurate;
- right to compensation for unauthorised access, loss or destruction of data.

Encryption technology

How secure are e-mails? When you order goods over the Internet and give your credit card number, it is obviously vital that this information cannot be intercepted by anyone. This can be achieved by **encrypting** the data. A common encryption system depends on being able to find the prime factors of two very large numbers, say 155 digits long. It is possible to devise an encryption key which is virtually impossible to break, and this is termed '**strong encryption**'. However, there are issues here; governments are wary of allowing strongly encrypted data to circulate, fearing that terrorists, criminals and spies could transmit messages which can never be decoded. So far, for example, it has proved impossible to factor 200-digit numbers. '**Weak encryption**' using fewer digits means the code is not breakable except by organisations with massive processing power and the will to do so – organised crime presumably included. In 1999 researchers proved that they could crack a code used by the majority of major international and financial institutions, which used 155-digit numbers. *Yesterday's strong encryption is today's weak encryption.*

E-mails and privacy issues

Standard e-mail is not private. It sits around on various computers on its way to you, and even after you delete an e-mail it will still be accessible to someone with a good utility program. The only way to ensure e-mail privacy is to use an encryption program.

Many employees have their own e-mail addresses at their places of work. How private is e-mail sent to and from these addresses? Commonly, e-mails sent out from these addresses goes out with the company footer, which makes it look as if they have been sanctioned by the firm.

In December 1999, twenty-three office staff from the New York Times were fired after managers discovered they had been e-mailing smutty jokes, pornographic pictures and jokes about bosses. The New York Times has a policy specifying that 'communications must be consistent with conventional standards of ethical and proper conduct, behaviour and manners'.

In 1997, Norwich Union paid £450,000 in an out-of-court settlement and had to make a public apology when an e-mail on the Intranet disparaging a competitor got out.

For information on privacy, try Privacy International http://www.privacy.org/pi/.

Module 2 Principles of Hardware, Software and Applications

Exercises

1. A company is storing details of its customers on a database. Describe **three** obligations the company has under the Data Protection Act.

2. Detailed information about individuals is stored on computer databases. It has become necessary for governments to pass laws to protect their citizens.

    Suggest three laws which might be necessary and give a reason for each.

3. Suppose you had moved house three years ago and have recently been receiving mail for the previous owners advertising water sports equipment. The previous owners tell you that they had entered a competition to win a scuba diving holiday about four years ago but had not won. Presumably, the competition organisers had passed on their name and address to the (independent) water sports company, although they had indicated on the form that they did not wish this to happen.

    Give two principles of Data Protection Legislation which would appear to have been broken here.

Chapter 24 – Health and Safety

Computers and health

Computers can be held responsible for a whole raft of health problems, from eyestrain to wrist injuries, back problems to foetal abnormalities, stomach ulcers to mental collapse. Articles appear regularly in the newspapers relating stories of employees who are suing their employers for computer-related illnesses.

Not so long ago it was thought that the widespread use of these fantastic machines, that could perform calculations and process data with lightning speed and complete accuracy, would free up humans to work maybe only two or three hours a day, while the computer did the lion's share. In fact, people seem to be working harder than ever, trying to keep up with the output of their computers. Human beings are the weak link in the chain, needing food, rest, a social life; prone to headaches, stress, tired limbs and mistakes.

Figure 24.1: Stress at work

Stress

Stress is often a major factor in work-related illness. Simply thinking about computers is enough to cause stress in some people. It is stressful to be asked to perform tasks which are new to you and which you are not sure you can cope with. It is stressful to know that you have more work to do than you can finish in the time available. It is stressful, even, to have too little to do and to be bored all day.

The introduction of computers into the workplace can have detrimental effects on the well-being of information workers at many different levels in an organisation. For example:

- some companies may use computers to monitor their workers' productivity, which often increases their stress levels. Symptoms include headaches, stomach ulcers and sleeplessness;
- many people are afraid of computers and fear that they will not be able to learn the new skills required, or that their position of seniority will be undermined by younger 'whizz kids' with a high level of competence in ICT;
- it can be almost impossible for some people to get away from work. Pagers, mobile phones, laptop computers and modems mean that even after leaving the office, there is no need to stop work – indeed, should you even *think* of stopping work? As a busy executive, can you afford to waste 45 minutes on the train to Ipswich reading the newspaper or just gazing out of the window, when you

could be tap-tap-tapping on your laptop, or infuriating your fellow passengers by holding long and boring conversations on your mobile phone?

- 'information overload' means that managers are often bombarded with far more information than they can assimilate, producing 'information anxiety'. Try typing the words 'Information Overload' into one of the World Wide Web's search engines and within seconds, it will have searched millions of information sources all over the world and come up with thousands of references all pre-sorted so that those most likely to be of interest are at the top.

- a survey of 500 heads of ICT departments revealed that over three quarters of respondents had suffered from failing personal relationships, loss of appetite, addiction to work and potential alcohol abuse. The continuing developments within ICT ensure that it is always in the minds of business executives and also that it is blamed for most corporate problems. The very speed of development, for which ICT is now famous, and the need to keep pace with this is also a major contributing factor to ICT stress-related illness.

Case study: Information overload

Val Kerridge is an ICT manager in an Engineering company:

"I have to monitor everything to do with computers that might affect the firm, from fax-modems to new operating systems or network capabilities. I'm always being asked what I think of new hardware or software products, so I feel obliged to read everything – computer magazines, e-mails, user group communications on the Internet, mailshots from suppliers – there was so much it made me ill. I couldn't sleep properly, I had constant headaches and neck pains from staring at a screen, and I never had time to eat properly in a 12 to 14 hour day at the office."

Peter Harris is a management consultant:

"I was away for four days and when I came back, there was a huge pile of mail and faxes and dozens of e-mail messages. I couldn't tell from the titles whether they were important or not, and I spent 10 hours or more in front of a screen dealing with it all. I didn't know what information overload was until I came across the research and then I thought, 'Yes, that's me.'

When I go into organisations I find it very common in all departments. There's too much information and not enough communicating.

I now have a survival strategy. I am very strict with the amount of information I use. I scan it and throw it away or file it. I've learned to say 'No, I don't need that information'".

Repetitive strain injury (RSI)

RSI is the collective name for a variety of disorders affecting the neck, shoulders and upper limbs. It can result in numbness or tingling in the arms and hands, aching and stiffness in the arms, neck and shoulders, and an inability to lift or grip objects. Some sufferers cannot pour a cup of tea or type a single sentence without excruciating pain.

Chapter 24 – Health and Safety

The Health and Safety Executive say that more than 100,000 workers suffer from RSI. It is not a new disease; Bernard Ramazzini, an Italian physician, noted of scribes and notaries in 1717:

> "The diseases of persons incident to this craft arise from three causes … constant sitting … the perpetual motion of the hand in the same manner, and the attention and application of the mind … constant writing also considerably fatigues the hand and the whole arm on account of the continual tension of the muscles and tendons."

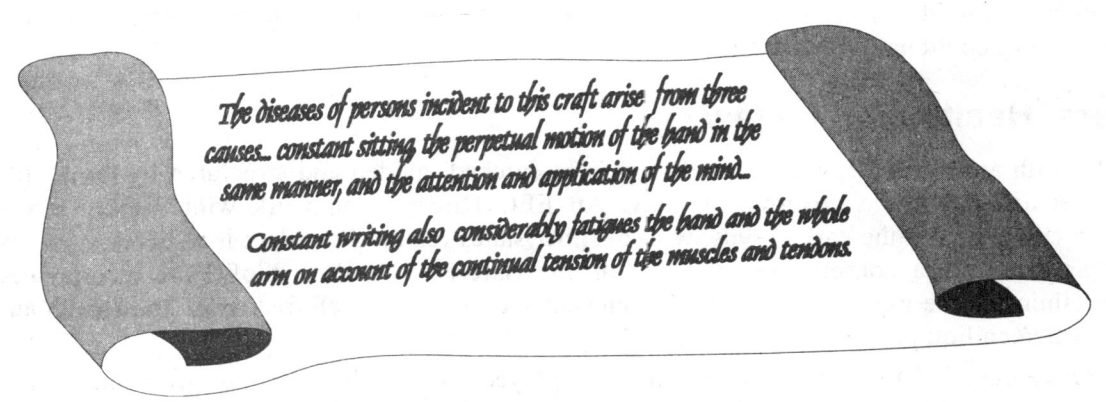

Figure 24.2: Recognition of RSI is not new!

Now, as then, the constant pain "can be removed by no medicines".

Case study: Bank staff 'driven to injury'

Keyboard operators at the Midland Bank's factory-style processing centre at Frimley, Surrey developed severe cases of repetitive strain injury after their work rate was sharply increased, a court was told yesterday.

Five former part-time workers who put cheque details into computers are claiming compensation for upper limb disorders including aches, stiffness and shooting pains in their arms, fingers, wrists, shoulders and necks.

The five former Midland workers, all women, were required to key in transaction records at an intensive stroke rate, on inadequately designed equipment, with a poor working posture and negligible training.

There was a lack of breaks or variation of tasks and there was strong pressure on staff to maintain and increase speed. The fastest operators – who keyed four strokes a second with their right hand, while holding cheques in their left – were awarded gold badges and their names were publicised by the bank.

In 1989, the Midland Bank had to pay £45,000 compensation to an RSI sufferer.

Source: Seumas Milne, The Guardian November 25 1997

> Q1: What factors were cited as contributing to the onset of RSI among the employees?

Eyestrain

Computer users are prone to eyestrain from spending long hours in front of a screen. Many computer users prefer a dim light to achieve better screen contrast, but this makes it difficult to read documents on the desk. A small spotlight focussed on the desktop can be helpful. There is no evidence that computer use causes permanent damage to the eyes, but glare, improper lighting, improperly corrected vision (through not wearing the correct prescription glasses), poor work practices and poorly designed workstations all contribute to temporary eyestrain.

Module 2 Principles of Hardware, Software and Applications

Extremely low frequency (ELF) radiation

In normal daily life we are constantly exposed to ELF radiation not only from electricity mains and computer monitors but also naturally occurring sources such as sunshine, fire and the earth's own magnetic field. Research into the effects of ELF radiation is increasing and seems to indicate that it may be connected to some health problems. Several studies have tried to establish whether there is a link between monitor use and problems in pregnancy such as early miscarriages. The results are not clear-cut, because although some studies seem to show a correlation between an increased rate of miscarriages and long hours spent at a VDU in the first trimester of pregnancy, other factors such as stress and poor ergonomic conditions could have played a part.

Computers, Health and the law

Occupational health and safety legislation in Britain is researched, guided and structured by the Health and Safety Executive (HSE), a government body. An EEC Directive on work with display screen equipment was completed in the early 1990s, with member states required to adapt it to become part of their own legislation. As a consequence, the Health and Safety at Work Act of 1974 incorporated legislation pertaining to the use of VDUs, and the relevant section is now referred to as The Health and Safety (Display Screen Equipment) Regulations 1992.

This legislation is intended to protect the health of employees within the working environment, and employers, employees and manufacturers all have some responsibility in conforming to the law.

Employers are required to:

- perform an analysis of workstations in order to evaluate the safety and health conditions to which they give rise;
- provide training to employees in the use of workstation components;
- ensure employees take regular breaks or changes in activity;
- provide regular eye tests for workstation users and pay for glasses.

Employees have a responsibility to:

- use workstations and equipment correctly, in accordance with training provided by employers;
- bring problems to the attention of their employer immediately and co-operate in the correction of these problems.

Manufacturers are required to ensure that their products comply with the Directive. For example, screens must tilt and swivel, keyboards must be separate and moveable. Notebook PCs are not suitable for entering large amounts of data.

Figure 24.3: Workstations must be ergonomically designed

The ergonomic environment

Ergonomics refers to the design and functionality of the environment, and encompasses the entire range of environmental factors. Employers must give consideration to:

- **lighting**. The office should be well lit. Computers should neither face windows nor back onto a window so that the users have to sit with the sun in their eyes. Adjustable blinds should be provided.
- **furniture**. Chairs should be of adjustable height, with a backrest which tilts to support the user at work and at rest, and should swivel on a five-point base. It should be at the correct height relative to a keyboard on the desk.
- **work space**. The combination of chair, desk, computer, accessories (such as document holders, mouse and mouse mats, paper trays and so on), lighting, heating and ventilation all contribute to the worker's overall well-being.
- **noise**. Noisy printers, for example, should be given covers to reduce the noise or positioned in a different room.
- **hardware**. The screen must tilt and swivel and be flicker-free, the keyboard must be separately attached.
- **software**. Software is often overlooked in the quest for ergonomic perfection. The EEC Directive made a clear statement about the characteristics of acceptable software, requiring employers to analyse the tasks which their employers performed and to provide software which makes the tasks easier. It is also expected to be easy to use and adaptable to the user's experience.

Software can be hazardous to your health

Bad software can be extremely stressful to use. Software that slows you down by crashing frequently, giving incomprehensible error messages, using non-standard function keys and displaying badly structured menus, for example, can leave a user longing to throw the computer through the nearest window. Repeated failure with a new software package very quickly becomes frustrating, boring and depressing. Feelings of inadequacy and alienation mean that people may begin to dread their daily encounters with the computer and productivity suffers.

Human-computer interaction is a growing field of study within computing and seeks to understand, among other things, what makes software difficult or unpleasant to use, and how it can be improved. The principles of good, usable software design are based on extensive research.

Exercises

1. State **four** Health and Safety issues which may arise for staff using computers.

2. State **three** responsibilities of an employer in relation to the health of employees who regularly use computer equipment.

Chapter 25 – General Purpose Packages

Word processing software

Word processing software is used to write letters, reports, books and articles, and any other document that in the past would have been typed on a typewriter. As the user keys in the text, it appears on the screen and is held in the computer's memory. The user can easily edit the text, correct spelling mistakes, change margins and so on before printing out the final version. The document can also be saved on disk for future amendment or use. Until the instruction is given to save, however, the document held in memory will be lost if for example there is a power cut. Memory is a **volatile** storage medium, and users are well advised to save their work frequently.

Below is a summary of some of the features offered by a word processing package such as MS Word.

- type, correct, delete and move text;
- change font size, align text left, right or centre, set tabs, set italics, bold and underline;
- find and replace text;
- insert graphics;
- check spelling and grammar;
- set up templates with type styles for different types of document;
- work in tables or columns;
- add headers and footers to each page;
- create indexes and tables of contents;
- type equations with maths symbols;
- mail merge to send personalised letters to people selected from a list held in Word or in a database.

Desktop publishing

Desktop publishing is an extension of word processing, although word processing packages are now becoming so powerful that the distinction between a 'word processing package' and a 'desktop publishing package' has become blurred. Desktop publishing packages such as Aldus PageMaker or Quark Express tend to be better at handling very long documents such as a book that combines several files. They also allow somewhat easier control over page layout in a newspaper or magazine-style publication. Graphics, scanned photographic images and text can be easily combined and laid out exactly as required. Using templates and wizards you can select a style suitable for a newsletter, poster, web page, advertisement, theatre program, business card, invitation, calendar or any of hundreds of types of publication. To create a web site, for example, Microsoft Publisher has a Web Site Wizard which enables you to easily add graphics, animation and hyperlinks to other pages or Internet sites.

A typical desktop publishing system includes a desktop computer, a laser printer and software.

There is no substitute for practical experience, so if at all possible you should use a desktop publishing package yourself and make notes on its capabilities.

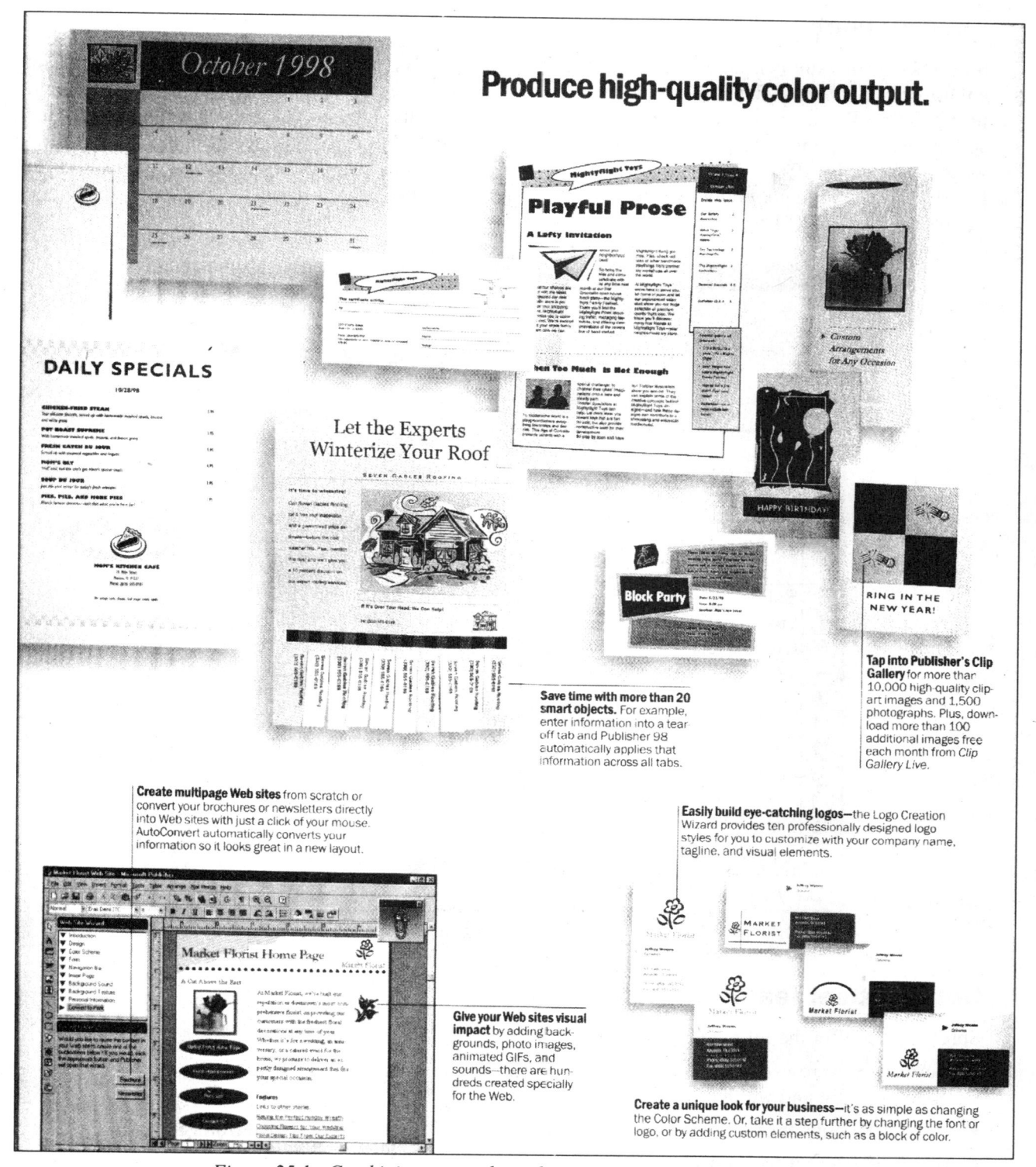

Figure 25.1 - Combining text and graphics using Microsoft Publisher

Module 2 Principles of Hardware, Software and Applications

Spreadsheets

Spreadsheet software is used by people who work with numbers: accountants, banks and building society employees, engineers, financial planners. The user enters the data and the formulae to be used in manipulating the data, and the program calculates the results. One of the most useful features of a spreadsheet is its ability to perform '**What If**' calculations: "What if we produce 30% more widgets and wages increase by 10% – how much will we have to charge in order to show a profit?" Spreadsheets are therefore often used in **planning and budgeting**, but are also widely used by anyone working with figures – for example, keeping a set of students' marks.

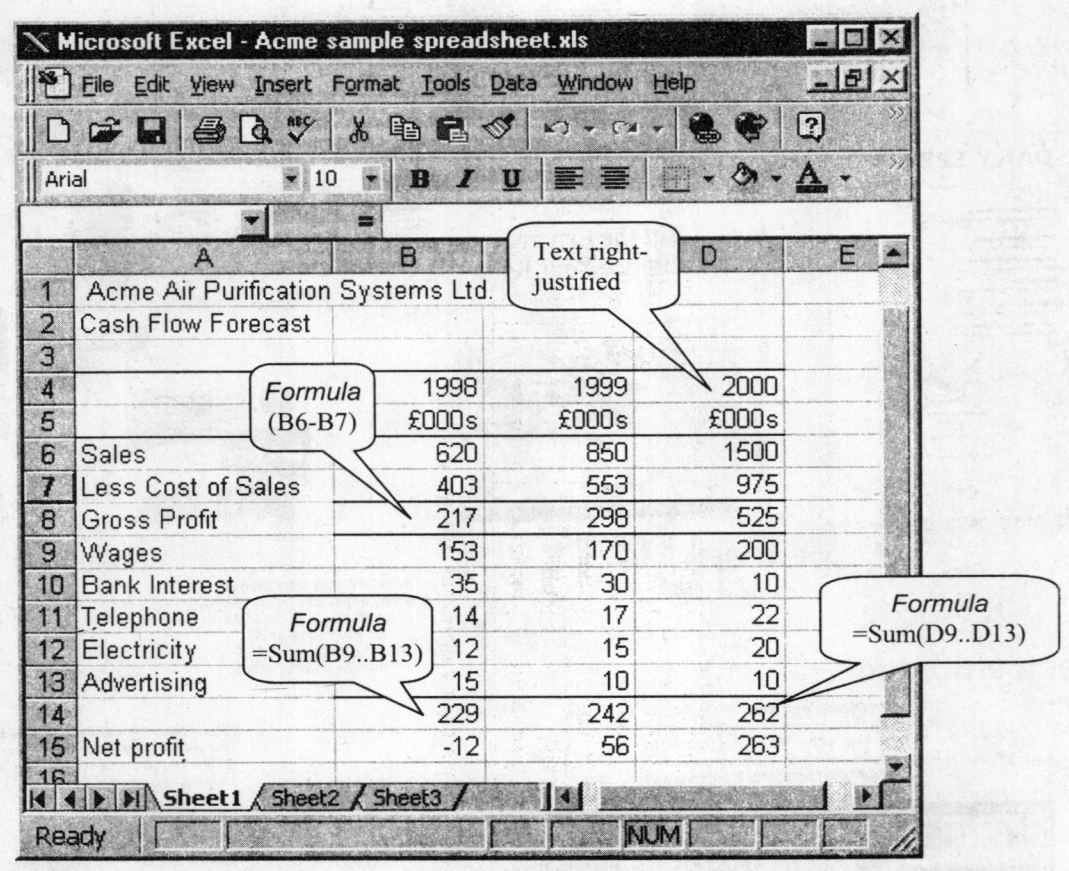

Figure 25.2: Spreadsheet containing numbers, text and formulae

Spreadsheet features

Spreadsheets offer the following facilities:

- format cells, rows and columns, specifying for example, the alignment of text, number of decimal places, height and width of cell;
- copy cell contents to other locations, with automatic adjustment of formulae from say b9 to c9, d9 etc.
- insert, move or delete rows and columns;
- use functions such as sum, average, max, min in formulae;
- determine the effect of several different hypothetical changes of data – this facility is termed 'what-if' calculation;
- create scenarios to examine the effects of changing a number of variables;

- create a simple database and sort or query the data to produce a report of, say, all females earning over £20,000 for a list of employees;
- write macros to automate common procedures;
- create templates – spreadsheets with formats and formulae already entered, into which new figures may be inserted;
- create 'multi-dimensional' spreadsheets using several sheets, and copy data from one sheet to another;
- create many different types of charts and graphs (see Figure 25.3).

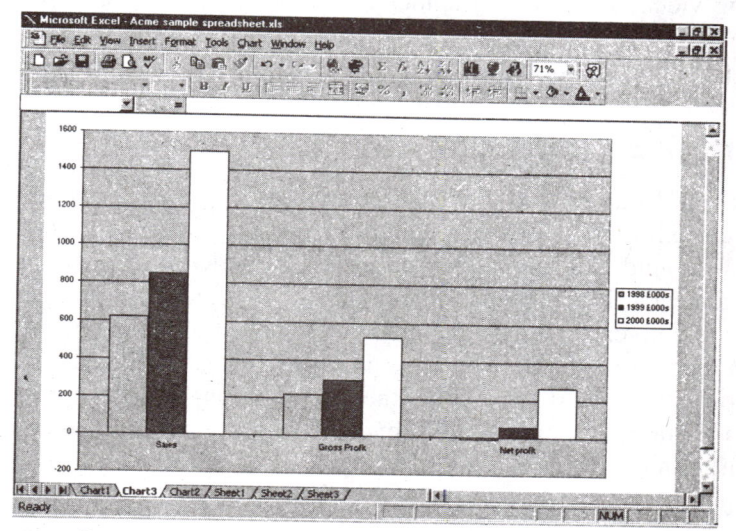

Figure 25.3: A chart created from spreadsheet figures

Electronic mail (e-mail)

E-mail systems allow you to send memos, letters and files containing data of all types from your computer to any other computer with an e-mail address and a modem, simply by typing the recipient's name and pressing the 'Send' button.

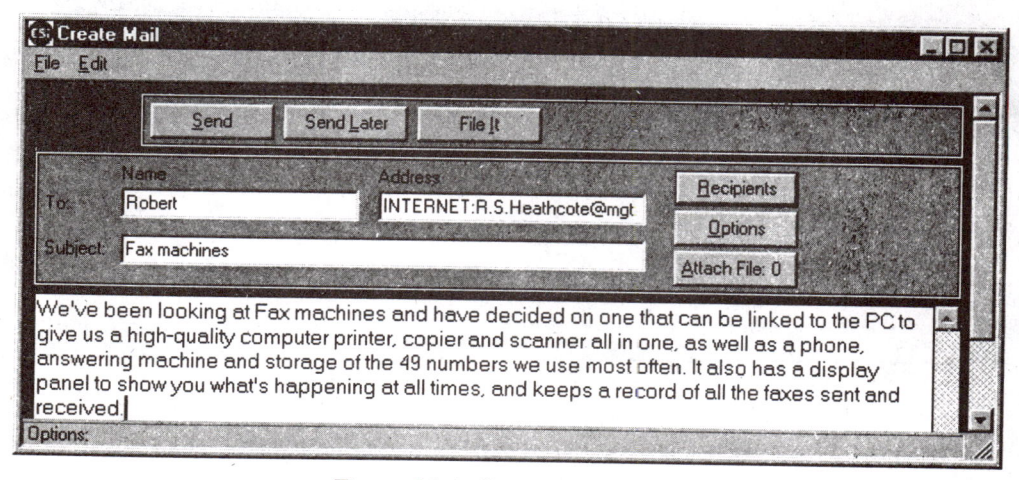

Figure 25.4: Creating an e-mail letter

Module 2 Principles of Hardware, Software and Applications

E-mail has many advantages over both ordinary mail and the telephone. For example:
- a message can be sent anywhere in the world for the price of a local call, without having to leave your desk;
- the same message can be sent simultaneously to a group of people;
- the message will arrive in at most a few hours, and can be picked up the next time the recipient looks at their e-mail;
- it is very easy to send a reply to an e-mail as soon as it is received, using a 'reply' button, or forward it to someone else with your comments;
- long files including video, sound and graphics can be sent automatically when the cheap rate starts after 6pm.

Graphics and text can be electronically transmitted and placed in a document by the recipient.

Presentation graphics software

Using graphics software such as PowerPoint or Lotus Freelance, professional-looking presentations can quickly and easily be designed. As well as showing text, clip art or scanned pictures and various types of chart, transition effects, sound and animation can easily be added. A transition effect determines how each new screen will appear – it could open like a curtain or blind, come in from left or right, etc. The presentation can then be delivered on a large screen attached to a computer, or by making sheets to be shown using an overhead projector. (Of course in this type of presentation, you can't use sound, animation or transition effects.) Alternatively, the presentation can be automated so that it moves continuously through the slides at a preset rate. This type of presentation is often used in shopping malls, tourist information centres and cinemas.

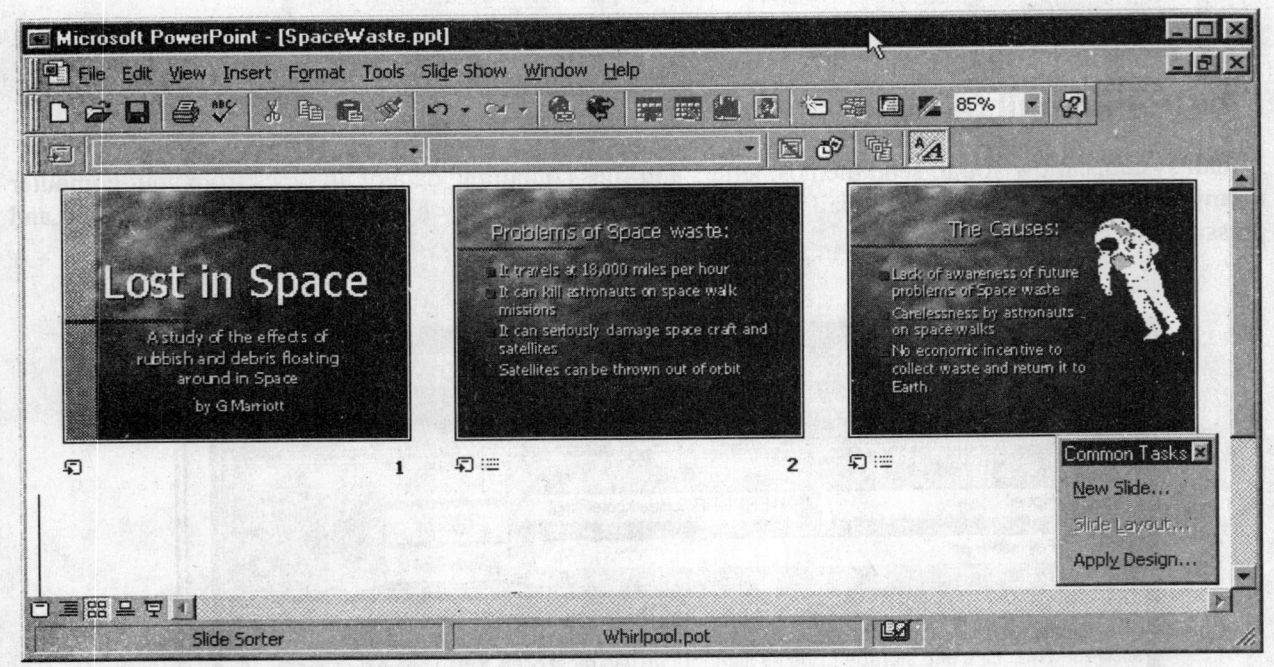

Figure 25.5: Creating a PowerPoint presentation

Integrated packages

An increasingly important feature of modern software is its ability to **integrate** with other packages. For example a user may have some figures stored in a database which he wants to import into a graphics package, or he may have prepared some figures in a spreadsheet which he wants to insert into a word processed document. **An integrated package** such as MS Works combines a spreadsheet module, a database module and a word-processing module in a single package and data can readily be transferred between modules.

Of course, it is also easy to transfer data between applications in many other software packages, whether they are described as 'integrated packages' or 'software suites' such as MS Office. The main difference is that in an integrated package, the different applications are all part of the same software package and you cannot buy one module separately.

Databases

Databases are covered in later chapters in this section.

Exercises

1. In one version of a spreadsheet a particular cell contains the formula
   =(G12+G13+G14+G15+G16)/5. Another version of the same spreadsheet uses the function
   =AVERAGE(G12:G16)

   (a) Compare the effectiveness of these two methods as the number of values whose average has to be calculated changes.

   (b) Outline **two** non-mathematical functions you would expect to find in a spreadsheet.

2. Identify two features of a software package which make it suitable for preparing a multimedia presentation.

3. State an appropriate application for a spreadsheet package in the office of a small manufacturing company, and describe *three* features of the package which would be beneficial within the context of this application.

4. A word processing package includes a global search and replace facility and a mail merge facility.

   (a) An operator uses the global search and replace facility to change all occurrences of *man* to *woman*.

   (i) Give an example to show how the use of this facility may not give the expected result.

   (ii) Suggest how this problem can be avoided.

   (b) Describe the stages involved in producing personalised letters using the mail merge facility.

5. Word Processing and Desktop Publishing software are being used in the home and in business to produce well-presented documents. Advantages to the user over non-computerised methods include the ease of error correction, and the range of formatting and presentation techniques available.

   (a) Give **three** further advantages to the user.

   (b) Give **one** reason why some people regret this trend.

Module 2 Principles of Hardware, Software and Applications

6. State **two** advantages and **one** disadvantage of sending a document by e-mail rather than by the traditional postal service.

7. A company wishes to buy a desk-top publishing package for its microcomputers. Describe **four** distinct features they might look for in choosing which package to buy.

8. The part of a spreadsheet given below holds a table of product details.

	A	B	C	D
1			**Mark up**	1.2
2				
3	**Product**	**Part Number**	**Cost Price**	**Selling Price**
4	Bar Code Reader 1000	BCR123	105	
5	CD ROM Drive 12 speed	CD1286	210	
6	Colour Scanner 24/600	CS24600	450	
7	Hard Disk 1.2 Gb external	HD12	300	
8	Ink Jet printer 100	IP100	120	
9	Keyboard II	KB185	43	
10	LaserWriter 4040	LW4040	675	
11	Monitor 15" Colour	M1536	185	
12	Midi Interface	M1267	56	
13	Mouse plus	MP34	20	
14	Performance Computer 456	PC456	645	
15				
16				
17				

The formula in cell D4 is: **=C4 * D1** (where the d1 is an absolute reference to cell D1). This formula is to be replicated down the column.

(a) (i) Briefly describe how to replicate the formula in D4 down the column to row 14.

   (ii) Why is it necessary to have the cell D1 as an absolute reference?

(b) A different part of the spreadsheet obtains the selling price for any given part number from this table using a lookup function. State the parameters needed by such a lookup function.

Chapter 26 – Records and Files

Hierarchy of data

An effective information system provides users with timely, accurate and relevant information. This information is stored in computer files, which need to be suitably organised and properly maintained so that users can easily access the information they need.

We'll look at the way that data is represented and structured in a computer, starting with the very lowest level.

BIT All data is stored in a computer's memory or storage devices in the form of binary digits or **bits**. A bit can be either 'ON' of 'OFF' representing 1 or 0.

BYTE Bits are grouped together, with a group of 8 bits forming a byte. One byte can represent one character or, in different contexts, other data such as a sound, part of a picture, etc.

There are different codes used for representing characters, one of the most common being ASCII (American Standard Code for Information Interchange). Using 8 bits it is possible to represent 256 (2^8) different characters.

FIELD Characters are grouped together to form **fields**. Data held about a person, for example, may be split into many fields including ID Number, Surname, Initials, Title, Street, Village, Town, County, Postcode, Date of birth, Credit Limit and so on.

RECORD All the information about one person or item is held in a **record.**

```
ID Number:    432768
Surname:      King
Initials:     DF
Title:        Mr
Street:       2 Burghley Crescent
Town:         Bath
County:       Avon
Post code:    BA3 5WT
Date of Birth: 14/8/78
Credit Limit:  £250
```

FILE A file is defined as a collection of records. A stock file will contain a record for each item of stock, a payroll file a record for each employee and so on.

DATABASE A database may consist of many different files, linked in such a way that information can be retrieved from several files simultaneously. There are many different ways of organising data in a database, and many different database software products for use on all types of computer from micros to mainframes.

Text and non-text files

The term file can be used in a broader sense to mean a data structure which could hold, for example:

- a source code program written in a high-level language;
- a binary file containing executable code;
- a bitmapped graphics file;
- a word processed letter;
- an ASCII text file.

For the rest of this chapter, the word *file* will be used in the sense of a *collection of records* such as a file of employees containing one record for each employee.

Primary key

Each individual record in a file needs to be given a unique identifier, and this is termed the **primary key**. It needs to be carefully chosen so that there is no possibility of two people or items having the same primary key; Surname, for example, is no use as an identifier. The primary key sometimes consists of more than one field: for example several stores in a national chain may each have a store number, and each store may have Departments 1, 2, 3 etc. To identify a particular department in a particular store, the primary key would be composed of both Store number and Department number.

> Q1: What would be a suitable primary key for:
> - a book in a bookshop?
> - a book in a library?
> - a hospital patient?
> - a car owned by a car-hire firm?

Secondary key

Other fields in a record may be defined as **secondary keys**. These fields are not unique to each record, but may be used to quickly locate a group of records. For example, the field **Department** may be defined as a secondary key on an Employee file.

Fixed and variable length records

In some circumstances records in a file may not all be the same length. **Variable length records** may be used when either:

- the number of characters in any field varies between records;
- records have a varying number of fields.

A variable length record has to have some way of showing where each field ends, and where the record ends, in order that it can be processed. There are two ways of doing this:

- use a special end-of-field character at the end of each field, and an end-of-record marker at the end of the record, as shown below. (* is used as the end-of-field marker, and # is used as the end-of-record marker.)

```
SH12345*laser printer*HP laserjet2100*750.00*999.99*7#
MH452*colour flatbed scanner*Microtek Scanmaker II*150.00*289.00*3#
```

- use a character count at the beginning of each field, and an end-of-record marker. In the implementation shown below, the byte holding the count is included in the number of characters for the field, and a real number is assumed to occupy 4 bytes, an integer 2 bytes. (You could also have a character count for the entire record instead of the end-of-record marker.)

```
8SH1234514laser printer15HP Laserjet21005270.005399.9937#
6MH45223colour flatbed scanner22Microtek Scanmaker II5150.005289.0033#
```

Advantages and disadvantages of variable length records

The advantages of variable length records are:
- less space is wasted on the storage medium;
- It enables as many fields as necessary to be held on a particular record, for example a field for each subject taken by an A Level student;
- it may reduce the time taken to read a file because the records are more tightly packed.

The disadvantages are:
- the processing required to separate out the fields is more complex;
- it is harder to estimate file sizes accurately when a new system is being designed.

Estimating file size

In a file of fixed length records, you can estimate the file size by multiplying the number of bytes in each record by the number of records. You need to know how many bytes in each field, and you need to add a few extra bytes for each **block** of records. Data is physically held on disk or tape in blocks of say 512 bytes. If the record length is 80 bytes, there will be a maximum of 6 records per block. Therefore 1000 records would occupy 1000/6 blocks, each of ½ Kb. Therefore the file will occupy 167/2 Kb, i.e. approximately 84Kb.

If the records are 102 bytes long, 5 records would probably not fit into a block of 512 bytes because a few bytes are required in each block for information about record size etc. However if you were asked to estimate file size in an exam question, this would be made very clear.

> Q2: Estimate the number of bytes used by a file of 800 records each of 120 bytes. You can assume that 4 records fit into each block of 512 bytes.

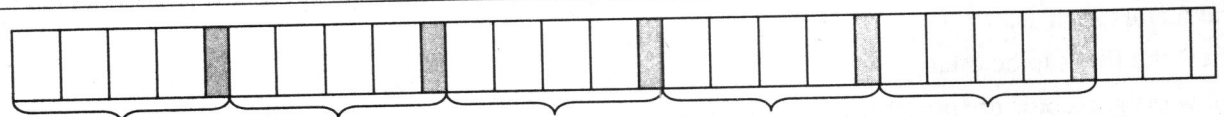

Each block contains 4 records of 120 bytes with some space left over

Exercises

1. When deciding which file structure to use for a particular application, one must choose between fixed length and variable length records.
   (a) State two advantages of using fixed length records.
   (b) Describe one example when it would be more appropriate to use variable length records.

2. Distinguish between the terms **primary key** and **secondary key** as applied to files and give an example of each from within an employee master file.

Chapter 27 – File Organisation

Master and transaction files

In the last chapter a *file* was defined as a collection of *records*. Most large companies have hundreds or even thousands of files that store data pertaining to the business. Some of the files will be **transaction files** and some will be **master files**.

Transaction files contain details of all transactions that have occurred in the last period. A period may be the time that has elapsed since business started that day, or it may be a day, a week, a month or more. For example a sales transaction file may contain details of all sales made that day. Once the data has been processed it can be discarded (although backup copies may be kept for a while).

Master files are permanent files kept up-to-date by applying the transactions that occur during the operation of the business. They contain generally two basic types of data:

- Data of a more or less permanent nature such as, on a payroll file, name, address, rate of pay etc.
- Data which will change every time transactions are applied to the file – for example, gross pay to date, tax paid to date, etc.

> Q1: A file of student records is to be kept holding student number, personal details such as name and address, course number and course grade (A-F). Design a record structure for the file, under the following headings:
>
> **Field description**   **Field length**   **Field type (character or numeric)**

File organisation

Files stored on magnetic media can be organised in a number of ways, just as in a manual system. There are advantages and disadvantages to each type of file organisation, and the method chosen will depend on several factors such as:

- how the file is to be used;
- how many records are processed each time the file is updated;
- whether individual records need to be quickly accessible.

Types of file organisation

The available methods include:
- serial;
- sequential;
- indexed sequential;
- random.

Note: A knowledge of indexed sequential file organisation is not required for the AQA/AEB syllabus.

Serial file organisation

The records on a serial file are not in any particular sequence, and so this type of organisation would not be used for a master file as there would be no way to find a particular record except by reading through the whole file, starting at the beginning, until the right record was located. Serial files are used as temporary files to store transaction data.

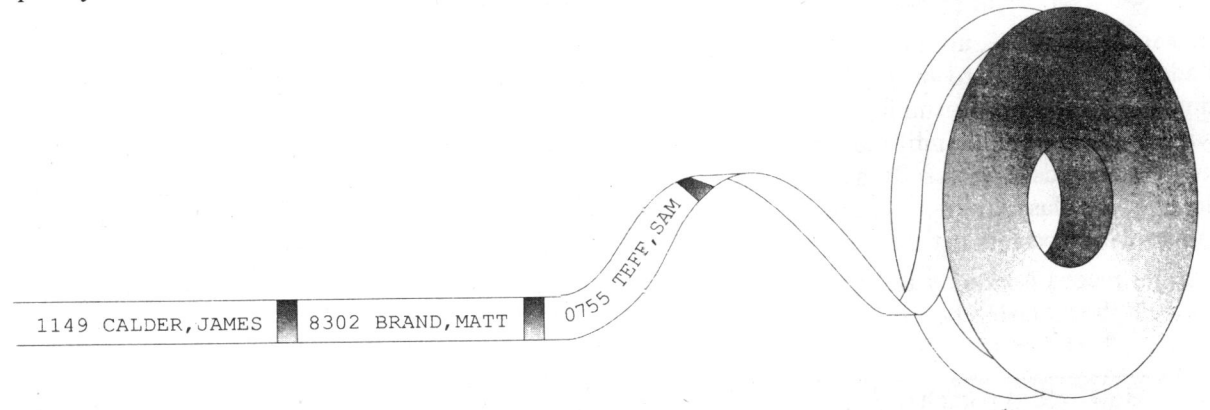

Figure 27.1: A serial file

Sequential file organisation

As with serial organisation, records are stored one after the other, but in a sequential file the records are sorted into **key sequence**. Files that are stored on tape are **always** either serial or sequential, as it is impossible to write records to a tape in any way except one after the other. From the computer's point of view there is essentially no difference between a serial and a sequential file. In both cases, in order to find a particular record, each record must be read, starting from the beginning of the file, until the required record is located. However, when the whole file has to be processed (for example a payroll file prior to payday) sequential processing is fast and efficient.

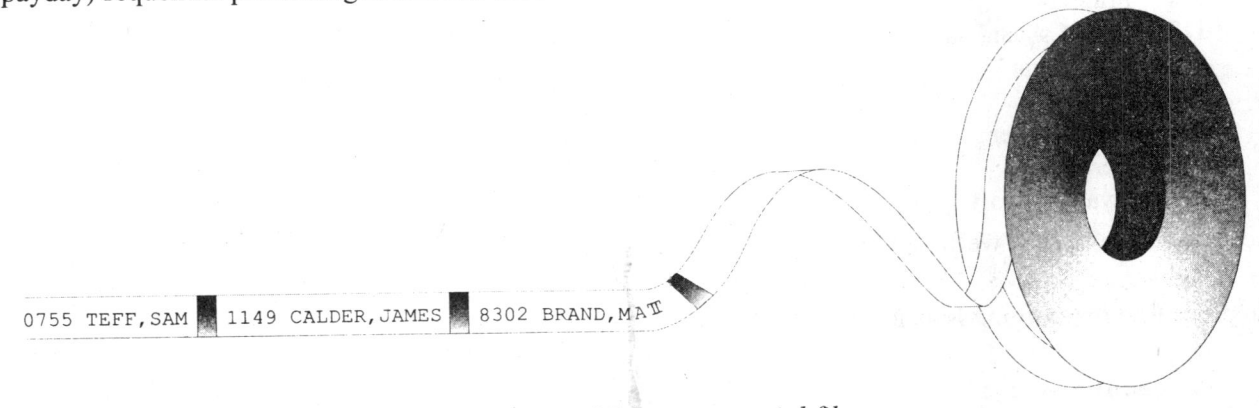

Figure 27.2: A sequential file

Adding and deleting records on a serial file

Most computer languages that are used for data processing include statements which allow the file to be opened at the end of existing records. Then, if one or more new records has to be added to a serial file, there is no problem; the new records can simply be appended to the end of the file.

Deleting a record is more complex. It is easy to understand the problem if you imagine the file is held on magnetic tape, and understand that in any particular program run you can **either** read from the tape **or** write to the tape. To find the record to be deleted, the computer has to read the tape from the beginning;

Module 2 Principles of Hardware, Software and Applications

but once it has found it, it cannot back up and 'wipe' just that portion of the tape occupied by the record, leaving a blank space. The technique therefore is to create a brand new tape, copying over all the records up to the one to be deleted, leaving that one off the new tape, and then copying over all the rest of the records.

Adding and deleting records on a sequential file

With a **sequential** file, all the records on the tape (or disk) are in order, perhaps of employee number, so just adding a new record on the end is no good at all. Of course the records could then be sorted but sorting is a very time-consuming process. The best and 'correct' way is to make a new copy of the file, copying over all records until the new one can be written in its proper place, and then copying over the rest of the records. It's exactly as if you had just made a list on a nice clean sheet of paper of all the students in the class in order of surname, and then discovered you had left out Carter, A.N. The only way to end up with a perfect list is to copy it out again, remembering to include Carter this time.

Deleting a record is exactly the same as for serial organisation. The file is copied to a new disk or tape, leaving out the record to be deleted.

> Q2:   How would you **change** a record on a sequential file held on magnetic tape? (e.g. if you had got Carter's initials wrong?)

Merging two sequential files

(Not required for AQA/AEB)

Sometimes it is necessary to merge two files which have exactly the same structure into one large file. For example, a garden centre may have kept two separate files, one for perennial plants and another for pot plants. It now decides it wants to put all plants into one file in order to produce a catalogue.

Suppose the two files have key fields as follows:

Perennial File (A)		**Pot Plant File (B)**	
111	Fragrant dianthus	156	Patio Dahlia
112	Dwarf shasta daisy	185	Cape Fuschia
117	Bellflower	187	Hanging Carnations
171	Bee balm	266	Begonia
200	Dwarf aster	268	Marguerite
201	Geranium		
203	Swallow-wort		

The merged file (which we'll call File C) will have records in the sequence 111, 112, 117, 156, 171, 185, 187, etc.

The procedure for merging is as follows:

```
Procedure Merge

Read a record from file A
Read a record from file B
Repeat
    If Key_of_A < Key_of_B then
        write Record A to File C
        if not end-of-file A then read another record from File A
        else set Key_of_A to HighValue
        endif
```

```
        else write Record B to File C
            if not end-of-file B then read another record from File B
            else set Key_of_B to HighValue
            endif
        endif
    until no more records on either file
```

In this procedure, HighValue is assumed to be a value higher than any of the keys on either file. In fact HighValue or a similar identifier is a reserved constant in some high level languages, used in this type of situation. The algorithm doesn't allow for one of the files being empty: it is left as an exercise to amend it to allow for this possibility!

Random files

A random file (also called a **hash file, direct** or **relative** file) has records that are stored and retrieved according to either their disk address or their relative position within the file. This means that the program which stores and retrieves the records has first to specify the address of the record in the file.

This is done by means of an **algorithm** or formula which transforms the record key into an address at which the record is stored. In the simplest case, record number 1 will be stored in block 1, record number 2 in block 2 and so on. This is called **relative** file addressing, because each record is stored at a location given by its key, relative to the start of the file.

More often, however, record keys do not lend themselves to such simple treatment. If for example we have about 1000 records to store, and each record key is 5 digits long, it would be a waste of space to allow 99999 blocks in which to store records. Therefore, a **hashing algorithm** is used to translate the key into an address.

One hashing method is the division/remainder method. Using this method, the key of the record is divided by the total number of addresses on the file, and the remainder is taken as the address of the record

For example, the address of record number 75481 would be calculated as follows:

    75481/1000 = 75 remainder 481.

    Address = 481.

> **Q3:** Calculate the addresses of records with keys 00067, 00500, 35648.

Synonyms

This method of file organization presents a problem: however cunning the hashing algorithm, synonyms are bound to occur, when two record keys generate the same address. One method of resolving synonyms is to place the record that caused the collision in the next available free space. When the highest address is reached, the next record can be stored at address 0. Another technique is to have a separate overflow area and leave a tag in the original location to indicate where to look next.

> **Q4:** On the same file as before, calculate the addresses of records with keys
> 12345
> 17998
> 56998
> 35345
> 88000
> 54999 entered in that order.

Properties of a good hashing algorithm

A hashing algorithm needs to be chosen so that it gives a good spread of records. This will partly depend on the properties of the record keys. Sometimes, to obtain a better spread of record addresses, a prime number close to the number of records to be stored on the file is chosen and the key of the record is divided by this number to obtain the remainder. For example, on the file of 1000 records discussed above, you could try dividing the keys by the prime number 997 instead of 1000 before taking the remainder.

The algorithm should be chosen so that:

- It can generate any of the available addresses on the file;
- It is fast to calculate;
- It minimises 'collisions' (synonyms).

Adding and deleting records from a random file

To add a record to a random file, its address first has to be calculated by applying the hashing algorithm. If that address is already full, the record can be put in the next available free space. Thus referring back to Q4, record 56998 would be stored in address 999 because 998 is already full. When searching for a record, the search has to continue until either the record is found or a blank space is encountered.

This poses a problem for deleting records. If for example the record 17998 were subsequently deleted, 56998 would not be found as its proper address 998 would be empty. The way round this problem is to leave the deleted record in place, and to set a flag labelling it as deleted. In other words, although *logically* deleted, the record is still *physically* present. A '**flag**' is simply an extra variable, e.g. a Boolean variable, stored with each record as an extra field. When the file is initialised and contains no records, the flag in each address can be set to 0, meaning that the record position is empty. When a record is written to an address, the flag is set to 1. When the record is deleted, the only change made to the record is to set the flag back to 0. When looking for a particular record, if the record key is found but it has a flag of 0, it is considered to be logically 'not there'. It's as though it's been crossed out, so it is to be ignored, but we can still see that there was a record there at one time. This means the space can be reused if a new record with a key hashing to this address is to be added to the file, but because the space is not actually empty, the search for a record that may have overflowed to the next address will still continue until either the record is found or an empty space is encountered.

Indexed sequential files

(Not required for AQA/AEB)

In an indexed sequential file, an index is held at the front of the file showing the highest key stored in each physical block of records. The records themselves are held in sequence in blocks, and often some space is left in each block when the file is created so that additional records can be added and the correct sequence of records maintained. Records that will not fit into the home block have to be placed in an overflow area and a 'tag' giving the record key and its overflow address left in the home block to show where the record is.

An indexed sequential file, therefore, consists of three areas:

1. a **home** area where the records are initially stored;
2. an **index** area containing an entry giving for each block address, the highest key in the block;
3. an **overflow** area to hold records that have been subsequently added and will not fit into the correct home block.

The great advantage of indexed sequential files is that since the records are held in sequence, but are also indexed, they can be processed either randomly or sequentially, depending on what is required.

Chapter 28 – File Processing

The role of various files in a computer system

All data processing systems except the most trivial will need to store data in files. These files can be categorised as:

- master files,
- transaction files (sometimes called **movement** files) or
- reference files.

Master and transaction files were defined in the previous Unit. A **reference file** is a file that contains data used by a program during processing. For example, in a payroll system:

- the **master file** contains details on each employee
- the **transaction file** contains details of the hours worked, holiday and sick days etc last period
- the **reference file** contains data on tax bands, union rates, etc.

> Q1: In an electricity billing system, briefly outline the contents of the customer master file, the transaction file and a reference file.
>
> Q2: Why not hold the data in the reference file either on the customer master file or within the program which calculates the customers' bills?

Operations on files

The following operations are commonly carried out on files:

- Interrogating/referencing
- Updating
- Maintaining
- Sorting.

Interrogating or referencing files

When a file is interrogated or referenced it is first searched to find a record with a particular **key**, and that record is then displayed on a screen, printed out or used in further processing, without itself being altered in any way.

How the record is located will depend entirely on how the file is organised. If the file is **sequential**, each record will have to be read until the required one is found. If the file is **indexed**, the indexes will first be read and the address of the record obtained so that the record can be read directly. If the file is **random** the hashing algorithm will be applied to get the address of the record.

Note that **database** systems are organised differently from the individual files discussed in this chapter and the previous one, and are considered separately in a later chapter.

Module 2 *Principles of Hardware, Software and Applications*

> **Q3:** A bicycle shop selling bicycles and spare parts has a computerised stock control system so that the salespersons can see whether any item is in stock via a terminal in the shop. What file organisation would you recommend for the master file of all stock items? Justify your answer.

Updating files

A master file is **updated** when one or more records is altered by applying a transaction or a file of transactions to it. First of all the correct record has to be located and read into memory, then updated in memory, and written back to the master file.

Once again, the method of doing this will depend on the file organisation.

If the master file is sequentially organised, it is impossible to read a record into memory, update it and then write it back to the same location.

The method used to update a sequential file was developed when virtually all master files were stored on magnetic tape (or even on punched cards or paper tape!). Although disks are often used nowadays to store sequential files, the same method is still used because it is very efficient under certain circumstances.

The method is called '**updating by copying**' and it requires the transaction file to be sorted in the same order as the master file.

The following diagram illustrates the process.

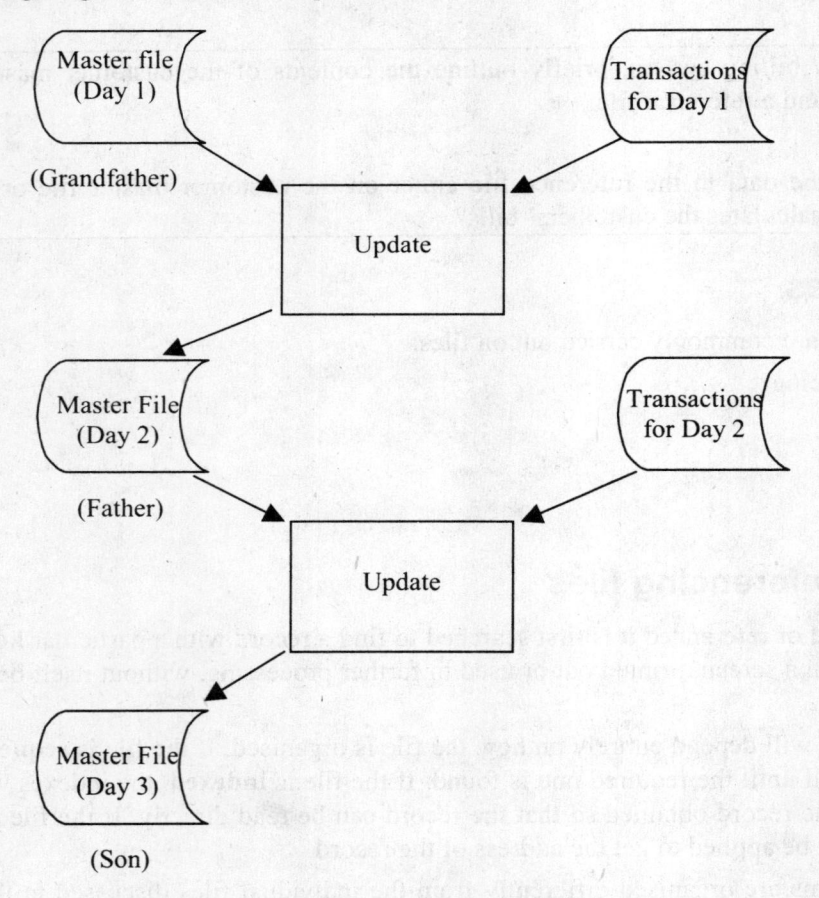

Figure 28.1: Grandfather-Father-Son method of updating

The steps are as follows:

1. A record is read from the master file into memory
2. A record is read from the transaction file into memory
3. The record keys from each file are compared. If no updating is required to the master file record currently in memory (the master key is less than the transaction key) the master record is copied from memory to a **new master file** on a different tape or area of disk, and another master file record is read into memory, overwriting the previous one. This step is then repeated.
4. If there **is** a transaction for the master record currently in memory, the record is updated. It will be retained in memory in case there are any more transactions which apply to it. Steps 2-4 are then repeated.

After a sequential file has been updated, two versions or **generations** of the master file exist; the **old master file**, still in the same state it was in prior to the update, and the **new master file** just created. The next time the file is updated, a third version of the master file will be created, and so on.

It is obviously not necessary to keep dozens of out-of-date master files, and the general practice is to keep three generations, called **grandfather, father** and **son** for obvious reasons, and then reuse the tapes or disk space for the next update that takes place.

Updating by overlay

If the file to be updated is indexed sequential or random, it is possible to access a record directly, read it into memory, update it, and write it back to its original location. This is called **updating by overlay**, **updating in place** or **updating in situ** if you are a Latin speaker. It is possible to do this because unlike in sequential file processing, the record is accessed by means of its address on the file and so can be written back to the same address.

File maintenance

File maintenance is similar to file updating, but refers to the updating of the more permanent fields on each record such as in a stock file, for example, the description of the item, price, location in warehouse, etc. It also involves adding new records to the file and deleting records for items that are no longer held.

Once again, depending on the file organisation, either the grandfather-father-son technique will be used, or, if the file is indexed or random, **updating by overlay** may be used.

File access methods

How a file is **organised** determines how it can be **accessed**:

- a sequential file can only be accessed sequentially;
- a random file would normally only be accessed randomly (it *could* be accessed serially but the records would not be in any particular sequence so this would be unusual);
- an indexed sequential file can *either* be accessed sequentially *or* randomly.

An indexed sequential file is thus the most versatile file organisation, and before the widespread use of databases was used in many different situations. One example would be customer billing systems (electricity, gas, etc) where the master file can be processed sequentially when sending out bills to all customers, and randomly when payments come in in dribs and drabs. Indexed sequential files are still used in older installations using COBOL programs but more up to date organizations use databases instead!

Criteria for use of sequential and direct access files

The choice of file organization (or more likely today, database design) is one of the most important decisions made by the system designer. A number of questions needs to be answered, including:

- Must the user have immediate access to the data, with a response time of no more than a few seconds?
- Must the information be completely up to date, or will last night's or last week's information be sufficient?
- Can requests for information be batched, sequenced and processed all together?
- Are reports needed in a particular sequence?
- What is the most suitable storage medium for the volume of data involved?
- What will happen if the information on the files is lost or destroyed?

In addition two further factors need to be considered; hit rate and volatility.

Hit rate

Hit rate measures the proportion of records being accessed on any one run. It is calculated by dividing the number of records accessed by the total number of records on the file, and expressed as a percentage.

For example, on a payroll run if 190 out of 200 employees were to be paid the hit rate would be 95%. In a system for processing car insurance renewals in weekly batches, the hit rate would be about 2% if renewals were spread more or less evenly through the year.

Sequential updating is inefficient with a low hit rate; random access would be better.

Use of serial files

Serial files are normally only used as transaction files, recording data in the order in which events take place; for example, sales in a shop, customers taking cash from a cash machine, orders arriving at a mail order company. The transactions may be batched and the master files updated at a later time, or alternatively in a real-time system, the files may be updated straight away but the transaction file is kept for record-keeping purposes. It will also be used in the event of a disaster like a disk head crash, to restore the master file from the previous night's backup.

Use of sequential files

Sequential files are used as master files for high hit rate applications such as payroll. The main bulk of processing time is taken up with the weekly or monthly payroll, when every employee's record needs to be accessed and the year-to-date fields brought up to date, and sequential organisation is fast and efficient. It is **not** efficient when only a few records need to be accessed; for example if an employee changes address and the record needs to be updated, since the entire file has to be read and copied over to a new master file. However as this happens relatively infrequently it still makes sense to use a sequential file organisation.

Use of indexed sequential files

Indexed files are extremely useful as they can be sequentially processed when all or most of the records need updating or printing, and randomly when only a few need to be directly accessed. They are suitable for real-time stock control systems, because each time a customer makes a purchase, the master file can be looked up, using the index, to find the appropriate record and ascertain the description and price to print on the receipt. The quantity in stock can be immediately updated, and the record written back to the file ('updating in situ'). When reports of sales or stock are needed in stock number sequence, the file can be processed sequentially, not using the index at all. Sequential processing of an indexed file is fast, but not as fast as the processing of a sequential file because each block probably contains some empty space, and some records will be in a separate overflow area; the records are not all in **physical** sequence even though they are in **logical** sequence (i.e. they appear to the user/programmer to be in sequence).

Use of random files

Random files are used in situations where extremely fast access to individual records is required. To find a record, the hashing algorithm is applied to the record key and the record address immediately found, so no time is wasted looking up various levels of index. In a network system, user ids and passwords could be stored on a random file; the user id would be the key field from which the address is calculated, and the record would hold the password (encrypted for security reasons) and other information on access rights. Random file organisation might also be used in an airline booking system, where thousands of bookings are made every day for each airline from terminals all over the country. A fast response time to the desired record is crucial here. Note that random file organisation is **not** suitable if reports are going to be needed in key sequence, as the records are scattered 'at random' around the file.

Exercises

1. Describe how a new record can be added to, and subsequently deleted from, a direct (random) file.

2. Explain each of the following file structures, giving an example of its use. In each case, describe how a new record is inserted:
   (i) serial access file;
   (ii) sequential access file
   (iii) random access file.

3. (a) Briefly explain two applications in which it is appropriate to process a file serially. Explain why serial processing is appropriate in each case.
   (b) Briefly describe an application which requires serial access to a master file on one occasion and direct access on another.

4. Records within a master file can be *retrieved* or the master file may be *updated*.
   (a) (i) Explain what is meant by retrieving.
       (ii) Give **two** ways in which records are processed when the master file is updated.
   (b) A new record needs to be inserted into a sequential file in one pass. Describe, in pseudocode, an algorithm for this process.

5. In a stock control filing system for some 500 different items of stock, a hashing algorithm is applied to a seven digit stock number to generate the disk address of the block which stores the data for each item of stock.
   (a) (i) State one problem that would arise if the seven digit stock number were to be used directly as a disk address for this application.
       (ii) Explain how the hashing algorithm overcomes this problem.
   (b) With a disk block limited to holding the data for only one item of stock, how could the system deal with storing the data for two items of stock which generate the same disk address?

Chapter 29 – File Security Methods

Threats to information systems

Computer-based information systems are vulnerable to crime and abuse, natural disaster and human error. In this chapter we'll look at some of the ways that an organisation can protect the **security** of data from theft or destruction.

Data security

Maintaining data security means keeping data safe from the various hazards to which it may be subjected. These include:

- natural hazards such as fire, floods, hurricanes or earthquakes
- deliberate corruption or destruction of data by malicious or terrorist acts
- illegal access to data by 'hackers'
- accidental destruction of data by hardware failure or program or operator error.

> Q1: Suggest measures to minimize the danger of loss of data from natural hazards.

Keeping data secure from fraudulent use or malicious damage

Data may be at risk not only from outside 'hackers' but from employees within the company. Organisations are often exposed to the possibility of fraud, deliberate corruption of data by disgruntled employees or theft of software or data which may fall into the hands of competitors. Measures to counteract these risks include the following:

- careful vetting of prospective employees;
- immediate removal of employees who have been sacked or who hand in their resignation, and cancellation of all passwords and authorisations;
- 'separation of duties'; i.e. trying to ensure that it would take the collusion of two or more employees to be able to defraud the company. The functions of data preparation, computer operations and other jobs should be separate, with no overlap of responsibility;
- prevention of unauthorised access by employees and others to secure areas such as computer operations rooms, by means of machine-readable cards or badges or other types of locks;
- the use of passwords to gain access to the computer system from terminals;
- educating staff to be aware of possible breaches of security, and to be alert in preventing them or reporting them. This can include politely challenging strangers with a "May I help you?" approach, not leaving output lying around, machines logged on, or doors unlocked;
- appointing a security manager and using special software which can monitor all terminal activity. Such software can enable the security manager to see, either with or without users' knowledge, everything being typed on any screen in a network. It will also record statistics such as number of logins at each terminal, hours of login time, number of times particular programs or databases were accessed and so on. It will even log the security manager's activities!

Password protection

Most password schemes use tables to store the current password for each authorised user. These tables will be stored on disk and will be backed up along with other vital system files, and in addition may be printed out in a dump of system files. For this reason password lists should not be stored in plain form but should be **encrypted**, and held in an irreversibly transformed state.

User IDs and passwords

Each user in an organisation who is permitted to access a company database is issued with a user id and a password, which will normally give them a certain level of access rights set by the database manager. Common rules issued by companies regarding passwords include the following:

- Passwords must be at least 6 characters;
- Password display must be automatically suppressed on screen or printed output;
- Files containing passwords must be encrypted;
- All users must ensure that their password is kept confidential, not written down, not made up of easily-guessed words and is changed regularly, at least every 3 months.

> Q2: Describe several ways by which a password may become known to an unauthorised person.
> Q3: If the encrypted passwords cannot be decoded, how will the system be able to compare a password entered by the user with the coded password held in the password table?
> Q4: What happens if the user forgets his password?

When a user types a password at a keyboard, the password is usually concealed in some way, for example by not echoing it on the screen. However, it can still be observed by wire-tapping. Passwords can be protected during transmission by encrypting them, but this is costly.

Communications security

Telecommunications systems are vulnerable to hackers who discover a user id and password and can gain entry to a database from their own computer. One way of preventing this is to use a call-back procedure so that when a remote user logs in, the computer automatically calls them back at a pre-arranged telephone number to verify their access request before allowing them to log on.

Data encryption can also be used to 'scramble' highly sensitive or confidential data before transmission.

Data encryption

Data on a network is vulnerable to wire-tapping when it is being transmitted over a network, and one method of preventing confidential data from being read by unauthorised hackers is to **encrypt** it, making it incomprehensible to anyone who does not hold the 'key' to decode it.

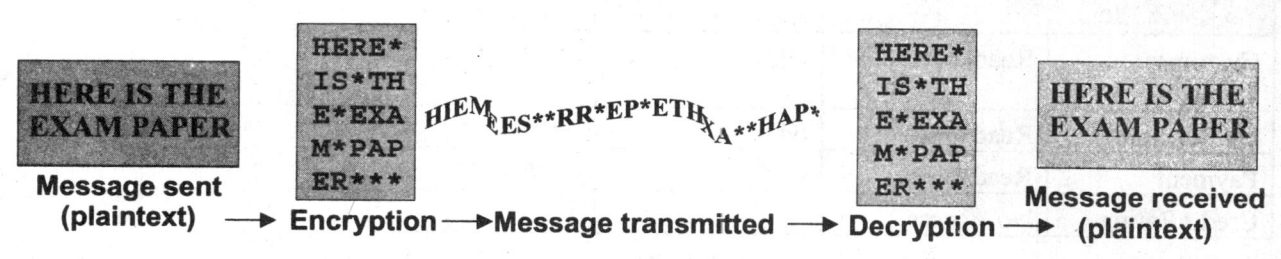

Figure 29.1: Data encryption

Module 2 *Principles of Hardware, Software and Applications*

There are many ways of encrypting data, often based on either **transposition** (where characters are switched around) or substitution (where characters are replaced by other characters).

In a **transposition** cipher, the message could be written in a grid row by row and transmitted column by column. The sentence 'Here is the exam paper' could be written in a 5 x 5 grid:

```
H E R E *
I S * T H
E * E X A
M * P A P
E R * * *
```

And transmitted as HIEMEES**RR*EP*ETHXA**HAP*

> **Q5:** Using the same grid, decode the message ITT*O*E*HRWDNIYA*OS*NITT*

Using a substitution cipher, a 'key' that is known to both sender and receiver is used to code the message. A very simple example is to substitute each letter with the next one in the alphabet.

In practice, since the key must be difficult to break, a much more sophisticated algorithm must be used, with frequent changes of key. (See also discussion of strong and weak encryption in Chapter 23.)

Cryptography serves three purposes:

- it helps to identify authentic users;
- it prevents alteration of the message;
- it prevents unauthorised users from reading the message.

Access rights

Even authorised users do not normally have the right to see all the data held on a company database – they can only see that which they need to do their job. In a hospital, for example, receptionists may have the right to view and change some patient details such as name, address and appointments but may not access the patient's medical records. In a stock control system, salesmen may be permitted to view the price, description and quantity in stock of a particular item, but not to change any of the details held.

Access rights to a particular set of data could typically be set to Read-Only, Read/Write, or No Access. This ensures that users within a company can only gain access to data which they are permitted to see, and can only change or delete data on the database if they are authorised to do so.

Likewise, the computer can also be programmed to allow access to particular data only from certain terminals, and only at certain times of day. The terminal in the database administrator's office may be the only terminal from which changes to the structure of a database may be made. An 'access directory' specifying each user's access rights is shown in Figure 29.2.

Access Profile: User ID 26885

Data	Access right	Terminal number	Permitted time	Security level
Customer Number	Read only	04,05	0830-1800	7
Credit Limit	Read Write	04	0830-1800	10
Payment	Read/Write	04,05	0830-1700	7
Credit Rating	No Access			12

Figure 29.2: A security access table as part of a database

Biometric security measures

Passwords are only effective if people use them properly: if obvious passwords are used, or people tell them to their friends or write them down on a piece of paper blue-tacked to the computer, they are useless. *Biometric* methods of identifying an authorised user include fingerprint recognition techniques, voice recognition and face recognition. One such system uses an infra-red scanner to capture the unique pattern of blood vessels under the skin, and can even differentiate between identical twins by comparing the scan with the one on disk stored for each person.

> **Case study: Iris recognition technology**
>
> The Nationwide Building Society started customer trials in March 1998 of 'iris recognition technology' – cash machines which are capable of recognising an individual's unique 'eye-print'. Special cameras are installed at the counter of the Swindon Head Office branch and at the cash machine. The camera captures a digital image of a person's iris, and from then on, every time a customer uses the cash machine, the system verifies their iris record within seconds.
>
> However, retina verification can be unreliable, as checking the iris requires a person to look into a device at exactly the same angle each time.

Disaster planning

No matter what precautions are taken against fire, flood, power surges, and deliberate or accidental destruction of data, the possibility always exists that data will be destroyed. A simple disk head crash can destroy a disk pack in a fraction of a second. System designers must provide a reasonable backup facility that does not degrade the performance of the system and does not cost too much.

The cost of lack of planning for computer failure can be ruinous. IBM estimates that 70% of organisations that experience a failure (caused by fire, flood, power failure, malice etc) cease operating within 18 months. The main consequence of a computer failure is loss of business, but other problems include loss of credibility, cashflow interruptions, poorer service to customers and loss of production.

Periodic backups

The most common technique used to ensure that data is not lost is to make **periodic backups**, by copying files regularly and keeping them in a safe place. This scheme has several weaknesses:

- All updates to a file since the last backup may be lost;
- The system may need to be shut down during backup operations;
- Backups of large files can be extremely time-consuming;
- When a failure occurs, recovery from the backup can be even more time-consuming.

A **benefit** of periodic backups is that files which may have become fragmented by additions and deletions can be reorganised to occupy contiguous space, usually resulting in much faster access time.

An important feature of all backup systems is the safe storage of the backup copies: it is usually necessary to store one backup copy in a fire-proof safe in the building, and another copy off-site.

Recovery procedures

A contingency plan needs to be developed to allow rapid recovery from major disruptions. In addition to file back-up procedures, it is necessary to:

- identify alternative compatible equipment and security facilities, or implement a service agreement which provides replacement equipment when needed. This may also include putting up temporary office space;
- have provision for alternative communication links.

Module 2 Principles of Hardware, Software and Applications

Exercises

1. An on-line information retrieval system holds confidential personal data.
   - (a) What precautions should be taken to
     - (i) minimise unauthorised access
     - (ii) detect unauthorised access?
   - (b) Why might different users be given different access privileges?
   - (c) Explain how the data should be protected from corruption.

2. Briefly describe the safeguards a company could use for each of the following threats to its computer system.
   - (i) Power failure of on-line systems
   - (ii) Disk corruption
   - (iii) Illegal tapping of data on telephone lines
   - (iv) Fire
   - (v) Viruses

3. (a) Computer crime of various types is seen as an increasing problem. Northland Bank takes considerable care to ensure that it employs staff who are honest.

   Assume, however, that a programmer in the Computing Section of Northland Bank is dishonest.
   - (i) Describe two ways in which this person might illegally benefit from his or her position.
   - (ii) Other than using passwords, describe **two** measures that the Bank could introduce to try to prevent its computer staff benefiting from such illegal activity.

   (b) Passwords are used extensively in the Bank's computer system. Describe **three** ways in which the use of passwords can be made as secure as possible.

   (c) It is quite common for an organisation to adopt some type of *code of practice* to try to guide the behaviour of its staff. In the case of Northland Bank, all employees have to sign a form agreeing to comply with the Bank's code of conduct. Describe whether a code of conduct would be likely to help the bank deal with a dishonest employee.

4. (a) Describe how computer security can be improved by using data encryption.

   (b) In addition to encryption, many measures are taken in the attempt to make computer systems more secure. For instance, passwords are used. Apart from the use of data encryption and passwords, describe **three** ways in which a computer system can be made more secure against unauthorised access.

   (c) Outline the need for recovery procedures in a computer system.

Chapter 30 – Data Processing Integrity Methods

Data integrity

This refers to the **correctness** of the data. The data held in a computer system may become incorrect, corrupted or of 'poor quality' in many different ways and at many stages during data processing.

1. **Errors on input.** Data that is keyed in may be wrongly transcribed. A batch of transaction data could go astray, or be keyed in twice by mistake.

2. **Errors in operating procedure.** An update program could for example be run twice in error and quantities on a master file would then be updated twice.

3. **Program errors.** These could lead to corruption of files; a new system may have errors in it that will not surface for some time, or errors may be introduced during program maintenance.

4. **Viruses.** Files can be corrupted or deleted if a disk becomes infected with a virus.

5. **Transmission errors.** Interference or noise in a communications link may cause bits to be wrongly received.

Standard clerical procedures

To protect against input and operating procedure errors, standard procedures may be documented and followed for both input and output.

Input

- Data entry must be limited to authorised personnel only.
- In large volume data entry, data may be verified (keyed in twice by different operators) to guard against keying errors.
- Data control totals must be used wherever possible to verify the completeness and accuracy of the data, and to guard against duplicate or illegal entry.

Output

- All output should be inspected for reasonableness and any inconsistencies investigated.
- Printed output containing sensitive information should be shredded after use.

Data entry methods

Methods of 'direct data capture' which cut out the need to key in data from input documents are likely to have advantages in terms of speed, accuracy and cost, and so are becoming more and more common. However, we are a long way off from escaping the chore of filling in forms of one sort or another, a large number of which will then have to be keyed into a computer system.

> **Q1:** Name (a) some applications which use direct data entry, eliminating the need for keying in data and
> (b) applications which require data to be keyed in.

Module 2 Principles of Hardware, Software and Applications

Types of input error

Figure 30.1 shows an example of an order form filled in by customers of a mail order company.

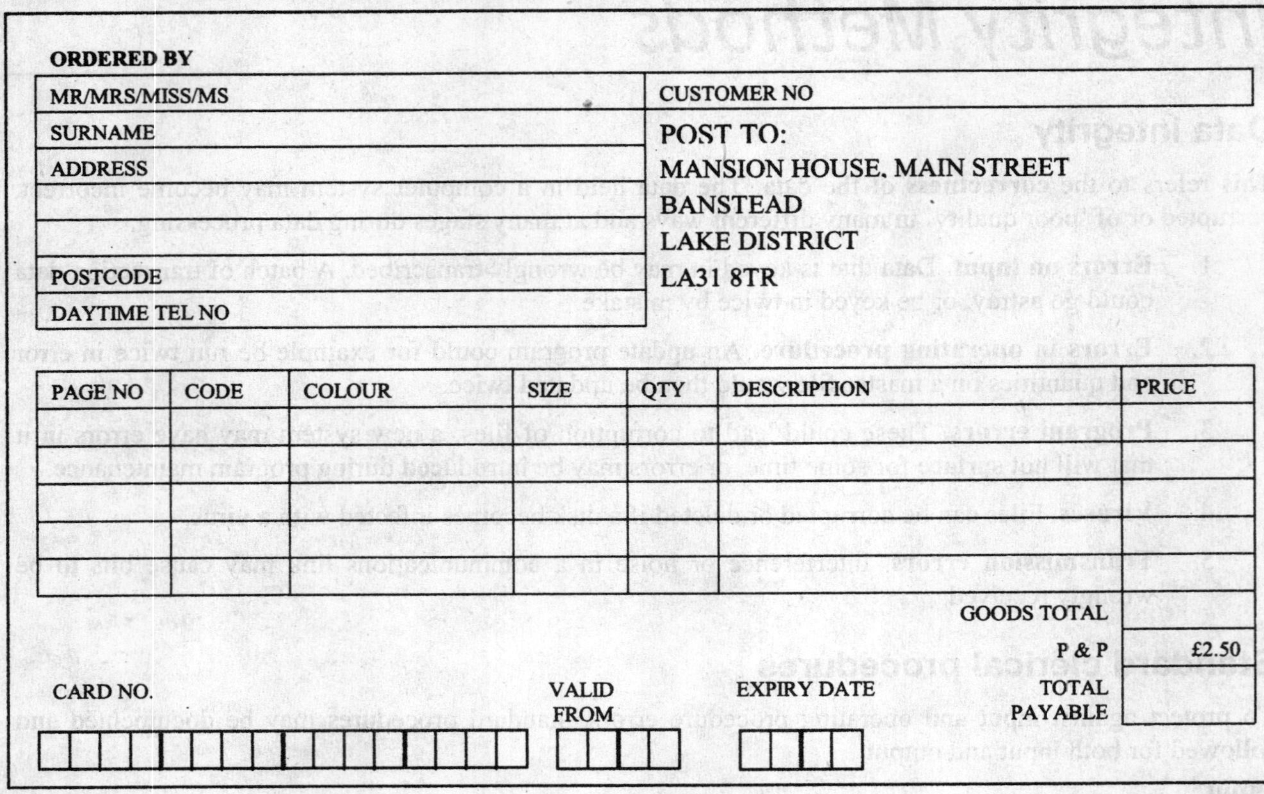

Figure 30.1: A Mail Order form

The information from this form will be keyed in to the computer and then processed to produce a set of documents including a delivery note and invoice for the customer, as well as updating stock and sales records. There are several possible sources of error before the data are processed:

- the customer could make a mistake, entering the wrong product codes, adding up the total cost wrongly, forgetting to enter their address or card expiry date, etc.
- the person keying in the data could make a **transcription** error, keying in the wrong product code or quantity, misreading the customer's name, adding an extra couple of 0's to the total price by keeping a finger down too long, and so on;
- a form could be blown into the bin by a sudden draught as a fan starts up or someone flounces out, slamming the door – or the operator might decide the writing was so bad it simply wasn't worth the effort of struggling with it, and bin it;
- a bored keypunch operator, chatting to a colleague, could enter the same form twice without realising it;
- a faulty connection between hardware components such as the processor and the disk drive could mean that some characters are wrongly transmitted.

Now clearly a mail order company would not stay in business very long if this was how the operation worked! So what can be done to minimise the possibility of error?

Batch processing

In a batch processing system, documents such as the sales orders described above are collected into batches of typically 50 documents. A **data control clerk** has the responsibility of:

- counting the documents;
- checking each one visually to see that the customer has entered essential details such as their name and address, and card details if that is the payment method;
- calculating a **control total** of some crucial field such as Total Payable, for the entire batch of 50 documents;
- calculating **hash totals** of other fields such as size or quantity (see below):
- filling in a batch header document which will show, for example:
  - batch number
  - number of documents in batch
  - date received
  - control total
  - hash total
- logging the batch in a book kept for this purpose.

A *hash total* is a sum of values calculated purely for validation purposes. For example, if the sizes of all garments ordered on a batch of forms (12,10, 12, 34, 36, etc.) are added together and the total entered on the batch header and keyed in, the computer will be able to perform the same calculation and if the figures don't match, then the batch must have an error in it somewhere.

Control totals and hash totals have a similar purpose; the data from the batch header is keyed in as well as the contents of all the documents in the batch, and the computer performs the same summing calculations that the data entry clerk made manually. If there is any discrepancy, then an error is reported and the batch is rechecked. The difference between the two types of total is only that a hash total has no meaning, whereas a control total (e.g. number of documents in the batch) does.

The stages in batch processing are discussed in the next chapter.

Validation checks

As the data is being keyed in, a computer program controlling the input can perform various validation checks on the data. For example:

1. **Presence check.** Certain fields such as customer number, item code, quantity etc must be present. The data control clerk may have visually checked this but the program can perform a second check. Also, if this is a new customer, a number could be automatically assigned.
2. **Format check** (also called **picture check**). For example the code perhaps has a pattern of 2 letters followed by 4 numbers. The quantity and price must be numeric.
3. **Range check.** The expiry date of a card must have a month number between 1 and 12, and the date must be later than today's date.
4. **File lookup check.** If the customer has filled in their customer number, the computer can look this up on the customer file and display the name and address. The data entry operator can check that it tallies.
5. **Check digit check.** (on the next page).
6. **Batch header checks.** The total number of records in the batch should be calculated by the computer and compared with the figure on the batch header. The control totals and hash totals are also calculated and compared.

Module 2 Principles of Hardware, Software and Applications

Check digits

Code numbers such as a customer number, employee number or product number are often lengthy and prone to error when being keyed in. One way of preventing these errors occurring is to add an extra digit to the end of a code number which has been calculated from the digits of the code number. In this way the code number with its extra check digit is self-checking.

The best-known method of calculating check digits is the modulus-11 system, which traps over 99% of all errors. The calculation of a check digit is shown below.

1. Each digit of the code number is assigned a 'weight'. The right hand (least significant) digit is given a weight of 2, the next digit to the left 3 and so on.
2. Each digit is multiplied by its weight and the products added together.
3. The sum of the products is divided by 11 and the remainder obtained.
4. The remainder is subtracted from 11 to give the check digit. The two exceptions are:
   - If the remainder is 0, the check digit is 0, not 11.
   - If the remainder is 1, the check digit is X, not 10.

Example:

To calculate the check digit for the number 1587:

Original code number	1	5	8	7
Weights	5	4	3	2
Multiply digit by its weight	5	20	24	14
Add products together		5 + 20 + 24 + 14 = 63		
Divide by 11		5 remainder 8		
Subtract remainder from 11		11 - 8 = 3		

Check digit = 3. The complete code number is 15873.

To check that a code number is valid, it is not necessary to recalculate the check digit completely. If the check digit itself is assigned a weight of 1, and the products of the digits (including the check digit) and their respective weights are calculated, their sum will be divisible by 11 if the check digit is correct.

All books have an ISBN number which has a modulus-11 check digit. Try checking whether the ISBN number 1-85805-170-3 is valid. (Ignore the hyphens.)

Verification

Verification is the process of entering data twice, with the second entry being compared with the first to ensure that it is accurate. It is common in batch processing for a second data entry operator to key in a batch of data to verify it. You have probably come across another example of verification when setting a password; you are asked to key the password in a second time to ensure that you didn't make a keying error the first time, as it is not echoed on the screen.

Detecting transmission errors

In order to guard against the possibility of data being wrongly transmitted between the various hardware components of a computer, a **parity bit** is added to each character. In an even parity machine, the total number of 'On' bits in every byte (including the parity bit) must be an even number. When data is moved from one location to another, the parity bits are checked at both the sending and receiving end and if they are different or the wrong number of bits are 'On', an error message is displayed.

Thus a character code of 1101010 will have a parity bit of 0 appended to it, and a character code of 1101110 will have a parity bit of 1 appended. (See Chapter 18, Figure 18.3.)

Data is transmitted over a transmission line between computers in **blocks** of say 256 bytes. A **checksum** may be calculated by adding together the numeric value of all the bytes in a block, and this sum transmitted with the data, to be checked again at the receiving end.

Protection against viruses

Steps can be taken which minimise the risk of suffering damage from viruses. These include:

- making sure that all purchased software comes in sealed, tamper-proof packaging;
- not permitting floppy disks containing software or data to be removed from or brought into the office. (This is a sackable offence in some companies);
- using anti-virus software to check all floppy disks before use.

Write-protecting disks

A simple measure such as write-protecting disks and tapes so that they cannot be accidentally overwritten can be effective in guarding against operator error. Both disks and tapes have write-protect mechanisms.

When the write-protect notch is open, the disk contents cannot be altered

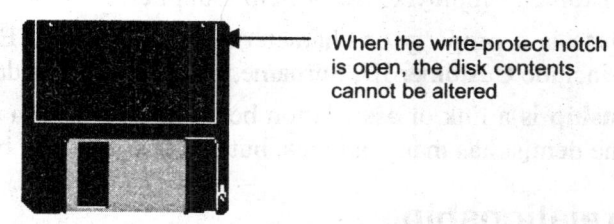

Figure 30.3: Write-protecting a floppy disk

Exercises

1. Explain the difference between data security and data integrity with specific reference to a database which might be used in a local health centre.

2. Parity bits and checksums are commonly used to detect errors during data transmission. Comment on the effectiveness of each of these methods in error detection.

3. Validation checks are used to detect errors in data. State three different validation checks that could be used on data entering a system, giving, for each, a clear example of an error which it should successfully detect.

4. In a library the ISBN for a reserved book has been recorded as **1 870941 39 1**. Showing all your working, determine whether this ISBN is valid or invalid.

Module 2 Principles of Hardware, Software and Applications

Chapter 31 – Entity-Relationship Modelling

(The material in this chapter is not examined in the first year. However, if you are doing practical database work in your first year, you will find it essential!)

The conceptual data model

When a systems analyst sits down to design a new system, one crucial task is to identify and state what **data** needs to be held. From the statement of data requirements a <u>conceptual data model</u> is produced. This describes how the data elements in the system are to be grouped. Three terms are used in building a picture of the data requirements.

1. An **entity** is a thing of interest to an organisation about which data is to be held. Examples of entities include Customer, Employee, Stock Item, Supplier.

2. An **attribute** is a property or characteristic of an entity. Examples of attributes associated with a Customer include Customer ID, Surname, Initials, Title, Address, Credit Limit.

3. A **relationship** is a link or association between entities. An example is the link between Dentist and Patient; one dentist has many patients, but each patient only has one dentist.

Types of relationship

There are only three different 'degrees' of relationship between two attributes. A relationship may be

- **One-to-one** Examples of such a relationship include the relationship between Husband and Wife, or between Householder and Main Residence.
- **One-to-many** Examples include the relationship between Mother and Children, between Customer and Order, between Borrower and Library Book
- **Many-to-many** Examples include the relationship between Student and Course, between Stock Item and Supplier, between Film and Film Star.

Entity-relationship diagrams [ERD]

An entity-relationship diagram is a <u>diagrammatic way of representing the relationships between the entities in a database</u>. To show the relationship between two entities, both the **degree** and the **name** of the relationship need to be specified. E.g. In the first relationship shown below, the **degree** is *One-to-one*, the **name** of the relationship is *Drives*:

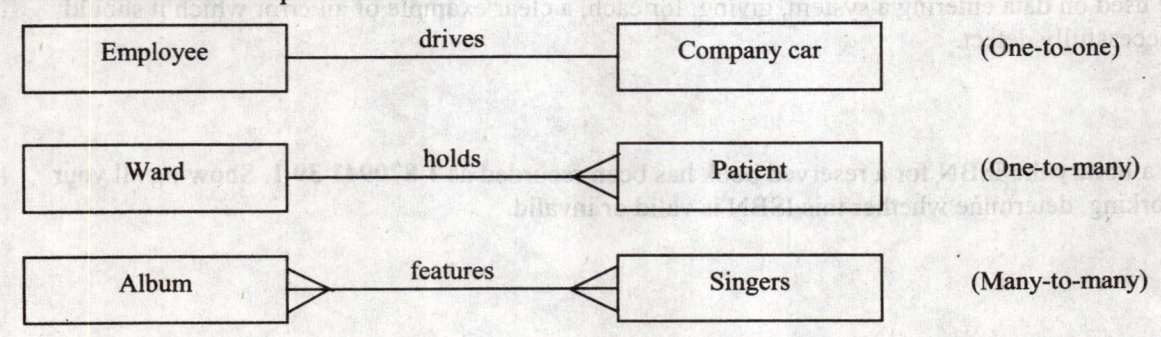

Employee	— drives —	Company car	(One-to-one)
Ward	— holds —<	Patient	(One-to-many)
Album	>— features —<	Singers	(Many-to-many)

Figure 31.1: Entity-relationships

Sometimes it can be tricky to establish the degree of the relationship. For example, several employees may use the same company car at different times. A single employee may change the company car that he uses. The relationship will depend upon whether the data held refers to the current situation, or whether it is a historical record. The assumption has been made above that the database is to record the current car driven by an employee.

Example:

The data requirements for a hospital in-patient system are defined as follows:

A hospital is organised into a number of wards. Each ward has a ward number and a name recorded, along with a number of beds in that ward. Each ward is staffed by nurses. Nurses have their staff number and name recorded, and are assigned to a single ward.

Each patient in the hospital has a patient identification number, and their name, address and date of birth are recorded. Each patient is under the care of a single consultant and is assigned to a single ward. Each consultant is responsible for a number of patients. Consultants have their staff number, name and specialism recorded.

State four entities for the hospital in-patient system and suggest an identifier for each of these entities.

Draw an entity-relationship diagram to show the relationship between the entities.

Answer:

Entity	Identifier
WARD	Ward number
NURSE	Staff number
PATIENT	Patient identification number
CONSULTANT	Staff number

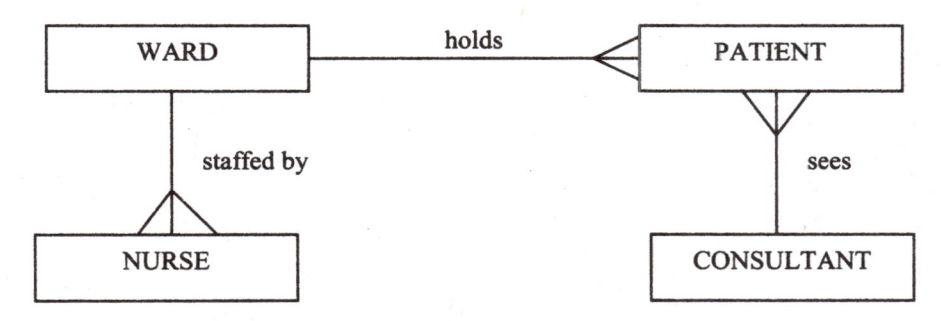

```
   ┌────────┐   holds   ┌─────────┐
   │  WARD  │───────────│ PATIENT │
   └────────┘           └─────────┘
       │                     │
  staffed by                sees
       │                     │
   ┌────────┐           ┌────────────┐
   │ NURSE  │           │ CONSULTANT │
   └────────┘           └────────────┘
```

Note that a one-to-many relationship does not necessarily imply that **every** ward, for example, has many patients, merely that is possible that at least one ward has more than one patient. It is possible that some wards have no patients at all.

> **Q1:** Draw entity-relationship diagrams to illustrate the relationships between
> (a) Product and Component
> (b) Home-owner and Main Residence
> (c) Pet-owner and Pet
> (d) Racehorse owner and Racehorse

Module 2 Principles of Hardware, Software and Applications

Once again there may be some argument about these relationships. Can a pet have more than one owner? For the purposes of a vet's database, probably not. A racehorse, on the other hand, is such a valuable animal that it is quite common for several people to have 'shares' in the horse.

When you are designing a database, it can often be quite hard to decide what is an entity and what is an attribute. Is **pet** an attribute of **owner**, or is **owner** an attribute of **pet**?? Or is neither the case, since both are entities in their own right? The latter statement is probably the correct interpretation of the real world situation.

> Q2: In a database system used by a car dealer, **Car** is one entity, and it has a primary key **RegistrationNumber**. Is **Manufacturer** an attribute of car, or is it an entity?

Exercises

1. A library plans to set up a database to keep track of its members, stock and loans.
   (a) State an identifier (primary key) for each of the entities MEMBER, STOCK and LOAN.
   (b) Draw an entity-relationship diagram showing the relationships between the entities.

2. In the context of a student records system, identify three typical entities and describe two different types of relationship that might exist between them.

Chapter 32 – Database Concepts

Traditional file approach

In the early days of computerised data processing, an organisation's data was duplicated in separate files for the use of individual departments. For example the Personnel Department would hold details on name, address, qualifications etc. of each employee, while the Payroll Department would hold details of name, address and salary of each employee. Each department had its own set of application programs to process the data in these files. This led to:

- **duplicated data**, meaning wasted space;
- **inconsistency problems**, where for example an address was updated on one file but not on another; e.g. Mr Johnstone moves house and passes his new address to Personnel who update their file. Unfortunately no one tells the Payroll Department and his next payslip is sent to the old address.
- **the data was not shareable**; if one department needed data that was held by another, it was awkward to obtain it.

The database approach

In an attempt to solve the above problems, the data from the various departments was centralised in a common pool so that **all applications had access to the same set of data**. For example all the details about stock held by a garden centre would be held in a database which was accessible by all applications using the data. The Sales department would update quantities in stock, the Marketing department would use the data to produce a catalogue, the Reorder system would use it to decide what stock to reorder.

Although this solved problems of duplication and inconsistency, it introduced two major new problems:

- **unproductive maintenance**; if one department needed some change to the number or length of fields in a record on one of the common files, every department had to change its application programs to take this change into account, even if the field was not one used by that department. In other words, the programs were still dependent on the record structure, and all departments were affected by even minor changes in another department.
- **Problems of security**; even confidential or commercially sensitive data was accessible by every application, because the data was centrally held.

A **database**, therefore, is defined as a collection of non-redundant data sharable between different application systems.

Validation of input data

Almost every field in a database can be put through some type of **validation** to ensure that data entry is accurate (see Chapter 30.) There are several types of validation check that may be specified, for example:

- Presence check – must data be entered in this field?
- Range check – is there a low/high limit? (e.g. the date must be greater than or equal to today's date in a theatre booking file, the price of a new car from a particular manufacturer must be between £6,000 and £30,000 in a car sales database.)
- Format check – must the data be in a particular format? (e.g. a National Insurance number must be 2 letters followed by 6 digits and a letter.)
- Is there a list of valid values? (e.g. Sex must be either M or F.)

Relational database design

In a relational database, data is held in tables (also called relations) and the tables are linked by means of common fields.

Conceptually then, one row of a table holds one record. Each column in the table holds one attribute.

e.g. A table holding data about an entity BOOK may have the following rows and columns:

BOOK

Accession Number	Dewey Code	Title	Author	Date published
88	121.9	Let's Cook!	Chan, C	1992
123	345.440	Electricity	Glendenning, V	1995
300	345.440	Riders	Cooper, J	1995
657	200.00	Greek in 3 weeks	Stavros, G	1990
777	001.602	I.T. in Society	Laudon, K	1994
etc				

Figure 32.1: A table in a relational database

There is a standard notation for describing a table in a relational database. For example, to describe the table shown above, you would write

BOOK (<u>Accession Number</u>, Dewey Code, Title, Author, Date Published)

Note that:

The entity name is shown in uppercase letters;

The primary key field (unique identifier) is underlined;

The attributes are shown in brackets, separated by commas.

Primary and secondary keys

Each entity in a database must have a unique key field known as the **primary key**. The key field in the above table is accession number. In a database holding data about students, the key field in a table about students could be a unique student number.

In order that a record with a particular key field can be quickly located in a database, an **index** of key fields will be automatically maintained by the database software, giving the position of each record according to its primary key.

If a database table often needs to be searched on a different field, for example, title or author, these can be defined as **secondary keys** so that the table will also be indexed on these fields.

Indexing

A database table can have indexes on as many fields as you choose. An index is, in effect, a list of numerical values which gives the order of the records when they are sorted on a particular field. An index on the Title field in the table shown in Figure 32.1, assuming it had only 5 records, would have entries 2, 4, 5, 1, 3. The DBMS constructs and maintains all the indexes automatically. There are advantages and disadvantages to having multiple indexes:

- in large tables they speed up queries considerably;
- when a report is required in the sequence of the indexed field, they avoid having to sort the database;
- on the negative side, they slow down data entry and editing, because the indexes have to be updated each time a record is added or deleted.

Linking database tables

Tables may be linked through the use of a common field. This field must be a key field of one of the tables, and is known as a **foreign key** in the second table. An example best illustrates this.

In a library database, two entities named BOOK and BORROWER have been identified. There is a one-to-many relationship between these two entities, because one borrower may borrow several books, but the same book cannot be taken out by many borrowers simultaneously.

The BORROWER table can be described using standard notation as follows:

BORROWER (<u>Borrower ID</u>, name, address)

In order to link the two entities, the key field Borrower ID needs to be added to the BOOK table as a *foreign key*. The BOOK table can be described as

BOOK (<u>Accession Number</u>, Dewey Code, Title, Author, Date Published, *Borrower ID*)

Note that a foreign key is shown in italics.

Querying a database

Information can be obtained from a database using **Query by Example** (**QBE**).
Using this method the user may

- combine into one table information from two or more related tables;
- select which fields are to be shown in the 'Answer' table;
- specify criteria to search on;
- save the query so that it can be executed whenever required;
- save the results of the query (the 'Answer' table).

The figure below shows a **query by example** window in the MS Access database.

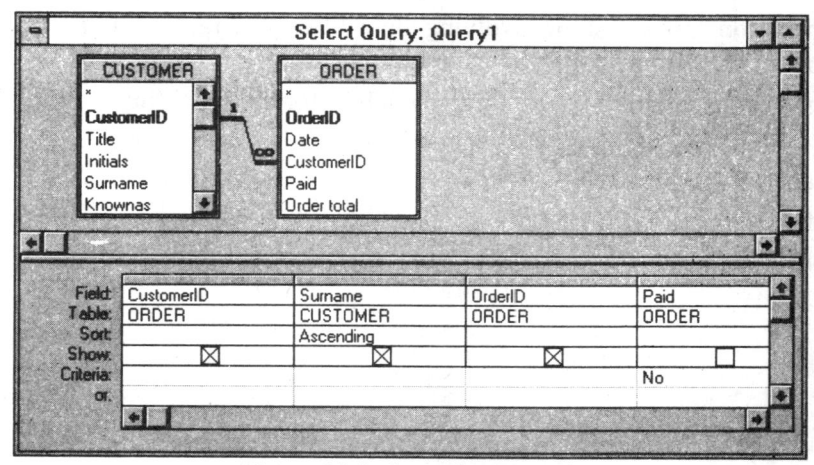

Figure 32.2: Query by Example

The query writes to an Answer table the Customer ID, Surname and Order ID of unpaid orders. (The Answer table is a new table created automatically when the query is run for the first time.)

Module 2 Principles of Hardware, Software and Applications

Exercises

1. Most database management packages allow conditions to be associated with the fields of a record. These conditions are specified during the design stage.

    An application using such a package has records containing the following fields:

    Part_number, description, number_in_stock, unit_cost, value_of_stock.

    Explaining your decision, choose from these fields:
    (a) one which must be unique;
    (b) one which must be calculated;
    (c) one which is always required (mandatory).

2. The data requirements for a booking system are defined as follows.

    An agency arranges bookings of live bands for a number of clubs. Each band is registered with the agency and has its name (unique) recorded, together with the number of musicians, the type of music played and hiring fee. Each band is managed by a manager. A manager may manage several bands. Each manager is assigned an identification number and managers have their name, address and telephone number recorded. Each club is assigned an identification number and clubs have their name, address and telephone number recorded.

    The agency records details of each booking made between a band and a club for a given date. A band will never have more than one booking on any particular date.

    (a) In database modelling, what is:
       (i) an attribute;
       (ii) a relationship?
    (b) Four entities for the booking system are Manager, Club, Band and Booking.
       (i) Suggest an identifier, with justification, for **each** of the entities Manager, Club and Band.
       (ii) Describe **four** relationships involving the entities Manager, Club, Band and Booking that can be inferred from the given data requirements.
    (c) A relational database is to be used. Describe tables for the following entities underlining the primary key in each case:
       (i) Manager;
       (ii) Band;
       (iii) Booking.

Chapter 33 – Operating Systems

What is an operating system?

Computers require two types of software: **applications software** such as word processing, spreadsheet or graphics packages, and **operating systems software** to control and monitor the running of application programs, and to allow users to communicate with the computer.

The operating system consists of a number of programs which are typically 'bundled' with the hardware; in other words, when you buy a new PC, for example, you will also be supplied with a CD containing the latest version of the Windows operating system. This then has to be installed by running a special installation program supplied on the CD, which will copy the operating system to your hard disk and customise it to your particular hardware configuration.

Each time you switch on your PC, the operating system kernel (the part you need in memory at all times) will be copied from the hard disk into memory, which takes a few minutes.

Functions of an operating system

Obviously the operating system (OS) for a standalone microcomputer system will be very much simpler than that of a supercomputer which is controlling hundreds of terminals and running many different kinds of job simultaneously. Nevertheless, all operating systems perform certain basic functions, including:

- **Memory management.** Most computers nowadays are capable of holding several programs in memory simultaneously so that a user can switch from one application to another. The operating system has to allocate memory to each application – as well as to itself!

- **Resource allocation and scheduling.** In larger computer systems which are capable of running several programs at once (**multiprogramming**), the OS is responsible for allocating processing time, memory and input-output resources to each one. While one program is executing, the operating system is scheduling the use of input and output devices for other jobs. Not all jobs are performed in the order they are submitted; the operating system schedules them in order to make the best possible use of the computer's resources.

- **Backing store management.** The OS controls the transfer of data from secondary storage (e.g. disk) to memory and back again. It also has to maintain a directory of the disk so that files and free space can be quickly located.

- **Interrupt handling.** The OS detects many different kinds of interrupt such as for example a user pressing the Enter key on the keyboard, a printer sending a message that it is out of paper, the real-time clock interrupting to indicate that the processor should be allocated to the next user in a multi-user system, a hardware or software malfunction.

- **Allowing a user to communicate with the computer.** The user gives instructions to the computer to start a program, copy a file, send a message to another user, and so on by typing in commands recognised by the operating system or by using a mouse to point and click in a graphical user interface such as Windows 98 or 2000.

Multi-programming

The most important operating system capability for sharing computer resources is **multi-programming**. This permits multiple programs to be active at the same time, with the operating system allowing each one a small 'time-slice' of processor time in turn. Using a technique known as **virtual memory**, the operating system divides each program into fixed-length portions called **pages**, storing only a few pages of the program in memory at any one time. All the other pages are stored on disk until they are needed, at which point the operating system brings in the new page, moving an unwanted page out to disk if necessary. This means that one or more large programs, which far exceed the computer's memory capacity, can execute concurrently.

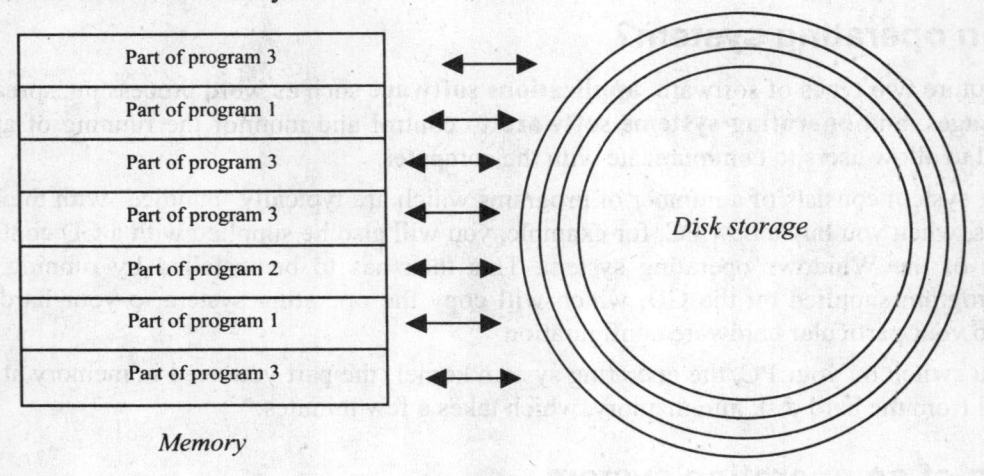

Figure 33.1: Virtual memory

Provision of a virtual machine

The operating system functions in such a way as to hide from the user all the complexities of the hardware. The average user is completely unaware of the operating system working away behind the scenes, and sees only a machine which (with luck) simply does what it is instructed no matter how complex the tasks involved. Switching from one window to another, from one printer to another, creating a new folder or making a backup is simply a matter of a few mouse clicks, as far as the user is concerned. This easy-to-use machine is sometimes referred to as the 'virtual machine'.

Operating systems can be classified into different types, some of which are described below.

Batch

The technique of multi-programming was developed when computers were operated in **batch-processing** mode. In batch-processing mode, **processing is carried out from beginning to end without user interaction**.

Jobs prepared in this way have all their processing requirements defined in advance. By using multi-programming, a batch of several jobs can be loaded so that when executed over the same time period the processor is kept as busy as possible by switching between the jobs as and when necessary. This increases **throughput**, i.e. the total number of jobs completed per unit time, and reduces the **turnaround time**, i.e. time between job submission and job completion. There is a significant delay of say, several hours between submitting a job and receiving the output.

Interactive

With this type of processing the user interacts directly with the system to supply commands and data as the application program undergoes execution and receives the results of processing immediately. An operating system which allows such interaction is said to support **interactive processing**. Such an operating system allows the user and the computer to be in **direct two-way communication**.

Chapter 33 – Operating Systems

Real-Time

Real time operating systems are characterised by four requirements:

- they have to support application programs which are non-sequential in nature, i.e. programs which do not have a START- PROCESS - END structure;
- they have to deal with a number of events which happen in parallel and at unpredictable moments in time (for example, a user clicking a mouse button);
- they have to carry out processing and produce a response within a specified interval of time;
- some systems are safety-critical, meaning they must be fail-safe and guarantee a response within a specified time interval.

Examples of real-time operating systems are:

- airline reservation system – up to a 1000 messages per second can arrive from any one of 11000-12000 terminals, situated all over the world. The response time must be less than 3 seconds.
- Process control system – up to 1000 signals per second can arrive from sensors attached to the system being controlled. The response time must be less than one thousandth of a second.

Network

A network operating system is required when a number of computers are connected together in a network. The operating system controls who logs on to the network by means of user names and passwords, in order to protect the data and programs stored on the network. It also makes the network transparent to the user, allowing any user with the appropriate access rights to use software stored on the network's file server, and to store data either on the file server or on a local hard or floppy disk.

File Management

An important part of a computer's operating system is the **file manager** or **file management system**. A file may be a document created in Word, Excel or other software, or it may be an **executable** file, i.e. a program which can be executed. When the user gives an instruction to save a file, giving it a name and specifying where it is to be saved, it is the job of the file manager to find a space on disk.

The file manager will typically hold the following information about each file or folder:

- file type – e.g., folder file, system file, hidden file, batch, executable, text;
- information indicating the location of the file on secondary storage – e.g., disk address of the first block in the file;
- file size in bytes;
- access rights – who can access the file and how it can be accessed: e.g., read only, read-write, write-only, delete permission;
- date information – e.g., data of creation, date of last access, date of last amendment, purge date;

Using the access rights the file manager is able to control who can share a particular file, and protect that file against unauthorised alteration.

Drives, folders and files

A drive is the hardware that seeks, reads and writes information from and to a disk. A hard disk and its drive are one inseparable unit, unlike a floppy disk which can be separated from its drive. Drives are given letter names like A, B, C etc. Frequently a large hard disk is 'partitioned' by the user or computer technician when the drive is initially formatted so that although there is only one physical drive, there are

Module 2 Principles of Hardware, Software and Applications

several 'logical drives' called, for example, F, G, X, Y, Z. This is done for convenience so that different types of work can be held on separate logical drives.

A hard disk is divided into a number of **folders** (called directories in early versions of Windows). Folders can be added and deleted by the user whenever necessary, and they are used to help keep all the thousands of files held on a disk organised so that they can be quickly located when needed. Folders can contain both files and subfolders.

Folder and file names in Windows 2000 can be up to 255 characters in length. In addition, they usually have an extension which is added automatically by the particular software package in which they were created, and which identifies them as being, for example, a Word document, an Excel spreadsheet or a Pascal program.

e.g. **BensProject.doc** (The extension .doc identifies this as a Word document.)

ProgSquares.exe (The extension .exe identifies this as an executable file.)

Pathnames

Folders (or so-called directories) are organised in a tree structure, with the folder at the top (bottom?) of the tree being known as the **root**. To refer to a particular file in a particular folder, you have to give it its full pathname, which shows exactly which folder it is in.

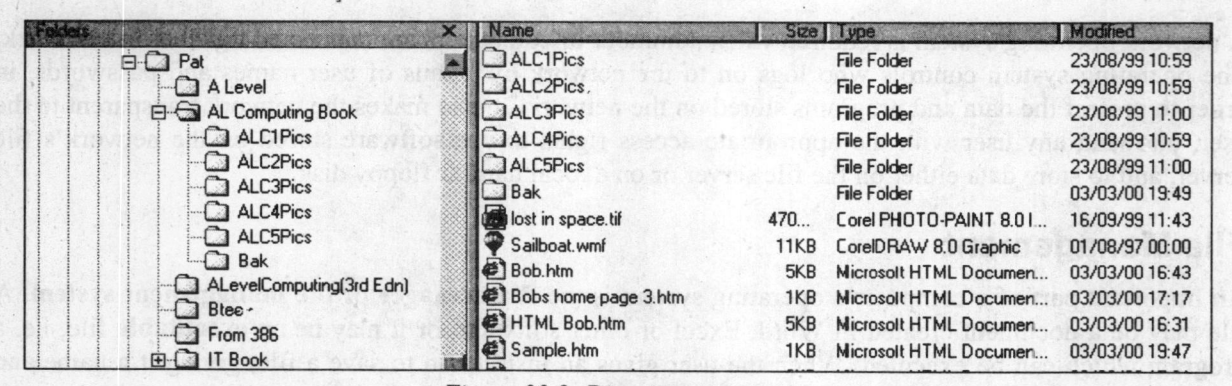

Figure 33.2: Directory structure

In the screenshot above taken from a Windows Explorer screen, the folder **Pat** is a subfolder of the **My Documents** folder (not shown) on the C drive. Within **Pat** there are subfolders named **A Level**, **AL Computing Book**, etc. The folder **AL Computing Book** has subfolders **ALC1Pics**, **ALC2Pics** etc and it also contains several files which you can see on the right hand side of the screenshot – **lost in space.tif**, **sailboat.wmf** etc.

The full name of the file **Bob.htm** is

C:\My Documents\Pat\A Level\AL Computing book\bob.htm

Access rights and other attributes

The file manager enables access rights to be set for particular files or folders. Depending on a user's ID and password, they may for example be given any of the following access rights to a file or folder:

Read	Allows the user to view the contents of a data file
Read & Execute	Allows the user to run a program file
Write	Allows the user to change the contents of a file
Modify	Allows a user to read, change or delete the file
Full control	Allows full control of the file

Backing up and archiving

The operating system Windows 2000 comes supplied with a program called **Backup** which can be used to back up files from the hard disk onto another hard disk on a network, tape or floppy disk. Individual files, folders or entire drives can be selected for backup. The program supports five common backup types: *normal*, *incremental*, *differential*, *copy* and *daily*.

- A *normal* backup copies all selected files to the backup medium, and clears the **archive** attribute for each file to mark it as backed up.

- An *incremental* backup copies only selected files that have changed since the most recent backup, and clears the archive attribute for each file.

- A *differential* backup copies only selected files that have changed since the most recent backup, but does not clear the archive attribute. Successive differential backups therefore copy all the files that have changed since the last normal or incremental backup.

- A *copy* backup copies all selected files, but does not clear the archive attribute. This means that a copy of a file can be made without affecting the normal backup routine.

- A *daily* backup copies all selected files that changed on the day the backup is made, and does not clear the archive attribute.

The main point to understand is that the Archive attribute is used by the operating system to decide which files to back up when the user selects a particular type of backup.

Choosing **File, Properties** in the Windows Explorer window causes the following dialogue box to be displayed, so that you can see the Archive attribute:

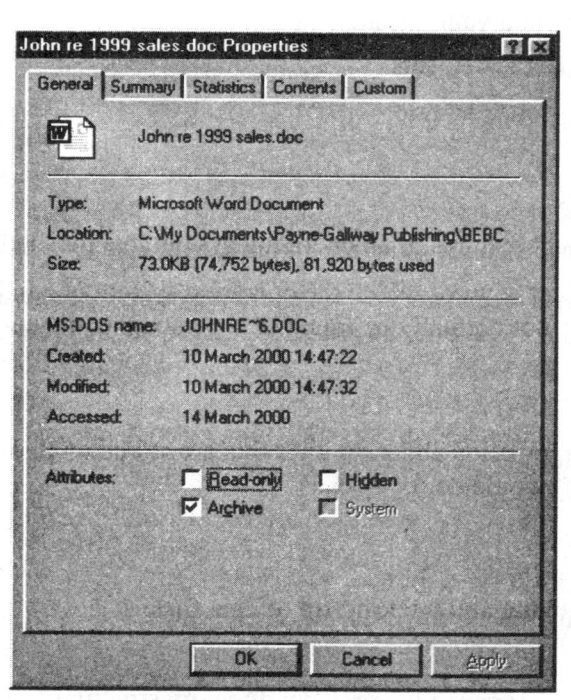

Figure 33.3: Examining the properties of a file

A common strategy for backups is to combine normal and differential backups as follows:
- at some regular interval, such as once a week, a normal backup is performed;
- at the end of each day, a differential backup is performed.

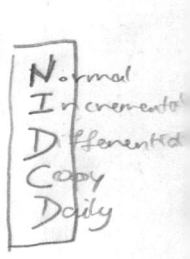

Module 2 Principles of Hardware, Software and Applications

The word *archive* is used here in a somewhat different sense from the normal meaning of the word. Archiving normally means making a backup of data, say on a writeable CD, which will not be changed again. For example, old invoices or purchase orders might be archived in order to make a permanent record of such documents. Backups, on the other hand are performed to make sure that data can be restored if a disaster occurs.

Exercises

1. (a) Explain the term *on-line processing*.

   (b) The phrase *real-time processing* can apply to two quite different computing environments.

   An example of the first environment is a *real-time airline booking system*.

   An example of the second environment is a *real-time control system* used to fly the aircraft.

   Explain the term *real-time processing*, making clear the difference between these two environments.

2. Describe three housekeeping utilities normally provided with the operating system for a single-user personal computer. Your description should include a typical task for which each utility is used.

3. For each of the following activities choose which of *Batch* or *Real Time* operating systems would be most suitable. Carefully explain your decision.

   (a) Producing monthly bank statements

   (b) Controlling a nuclear power station.

4. (i) Describe **two** important features of an operating system in a personal computer.

   (ii) Describe two additional features which the operating system of a mainframe computer might include, which would not normally be found on a personal computer.

5. Disk directories record information about the files that are stored on disk. State **three** items of information that, typically, would be recorded.

6. Distinguish between **archiving** and **backing-up** of data files.

7. Describe, with the aid of a diagram, a hierarchical directory structure.

Chapter 34 – Input Devices

Keyboard data entry

The keyboard is the most common input device, suitable for a wide range of applications from entering programs to typing all kinds of documents using a word processor, or entering personal details of customers or patients at a hospital, etc. Data entered at a keyboard is commonly copied from a source document, and as such has disadvantages:

- It is easy to make **transcription** errors – that is, copy the data wrongly from the document.
- It is time-consuming.
- Data entry operators who enter data all day every day are prone to **repetitive strain injury** (RSI), a condition which renders them unable to do any further data entry or even perform everyday tasks such as pouring a cup of tea.

Voice data entry

The user speaks the text into a microphone and special software such as IBM's VoicePad or Dragon's Naturally Speaking interprets the text and displays it on a screen, where it may be edited using the keyboard and exported to a word processing package such as Word. The accuracy of the voice recognition system is improved by 'training' it to a particular user's voice – an embarrassing process of speaking a given set of a few hundred short sentences to your computer, repeating any that are not accurately interpreted.

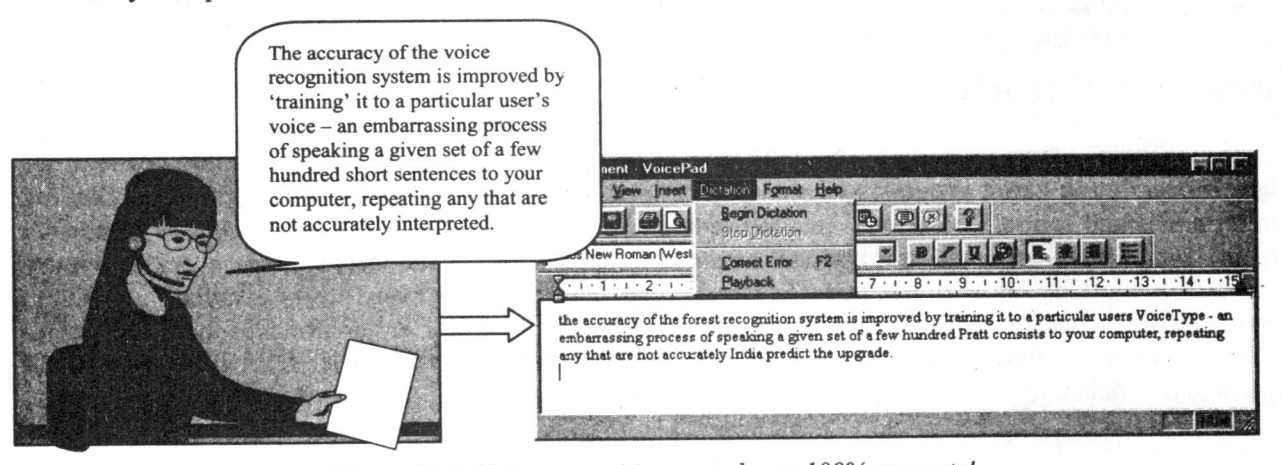

Figure 34.1: Voice recognition: not always 100% accurate!

Scanners and OCR

An optical scanner can be used to scan graphical images and photographs, and software can then be used to edit or touch up the images. Scanners can also be used to read typed or even hand-written documents and OCR (Optical Character Recognition) software can then be used to interpret the text and export it to a word processor or data file. Scanners are also used to input large volumes of data on preprinted forms such as credit card payments, where the customers account number and amount paid are printed at the bottom of the payment slip.

Module 2 Principles of Hardware, Software and Applications

> ### Case study: Automating college enrolment
>
> Enrolling thousands of college students on hundreds of different courses is a year-long administrative headache for colleges. Unravelling the mysteries of what students and staff have written on the enrolment forms and then entering all this information onto computer, checking it and resolving it can take weeks. One college has slashed this time and eliminated many of the errors by investing in a scanning solution from Formic.
>
> Formic has a proven track record in scanning survey questionnaires using graphical imaging and intelligent character recognition technologies which produce clean, validated data with minimal human intervention. Its new ACE product (Automated College Enrolment) links a scanner with a digital camera and identity card printer to offer immediate and complete enrolment in the presence of the student.
>
> Students select their courses with the help of teaching staff, who then attach official peel-off stickers to the form. Stickers are preprinted with course names and barcodes for reliable scanning. This simple procedure has eliminated much administrative frustration of trying to identify which course a student really meant to enrol for, and made it impossible for students to enrol on courses that do not exist.
>
> Students present themselves at the enrolment desk for their form to be scanned by computer. Handwriting is converted to letters and numbers, answers are checked and validated against a postcode database. This way, all omissions and inconsistencies are picked up and resolved while the student is still there. Finally, a plastic identity card is produced bearing the student's name, enrolment number and smiling face in full colour etched securely into its tough surface. The same digital picture is stored for use later. The whole process typically takes two to three minutes from start to finish.
>
> *Source: Tim Macer, Formic magazine*
>
> ➢ Q1: What are the benefits of the scanning system? What output could be obtained from the information gathered at enrolment time? What other use could be made of the digital photographs?

Key-to-disk systems

In organisations where large amounts of data are collected on forms which then have to be keyed in for later processing (a **batch processing** system) an entire computer system consisting of a processor, dozens of terminals and central disk storage may be dedicated entirely to data entry. One terminal is nominated as the supervisor's terminal, from whose screen the supervisor can see exactly what every data entry operator is working on and how many keystrokes per hour and how many errors everyone is making. Completed batches of data are stored on disk from where they are either downloaded to the main computer over a communications link, or transferred to magnetic tape which is physically removed and taken to the main computer room.

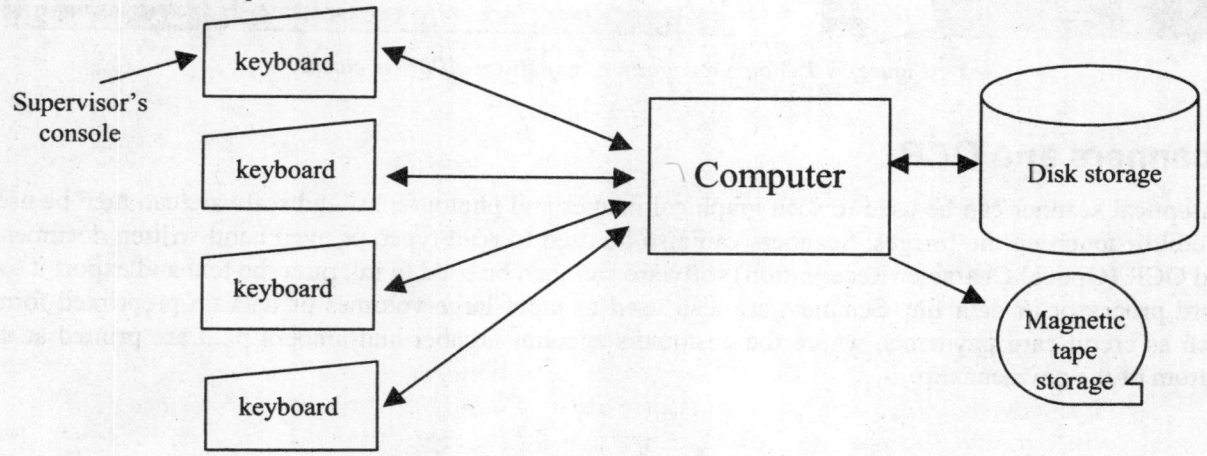

Figure 34.2: A key-to-disk system

Using a key-to-disk system, each data entry operator calls up the data entry program for their particular batch of data (e.g. payroll data entry, Council Tax payments, student grant applications) and keys in the data, which is automatically validated by the computer program.

When the batch of data has been entered and stored on disk, the source documents are passed to a second data entry operator who switches their machine to **verify** mode and keys in the data a second time. The keystrokes are compared with the data already stored on disk and any discrepancy causes the machine to beep so that the error can be corrected.

Mouse, joystick, light pen, touch screen

The mouse and its variants such as a trackball is well known to all users of PCs. A light pen is a device which incorporates a light sensor so that when it is held close to the screen over a character or part of a graphic, the object is detected and can be moved to create or modify graphics.

A touch screen allows the user to touch an area of the screen rather than having to type the data on a keyboard. They are widely used in tourist centres, where tourists can look up various local facilities and entertainments, in fast food stores such as McDonald's for entering customer orders, in manufacturing and many other environments.

Magnetic Ink Character Recognition (MICR)

All banks use MICR for processing cheques. Along the bottom of a cheque the bank's sort code, customer account number and cheque number are encoded in special characters in magnetic ink. The amount of the cheque is encoded in magnetic ink when it is handed in at a bank. The cheques can then be processed extremely fast by high-speed MICR devices that read, sort and store the data on disk. MICR has several advantages for processing cheques:

- it is hard to forge the characters;
- the characters can be read even if the cheque is crumpled, dirty or smudged;
- the characters are readable by humans, unlike bar codes.

Magnetic stripe

Cards with magnetic stripes are used as credit cards, debit cards, railway tickets, phone cards and many other applications. The magnetic strip can be encoded with up to 220 characters of data, and there are over 2.4 billion plastic card transactions every year in Britain, with 83% of adults owning at least one card. Nevertheless, three factors threaten to destroy the lucrative business that high street banks have made out of plastic: crime, the cost of cash and competition. In 1996 card fraud cost the banks £97.1 million, with £13.3 million of it from fake magnetic stripe cards. The 220 characters are simply too easy to copy, which is why the stripes will eventually disappear and be replaced by a chip, which is almost impossible to fake.

Smart cards

Smart cards look similar to plastic cards with a magnetic stripe, but instead of (or as well as) the magnetic stripe, they contain a 1-millimetre square microprocessor embedded in the middle, behind a small gold electrical contact. Instead of swiping the card, you plug it into a reader.

Chip cards cost only about £1 to produce, and can hold millions of characters of data. Banks plan to introduce a 'supercard' which in addition to debit and credit facilities, can be loaded with digital cash so that smaller items such as bread, milk and newspapers can be bought without the need to carry cash. BT will adapt local payphones in a trial area to load the cards, and NCP car parks will accept the cards. When your card runs out of digital cash, you reload it from a cashpoint machine.

Module 2 Principles of Hardware, Software and Applications

The Mondex card was introduced in Swindon in 1994 for a trial period, and incorporates the 'electronic purse' idea but no debit or credit facilities. However even this card has proved not to be entirely tamper-proof, which leaves open the possibility that dishonest users could simply load their cards with as much money as they like.

Figure 34.3: The Mondex Smart card

> **Q2:** It has been suggested that other information such as kidney donor record and driving license could be held on the same chip card that allows you to withdraw cash and pay for goods.
> What would be the benefits of doing this?
> What other information would it be useful to hold on a card of this sort?

Optical Mark Recognition (OMR)

An optical mark reader can detect marks made in preset positions on a form. It is widely used for marking multiple-choice exams and market research questionnaires.

Bar code reader or scanner

Bar codes appear on almost everything we buy. The pattern of thick and thin represents the 13-digit number underneath the bar code. There are four main pieces of information on a bar code.

The first two (or sometimes three) digits indicate in which country the product has been registered. The code for the UK and Ireland is 50.

The next five digits represent the manufacturer's code – Cadbury's, for example, is 00183.

The second group of five numbers represents the product and package size, but not the price.

The last digit is a check digit, which is calculated from the other digits in the code and ensures that the barcode is keyed in or read correctly.

Figure 34.4: A product bar code

> **Q3:** A supermarket has a file of all stock items, which is on-line to the point-of-sale terminals at each check-out. What data is held on the stock file? What processing takes place when an item is scanned by the barcode reader? What is the output from the process?

Hand-held input devices

Portable keying devices are commonly used in such applications as reading gas or electricity meters, where the meter reader displays the next customer name, address and location of meter on a small screen, then reads the meter and keys in the reading. At the end of the day all the readings can be downloaded via a communications link to the main computer for processing.

Digitiser (Graphics tablet)

Professional quality illustrations can be drawn on a digitiser, which is a flat rectangular slab of material onto which a stylus is placed. The position of the stylus can be detected by the computer. As well as, or instead of a stylus, a 'puck' may be used to click on a special template which covers part of the tablet.

Graphics tablets come in a wide range of resolutions and types, from those used by primary school children to create drawings, to those used by engineers and architects in conjunction with computer-aided design (CAD) software. The graphics tablet shown in Figure 34.5 is a high-resolution tablet that translates x-y dimensional data into readable format and transfers it to a computer.

Photograph courtesy of Kye Systems UK Ltd

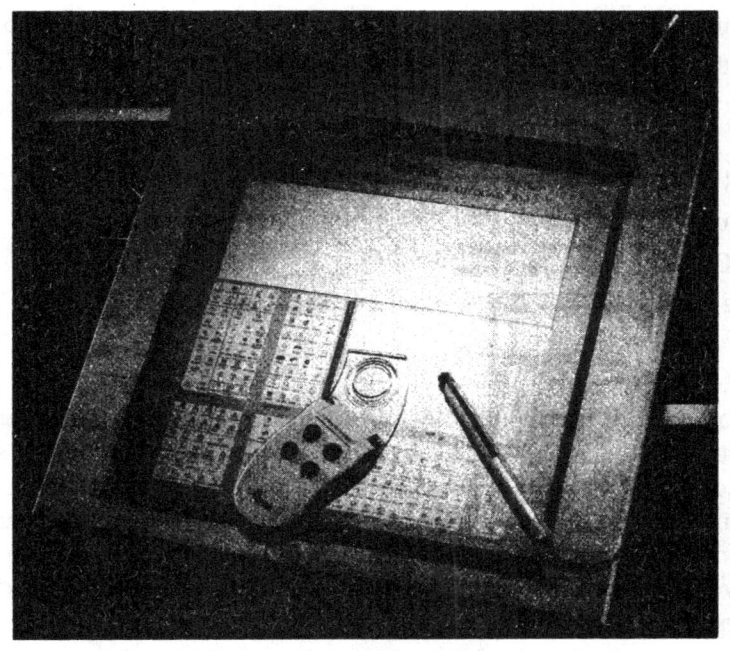

Figure 34.5: A graphics tablet with puck and stylus

Module 2 Principles of Hardware, Software and Applications

Exercises

1. "In the future computer keyboards will be obsolete as every computer will be capable of direct speech input".

   State whether or not you agree with this claim and give **two** distinct reasons to support your answer.

2. Most banks now dispense cash via Automated Teller Machines (ATMs). After inserting a plastic card which is read by the ATM, the customer types requests and responses on a special keypad.
   (a) Describe fully the procedure that the customer follows when making a cash withdrawal.
   (b) The information on the card is encoded onto a magnetic strip. Name three customer attributes that are stored on the strip.

3. (a) Give one application for which an Optical Mark Reader (OMR) is a suitable input device.
   (b) Explain why the OMR is a suitable input device for this application.

4. (a) Why is MICR used in preference to OCR in cheque processing systems?
   (b) Why is OCR used in preference to MICR in invoicing systems?
   (c) (i) What is Optical Mark Reading (OMR)?
       (ii) Give **one** situation where OMR might be used.

5. A particular company operates a manual clocking on and off system in which each employee has a time card. At the start and end of a shift, each employee takes their card out of an envelope beside the time clock, places it in a slot where the current time and date are stamped in ink on the card and replaces the card in the envelope. Each Friday evening the cards for the week are collected and replaced by new ones for the next week. The details from each card are used to work out how many hours each employee has worked so that each employee's pay can be calculated. Workers are paid one week in arrears.

   A computerised system is being proposed in which the time clock will be replaced by an on-line device through which each employee will pass a swipe card instead of clocking in or out. In addition, employees will be able to use the swipe cards to purchase refreshments at a number of on-line automatic dispensers. The cost of these refreshments will be deducted from each employee's pay.

   (a) The current manual system gives rise to a number of problems. Describe three different problems which may arise and suggest one way in which each problem could be eliminated while still using the current time clock and cards.
   (b) List the details which will be recorded on the swipe card and suggest two other uses to which the swipe card might be put.
   (c) Describe two significant problems the proposed system may give rise to and suggest a way in which each of these problems might be resolved.
   (d) Outline three advantages the proposed system will bring to the company's payroll system.

Chapter 35 – Output Devices

Printers

Printers come in all shapes and sizes, and the type of printer chosen will depend on several factors such as:

- **volume of output** – for high volumes, a fast, heavy-duty printer is required;
- **quality of print required** – business letters and reports to clients, for example, will require a high quality print, probably on special headed stationery;
- **location of the printer** – if the printer is going to be situated in a busy office, the noise that it makes is an important consideration;
- **requirement for multiple copies** – some printers cannot produce multiple copies;
- **requirements for colour** – does the output need to be in colour?

Dot matrix printer

A dot matrix printer is an **impact printer**, producing its image by striking the paper through a ribbon. Its print head consists of a number of small pins, varying between 9 and 24 depending on the manufacturer. A 24 pin print head will produce a better quality of print than a 9 pin print head because the dots are closer together.

As the print head moves across the page, one or more pins strike the ribbon and make a dot on the paper. The figure below shows how the letter F is produced.

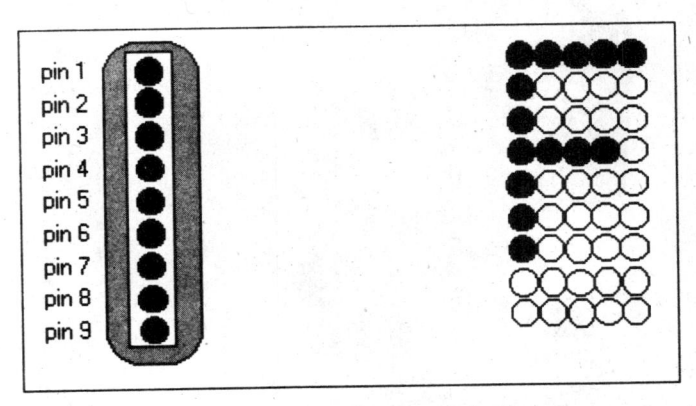

Figure 35.1: Dot matrix print head

In order to produce 'near letter quality' (**NLQ**) print, a line is printed twice, with the print head being shifted along very slightly in the second printing so that the spaces between the dots are filled in. The disadvantage of this technique is that the document then takes approximately twice as long to print. Many dot matrix printers are 'bidirectional', meaning that they can print in either direction, thus eliminating the need to start printing each line from the left hand side of the page.

Dot matrix printers are extremely versatile, with most of them able to print in condensed, standard and enlarged mode, in 'bold' or normal print. They are useful in situations where several copies of a document need to be routinely produced on 2-, 3- or 4-part stationery.

Module 2 *Principles of Hardware, Software and Applications*

Many dot matrix printers have a graphics mode that enables them to print pictures and graphs by activating individual print head pins separately or in combination to produce any shape or line. With appropriate software any typeface can be produced, and using a special 4-colour ribbon (red, yellow, blue and black), colour output for, say, a graphical presentation can be produced. However the quality of colour is not as good as that produced by other types of colour printer.

One of the main drawbacks of a dot matrix printer is its noise; in an office environment it can be an irritating distraction. Covers can be obtained to cut down the noise, but it is still audible.

Ink jet printers

Ink jet printers are a popular type of non-impact printer, with prices ranging between £150 and £1500; a popular colour inkjet printer such as Hewlett Packard's DeskJet 690C costs around £150. They are compact and quiet, and offer resolution almost as good as a laser printer. However, they are slow in operation; on average 3 pages per minute are printed, but a complex combination of text and colour can take several minutes for a single sheet.

Inkjet printers such as the HP Deskjet fire a droplet of ink at the page by boiling it in a microscopic tube and letting steam eject the droplet. Heating the ink can damage the colour pigments and matching the ink chemistry to the broad range of papers used in the office is a technical challenge. Large areas of colour can get wet, buckle, and the ink may smear. Printing an ink jet colour page can cost as much as 75p if all colour inks are supplied in a single cartridge; more thrifty printers will use separate red, blue, yellow and black cartridges which can be individually replaced. Although ordinary photocopy paper can be used, special smooth-coated paper may produce a more satisfactory result.

Figure 35.2: A Canon Bubble Jet Printer BJC7000

Laser printers

Laser printers are becoming increasingly popular, with prices dropping rapidly to under £500 for a PostScript printer suitable for desktop publishing applications. Laser printers use a process similar to a photocopying machine, with toner (powdered ink) being transferred to the page and then fused onto it by heat and pressure. A laser printer produces output of very high quality at a typical speed in the region of ten pages per minute, and is virtually silent in operation. The main running expenses are the toner, which costs about £75 for a cartridge lasting for around 5,000 copies, and a maintenance contract which is typically up to £300 per annum.

A high quality colour laser printer may cost between £4,000 and £5,000.

Plotters

A plotter is an output device used to produce high quality line drawings such as building plans or electronic circuits. They are generally classified as pen (vector plotters) or penless (raster plotters). The former use pens to draw images using point-to-point data, moving the pen over the paper. Pen plotters are low in price and hold a large share of the plotter market.

Penless plotters include electrostatic plotters, thermal plotters and laser plotters. They are generally used where drawings of high densities are required, for example drawings of machines, printed circuit boards or maps. Colour electrostatic plotters are increasingly being used in, for example, assembly drawings of machines and building plans, making them easier to read and understand.

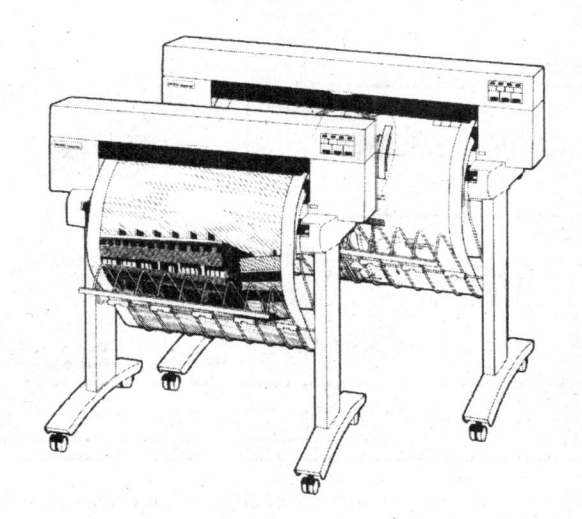

Photograph courtesy of Hewlett Packard Company

Figure 35.3: Hewlett-Packard plotters

Visual display unit (VDU)

A VDU has three basic attributes: size, colour and resolution. It has its own fixed amount of RAM associated with it to store the image being displayed on the screen, and the amount of RAM it has will determine the resolution and the maximum number of colours that can be displayed. Note that:

- the resolution is determined by the number of pixels (addressable picture elements) used to represent a full-screen image;
- the number of colours that can be displayed is determined by how many bits are used to represent each pixel. If only one bit is used to represent each pixel, then only two colours can be represented. To display 256 colours, 8 bits per pixel are required, and to display 65,536 (i.e. 2^{16}) colours, 16 bits (2 bytes) per pixel are needed. It is usually possible to adjust both the resolution and the number of colours - *if a high resolution is selected you won't be able to have as many colours because of the memory limitations of the VDU.*

For example, if a resolution of 800x600 pixels is selected together with 65,536 colours, the amount of video RAM required will be 800x600x2 bytes = 960,000 bytes, i.e. almost 1Mb. If 1Mb is all the video RAM supplied by the manufacturer, the resolution cannot be increased to say, 1000x800 unless the number of bytes used to represent each pixel is reduced, thus limiting the number of colours which can be displayed.

Module 2 Principles of Hardware, Software and Applications

On a PC, the number of colours and the resolution of the screen can be adjusted on the Display option of the Control Panel.

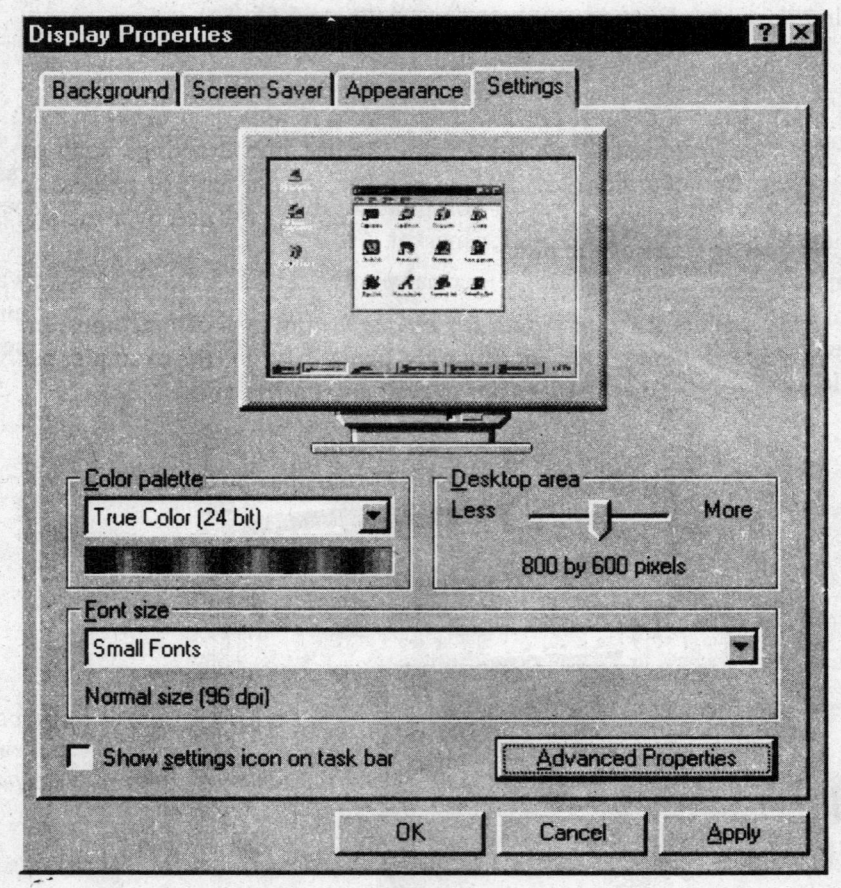

Figure 35.4: Adjusting the number of colours and resolution of a PC

Exercises

1. A printer fails to work or perform as the user expects when a document has been sent to be printed. The user has checked that the on-line light of the printer is illuminated and the printer paper is correctly inserted. Give two other possible reasons why the printing process failed.

2. Explain the relationship between the resolution of a screen and the number of colours that it can display.

3. State one advantage and one disadvantage of an ink jet printer compared with a laser printer.

Chapter 36 – Storage Devices

Primary and secondary storage

A computer's main memory (RAM) is known as **primary storage**. In order to execute a program, the program instructions and the data on which it is to operate have to be loaded into main memory. Primary storage, however, is **volatile**; when the computer is switched off, all the contents of memory are lost. This is one good reason to perform frequent saves to disk when working on, for example, a word processed document.

A more permanent, **non-volatile** form of storage is required by all computer systems to save software and data files. Magnetic tape, magnetic disks, CD-ROM (Compact Disk Read Only Memory), and microfilm are all examples of what is known as **secondary storage**.

File processing concepts

Data stored on secondary storage is typically stored in **files**, with a file of data being defined as a collection of records. A payroll file, for example, will contain a record for each employee, and a stock file will contain a record for each stock item. The manner in which these files are **processed** depends on whether every record in the file is to be processed one after the other, or whether individual records will be processed in no particular sequence. These two methods of processing are known as sequential and random processing. (See Chapter 28 for further details.)

Sequential processing. Each record in the file is read. If only the 200th record on the file needs altering, the first 199 records must be read anyway, and left as they are. Sequential processing is very fast and efficient for an application such as payroll where every record needs to be processed because every person in the company will be paid.

Random processing. Each record on the file has its own address, which can either be calculated from its unique key, or held in a separate index, so the record can be directly accessed. This type of processing is essential if, for example, you want to look up the price of an item of stock on a file of 20,000 items.

These two types of processing are similar to the different ways in which you would access a particular song on a cassette tape and on a CD. On a tape, you have to wind forward until you find the song you want, whereas on a CD, you just select the track and press the correct button. Note, however, that whereas you can 'process' a CD sequentially (listen to all the tracks from beginning to end) you cannot go directly to a particular song on a tape.

Similarly, some files need to be processed sequentially on some occasions, and randomly on others.

> **Q1:** Many files need to be processed sequentially on some occasions and randomly on others. When would the following files need to be processed (a) sequentially? (b) randomly?
> (i) Payroll file (ii) Electricity billing file (iii) Library book file

Module 2 Principles of Hardware, Software and Applications

Floppy disks

The standard 3½" floppy disk is a thin, flexible plastic disk coated in metal oxide, enclosed in a rigid plastic casing. A standard high density disk has a storage capacity of 1.44 Megabytes.

How data is stored

A diskette consists of two surfaces, each of which contains typically 80 concentric circles called tracks. Each track is divided into sectors. Microcomputer disks are soft-sectored: the sectors are not present when you buy a new floppy disk, but are defined when you first format the disk. If you reformat a disk that already has data on it, all the data will be erased (although you can also do a 'quick format' which erases only the file directory).

The tracks near the centre store the same amount of data as the outer tracks – the data is recorded more densely near the centre.

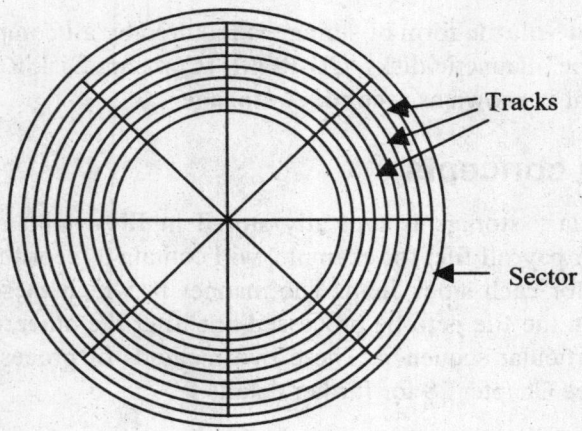

Figure 36.1: Tracks and sectors on a magnetic disk

Hard disks for microcomputers

The hard disk used with PCs consist of one or more disk platters permanently sealed inside a casing. Hard disks typically have a capacity of between 2Gb and 10Gb. (1Gb = 1,000Mb.)

Each surface has its own read-write head. The heads are mounted on a single spindle so they all move in and out together.

Figure 36.2: A microcomputer hard disk drive

External hard drives which can be plugged into a microcomputer are available as extra storage.

Hard disks for minis and mainframes

For large-scale applications storing huge amounts of data, several hard disk units will be required. The disks may be either fixed (sealed inside the unit) or removable. Fixed disks are faster, more reliable, and have a greater storage capacity.

As with other types of disk, data is stored on concentric tracks, with tracks being divided into sectors. All the tracks that are accessible from one position of the read-write heads form a **cylinder**; data is recorded cylinder by cylinder to minimise movement of the read-write heads, thereby minimising access time.

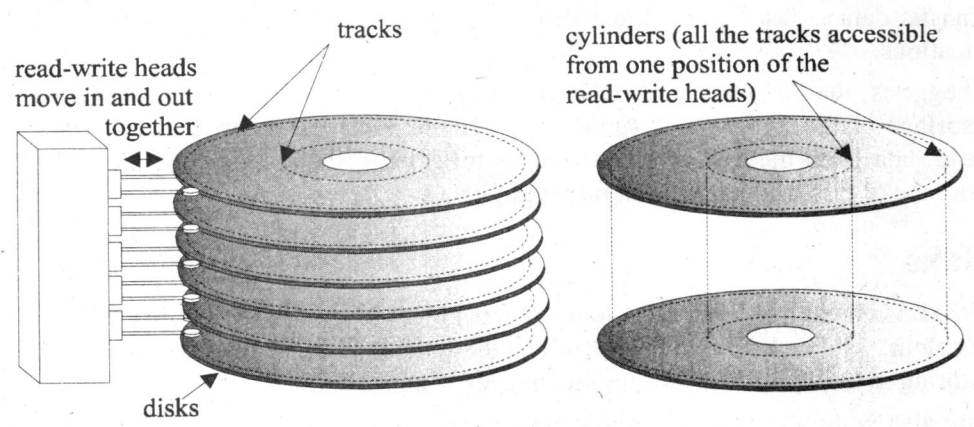

Figure 36.3: A disk drive

Magnetic tape

Data is recorded in 'frames' across the tape, with one frame representing one byte. The frames form tracks along the length of the tape, with 9 tracks being common, giving 8 data tracks and one parity track.

```
                              1 0 1        Track 1
                              1 1 1
                              0 1 1
                              0 0 0
                              1 1 0
                              1 1 0
                              0 0 1
                              0 0 1
                              0 0 1        Parity track
```

Figure 36.4: Tracks on a magnetic tape

Magnetic tape is a serial medium, meaning that an individual record can only be accessed by starting at the beginning of the tape and reading through every record until the required one is found. Likewise, it is impossible to read a record, amend it in memory, then backspace to the beginning of the block and overwrite the old record. Therefore, updating a magnetic tape file always involves copying the file to a new tape with the amendments made.

Uses of magnetic tape

Tape is a cheap and convenient medium for backup, and is also used for **archiving** past transactions or other data that may be needed again, such as for example, weather records collected over a number of years.

Cartridge tape drives are in common use for backing up the hard disk of personal computers, being much more convenient than using dozens of floppy disks. A single 36-track, 12" tape cartridge can store several gigabytes.

> **Q2: Discuss the relative advantages of hard disks, floppy disks and magnetic tape.**

Module 2 Principles of Hardware, Software and Applications

CD-ROM

CD-ROMs can store around 680Mb of data, equivalent to hundreds of floppy disks. The data may be in text form, or may be in the form of graphics, photographic images, video clips or sound files. Although they do not transfer data as fast as a hard disk drive, their speed is increasing every year and is acceptable for most applications.

As the name suggests, the disks are read-only. When the master disk is created, a laser beam burns tiny holes in the surface of the disk, which (unlike a magnetic disk) has a single spiral track divided into sectors. To read data from the disk, a laser beam is reflected off the surface of the disk, detecting the presence or absence of pits which represent binary digits.

WORM disks

Write Once, Read Many optical laser disks look similar to CD-ROM disks, but they are often gold rather than silver in colour. An end-user company can use these disks to write their own material, typically for archiving or storing say, graphic or photographic images which will not be changed.

These disks are also widely used for pirated software; whereas silver CDs are pressed in factories, gold CDs are usually written one at a time on PCs in garages and back bedrooms. A £5 blank disk can hold £20,000 worth of software and sell for £50 to £80, and they are sometimes used by less reputable PC manufacturers who install the software on their PCs to make a more attractive deal for the unknowing customer. However, because there is a lot of competition among pirates, these CDs sometimes carry viruses which can cause havoc on a hard drive.

Magneto-optical disks

Magneto-optical disks integrate optical and laser technology to enable read and write storage. A 5½" disk can store up to 1 Gb. These disks may in the future replace current magnetic disks, but at present the technology is still developing and the disks are too expensive, slow and unreliable to be in widespread use.

> ➤ **Q3:** What are some of the applications of CD-ROM? Why is CD-ROM particularly suitable for these applications?

Exercises

1. Why do many software manufacturers now prefer to sell their software on CD-ROM rather than on floppy disk?

2. Give one appropriate use with clear justification for:
   (a) floppy disks;
   (b) hard disks;
   (c) CD-ROMs

3. WORM (Write Once Read Many times) is an acronym sometimes used for certain types of data storage.

   Give **one** example of this type of storage and describe a typical use for your example.

   Give one feature of WORM type of storage which makes it appropriate for the example you have given.

Module 3

System Development

In this section:

Chapter 37 -   *The Classical Systems Life-Cycle*
Chapter 38 -   *From Design to Evaluation*
Chapter 39 -   *Human-Computer Interface*

Chapter 37 – The Classical Systems Life-Cycle

Overview of the systems life cycle

Large systems development projects may involve dozens of people working over several months or even years, so they cannot be allowed to proceed in a haphazard fashion. The goals of an information system must be thoroughly understood, and formal procedures and methods applied to ensure that the project is delivered on time and to the required specification.

The systems life cycle methodology approaches the development of information systems in a very methodical and sequential manner. Each stage is composed of certain well-defined activities and responsibilities, and is completed before the next stage begins. This approach was popular in the 1960s and 70s, when systems were largely transaction-processing systems and had a much heavier reliance on programming than most modern information systems, which are database-oriented.

There are several versions of the systems life cycle diagram; the stages include problem definition, problem investigation, feasibility study, analysis, design, construction/implementation (including programming, testing and installation, maintenance and evaluation. Most diagrams like the one below show only 5 or 6 main steps.

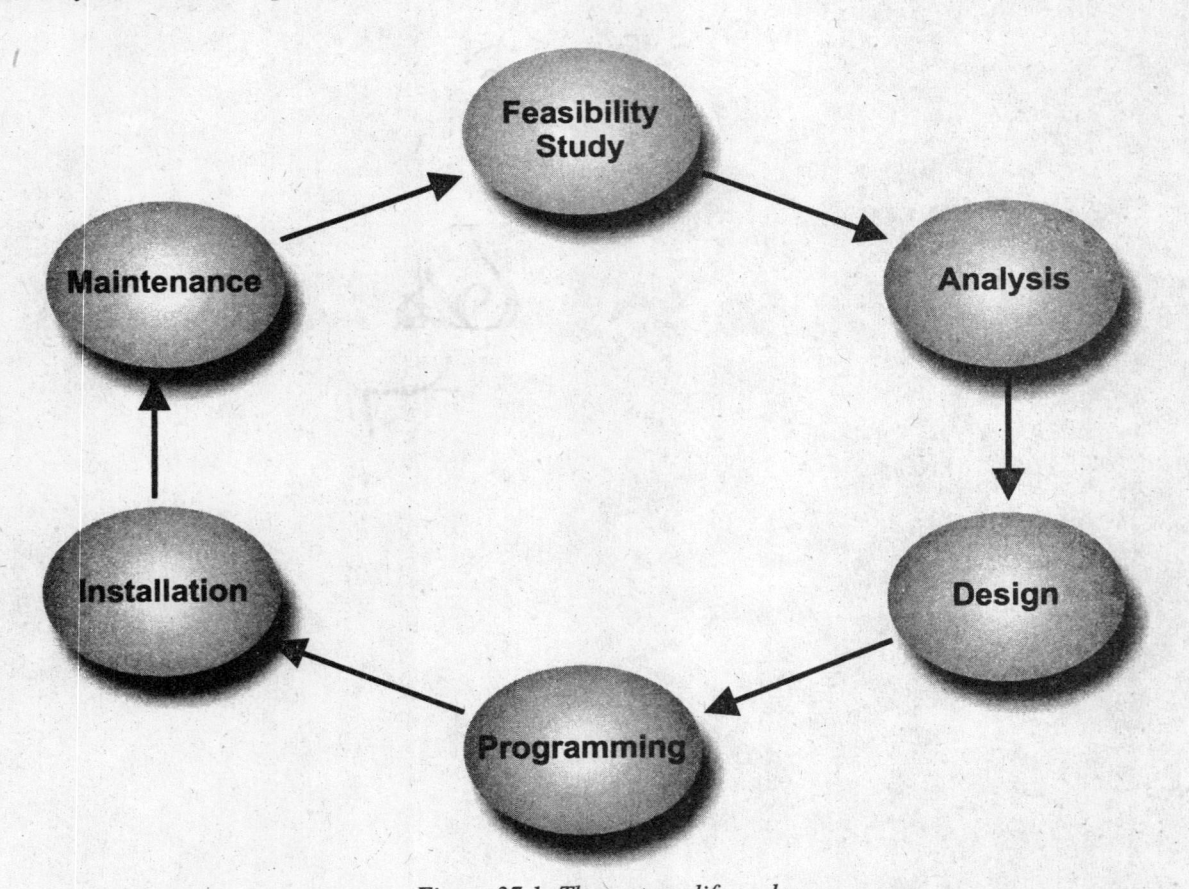

Figure 37.1: The systems life cycle

The waterfall model

The systems life cycle approach to development is also known as the 'waterfall model', and a variation on the basic diagram of 37.1 is shown in Figure 37.2.

Note that the arrows go up and down the 'waterfall', reflecting the fact that developers often have to rework earlier stages in the light of experience gained as development progresses.

A project milestone terminates each stage of a life-cycle-oriented approach. At this stage, the 'deliverable' resulting from that stage – such as the documentation for the analysis or the design, or the program code or finished database application, is *signed off* by all concerned parties and approval is given to proceed to the next stage. The 'concerned parties' usually include the end-users, management and developers, as well as other experts such as database administration personnel. This sequence continues until the evaluation stage has been completed and the finished system is delivered to the end-users.

In this model, the end-user has very little say in the development process, which is carried out by technical specialists such as systems analysts and programmers. He or she is presented with the finished system at the end of the development cycle and if it is not quite what was wanted, it is generally too late to make changes. Therefore, it is extremely important that the system requirements are very clearly specified and understood by all parties before being signed off.

Such levels of certainty are difficult to achieve and this is one of the major drawbacks of the 'waterfall model'.

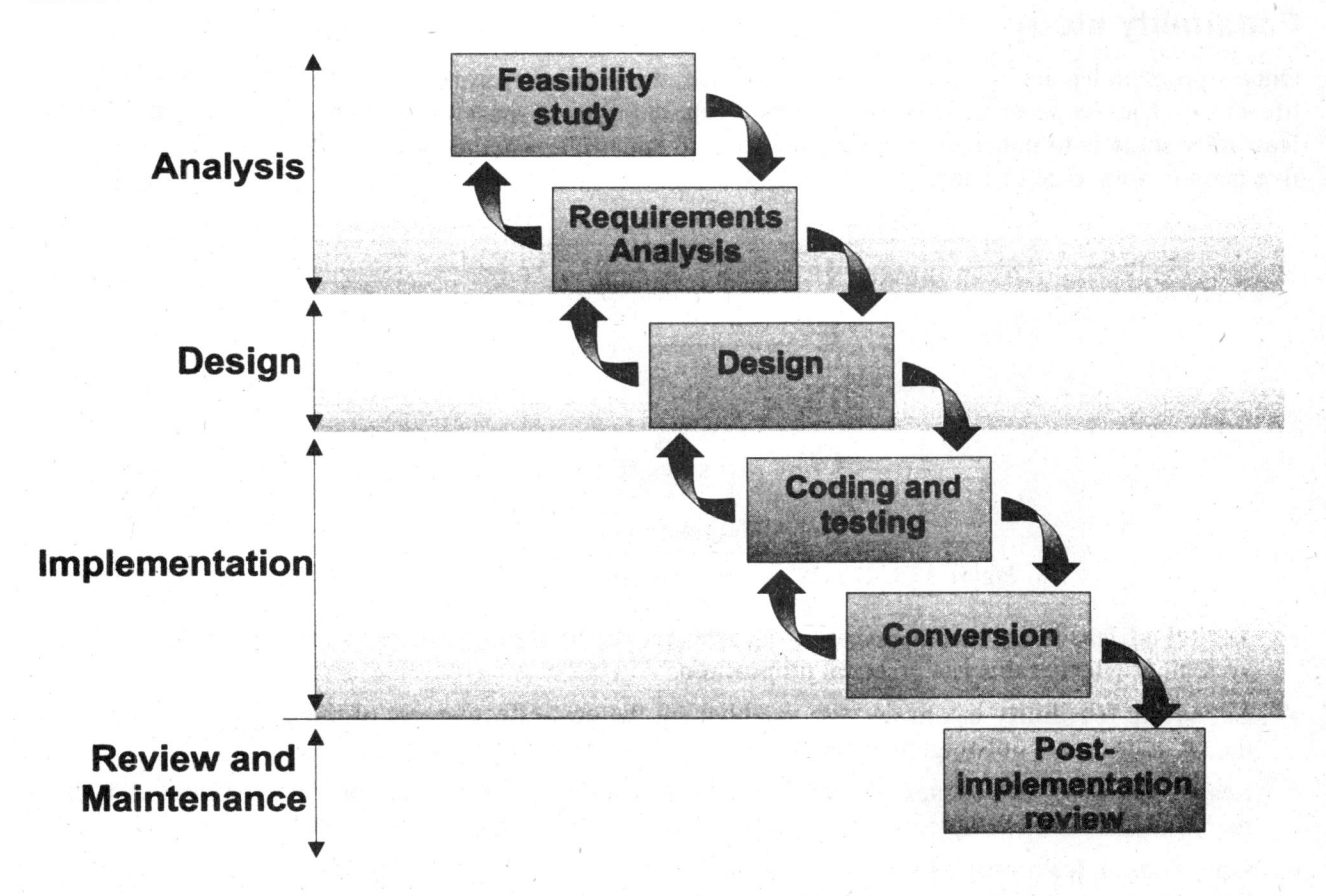

Figure 37.2: Systems development life cycle (the 'Waterfall model')

What prompts a new system?

The development of a new information system is a major undertaking and not one to be undertaken lightly. Wal-Mart, the American discount store which has recently taken over Asda, spent $700m on its computerised distribution system in the 1980s. Tesco, Sainsbury's and Marks and Spencer have spent massive sums of money on their computer systems in the past decade. Businesses must adapt to remain competitive. Some of the reasons for introducing a new system may be:

1. **The current system may be no longer suitable for its purpose.** Changes in work processes, expansion of the business, changes in business requirements or the environment in which the organisation operates may all lead to a reassessment of information system requirements.
2. **Technological developments may have made the current system redundant or outdated.** Advances in hardware, software and telecommunications bring new opportunities which an organisation cannot ignore if it is to keep ahead of its rivals.
3. **The current system may be too inflexible or expensive to maintain**, or may reduce the organisation's ability to respond quickly enough to customer's demands.

At the end of the millennium, many businesses with old systems that were susceptible to the 'millennium bug' took the opportunity to install new systems which would provide better information, rather than spend money on having external consultants patch up their old system.

Feasibility study

Once a problem has been recognised and identified, the **feasibility study** is the first stage of the systems life cycle. The **scope** and **objectives** of the proposed system must be written down. The aim of the feasibility study is to understand the problem and to determine whether it is worth proceeding. There are five main factors to be considered:

Technical feasibility
Economic feasibility
Legal feasibility
Operational feasibility
Schedule feasibility

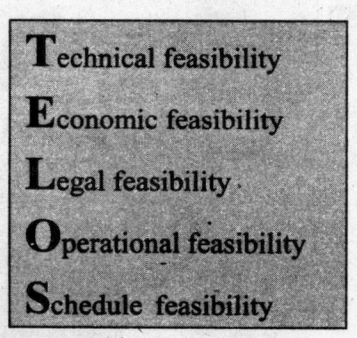

Figure 37.3: TELOS – a mnemonic for the five feasibility factors

- **Technical feasibility** means investigating whether the technology exists to implement the proposed system, or whether this is a practical proposition.
- **Economic feasibility** has to do with establishing the cost-effectiveness of the proposed system – if the benefits do not outweigh the costs, then it is not worth going ahead.
- **Legal feasibility** determines whether there is any conflict between the proposed system and legal requirements – for example, will the system contravene the Data Protection Act?
- **Operational feasibility** is concerned with whether the current work practices and procedures are adequate to support the new system. It is also concerned with social factors – how the organisational change will affect the working lives of those affected by the system.
- **Schedule feasibility** looks at how long the system will take to develop, or whether it can be done in a desired time-frame.

Chapter 37 – The Classical Systems Life-Cycle

The completion of this stage is marked by the production of a feasibility report produced by the systems analyst. If the report concludes that the project should go ahead, and this is agreed by senior managers, detailed requirements analysis will proceed.

Analysis/Requirements analysis

The second phase of systems analysis is a more detailed investigation into the current system and the requirements of the new system.

It is the job of the systems analyst to find out what the user's requirements are, to find out about current methods and to assess the feasibility of the new proposed system. Gathering details about the current system may involve:

- interviewing staff at different levels of the organisation from the end-users to senior management.
- examining current business and systems documents and output. These may include current order documents, computer systems procedures and reports used by operations and senior management.
- sending out questionnaires and analysing responses. The questions have to be carefully constructed to elicit unambiguous answers.
- observation of current procedures, by spending time in various departments. A time and motion study can be carried out to see where procedures could be made more efficient, or to detect where bottlenecks occur.

The systems analyst's report will examine how data and information flow around the organisation, and may use **data flow diagrams** to document the flow. It will also establish precisely, and in considerable detail, exactly what the proposed system will do (as opposed to how it will do it). It will include an in-depth analysis of the costs and benefits, and outline the process of system implementation, including the organisational change required. It must establish who the end-users are, what information they should get and in what form and how it will be obtained.

Alternative options for the implementation of the project will be suggested. These could include suggestions for:

- whether development should be done in-house or using consultants;
- what hardware configurations could be considered;
- what the software options are.

Data flow diagram (DFD)

A data flow diagram shows how data moves through a system and what data stores are used. It does not specify what type of data storage is used or how the data is stored.

The following four symbols are used in data flow diagrams:

External entity – data source or data destination, for example people who generate data such as a customer order, or receive information such as an invoice.

Process – an operation performed on the data. The two lines are optional; the top section of the box can be used to label the process, the middle to give a brief explanation, the bottom to say where the process takes place. An alternative convention is to use a circle for a Process.
Make the first word an active verb – e.g. **validate** data, **adjust** stock level.

Module 3 Practical Systems Development

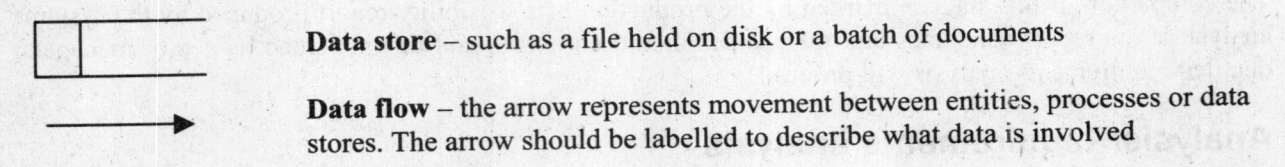

Data store – such as a file held on disk or a batch of documents

Data flow – the arrow represents movement between entities, processes or data stores. The arrow should be labelled to describe what data is involved

Example: A theatre uses a computerised booking system to keep records of customers, plays and bookings. A customer may make a booking in person, by telephone or by preprinted form. The booking clerk first has to check whether there are any seats free for the performance. If there are, the clerk reserves the seats, then checks whether the customer's details are already on file, and if not, types them in. The tickets are then printed out and handed or sent to the customer. Payment is made either in cash or by credit card.

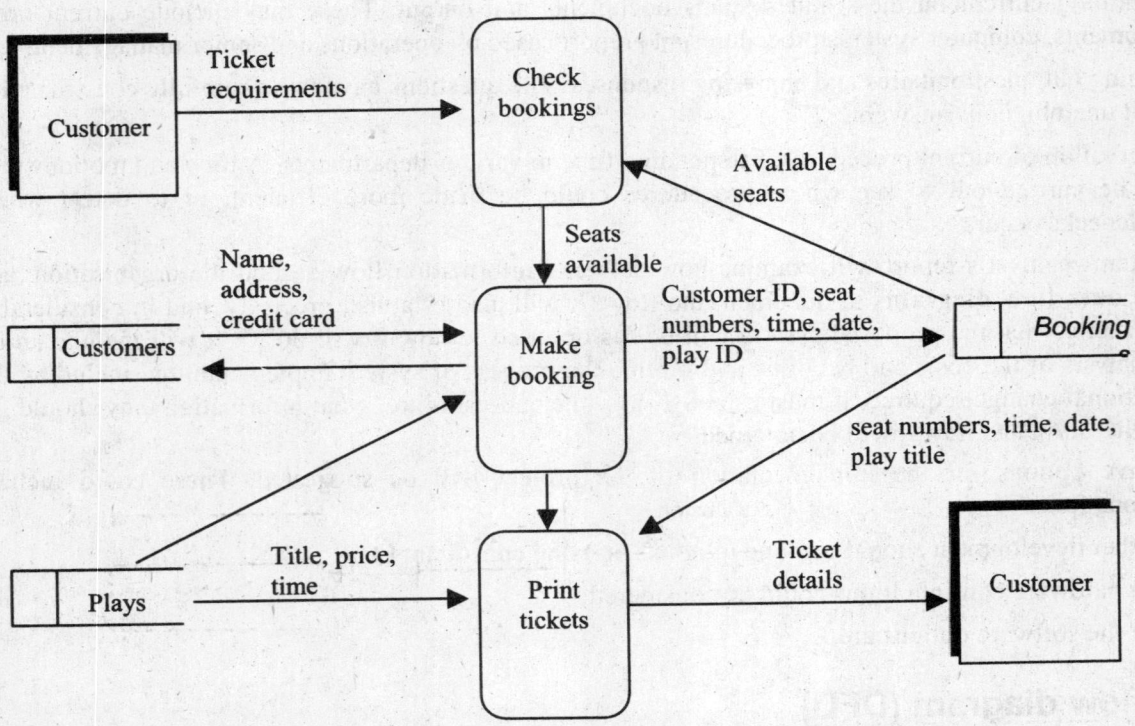

Figure 37.4: Data flow diagram of a theatre booking system

In the next chapter, the remaining stages of the system life cycle including design, implementation, testing, maintenance and evaluation will be considered.

Exercises

1. A feasibility study will often be carried out at an early stage of system development. As well as finding out if the proposal is technically possible the study will also consider economic and social feasibility.

   In the context of a feasibility study describe **one** cost, **one** benefit and **three** possible social effects that would be considered.

2. State **three** different methods of fact finding available during the systems analysis stage of the systems life cycle, and for **each** of these three methods, give **one** reason for its use.

3. Describe five main stages in the full life cycle of a computerised system.

4. A firm uses an existing database to send a word processed, personalised letter to all its customers telling them of a new product.

    (a) What is the term used for this process?

    (b) Draw a data-flow diagram for this process.

5. During system development a *data flow diagram* may be used to represent all or part of the system. Below is an outline of a data flow diagram for a system to produce gas bills where the meter readings, having been recorded using a hand held device, are processed against the customer master file to produce the printed gas bills for the customers and a printed error report.

    Give an appropriate label to **each** of the numbered elements A to E.

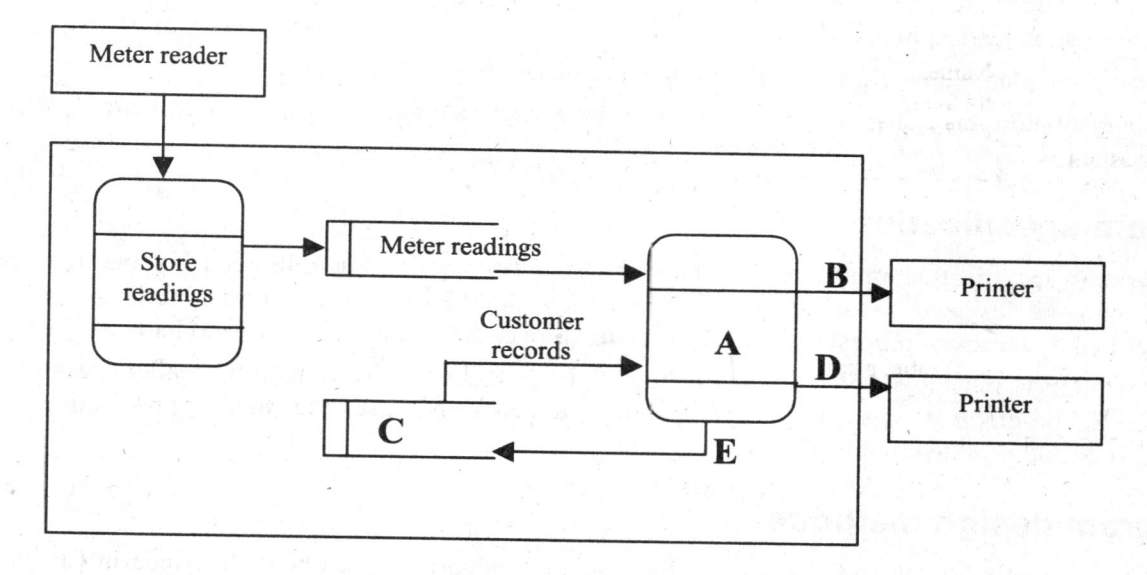

6. A proposed computerised information system will be used in a number of separate departments within a large organisation.

    (a) Suggest and justify **two** criteria which the systems analyst might use when selecting the personnel to be interviewed.

    (b) State **two** disadvantages of interviewing as a fact finding method.

Chapter 38 – From Design to Evaluation

System design

The design specifies the following aspects of a system:

- The hardware platform – which type of computer, network capabilities, input, storage and output devices.
- The software – programming language, package or database.
- The outputs – report layouts and screen designs.
- The inputs – documents, screen layouts and validation procedures.
- The user interface – how users will interact with the computer system.
- The modular design of each program in the application.
- The test strategy, test plan and test data.
- Conversion plan – how the new system is to be implemented.
- Documentation including systems and operations documentation. Later, a user manual will be produced.

System specification

The systems specification must describe how the new system will work. Screen layouts and report formats must be designed, file contents and organisation specified, and each program in the system must be described by means of program specifications, structure charts, pseudocode or flowcharts.

The programmers must then code, test and debug all the programs in the system. In smaller organisations the roles of programmer and analyst may overlap, and in some cases the 'analyst/programmer' may design, code and test the programs.

Program design methods

The use of structure charts and pseudocode for describing algorithms has been described in Chapters 8 and 9. An **algorithm** is a sequence of instructions to solve a given problem. **Pseudocode** is an intermediate stage between plain English and the programming language in which the solution will eventually be coded – it enables the writer to concentrate on the steps in the solution without worrying about the syntax rules of a particular language.

Prototyping

As in any other context, prototyping means building a working model of a new system in order to evaluate it, test it or have it approved before building the final product. When applied to computer systems, this could involve, for example, using special software to quickly design input screens and run a program (supplied as part of the prototyping package) to input and validate data using the screen format just created. This gives the user a chance to experience the 'look and feel' of the input process and to suggest alterations before going any further.

The prototype may then be discarded and the system built using the same or different software. This is termed **throw-away** prototyping.

Some organisations will use prototyping in the analysis stage, others in the design phase. Others may use it almost exclusively, going directly from preliminary investigation, via the prototype, to an implemented system. The analysts or programmers will simply keep refining the prototype until the user says it is acceptable. This is called **evolutionary** prototyping.

> ➤ Q1: What are the advantages and disadvantages of using prototyping as a tool of systems analysis and design?

Choosing a software solution

Many different solutions to a particular problem will have been looked at before a particular solution is chosen. The criteria on which the final choice is based will include:

- **Usability** – will the users find the system easy to use, will it save them time, cut out tedious repetitive tasks, give them quick access to information they need, or help them in some way? Or will it just give them extra work with no obvious benefits, or produce mountains of paperwork from which it is hard to extract useful information?
- **Performance** – will the system function in the way that was intended? Or will it suffer from 'bugs', slow access times when retrieving data from a database, screens that take minutes to change or redraw after a command is typed, hardware that is unreliable?
- **Suitability** – does the system really provide a solution to the problem, or was it considered because for example it was the 'cheapest' solution? Will it integrate with existing software, can current manual methods be adapted for the new system?
- **Maintainability** – will it be easy to upgrade the system, add new functionality, make modifications when required?

Testing strategies

When a new system is developed, it has to undergo rigorous testing before it is released. Typically, it may undergo several phases of testing including:

- **Dry run testing:** the programmer follows through the code manually using test data to check that an algorithm is correct. This technique is useful for locating run-time errors – it would normally be carried out on a part of a program rather than the whole program. A **trace table** (see Chapter 7) is useful for checking the values of variables while following through the logic.
- **Unit testing:** this refers to the testing of each individual subroutine or module in a suite of programs.
- **Integration testing:** this involves testing a complete suite of programs to ensure that they all function correctly when they are put together – for example, by being called from a menu program.

Test plan and test data

A test plan needs to be drawn up for each program in a system. This is usually in the form of a table showing each item that needs to be tested. It should cover every possible type of input including values which are too large, too small or invalid for other reasons such as an alphabetic character being entered instead of a number. The test plan needs to show for each test what the expected result is.

Technical documentation

Technical documentation helps to ensure that a system can be maintained after completion. All too often changes of staff within a company mean that no-one who was involved in the original design or programming of a system is still with the company. It is essential that proper documentation is kept to enable a newcomer to make necessary corrections, alterations or enhancements.

Contents of a documented system

- an accurate and up-to-date systems specification;
- Data Flow Diagrams showing the inputs to the system, files required, processes to be carried out, and output from the system;
- a description of the purpose of each program within the system;
- a structure diagram, flowchart or pseudocode for each program in the system;
- organisation, contents and layout of each file used;
- layout and contents of all output prints and displays;
- current version of each program listing;
- test data and expected results.

Implementation

This phase includes both the coding and testing of the system, the acquisition of hardware and the installation of the new system or conversion of the old system to the new one.

The installation phase can include:

- installing the new hardware, which may involve extensive recabling and changes in office layouts;
- training the users on the new system;
- conversion of master files to the new system, or creation of new master files.

Evaluation

When a new software system is complete, it is very important to evaluate it to ensure that it meets the user's original specifications and is satisfactory in all respects.

Minor programming errors may have to be corrected, clerical procedures amended, or modifications made to the design of reports or screen layouts.

The solution will be evaluated in terms of

- Effectiveness: does it do what it is supposed to do?
- Usability: is it easy to use?
- Maintainability: will it be easy to maintain?

Often it is only when people start to use a new system that they realise its shortcomings! In some cases they may realise that it would be possible to get even more useful information from the system than they realised, and more programs may be requested. The process of **system maintenance**, in fact, has already begun, and the life cycle is complete.

System maintenance

All software systems require maintenance, and in fact the vast majority of programmers are employed to maintain existing programs rather than to write new ones. There are differing reasons for this, and different types of maintenance.

- **Perfective maintenance**. This implies that while the system runs satisfactorily, there is still room for improvement. For example, extra management information may be needed so that new report programs have to be written. Database queries may be very slow, and a change in a program may be able to improve response time.

- **Adaptive maintenance**. All systems will need to adapt to changing needs within a company. As a business expands, for example, there may be a requirement to convert a standalone system to a multi-user system. New and better hardware may become available, and changes to the software may be necessary to take advantage of this. New government legislation may mean that different methods of calculating tax, for example, are required. Competition from other firms may mean that systems have to be upgraded in order to maintain a competitive edge.
- **Corrective maintenance**. Problems frequently surface after a system has been in use for a short time, however thoroughly it was tested. Some part of the system may not function as expected, or a report might be wrong in some way; totals missing at the bottom, incorrect sequence of data, wrong headings, etc. Frequently errors will be hard to trace, if for example a file appears to have been wrongly updated.

Exercises

1. Software developers use *prototyping* for different reasons in different situations.

    (a) What is prototyping?

    (b) Briefly explain **two** reasons for using prototypes.

2. Describe **two** methods of testing which will be used during the development of a new software system.

3. A typical software system will require both corrective and adaptive maintenance.

    (a) Describe the main difference between corrective maintenance and adaptive maintenance.

    (b) Explain how a software system should be developed in order to

    (i) Decrease the amount of corrective maintenance required.

    (ii) Ensure adaptive maintenance is as straightforward as possible.

4. (a) Explain why an error in the system specification is usually more expensive to correct if it is discovered during the maintenance phase than if it is discovered during the design phase.

    (b) Distinguish between evolutionary prototyping and throw-away prototyping.

Chapter 39 – Human Computer Interface

Introduction

The '**human computer interface**' is a term used to describe the interaction between a user and a computer; in other words, the method by which the user tells the computer what to do, and the responses which the computer makes.

It's important not to allow the word 'computer' to limit your vision to a PC sitting on an office desk. You also need to think in terms of a person getting cash from a cash machine, a pilot of a jumbo jet checking his instrument panels, the operator of a high-volume heavy duty photocopier, a scientist monitoring a chemical reaction, a musician composing a symphony using appropriate hardware and software.

> Q1: Name some other tasks for which computers are used, and for which special purpose interfaces are required.

The importance of good interface design

A good interface design can help to ensure that users carry out their tasks:

- **safely** (in the case of a jumbo jet pilot, for example);
- **effectively** (users don't find they have video taped two hours of Bulgarian clog dancing instead of the Cup Final);
- **efficiently** (users do not spend five minutes trying to find the correct way to insert their cash card and type in their PIN and the amount of cash they want, and then leave without remembering to extract their card);
- **enjoyably** (a primary school pupil using a program to teach multiplication tables).

Well-designed systems can improve the output of employees, improve the quality of life and make the world a safer and more enjoyable place to live in.

> Q2: In the early days of cash machines, it was found that users sometimes forgot to remove their cards after withdrawing their cash. What simple change was made to eliminate this fault?

Designing usable systems

In order to design a usable interface, the designer has to take into consideration:

- **who** will use the system. For example, will the users be computer professionals or members of the general public who may be wary of computers? For an educational program, will the users be young, for example primary school children, or teenagers on an A Level course? Will the system have to cater for both beginners and experienced users?
- **what tasks** the computer is performing. Is the task very repetitive, does the task require skill and knowledge? Do tasks vary greatly from one occasion to the next? A travel agent who spends most of the day making holiday bookings will require a different interface from an office worker who needs to be able to switch between word processing, accounts and accessing the company database.

- **the environment** in which the computer is used. Will the environment be hazardous (in a lifeboat setting out to rescue a stricken vessel), noisy (in a factory full of machinery), or calm and quiet (some offices)?
- **what is techologically feasible** (is it possible to simply dictate a letter to a word processor instead of typing it in?)

Interface styles

There is a number of common interface styles including:
- command line interface;
- menus;
- natural language;
- forms and dialogue boxes;
- graphical user interface (GUI).

Command-line interface

The command-line interface was the first interactive dialogue style and is still widely used in spite of the availability of menu-driven interfaces. It provides a means of expressing instructions to the computer directly using single characters, whole word commands or abbreviations.

With this type of interface very little help is given to the user, who has to type a command such as, for example, **Format a:** to format a disk. Commands enable a user to quickly and concisely instruct the computer what to do, but they do require the user to have a knowledge of the commands available and the syntax for using them.

> Q3: Identify TWO situations in which a command-driven interface would be appropriate.

Menus

There are several different types of menu interface, outlined below.

1. **Full screen menu.** This type of menu is often used as the 'front end' of an application. It stays on screen until the user makes a choice.

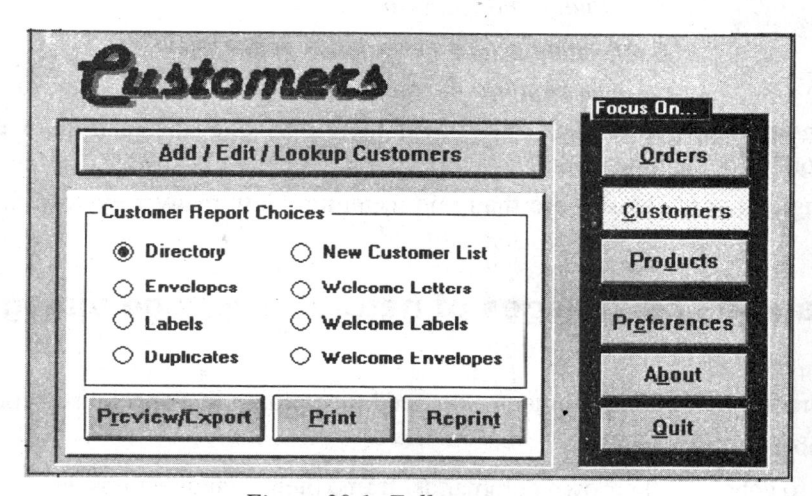

Figure 39.1: Full screen menu

2. **Pull-down menu.** This type of menu is displayed along the top of the screen, and when the user clicks on an item, a submenu appears. The menu is always present whatever screen the user is looking at in the application.

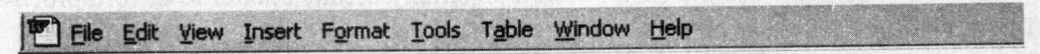

Figure 39.2: Pull-down menu

3. **Pop-up menu**. The menu pops up in response to, say, a click of the right mouse button on a particular area of the screen.

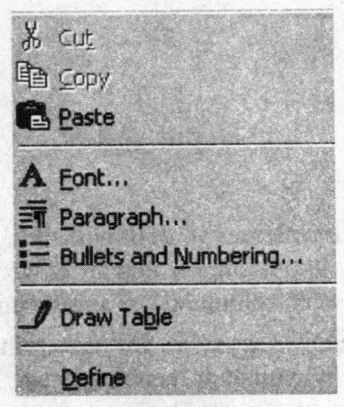

Figure 39.3: Pop-up menu

Natural language

It is a very attractive idea to have a computer which can understand natural language – 'plain English' in other words. *'How do I create an A5 folded leaflet in Word?'* is understandable to most people but does not elicit a sensible answer from the Office Assistant. (You can't, basically.) Unfortunately, the ambiguity of natural language makes it very difficult for a machine to understand. Language is ambiguous in a number of different ways. Firstly, the syntax, or structure of a sentence may not be clear – for example consider the sentences

James and Henrietta are married.

A salesman visited every house in the area.

The man hit the dog with the stick.

Are James and Henrietta married to each other? Was there only one salesman involved in the house-to-house sales operation? Who had the stick?

Secondly, many English words have more than one meaning. How many ways can the word 'match' be interpreted?

Advantages and disadvantages of natural language dialogue

Advantages:
- most natural form of dialogue for humans – no need for training in a specialised command language;
- extremely flexible and powerful;
- the user is free to construct their own commands, frame their own questions, etc.

Disadvantages:
- people find it difficult to stick to grammatically correct English;
- a well designed 'artificial language' can often say the same thing more concisely than 'natural language';
- a smooth, natural language can easily mislead the naive user into believing the computer is 'intelligent'.

Forms and dialogue boxes

When a user is required to enter data such as, for example, sales invoices or customer names and addresses, it is common to have a 'form' displayed on the screen for the user to fill in. The following points should be noted when designing forms of this type:

- the form should be given a title to identify it;
- the form should not be too cluttered – spaces and blanks are important;
- it should give some indication of how many characters can be entered in each field of data;
- the user should be given a chance to go back and correct any field before the data is accepted;
- items should appear in a logical sequence to assist the user;
- default values should wherever possible be prewritten onto the form so that a minimum of data entry is required;
- full exit and 'help' facilities should be provided – for example, users could enter '?' in a field if they require more information;
- lower case in a display is neater and easier to read than all upper-case;
- colours should be carefully chosen to be legible and easy on the eyes;
- 'attention-getting' devices such as blinking cursors, high-intensity, reverse video, underlining etc should not be over-used.

Dialogue boxes are a special type of form often associated with the Windows environment; an example shown below is the dialogue box which appears when the instruction to *Print* is given in Word 2000.

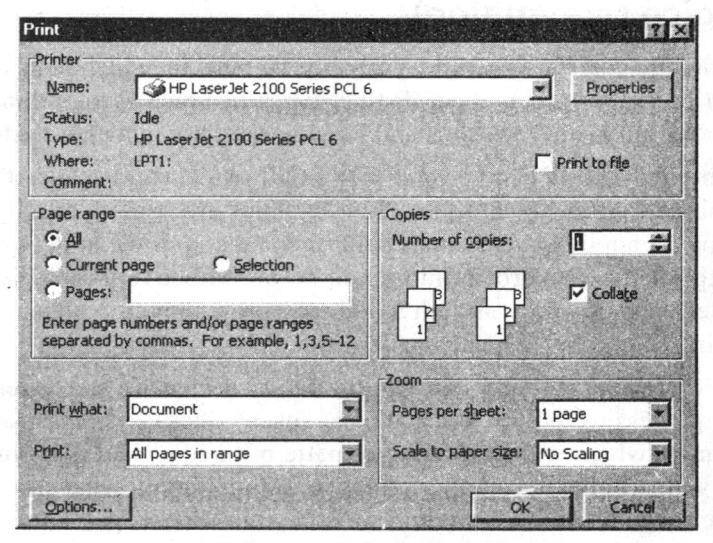

Figure 39.4: Dialogue box

The WIMP interface

WIMP stands for Windows, Icons, Mouse and Pull-down menus.

A **window** is an area on the screen through which a particular piece of software or a data file may be viewed. The window may occupy the whole screen, or the user can choose to have several windows on the screen with a different application running in each one. Windows can be moved, sized, stacked one on top of the other, opened and closed. A Windows environment mimics a desktop on which a worker may have several books or pieces of paper spread out for reference.

An **icon** is a small picture representing an item such as a piece of software, a file, storage medium (such as disk or tape) or command. By pointing with a mouse at a particular icon and clicking the mouse button the user can select it.

Microsoft Windows enables the user to run several different software packages such as MS Word (a word processor), MS Excel (a spreadsheet), MS Paint (a graphics package) simultaneously and to move data and graphics from one package to another. Software packages written by other manufacturers, such as Aldus PageMaker, have been written to run under Windows because of the convenience to the user of this easy-to-use environment.

Advantages of a common user interface

All the software packages mentioned above use a consistent interface and have a similar 'look and feel' so that a user familiar with one package can quickly learn a second. For example, in each package a single click of the mouse button **selects** an item, and a double click **activates** the item. In each package, the methods for opening, closing, sizing and moving windows is identical. The advantages can be summarised as:

- increased speed of learning;
- ease of use;
- confidence building for novice users;
- increased range of tasks solvable by experienced users;
- a greater range of software accessible to the average user.

Speech input (voice recognition)

The ultimate in user-friendly interfaces would probably be one in which you could simply tell your computer what to do in ordinary speech. Two distinct types of voice recognition system are emerging; small vocabulary command and control systems and large vocabulary dictation systems.

- **Command and control systems** can be relatively small and cheap because they need only a small, tightly defined vocabulary of technical terms. Such systems are coming rapidly into use as automatic call-handling systems for applications such as bank account enquiries. In PC systems, voice command can be used to bring up files, control printing and so on, effectively replacing the mouse. In some systems the computer is 'trained' by an individual user pronouncing a given vocabulary of words; it then stores a recording of the user's speech pattern for each word or syllable.

- **Large vocabulary dictation systems** can handle whole sentences and extensive vocabularies but need much greater processing power and memory space. These systems use elaborate probability distributions to estimate which word the acoustic pattern it has picked up is most likely to be, partly by looking at other words in the developing sentence and predicting what sort of word (noun or verb, for example) is likely to be used. Various voice recognition packages after suitable 'training' will take dictation at 70 words per minute and get about 97% of them correct. Voice recognition is however still an expensive technology and widespread use is some way off.

> **Q4:** Name some other situations in which voice input would be appropriate.

Speech/sound output

A speech synthesis system works as follows:

Individual words and sounds are spoken into a microphone by a human being and recorded by the system, thereby training it to speak. Output that would normally be printed can then be spoken, so long as the word is contained in its vocabulary. A second, more flexible method uses phonemes – the individual sounds from which all words are constructed in any particular language.

Such a system has limited use but could for example be used by a bank computer connected by telephone line to customers' homes and offices. The customer could key in his account number using the telephone keypad, and the computer could then access his account and speak out the customer's account balance.

Exercises

1. A company is designing a software package for use by pupils in infants' schools.

    Briefly describe and justify two appropriate features of the package's human-computer interface.

2. A college uses a range of software packages from different suppliers. Each package has a different user interface. The college is considering changing its software to one supplier and to a common user interface.
    (a) Give **four** advantages of having a common user interface.
    (b) Describe four specific features of a user interface which would benefit from being common between packages.
    (c) Discuss the issues involved, apart from user interfaces, in the college changing or upgrading software packages.

3. A railway station has a computer-based timetable enquiry system for use by passengers. Enquiries are entered from a keyboard and displayed on the screen-based form illustrated below.

```
Destination:
Date of Travel:
Latest arrival time:
```

Module 3 Practical Systems Development

Details of the train times are displayed at the bottom of the screen.
   (a) The exact format of the input required for this system is not clear. Redesign the form to make it clear.
   (b) Some users of the enquiry system find it difficult to use. Suggest *three* ways in which it could be made easier to use.

4. Briefly describe three important features of a well-designed user interface.

5. Two common approaches used to overcome the problem of communication between a user and the computer are command languages and forms dialogues.

   Briefly define both approaches, and in each case state **one** advantage and **one** disadvantage.

6. Describe two different features of a software user interface which would make it suitable for use by both experienced and inexperienced users.

7. A hospital is considering the introduction of voice recognition software for use by consultants in the production of medical reports about patients.
   (a) Outline **two** advantages of using voice recognition for this purpose.
   (b) Briefly describe **one** drawback in the general use of voice recognition software.

Module 4

Processing and Programming Techniques

In this section:

Chapter 40 - Structure and Role of the Processor
Chapter 41 - Number Bases and Representation
Chapter 42 - Floating Point Numbers
Chapter 43 - Assembly Language Instructions
Chapter 44 - Instruction Formats and Addressing modes
Chapter 45 - High Level Languages
Chapter 46 - Object-Oriented Programming
Chapter 47 - Prolog Programming (1)
Chapter 48 - Prolog Programming (2)
Chapter 49 - Recursion
Chapter 50 - Lists
Chapter 51 - Linked Lists
Chapter 52 - Queues and Stacks
Chapter 53 - Trees
Chapter 54 - Searching and Sorting
Chapter 55 - Operating System Classification
Chapter 56 - Operating System Concepts
Chapter 57 - Memory, File and I/O Management

Chapter 40 – Structure and Role of the Processor

Inside the CPU

We have seen that a computer consists of the processor, memory, input and output units. The processor itself consists of three main components:

- the arithmetic-logic unit (ALU) in which all arithmetic and logic operations are carried out;
- the control unit, which coordinates the activities taking place in the CPU, memory and peripherals, by sending control signals to the various devices;
- The system clock, which generates a continuous sequence of clock pulses to step the control unit through its operation. *[annotation: not inside CPU]*

In addition, the CPU contains circuitry controlling the interpretation and execution of instructions. Special storage locations called **registers** are included in this circuitry to hold information temporarily while it is being decoded or manipulated. Some of these special purpose registers are shown in the block diagram and explained below.

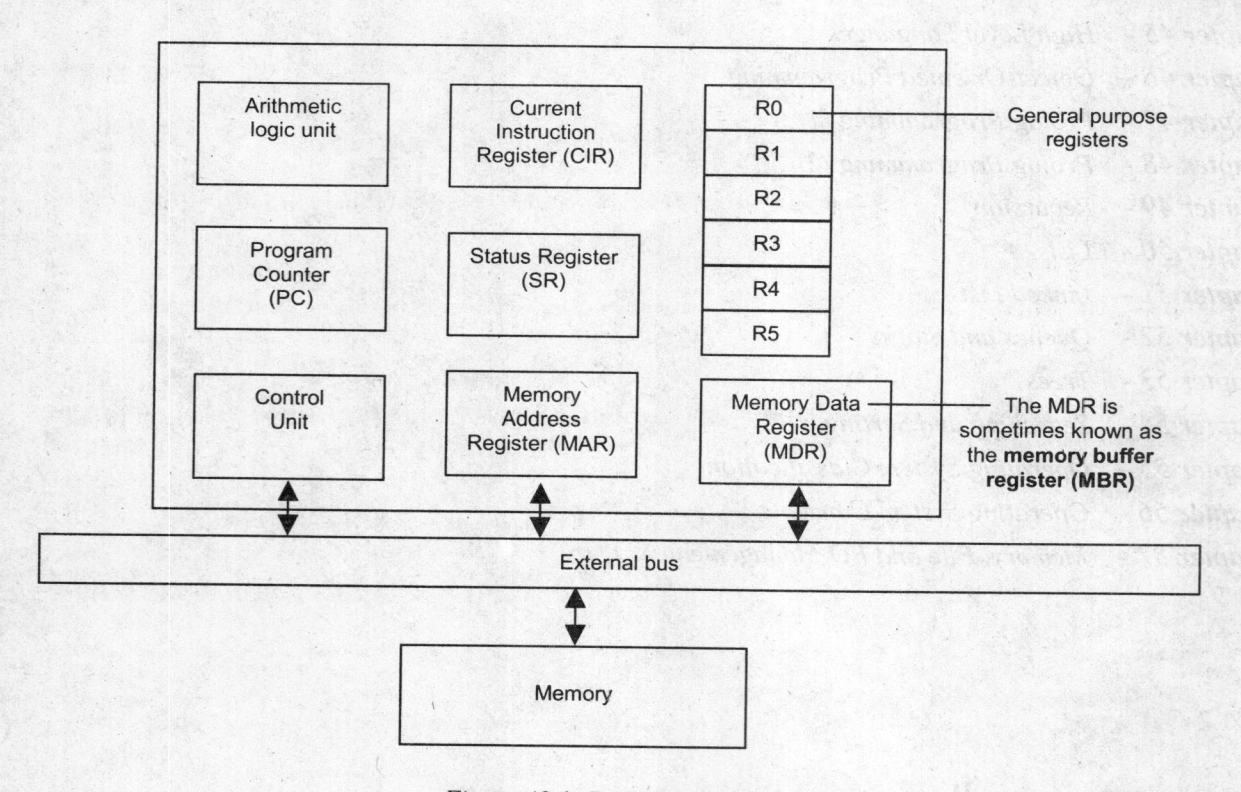

Figure 40.1: Registers inside the CPU

The registers shown in the block diagram above, which represents a 'typical' computer, each have a specific purpose, which is described below:

- the **program counter** (**PC**) holds the address of the next instruction to be executed. It is also known as the **sequence control register** (**SCR**) or the **sequence register**.

  When a sequence of instructions is being executed, the program counter is automatically incremented to point to the next instruction – that is, it holds the address of the next instruction to be executed. Depending on the length of the current instruction, this may mean that 1, 2 or 3 has to be added to its current contents. If the current instruction is a branch or jump instruction, then the address to branch to is copied from the current instruction to the program counter.

- The **general purpose registers** are used for performing arithmetic functions. In some computers, there is only one general purpose register, usually called an **accumulator**, which acts as a working area. Other computers have up to 16 general purpose registers.

  For example, an instruction to add the contents of memory locations 1000 and 1001 and store the result in location 1002 might be broken down into the instructions:

  ```
  Load contents of 1000 into the accumulator
  Add contents of 1001 to the accumulator
  Store contents of accumulator in 1002
  ```

- The **current instruction register** (**CIR**) contains both the **operator** and the **operand** of the current instruction. For example, a machine language instruction to load the contents of location 1000 into the accumulator might be written

        LDA 1000

  where LDA is the **operator**, and 1000 is the **operand**. → address

- The **memory address register** (**MAR**) holds the address of the memory location from which data will be read or to which data will be written. Remember that both instructions and data are held in memory, so that sometimes the MAR will hold the address of an instruction to be fetched, and sometimes it will hold the address of data to be used in an instruction. Thus when an instruction is to be 'fetched', the contents of the program counter are copied to this register so that the CPU will know where in memory to get the next instruction from.

- The **memory data register** (**MDR**) is used to temporarily store data read from or written to memory. The instruction (for example, LDA 1000) is placed here en route to the CIR where it will be decoded. When the instruction has been decoded, the operand, 1000, will be placed in the MAR and the contents of location 1000 will then be copied to the MDR.

  All transfers from memory to the CPU go via the memory data register. Both the memory data register and the memory address register serve as 'buffer' registers to compensate for the difference in speed between the CPU and memory.

- The **status register** (**SR**) contains bits that are set or cleared based on the result of an instruction. For example, one particular bit will be set if overflow occurs, and another bit set if the result of the last instruction was negative. Based on this information the CPU could make a decision on whether to branch out of a given sequence.

  Status registers (also known as **program status words** or **PSW**s) also contain information about interrupts, which are discussed later in this chapter.

The steps in the fetch-execute cycle

The sequence of operations involved in executing an instruction can be subdivided into two phases – the **fetch** cycle and the **execution** cycle. In addition to executing instructions, the CPU has to supervise other operations such as data transfers between input/output devices and main memory. When an I/O device needs to transfer data, it generates an **interrupt** and the CPU suspends execution of the program and

Module 4 Processing and Programming Techniques

transfers to an appropriate interrupt handling program. A test for the presence of interrupts is carried out at the end of each instruction cycle.

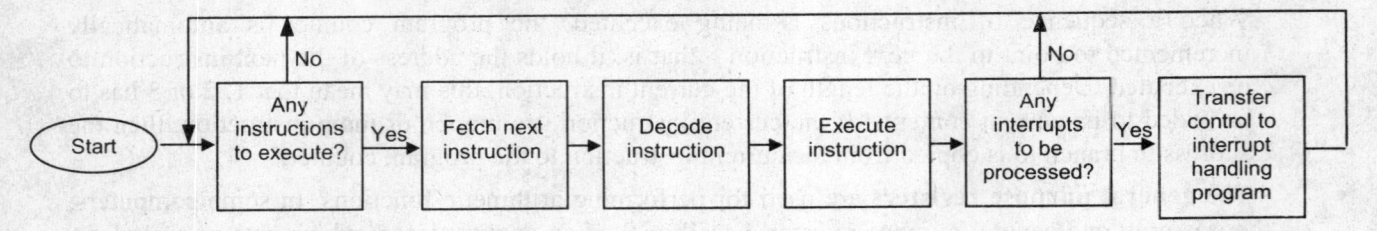

Figure 40.2: The fetch-execute cycle

How the CPU registers are used

The fetch-execute cycle may be broken down into a series of steps as follows:

(Fetch phase)

1. The address of the next instruction is copied from the PC to the MAR.
2. The instruction held at that address is copied to the MDR. Simultaneously, the content of the PC is incremented so that it holds the address of the next instruction.
3. The contents of the MDR are copied to the CIR.

(Execute phase)

1. The instruction held in the CIR is decoded.
2. The instruction is executed.

> Q1: Describe the sequence of events carried out during the fetch-execute cycle when obeying the first of the instructions below, showing the contents of each of the following registers during the cycle:
>
> program counter (PC), memory address register (MAR), memory data register (MDR), current instruction register (CIR), accumulator (ACC)
>
> ```
> Address   Contents     Type          Comment
> 500       LDA 1000     instruction   load contents of location 1000 into ACC
> 503       ADD 1001     instruction   add contents of location 1001 into ACC
> 506       STO 1002     instruction   store contents of ACC in location 1002
>
> 1000      3            data
> 1001      5            data
> 1002      0            data
> ```

The stack pointer

In addition to the registers mentioned above, most computers use a special register called a **stack pointer** which points to the top of a set of memory locations known as a **stack**. (A stack is a data structure which can only be accessed at the 'top', like a pile of plates). When execution of a program is interrupted for any reason the status of the interrupted program and the current contents of all the registers are saved on the stack, and the stack pointer updated.

Stacks may also be used instead of general purpose registers to store the intermediate results of arithmetic operations and to hold return addresses and parameter information when subroutines are called.

Whenever a subroutine is called in the program, the contents of the program counter, which contains the address of the next instruction after the CALL, is saved on the stack. A RETURN instruction fetches this value off the stack and loads it into the program counter so that execution continues from the correct instruction.

Recap: the accumulator and general purpose registers

It is important to understand that **all** operations take place in the accumulator or a general purpose register. Thus for example the machine code equivalent of

```
P := Q - R
```

will be something like

```
Load Q into the accumulator
Subtract R from the accumulator
Store the contents of the accumulator in P
```

> Q2: Write the machine code equivalent of (i) P := 100;   (ii) NUM1 := NUM2;

Interrupts

In Figure 40.2 you will see that at the end of each fetch/execute cycle the processor may be required to deal with an interrupt. *An interrupt is a signal from some device or source seeking the attention of the processor.* The interrupt signal is sent along a control line to the processor, and the currently executing program is suspended while control is passed to **an interrupt service routine**.

Types of interrupt

The following different types of interrupt may occur:
- **interrupts generated by the running process**. The process might need to perform I/O, obtain more storage or communicate with the operator.
- **I/O interrupts**. These are initiated by the I/O hardware and signal to the CPU that the status of a channel or device has changed. An I/O interrupt will occur when an I/O operation is complete, when an error occurs, or when a device is made ready.
- **Timer interrupts**. These are generated by a timer within the processor, and allow the operating system to perform certain functions at regular intervals. For example, each user in a multi-user system may be allocated a certain amount of processor time before a timer interrupt is generated and control of the processor passes to the next user in turn.
- **Program check interrupts**. These are caused by various types of error such as division by zero.
- **Machine check interrupts**. These are caused by malfunctioning hardware.

Interrupt priorities

There is a special register in the CPU called the **interrupt register**. At the beginning of each fetch-execute cycle, the interrupt register is checked. Each bit of the register represents a different type of interrupt, and if a bit is set, the state of the current process is saved and the operating system routes control to the appropriate interrupt handler.

Some interrupts, such as those generated by hardware failure, may need to be dealt with immediately, whereas others such as an I/O device signaling that it is ready for I/O, can be temporarily ignored. Interrupts are therefore assigned **priorities** so that when two interrupts are received simultaneously, the one with the highest priority is dealt with first. Only an interrupt with a higher priority is allowed to interrupt the servicing of another.

Examples of interrupt priorities are given below; one is highest priority, four is lowest.

Class of interrupt	Source of interrupt	Priority
Hardware failure:	Power failure – initiated when a decline in the internal voltages is detected, giving the OS a few milliseconds to close down as gracefully as possible.	1
	Memory parity error	1
Program:	Arithmetic overflow	2
	Division by zero	2
	Attempt to execute an illegal machine instruction	2
	Reference outside a user's allowed memory space	2
Timer	Generated by an internal clock within the processor	3
I/O	I/O device signals normal completion or the occurrence of an error condition	4

The interrupt handler

What happens when, for example, a key on the keyboard is pressed, thus generating an interrupt? A small program called an **interrupt service routine (ISR)** or **interrupt handler** is executed to transfer the character value of the key pressed into main memory. *A different ISR is provided for each different source of interrupt.* A typical sequence of actions when an interrupt occurs would be:

1. The current fetch-execute cycle is completed.
2. The contents of the program counter, which points to the next instruction of the user program to be executed, must be stored away safely so it can be restored after servicing the interrupt.
3. The contents of other registers used by the user program are stored away safely for later restoration.
4. The source of the interrupt is identified. (vector interrupt)
5. Interrupts of a lower priority are disabled. put at the back of queue
6. The program counter is loaded with the start address of the relevant interrupt service routine.
7. The interrupt service routine is executed.
8. The saved values belonging to the user program for registers other than the program counter are restored to the processor's registers. (from stack)
9. Interrupts are re-enabled.
10. The program counter is restored to point to the next instruction to be fetched and executed in user program. (from where it was stopped)

The vectored interrupt mechanism

Step 6 above requires the PC to be loaded with the start address of the relevant ISR. One method of locating the correct ISR is known as the **vectored interrupt mechanism**. The interrupting device supplies a number (an offset) which is added to a fixed number (the base address). This base address plus offset is the address of a **vector**, i.e. a pointer to the address of the ISR. The PC is therefore loaded with the vector at this address.

The advantage of this method is that new ISRs can be placed at any appropriate memory location and it is only necessary for the interrupting device to supply the correct offset for the vector to be located.

Processor performance

In the traditional computer (sometimes referred to as the **von Neumann machine**) instructions are fetched and executed one at a time in a serial manner. Data, instructions and addresses are transmitted between memory and the processor along **data and address buses.** A third type of bus called the control bus is used to send control and timing signals between the various components of the CPU and between the CPU and main memory (see Chapter 17, Figure 17.3).

The main features which distinguish one processor from another and which determine the performance of each are:

- Clock speed
- Word size
- Bus size
- Architecture

Clock speed

In order to synchronise the various steps carried out during the fetch-execute cycle, all processors have an internal clock which generates regularly timed pulses. All processor activities, such as fetching an instruction, reading data into the memory data register etc. must begin on a clock pulse, although some activities may take more than one clock pulse to complete. Typically, the clock pulse rate in 2000 is around 500 Megahertz (million cycles per second). The clock speed, therefore, is one of the factors which will influence the speed at which instructions are executed; a 600MHz processor will in general operate faster than a 500MHz processor.

Word size [32-bit or 64-bit "processor"]

The word size of a computer is the number of bits that the CPU can process simultaneously. Bits may be grouped into 8-, 16-, 32-, 64- or 128-bit 'words', and processed as a unit during input and output, arithmetic and logic instructions. A processor with a 32-bit word size will operate faster than a processor with a 16-bit word size. Word size is a major factor in determining the speed of a processor.

‹Bus size›

Both the addresses of data and instructions, and the data and instructions, are transmitted along **buses**. The width of the address bus determines the maximum address that can be directly referenced. For example, if the width of the address bus is 8 bits, the maximum address that can be transmitted is 11111111 in binary which is 2^8-1 or 255. In all 256 addresses, from 0 to 255, can be referenced.

The width of the data bus determines how many bits can be transferred simultaneously. This is usually but not always the same as the word size of the computer. Not all processors with a 32-bit word for example have a 32-bit **data bus**, and so the data may have to be fetched in two groups of 16 bits.

> Q3: Distinguish between the **data bus** and the **address bus**.
> Q4: What is the maximum address that can be directly addressed in a processor with a 16-bit address bus?
> Q5: What is the lowest address?
> Q6: Express the maximum number of directly addressable locations in kilobytes.

Module 4 Processing and Programming Techniques

Exercises

1. Name **one** register involved in the fetch part of the fetch-execute cycle.

2. (a) Briefly describe what is meant by an interrupt.
   (b) Give **four** different types of event that may cause an interrupt.
   (c) Briefly describe the role of priorities in the handling of interrupts.

3. When data is being sent to a printer an interrupt may occur.
   (a) State two reasons why an interrupt might occur in this case.
   (b) Interrupts can be given priorities. Give two examples of interrupts which are likely to have higher priorities than an interrupt from the printer.

4. State the purpose of the *program counter register*.

5. (a) Explain how each of the following can lead to faster execution of instructions in a computer:
      (i) modifying the width of the data bus;
      (ii) altering the clock rate.
   (b) State one other feature of processor design or configuration which improves processor performance and describe how the improvement is achieved.

6. A microprocessor *data bus* has 16 lines and its *address bus* has 24 lines. What is the maximum memory capacity that can be connected to the microprocessor?

Chapter 41 – Number Bases and Representation

The denary number system

Our number system is called the denary system and uses the 10 digits 0 to 9. In this system, as we move from right to left each digit is worth 10 times as much as its right-hand neighbour. Thus for example the number 583 represents

$$5 \times 100 + 8 \times 10 + 3 \times 1 = 583$$

The **number base** specifies how many digits are used and how much each digit is multiplied by as we move from right to left. The denary system is a **base 10** system.

The binary and hexadecimal number systems

The binary number system is a base 2 system using only the two digits 0 and 1. Each digit is worth twice as much as the one to its right. Thus the binary number 10011 represents

$$16 \times 1 + 8 \times 0 + 4 \times 0 + 2 \times 1 + 1 = 19$$

Binary numbers are ideal for representing numbers inside a computer because the digits 0 and 1 can be represented by 'off' and 'on' in electrical circuits. However, they are very inconvenient for humans to read as even a relatively small number such as 256 requires 9 binary digits to represent it.

In order to ease the task of examining the contents of memory or a computer file, binary numbers are commonly put into groups of 4 bits and printed out in the form of **hexadecimal** numbers. These are numbers to base 16, and use the digits 0-9 and letters A to F. The table below shows the numbers 1 to 16 in denary, binary and hexadecimal.

Denary	Binary	Hexadecimal
1	1	1
2	10	2
3	11	3
4	100	4
5	101	5
6	110	6
7	111	7
8	1000	8
9	1001	9
10	1010	A
11	1011	B
12	1100	C
13	1101	D
14	1110	E
15	1111	F
16	10000	10

Table 41.1: Numbers 1-16 in denary, binary and hexadecimal

Module 4 Processing and Programming Techniques

Denary to binary and hexadecimal

Suppose you are asked to translate the number 179 to binary. To translate from a denary number to binary, write down headings 1, 2, 4, 8 etc from right to left as follows:

128	64	32	16	8	4	2	1

128 is the largest of the above numbers to go into 179, so put a 1 under 128 and subtract 128 from 179 leaving 51. 32 is the largest number to go into 51, so put a 1 under 32 and subtract it from 51 leaving 19. You can repeat the process, or take a shortcut by observing that 19 = 16 + 2 + 1. Either way you end up with the following, after filling in blank spaces with 0s.

128	64	32	16	8	4	2	1
1	0	1	1	0	0	1	1

To translate the number 179 into hexadecimal, the easiest way is to first translate it into binary, and then translate each group of 4 digits into hexadecimal. Thus, 179 = B3 in hexadecimal.

Tip: It is useful to remember that 1010 in binary is 10 in denary and A in hexadecimal. Also remember that 1111 is 15 in binary and F in hexadecimal. You can work the other numbers out as required.

> Q1: Translate the denary number 124 into   (a) binary   (b) hexadecimal

Translating back to denary

To translate a binary number to denary, do exactly the same in reverse. Write the binary digits down under the headings 1, 2, 4, 8 etc and add up all the headings which have a 1 under them. For example, to translate the binary number 1001 0010 to denary, write down

128	64	32	16	8	4	2	1
1	0	0	1	0	0	1	0

This equals 128 + 16 + 2 = 146.

To translate the binary number 146 into hexadecimal, divide it into 2 groups of 4 digits (starting from the right. The number above is therefore 92 in hexadecimal. (Notice that this is the same as **9 x 16 + 2**. Each digit in a hexadecimal number is worth 16 times as much as the one on its right.)

> Q2: Translate the binary number 0110 1110 into   (a) denary   (b) hexadecimal

> Q3: The ASCII code for the letter N is 0100 1110. Show how this would be represented in
>   (a) denary
>   (b) hexadecimal

Representation of negative numbers using twos complement

Negative numbers are commonly represented using a system called **twos complement**. To understand how this works, imagine the mileometer of a car, set at 00000 miles. If the car goes forward one mile the reading becomes 00001. If the meter was turned **back** one mile the reading would be 99999 miles. This could be interpreted as '-1' mile.

Two's complement works in the same way:

```
11111101  =  -3
11111110  =  -2
11111111  =  -1
00000000  =   0
00000001  =   1
00000010  =   2
00000011  =   3
```

Notice that if the number starts with a 1, it represents a negative number.

Adding together the binary equivalents for 3 and -3, we obtain

```
      11111101
   +  00000011
   -----------
(1)   00000000     The 'carry' of 1 is ignored.
```

Converting a negative denary number to binary

The rules for converting a negative denary number to binary can be stated as follows:

- Find the binary value of the equivalent positive decimal number
- Change all the 0s to 1s and all the 1s to 0s.
- Add 1 to the result.

An even simpler way of changing the sign of a binary number can be stated as:

- Starting from the right, leave all the digits alone up to and including the first '1'.
- Change all the other digits from 0 to 1 or from 1 to 0.

Example: - 00110100 = 11001100

> **Q4:** Convert the following numbers to binary:
>   (i) - 5   (ii) - 10   (iii) - 20
>
> **Q5:** What is the largest negative number that can be held in 8 bits, assuming the leftmost bit is a sign bit?

Binary subtraction

The easiest way of performing binary subtraction is to first convert the number to be subtracted to a negative number, and then add it. Thus, to subtract 12 from 15, using 1 byte for each number,

```
  12  =      00001100  in binary
- 12  =      11110100
  15  =      00001111
      add    11110100
             ----------
             00000011
```

> **Q6:** Subtract 23 from 123 in binary.

Exercises

1. The hexadecimal codes for the characters C, A, T are 43, 41 and 54. What are the equivalent binary codes? Why are ASCII codes often represented in hexadecimal rather than binary in printouts of the contents of sections of memory?

2. Translate the numbers 101 and -73 into binary using two's complement. Show in binary the result of adding these two binary numbers.

3. In a particular computer, integers are represented in two's complement form using 8 bits.
    (a) Show how the decimal numbers +63 and –65 will be represented.
    (b) Show the result obtained when +63 is added to +65 using this representation and comment on your answer.

4. (a) How would the decimal number 1025 be stored in binary in a 16 bit register?
   (b) Using hexadecimal as a shorthand notation, how would you write your binary number?
   (c) The hexadecimal character code for the digit 1 is 31. State how 1025 would be represented using this coding system.

Chapter 42 – Floating Point Numbers

Fixed point binary numbers

So far we have considered only **integers** – that is, whole numbers. The system can easily be extended to include fractions, as shown by the following example:

100	10	1	.	1/10	1/100
1	3	6	.	7	5

The number 136.75 represents 1 hundred, 3 tens, 6 units, 7 tenths and 5 hundredths.

In binary, the equivalent column headings are

128	64	32	16	8	4	2	1	.	1/2	1/4	1/8	1/16

The number 136.75 can be expressed as $136 + 1/2 + 1/4$, and using the column headings above converts to

128	64	32	16	8	4	2	1	.	1/2	1/4	1/8	1/16
1	0	0	0	1	0	0	0	.	1	1	0	0

Notice that the first digit after the point (called the 'binary point') is worth one half, whereas in the decimal system the equivalent digit is only worth one tenth. This means that with the same number of digits after the point, the binary system is less accurate. For example, if we write down an amount in pounds to 2 decimal places, the amount is accurate to the nearest penny. If we converted the amount to binary and only allowed two digits after the binary point, we can only hold .00 (0 pence), .01 (25 pence), .10 (50 pence) or .11 (75 pence) as the fractional part, so the amount is only accurate to the nearest 25 pence.

The following table shows some decimal fractions and their binary equivalent:

Binary fraction	Fraction	Decimal fraction	Binary fraction	Fraction	Decimal fraction
0.1	1/2	0.5	0.000001	1/64	0.015625
0.01	1/4	0.25	0.0000001	1/128	0.0078125
0.001	1/8	0.125	0.00000001	1/256	0.00390625
0.0001	1/16	0.0625	0.000000001	1/512	0.001953125
0.00001	1/32	0.03125	0.0000000001	1/1024	0.0009765625

> ➢ **Q1:** Using 1 byte to hold each number, with an imaginary binary point fixed after the fourth digit, convert the following decimal numbers to binary:
> (i) 4.25   (ii) 7.1875   (iii) 3.5625   (iv) 3.5627
>
> ➢ **Q2:** Convert the following numbers to decimal, assuming 4 bits after the point:
> (i) 0000000001101000   (ii) 0000000000110010
>
> ➢ **Q3:** What is (i) the largest number   (ii) the smallest positive number
> that can be held in two bytes, assuming 4 bits after the point?

Floating point binary

Fixed point representation allows the computer to hold fractions, but the range of numbers is still limited. Even using 4 bytes (32 bits) to hold each number, with 8 bits for the fractional part after the point, the largest number that can be held is just over 8 million. Another format is needed for holding very large numbers.

In decimal, we can show very large numbers as a **mantissa** and an **exponent**. For example

$$1{,}200{,}000{,}000{,}000 \quad \text{can be written as} \quad 0.12 \times 10^{13}$$

Here, 0.12 is called the **mantissa** and 13 is called the **exponent**. The mantissa holds the digits and the exponent defines where to place the decimal point. In the example above, the point is moved 13 places to the right.

The same technique can be used for binary numbers. For example, two bytes (16 bits) might be divided into 10 bits for the mantissa (1 sign bit and 9 digits) and 6 for the exponent.

sign	mantissa	exponent
0	110100000	000011

The sign bit (0) tells us that the number is positive. The mantissa represents 0.1101 and the exponent tells us to move the point 3 places right, so the number becomes 110.1, which converted to decimal is 6.5. Note that the point starts off between the sign bit and the first bit of the mantissa.

> **Q4:** Convert the following binary numbers to denary:
> (i) 0 101010000 000010   (ii) 0 110110000 000100

If the *exponent* is negative (indicated by a 1 in its leftmost bit), the binary point is moved *left* instead of right. So, for example,

sign	mantissa	exponent
0	100000000	111110

represents a mantissa of 0.1 and an exponent of 111110 (-2), so the whole number represents 0.001, that is, one eighth or 0.125.

The rules for converting a positive binary floating point number to decimal can be summarised as follows:

- place the point between the sign bit and the first digit of the mantissa
- convert the exponent to its equivalent decimal form (positive or negative)
- move the point right if the exponent is positive, or left if the exponent is negative, the appropriate number of places
- convert the resulting binary number to denary.

> **Q5:** Convert the following binary numbers to decimal:
> (i) 0 101000000 111111   (ii) 1 001101000 000110

Normalisation

The **precision** of the floating point representation described above depends on the number of digits stored in the mantissa. Looking once again at the more familiar decimal system:

the number 34,568,000 can be expressed as $.34568 \times 10^8$, allowing 5 digits for the mantissa,

or as $.3457 \times 10^8$, allowing only 4 places for the mantissa.

Some accuracy has been sacrificed here.

The number could also be written as .034568 x 10⁹, but then we need 6 places in the mantissa to achieve the same accuracy. In order to achieve the most accurate representation possible for a given size of mantissa, the number should be written with no leading zeros to the left of the most significant bit.

In binary, the same principle is used. Thus using a mantissa of 9 bits plus a sign bit, the number 0.000001001 would be represented in the mantissa as 0.100100000, with an exponent of 111011 (-5).

This is known as **normalised form**, and in the case of a positive number, is the form in which the first bit of the mantissa, not counting the sign bit, is 1.

Note that the mantissa of a positive number in normalised form always lies between ½ and 1.

Example: Normalise the floating point binary number 0 000110101 000010

    Step 1: Put in the assumed binary point, and convert the exponent to decimal, giving

        0.000110101   Exponent = 2.

    Step 2: Shift the number left 3 places so that the binary point immediately precedes the first 1, and subtract 3 from the exponent.

        0.110101000   Exponent = 2 - 3 = -1.

    Answer: 0.110101000 111111

> **Q6:** Normalise the following numbers, which are held with a 10-bit mantissa and a 6-bit exponent.
> (i) 0 000000110 000111   (ii) 0 000010111 000110

Negative floating point numbers

With negative numbers, the normalised form is the one in which the first bit of the mantissa, not counting the sign bit, is 0. To normalise a negative number, therefore, shift the number left until the first bit (not counting the sign bit) is 0, and adjust the exponent accordingly.

Note that the mantissa of a negative number in normalised form always lies between -1/2 and -1.

Example: Normalise the following number: 1 111100100 000011

    Step 1: Insert the assumed binary point to the right of the sign bit, and convert the exponent to decimal, giving

        1.111100100   Exponent = 3

    Step 2: Shift the number left 4 times so that the first bit of the mantissa is 0, and subtract 4 from the exponent, giving

        1.001000000   Exponent = 3 - 4 = -1

    Answer: 1 001000000 111111

> **Q7:** Normalise the following numbers:
> (i) 1 111110111 000000   (ii) 1 111111010 000011

Exercises

1. The binary pattern 1010 1011 0111 can be interpreted in a number of different ways.

   (a) State its hexadecimal representation.

   (b) State its value in denary if it represents a two's complement floating point number with an eight bit mantissa followed by a four bit exponent.

Chapter 43 – Assembly Language Instructions

The instruction set

Instructions in machine language are in the form of binary codes, with each different processor using different codes for the instruction set supported by its hardware. The instruction set of a typical computer includes the following types of instructions:

- **data transfer** such as MOVE, LOAD, STORE
- **arithmetic operations** such as ADD, SUBTRACT, MULTIPLY, DIVIDE, SHIFT
- **logical operations** such as AND, OR, NOT, exclusive-OR
- **test and branch instructions**; unconditional, conditional, subroutine calls and returns.

Data transfer instructions

Examples of data transfer instructions include:

- moving data from memory to a register, or from register to register;
- moving data from a register to memory or to an output unit;
- moving data from an output unit to a register.

Typically, two-, three- or four-character **mnemonics** are used for all machine code instructions, such as

```
MOV  R1, R2    Move contents of register R2 to R1
LD   R1, #32   Load the number 32 into R1
STO  X, R1     Store contents of R1 in memory location X
```

Arithmetic instructions

Some microprocessors offer only addition and subtraction as the basic arithmetic operations. Others offer a more comprehensive set such as:

ADD	addition	SUB	subtraction
MPY	multiplication	DIV	division
INC	increment	DEC	decrement
NEG	sign change	ABS	absolute value

After an arithmetic operation has been carried out, it is often useful to be able to test the result to see whether it was, say, zero or negative, or whether 'carry' or overflow occurred. The status register in some processors includes 4 bits referred to as N, Z, V and C which are set to 1 or 0 depending on the result of the previous operation, as follows:

If result is negative, N = 1

If result is zero, Z = 1

If overflow occurred, V = 1

If carry occurred, C = 1

These bits are called **status bits** or **condition codes**. Conditional branch instructions such as BZ (Branch if zero) check the status of the relevant status bit (often called a 'flag') and branch accordingly.

Carry and overflow

In a microprocessor using 8-bit registers, the range of integers that can be held in one register is from -128 to 127, and if the result of an arithmetic operation falls outside that range, the overflow bit will be set to 1, otherwise it will be set to 0.

Example: 0100 0000 (64)
         +   0100 0001 (65)

             1000 0001 (-127)

The sign bit has changed to 1, and the result is negative. This situation can be detected by examining the overflow bit, which will have been set by this operation.

The carry bit will **not** have been set, because there is no external carry – that is, all the binary digits still fit into the 8-bit register.

Adding two large negative numbers will cause both the overflow bit and the carry bit to be set, as shown below:

Example: 1100 0000 (-64)
         +   1011 1111 (-65)
             ----
        (1) 0111 1111 (+127)

In some situations the carry bit will be set and the overflow bit will not be set.

Example: 1111 1111 (-1)
         +   1111 1111 (-1)
             ----
        (1) 1111 1110 (-2)

Here, -2 is the correct answer and the carry bit can be ignored.

The overflow bit, then, warns that the sign of the result has been accidentally changed and action must be taken. The carry bit indicates that a ninth bit has been set and action may or may not be needed, as we shall see when performing double precision arithmetic.

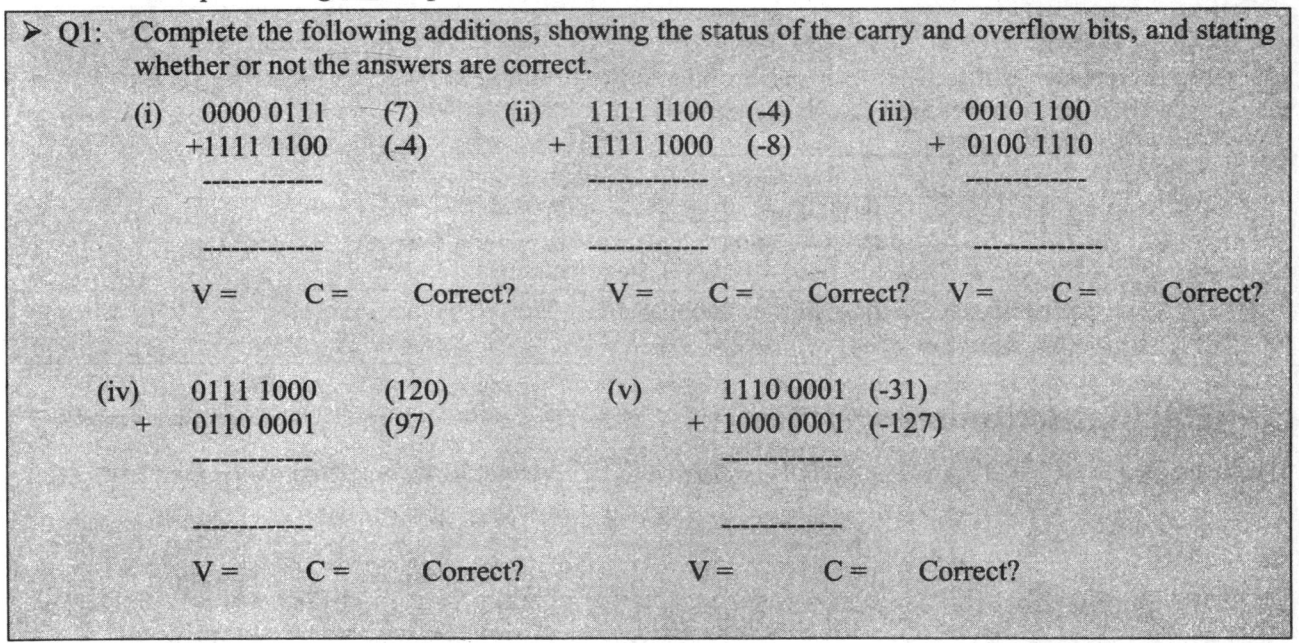

> **Q1:** Complete the following additions, showing the status of the carry and overflow bits, and stating whether or not the answers are correct.
>
> (i)   0000 0111 (7)   (ii)   1111 1100 (-4)   (iii) 0010 1100
>   + 1111 1100 (-4)   + 1111 1000 (-8)   + 0100 1110
>   ---------   ---------   ---------
>
>   ---------   ---------   ---------
>   V =   C =   Correct?   V =   C =   Correct?   V =   C =   Correct?
>
> (iv) 0111 1000 (120)   (v)   1110 0001 (-31)
>   + 0110 0001 (97)   + 1000 0001 (-127)
>   ---------   ---------
>
>   ---------   ---------
>   V =   C =   Correct?   V =   C =   Correct?

Module 4 *Processing and Programming Techniques*

Shift instructions

There are generally 2 or 3 different shift operations available: **logical**, **arithmetic** and **rotate**.

A **logical** shift right causes the least significant bit (lsb) to be shifted into the carry bit, and a zero moves in to occupy the vacated space.

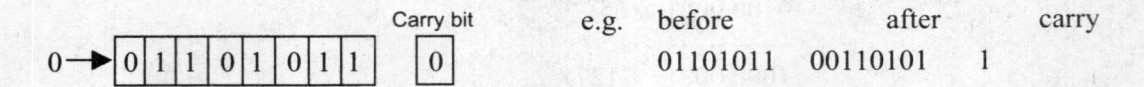

```
                                    Carry bit      e.g.   before       after      carry
0 → [0|1|1|0|1|0|1|1]                 [0]                 01101011    00110101     1
```

It is useful for examining the least significant bit of a number. After the operation, the carry bit can be tested and a conditional branch instruction executed.

> **Q2:** Shift the binary pattern 0100 0111 right once and then left once, showing the contents of the carry bit after each shift.

An **arithmetic shift** is similar but it takes into account the value of the sign bit, which always remains the same. Shifting right has the effect of dividing by 2, and shifting left multiplies by 2. In a right shift, if the sign bit is 1, 1 is moved in from the left instead of 0.

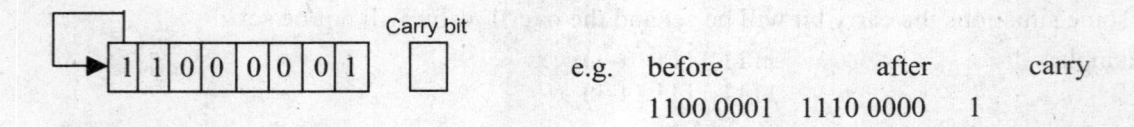

```
                                    Carry bit      e.g.   before       after      carry
  → [1|1|0|0|0|0|0|1]                 [ ]                 1100 0001   1110 0000    1
```

> **Q3:** Convert the number 12 to binary, and then multiply it by 4 using arithmetic shifts. Convert the result back to decimal.

> **Q4:** Convert the number -16 to binary, and divide by 8 using arithmetic shifts.

A **rotate** or **circular** shift is useful for performing shifts in multiple bytes. In a circular right shift, the value in the carry bit is moved into the vacated position.

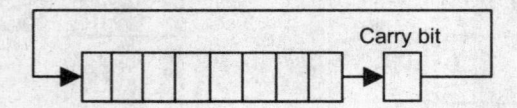

```
                                    Carry bit
  → [ | | | | | | | ] →               [ ]
```

> **Q5:** Show the result of a circular shift on the bit pattern 0100 1100, assuming the carry bit was set to 1 before the operation.

Logical instructions

The instructions OR, NOT, AND and XOR (exclusive OR) have the following effects:

		OR	NOT	AND	XOR
Inputs	– A	1010	1010	1010	1010
	– B	1100		1100	1100
		----	----	----	----
Result		1110	0101	1000	0110

The NOT function can be used to find the two's complement of a number:

```
        A            0110 0111
        NOT A        1001 1000
        add 1                 1
                     --------------
        2's complement 1001 1001
```

The assembly language instructions to carry out this operation would be similar to those shown below:

```
LDA  #01100111B    ;load binary number into accumulator
COMA               ;complement the number in the accumulator
ADDA #1            ;add 1 to the accumulator
```

The OR function can be used to set certain bits to 1 without affecting the other bits in the binary code. For example, a system has eight lights that can be turned on (output 1) or off (output 0), controlled by an 8-bit binary code. At present, lights 1 to 4 are on. We now wish to turn on lights 5 and 7 as well.

```
Light number      1 2 3 4 5 6 7 8
Present output    1 1 1 1 0 0 0 0
OR with           0 0 0 0 1 0 1 0
                  ------------------
Result            1 1 1 1 1 0 1 0
```

The assembly language code for this operation could be

```
LDA  LIGHT     ;load contents of LIGHT into accumulator
ORA  #1010B    ;OR operation with binary 1010
STA  LIGHT     ;store result back in LIGHT
```

The AND function can be used for masking out certain bits of a number. For example, if we input the ASCII character 3 at the keyboard, the ASCII pattern 00110011 is input. In order to change this to a pure binary number, we need to mask out the first 4 bits.

> Q6: Use an AND operation to convert an ASCII digit to a pure binary number.

> Q7: Devise an OR operation that will convert a pure binary digit to its equivalent ASCII code.

An XOR function can be used to 'toggle' bits on and off. All 1s become 0s, and all 0s become 1s.

> Q8: Use an XOR function to find the 2's complement of a number held in NUM. Store it in NEGNUM.

Conditional branches

These instructions may test the flags in the status register; typical instructions are to 'Branch if the last result was zero', 'Branch if there was a carry' and so on, with mnemonic codes such as BZ, BC etc.

Compare instructions may be used to compare the contents of two registers. If the contents of the two registers are equal, the zero flag in the status register is set to 1 and may be tested.

Example: Write assembly code instructions to branch to LABEL1 if the contents of registers R1 and R2 are equal.

Solution:
```
CMP R1,R2      ;compare contents of R1 and R2
BZ  LABEL1     ;branch if they are equal to LABEL1
```

Unconditional branches

An instruction such as JUMP 1000 causes an unconditional branch to an instruction held in location 1000. The contents of the program counter (PC) will be changed to hold the address 1000. In the case of a subroutine call, the return address has to be stored so that control can be returned to the next instruction after the CALL. This is usually done by pushing the address of the next instruction onto the **stack**, and updating the stack pointer. When the RETURN from the subroutine is encountered, the address is popped from the stack and loaded into the PC.

Exercises

1. Write the assembly language equivalent of the following block of high level language code, taking care to comment each instruction where its meaning may not be clear.

    x ← 0;
    Repeat
       x ← x + 1;
    Until x = 100000;

2. Write the sequence of key assembly language instructions, with annotation, which corresponds to the following block of high level language code:

    If N = 10
       Then N ← 1
       Else N ← N + 1
    EndIf

3. An eight bit register contains two four-bit codes (bits 0 to 3 and bits 4 to 7).

7	6	5	4	3	2	1	0

    Describe how, using shifting and masking, copies of each of these four-bit codes can be obtained from the register.

4. What would be the result of performing **each** of the following logical operations?
    - (i) NOT 00110110
    - (ii) 00110010 AND 00001111
    - (iii) 00000011 OR 11110000
    - (iv) 00010011 XOR 00010011

Chapter 44 – Instruction Formats and Addressing Modes

Instruction format for an 8-bit microprocessor

Machine code instructions, just like numbers, letters and other symbols, are stored as an arrangement of bits in a binary code. In an 8-bit microprocessor, some instructions may occupy just one byte, while others will occupy two or three bytes. The first byte will always contain the 'op code' – the code for that particular operation or instruction.

> Q1: How many different instruction formats are possible if 8 bits are used for the op code?

Zero address instructions

Instructions which occupy one byte do not involve an address – they are instructions such as

```
HALT    ; stop execution
CCF     ; clear the carry flag
CCC     ; clear all status flags
SL      ; shift the contents of the accumulator left one bit
```

PC [| | | | | | |] op code

One address instructions

One address instructions occupy two bytes; examples of such instructions are

```
ADD  X     ; add the contents of X to the accumulator
LDI  #23   ; load the number 23 into the accumulator
BN   L1    ; branch to label L1 if contents of accumulator are negative
```

PC   [| | | | | | |] op code

PC + 1 [| | | | | | |] operand

Two address instructions

Two address instructions occupy three bytes, either because the instruction involves two operands, or because the address of the operand is too large to fit into one byte. Examples of such instructions are

```
LDA MEM2      ; load contents of MEM2 (eg location 0DFF hex) into acc.
ADD C, MEM1   ; add contents of location MEM1 to register C
EXOR A, MASK  ; exclusive OR contents of A with MASK
```

PC   [| | | | | | |] op code

PC + 1 [| | | | | | |] low address or operand 1

PC + 2 [| | | | | | |] high address or operand 2

In the first example above, FF will be stored in PC+1, and 0D in PC+2. The processor will determine from the op code how to interpret all the bytes making up the instruction.

A 16-bit instruction format

Machines which use 16-bit words also make use of 0-address, 1-address and 2-address formats, taking up one, two or three words. However, with 16 bits obviously more information can be stored in each word, and a typical instruction format is shown below.

1-word instruction

0 1 2 3	4 5	6 7 8 9 10 11 12 13 14 15
Function code	Mode	Operand address

The first 4 bits are used for the op code, and bits 4 and 5 are used to indicate the **addressing mode** being used (see below).

Microprocessors may have more than one instruction format for the one-word instructions, depending on the type of instruction being used. Instruction formats indicate not only what operation is to be performed but also how many locations are being used to hold the actual instruction, so that the PC (program counter) can be correctly incremented. The number of memory locations used for the address will depend partly on the mode of addressing being used.

> **Q2:** Does the number of words occupied by an instruction have any bearing on how fast the instruction will execute? Explain your answer.

Addressing modes

There are several different ways in which the computer can calculate the addresses holding the source and/or destination of the data being processed in a particular instruction. These are called **addressing modes**, and are described below, starting with immediate addressing.

Immediate addressing

In some instructions, the data to be operated on is held as part of the instruction format. In a 2-byte instruction format, the operand is therefore not an address at all, but a value (indicated by #). Typical instructions using immediate addressing are:

```
LDAI #35H     ; load the hexadecimal value 35 into the accumulator
MVI  C, #8    ; move the value 8 into register C
```

This type of addressing could be used, for example, to initialise a counter to a particular value.

Direct addressing

In this mode, the operand gives the address of the data to be used in the operation. For example:

```
LDA MEM       ; load contents of location MEM into the accumulator
```

The number of locations which can be addressed using direct addressing is limited because only say, 10 out of 16 bits are available to hold the address, and often more than one word is used for holding the address.

This type of instruction is slow, for locating the data involves three or maybe four memory operations; three to load the 3-byte instruction, and then another to go and get the data to be operated on.

> **Q3:** If 16 bits are allowed for an address, what is the maximum memory address that can be referenced using direct addressing?

Indirect addressing

With this type of addressing, the address of the data in memory is held in one of the registers, and the operand of the instruction holds the number of the register to refer to.

```
LDA  (7)       ; load the contents of the memory location
                 whose address is in register 7.
```

Generally, the 8-bit or 16-bit op code contains all the information needed; what operation is to be performed, and which register holds the data address.

> **Q4:** The store locations 100 and 120 contain the values 120 and 200 respectively. What value would be loaded into the accumulator by **each** of the following instructions?
> (i)   LDAI 100   ; LOAD immediate 100
> (ii) LDA 100   ; LOAD direct 100
> (iii) LDA (100)   ; LOAD indirect 100

Indexed addressing

This is a variation on indirect addressing, where the operand address is calculated by adding to a base address the value held in an index register. Using this mode of addressing, the address of the operand can be modified by operating on the contents of the index register.

For example, suppose we wish to set to zero the contents of TABLE to TABLE + 99. Using an index register X, the following instructions can be used:

```
        LDA #0        ;load 0 into the accumulator
        LDX #0        ;load 0 into the index register
LOOP    STA TABLE(X)  ;store contents of accumulator in TABLE + X
        INX           ;increment the index register
        CPX #99       ;compare X with 99
        BNE LOOP      ;branch if not equal to LOOP
```

Relative addressing

This type of addressing is often used in branch instructions to specify where the next instruction is located relative to the instruction whose address is held in the PC. An example is:

```
        JMP    +10    ;branch to the instruction 10 bytes on.
```

A 'jump relative' with a one-byte operand can only jump forwards or backwards 127 bytes. Relative jumps allow the code to be **relocatable** anywhere in memory.

Exercises

1. A 32 bit instruction has 8 bits allocated to the operation code and the remaining 24 bits allocated to the operand. Discuss briefly the consequences of reducing the number of bits allocated to the operation code by 1.

2. Stating any assumptions you are making, explain the meaning of the assembly language instruction **ADD 146** where the address is
   (a) An indirect address.
   (b) An indexed address.

Module 4 Processing and Programming Techniques

3. Distinguish between direct addressing and indirect addressing in machine code.

4. (a) A particular computer uses a 24-bit word length.
   (i) Suggest an allocation of the 24 bits for a single address instruction explaining the significance of the allocation you have chosen.
   (ii) Suggest an allocation of the 24 bits for a two address instruction where one of the addresses refers to one of 7 available registers and the other refers to a memory location.
   (4)

   (b) A particular assembly language program is being processed using the fetch execute cycle. The last statement in this program is a conditional jump statement.
   (i) List the steps in the fetch phase of the cycle, identifying the main registers involved.
   (ii) Describe how an unconditional jump statement is executed.
   (iii) Explain why the position of the conditional jump statement as the last statement in this program is probably due to a mistake and suggest two types of statement which you would expect to see as the last statement in an assembly language program.

Chapter 45 – High Level Languages

High and low level languages

Computer languages may be classified as being either **low level**, (such as assembly language) or **high level** (such as Pascal, BASIC, PROLOG or 'C').

The characteristics of a **low level language** are:

- they are machine oriented; an assembly language program written for one machine will not work on any other type of machine (unless it happens to use the same processor chip);
- each assembly language statement (apart from macros) generally translates into one machine code instruction. Hence, programming is a lengthy and time-consuming business.

Assembly language is generally used when there is a requirement to manipulate individual bits and bytes, write code that executes as fast as possible, or occupies as little memory as possible. An example of an application with all three of these requirements is a **device driver**; that is, a program which allows the computer to interface with an external device such as a printer. When you buy a printer to use with a PC, for example, it will come with an appropriate printer driver supplied on a floppy disk, and the driver has to be installed on the hard disk before the printer can be used.

The characteristics of a **high level language** are:

- They are not machine oriented; in theory they are portable which means that a program written for one machine will run (with minor modifications) on any other machine for which the appropriate compiler or interpreter is available.
- They are problem oriented; each high level language has structures and facilities appropriate to a particular use or type of problem. For example FORTRAN was developed for use in solving mathematical problems, whereas COBOL was written especially for data processing applications. Some languages such as Pascal were developed as general purpose languages.
- Statements in a high level language generally resemble English sentences or mathematical expressions and these languages tend to be easier to learn and understand than assembly language. Each statement in a high level language will be translated into several machine code instructions.

Typical high level language facilities

High level languages have many facilities not found in low level languages; for example:

- selection structures such as **if .. then .. else**, **case**;
- iteration structures such as **while .. endwhile**, **repeat .. until** and **for .. endfor**. Instead of selection and iteration statements, assembly language programmers must use conditional branch statements such as **branch if equal, branch if non-zero**, etc.
- built in routines to simplify input and output (e.g. **readln**, **writeln** in Pascal);
- built in functions such as **sqr, log, chr**;
- data structures such as **string, array, record**.

Procedural (imperative) languages

High-level languages such as Pascal, C, COBOL and BASIC are classified as **procedural** or **imperative** languages. The program consists of a sequence of instructions which the computer will execute in a specified order. There are dozens of procedural languages in use today, including:

- **Pascal**, which was developed in the 1970s to teach structured programming.
- **FORTRAN (FORmula TRANslation)** developed for use in scientific and engineering applications in the 1950s and still used. The features which make it suitable for mathematical applications include the following:
  - it has a large library of inbuilt mathematical functions such as log, sqrt, sin, arctan etc.;
  - comprehensive libraries of statistical, scientific and engineering routines are readily available, well-documented and easy to incorporate into the user's program;
  - double precision arithmetic (using, say, 64 bits instead of 32 bits to represent a real number) means that calculations can be performed with great accuracy;
  - good array handling capabilities mean that it is suitable for solving, for example, large sets of simultaneous equations.
- **COBOL (COmmon Business Oriented Language),** developed in the 1950's (see Chapter 4). A new version of COBOL called COBOL97 was issued in 1997 so in spite of predictions that it would be dead and buried before the end of the century, it looks set to continue for some time yet! It has many facilities which make it suitable for data processing applications, including:
  - good validation facilities;
  - a **sort** verb to allow files to be sorted into any sequence;
  - excellent file-handling capabilities;
  - good report-formatting facilities;
  - facility to access databases from within a COBOL program.
- **C**, developed by Dennis Richie at Bell Laboratories in the USA around 1972. It was originally developed for systems programming for the operating system UNIX. It is a relatively low-level language which has many of the advantages of Assembly language (facilitating very efficient programs for operating systems, text processing and compilers) and at the same time has the advantages of a high level language in that it is easy to learn, portable and hides the details of the computer's architecture from the user.

Object-oriented languages

Languages such as Java, C++ and Delphi are called **object-oriented** languages. In this type of language, the programmer uses objects, which are data items with all the processing possible on the data item attached to it. These languages are widely used for developing Windows applications. Object-oriented programming is discussed in more detail in the next chapter.

Declarative languages

There is another class of programming language called **declarative** languages which consist of a series of facts and rules about a particular subject, rather than a sequence of instructions. Prolog is an example of a declarative language, and is discussed in more depth in Chapters 47 and 48.

Languages for real-time embedded systems

As computers have become smaller, faster and more reliable, their range of applications has widened. One of the fastest expanding areas of computer applications is **embedded systems**, in which the computer is just one component within a larger engineering system. Such systems include:

- a microprocessor-controlled washing machine or video recorder;
- a modern jet aircraft;
- a system for controlling traffic lights;
- a process control system for controlling the flow of water along a pipe by means of a valve;
- a robot used in a car assembly plant.

Some of these systems may be extremely large and complex; for example the US Air Force C-17 transport aircraft has 19 different embedded computers incorporating over 80 microprocessors on board which utilise about 1.35 million lines of software code.

Languages for programming real-time systems need the following facilities:

- **real-time control facilities.** The programmer needs to be able to specify times at which actions are to be performed or completed, or take readings at regular time intervals, say every 5 seconds. For example an electric power station needs to increase supply at 5pm on Monday to Friday to cope with the surge in demand caused by families returning home, switching on lights, cooking dinner and so on. Traffic lights at an intersection may change every 30 seconds or less if an oncoming car is detected coming from a particular direction.

  An embedded system also needs to be able to recognise and act upon the **non-occurrence** of some external event. For example, a temperature sensor in a nuclear reactor may be required to log a new reading every second, with the failure to give a reading within 10 seconds being defined as a fault. The programmer has to be able to code a **timeout**; that is, what action to take after the 10 seconds are up.

- **interaction with hardware interfaces.** The language must contain statements to monitor sensors and control actuators (which make something happen). It also needs to be able to identify and handle interrupts from devices such as the sensor detecting oncoming traffic.

- **ability to support concurrent programming.** More than one action may need to be carried out simultaneously.

The languages C, Ada, Modula-2 and Occam all contain these facilities.

Criteria for selecting a programming language

A programming task can be made considerably easier, faster to complete, and more maintainable when a suitable language for the task is chosen. Criteria for making this choice will include:

- the nature of the application;
- the availability of facilities within the language for implementing the software design;
- the availability of a suitable compiler/interpreter for the hardware;
- the expertise of the programmers.

Exercises

1. When designing a solution to a particular problem, a systems analyst may have to choose an appropriate high level language. Give **two** criteria which the analyst might consider in making this choice, justifying the choice of each of these criteria.

Module 4 Processing and Programming Techniques

Chapter 46 – Object-Oriented Programming

Windows applications

At the beginning of the twenty-first century, Windows applications are to be found running on virtually every PC in every office in the country. These applications function in a completely different way from programs written using procedural languages such as COBOL, FORTRAN or Pascal. Such programs started at the beginning and ran to completion in a sequence determined by the programmer, looping and branching according to the programmed instructions and the data presented to the program. Windows programs, on the other hand, are **event-driven** – nothing happens until the user moves the mouse, presses a key, selects from a menu, presses a command button, clicks a tool on a toolbar etc.

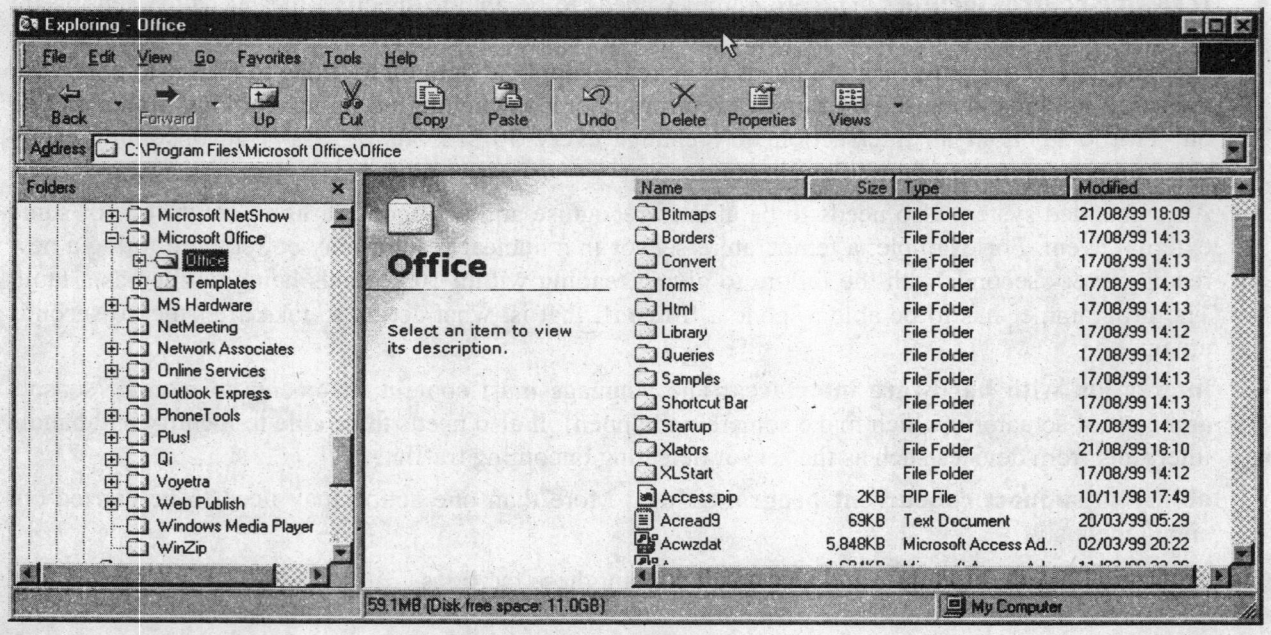

Figure 46.1: A Windows 98 screen with objects

Traditional programming methods and the languages they use are not suitable for a Windows environment. Instead, **object-oriented programming** (OOP) languages such as Visual Basic, Visual C++ and Delphi have been developed to write Windows applications.

Objects and classes

An object class is the collection of attributes and activities (called **methods** in Delphi and Visual Basic) that an object within the classification can have or perform. For example, HUMAN is a real-world classification, and individuals in this class have attributes like height, eye-colour and gender. Members of this class have activities associated with them – they eat, breathe, sleep and think. Once you have defined a class in an object-oriented language, you can then define instances of the object class. Nelson Mandela, Michael Owen and Gwyneth Paltrow are all instances of the human class. (Note that 'boy' and 'girl' are not instances of the human class – they are **subclasses**.)

218

Chapter 46 – Object-Oriented Programming

> ➤ Q1: 'PC' is a real-world classification. Name several attributes and activities associated with this class. Identify several instances of the class.
>
> ➤ Q2: Think of some other classes, and list the attributes and activities associated with each class. Identify instances of each class.

Objects in Windows

An **object** can be thought of as an independent procedure that contains both the instructions and data to perform some task, and the code necessary to handle various messages it may receive. Objects in Windows include forms, dialogue boxes, command buttons, list boxes and text boxes.

For example, a dialogue box in Windows is physically distinct from any other object. The code for the dialogue box contains all the instructions necessary to draw the box on the screen, display a text string in the title bar, and include a control-menu box in the top left-hand corner. The dialogue box object has **attributes** which are given values to define its colour and the thickness of its border. The object also contains all the procedures needed to react to events which might occur, such as a user dragging the box or clicking the **Yes** button.

When a dialogue box is called up, other objects such as a message string and command buttons are also displayed. (See figure below.) Each of these is an entirely separate and independent object with its own attributes and methods.

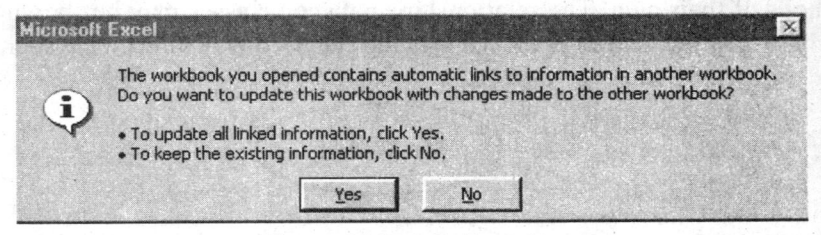

Figure 46.2: A dialogue box

> ➤ Q3: The command buttons marked **Yes** and **No** in the figure above are objects that have attributes such as **Name, Caption, Width, Height, Position**. They each have a different **On Click** method (i.e. procedure that is executed when the button is clicked). Can they be members of a common class of **Command Buttons**?

Encapsulation

In traditional third-generation languages such as Pascal, the programmer can choose to write structured, modular programs and divide the code up into a number of procedures. However it is often a matter of personal preference whether a particular task is broken up into one, two or three procedures.

In object-oriented programming, an object usually represents some real concept such as a dialogue box, command button or list. It is therefore much more intuitive to decide what procedures are needed for the events which may affect the object.

An object contains all that is needed to make that particular aspect of the program carry out its tasks:

- the procedures (methods) that are needed to respond to events that may occur;
- the data that is needed by these procedures.

The process of bundling together procedures and data is referred to as **encapsulation**.

Figure 46.3 below shows the data and procedures for a command button object.

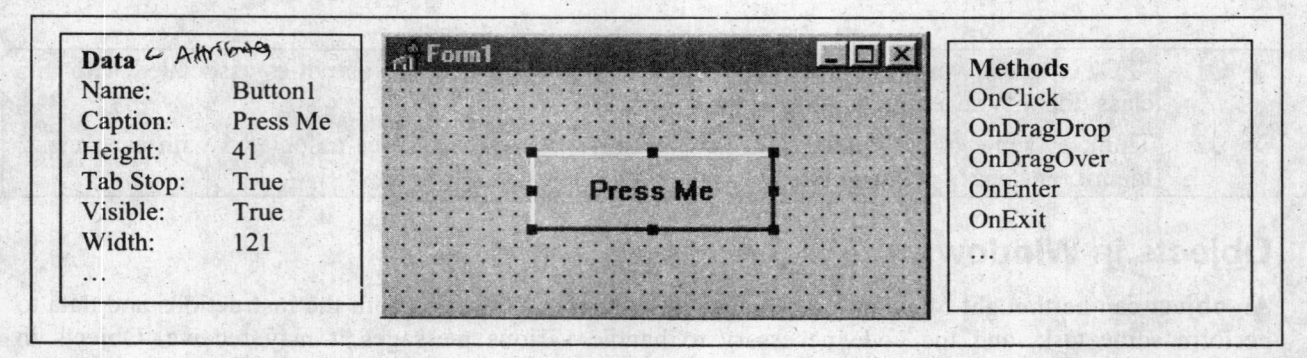

Module 4 Processing and Programming Techniques

Data ← Attributes		Methods
Name:	Button1	OnClick
Caption:	Press Me	OnDragDrop
Height:	41	OnDragOver
Tab Stop:	True	OnEnter
Visible:	True	OnExit
Width:	121	...
...		

Figure 46.3: Data and procedures for command button object

Inheritance

Many objects are related to other objects in some way. For example, a sports car and a lorry are both types of vehicle. Humans, tigers and whales are all members of the MAMMAL class. You can often define a new type of object by amending the definition of some other object. In object-oriented programming, this has the advantage of allowing the reuse of existing code, and is known as **inheritance**.

The class that you start with is called the **base class**. From the base class you can derive other classes which inherit all the properties and methods of the base class. In addition the new classes can have new properties and methods of their own. The relationships between classes may be shown in an **Inheritance diagram**. Notice which way the arrows point – this is the standard way of drawing such a diagram.

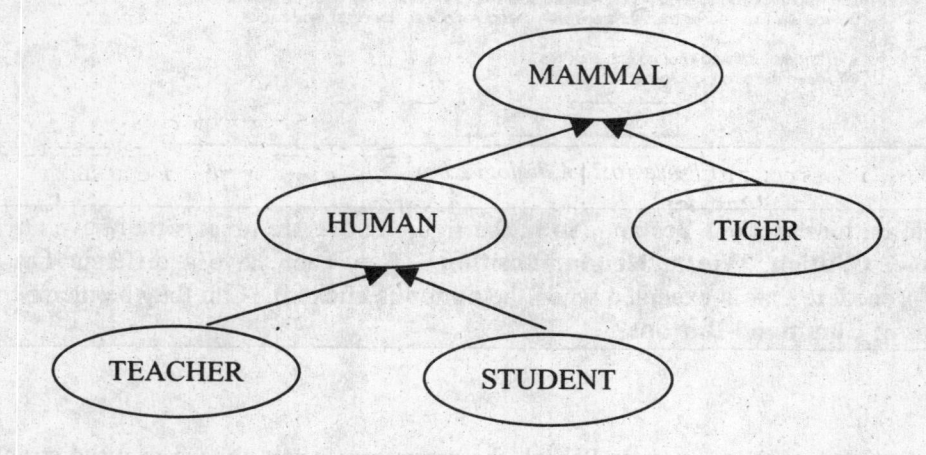

Figure 46.4: An Inheritance diagram

Another way of drawing an Inheritance diagram, showing more detail, is shown below.

Chapter 46 – Object-Oriented Programming

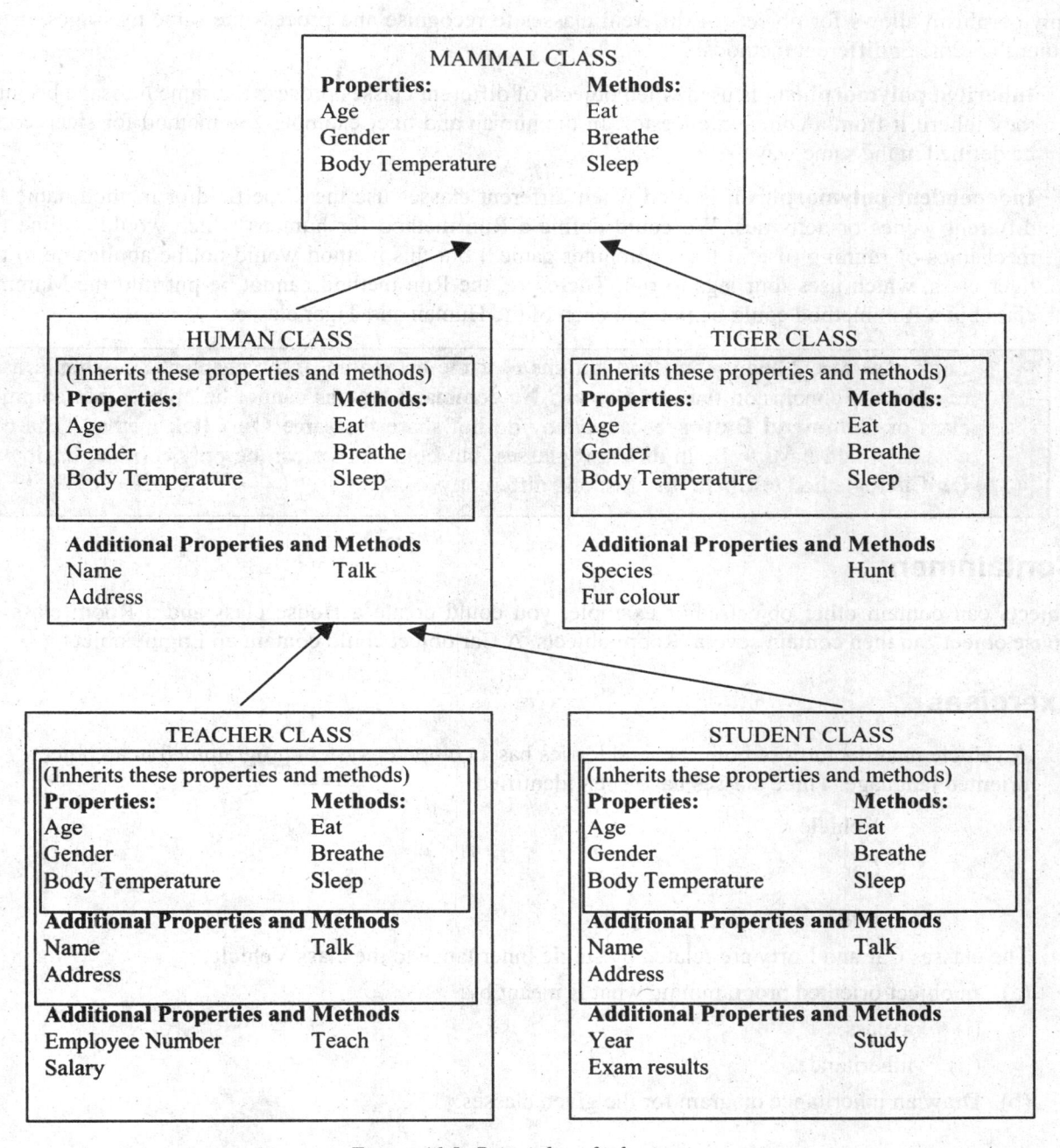

```
                    MAMMAL CLASS
         Properties:          Methods:
         Age                  Eat
         Gender               Breathe
         Body Temperature     Sleep
```

HUMAN CLASS
(Inherits these properties and methods)
Properties:	Methods:
Age	Eat
Gender	Breathe
Body Temperature	Sleep

Additional Properties and Methods
Name	Talk
Address	

TIGER CLASS
(Inherits these properties and methods)
Properties:	Methods:
Age	Eat
Gender	Breathe
Body Temperature	Sleep

Additional Properties and Methods
Species	Hunt
Fur colour	

TEACHER CLASS
(Inherits these properties and methods)
Properties:	Methods:
Age	Eat
Gender	Breathe
Body Temperature	Sleep

Additional Properties and Methods
Name	Talk
Address	

Additional Properties and Methods
Employee Number	Teach
Salary	

STUDENT CLASS
(Inherits these properties and methods)
Properties:	Methods:
Age	Eat
Gender	Breathe
Body Temperature	Sleep

Additional Properties and Methods
Name	Talk
Address	

Additional Properties and Methods
Year	Study
Exam results	

Figure 46.5: Principles of inheritance

Polymorphism

Two or more classes that are derived from the same base class are said to be **polymorphic**. Polymorphism simply means that two objects may share many characteristics but have unique features of their own.

> ➢ Q4: Which classes in the above inheritance diagram are polymorphic?

When new classes are derived from a base class they may redefine some of the base methods. Polymorphism allows for objects of different classes to recognise and process the same messages, using either the same or different methods.

- **Inherited polymorphism** is used when objects of different classes process the same message because they inherit it from a common ancestor. In the human and tiger example, the method for sleep could be defined in the same way.

- **Independent polymorphism** is used when different classes use the same field or method name for different values or activities. We could define a Run method for humans which would outline the mechanics of running (useful for a computer game?) but this method would not be applicable to the tiger class, which uses four legs to run. Therefore, the Run method cannot be put into the Mammal class but a Run method could be put into each of the Human and Tiger classes.

> Look back at Q2 about command buttons near the beginning of the chapter. You should have reached the conclusion that the **Yes** and **No** command buttons cannot be objects in a common class of **Command Button** because they do not share the same **On Click** method. The two objects would have to be in different classes, but both classes can be polymorphic, having an **On Click** method to which they respond differently.

Containment

Objects can contain other objects. For example, you could create a House class and a Room class. A House object can then contain several Room objects. A Car object could contain an Engine object.

Exercises

1. A vehicle manufacturer of both cars and lorries has a computer system programmed in an object-oriented language. Three classes have been identified:

    Vehicle

    Car

    Lorry

    The classes Car and Lorry are related by single inheritance to the class Vehicle.

    (a) In object-oriented programming what is meant by:
    - (i) a class;
    - (ii) inheritance?

    (b) Draw an inheritance diagram for the given classes.

2. (a) For a language to be classified as object-oriented, it must satisfy **three** requirements. State these requirements.

    (b) In object-oriented programming what is meant by
    - (i) a *class*?
    - (ii) *inheritance*?

Chapter 47 – Prolog Programming (1)

Procedural and declarative languages

Human beings possess two different kinds of knowledge:

- **declarative** knowledge – facts about people, objects and events and how they relate to each other;
- **procedural** knowledge – how to do things, how to use their declarative knowledge, and how to work things out.

Computers may also be programmed with these two different kinds of knowledge.

High level languages such as Pascal, COBOL or FORTRAN are all examples of **procedural** languages, where the program consists of a sequence of instructions telling the machine what to do. The programmer has to show exactly what steps must be executed in order to solve the problem, and in what order, for any given set of data. As instructions are executed, program variables are modified using assignment statements.

Declarative languages such as **Prolog** work in a different way.

Prolog

Prolog (which stands for PROgramming in LOGic) is a particular type of declarative language known as a **logic** programming language. It has the following characteristics:

- Instead of defining **how** a problem is solved, the programmer states the facts and rules associated with the problem. A **fact** is something that is always unconditionally true, and a **rule** is true depending on a given condition.

- The **order** in which the rules and facts are stated is not important, unlike the statements in an imperative (i.e. procedural) language. It is therefore easy to add new rules, delete rules or change existing rules.

- Executing a Prolog program involves stating a goal to be achieved and allowing Prolog to determine whether the goal can be achieved with the given facts and rules.

- The route through the program does not have to be explicitly stated by the programmer. Like Theseus with his ball of string in the Minotaur's maze, who could select a route at a junction and always find his way back if it proved to be a dead end, Prolog will select a possible route through a program and if that fails, it will **backtrack** to that point and try another route until either the goal is achieved or there are no further routes to try.

Prolog is especially well suited to programming **expert systems**, which embody the facts and rules about a particular field of knowledge such as oil prospecting, social security regulations or medical diagnosis. In an expert system, facts and rules are described in the program to form the 'expert knowledge', and a user can then query the program to obtain answers to problems, given that certain facts or conditions are true.

It is also suited to the **processing of natural language** (trying to get a computer to understand ordinary English, Chinese or Urdu) because each of these languages has its own syntax rules which can be stated in the program to help the computer decide whether a group of words make a sentence, and what it means.

Module 4 Processing and Programming Techniques

The example of a Prolog program which follows can be used to determine relationships between members of a family – useful perhaps in one of those 500-page family sagas when you can never remember who is related to whom...

The 'knowledge' that has to be programmed is a representation of the family tree below, and rules about relationships.

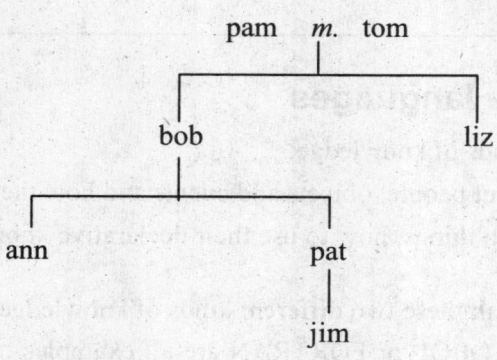

```
            pam  m.  tom
               |
       ┌───────┴───────┐
      bob              liz
       |
   ┌───┴───┐
  ann     pat
           |
          jim
```

A Prolog program

```
/* Family tree: program by Matthew Todd, 1.12.93 */
/* facts */
    parent(pam,bob).
    parent(tom,bob).
    parent(tom,liz).
    parent(bob,ann).
    parent(bob,pat).
    parent(pat,jim).
    female(pam).
    male(tom).
    male(bob).
    female(liz).
    female(pat).
    female(ann).
    male(jim).

/*rules*/
    grandparent(X,Y):-              (ie X is a grandparent of Y if
        parent(X,Z),                    X is a parent of Z and
        parent(Z,Y).                    Z is a parent of Y)

    mother(X,Y):-                   (X is the mother of Y if
        parent(X,Y),                    X is a parent of Y and
        female(X).                      X is female)

    father(X,Y):-
        parent(X,Y),
        male(X).

    sister(X,Y):-
        parent(Z,X),
        parent(Z,Y),
        female(X).
```

```
brother(X,Y):-
           parent(Z,X),
           parent(Z,Y),
           male(X).
```

Queries can now be made to find out relationships; for example if the user wants to know "Does Liz have a brother?" the query is typed in at the **?** prompt as follows:

       `?- brother(X,liz).`   and the program will respond

       `X=bob`

To ask "Who is the mother of Bob?" type

       `?- mother (X,bob).`   and the program will respond

       `X=pam`

Type   `?- grandparent(bob,Who)` and the program will respond

       `Who=jim`

       `?- brother(Who,ann)`   and the program will respond

       `no`   `(because ann has no brother)`

Practical Prolog

It will be very helpful to have some practical experience of programming in Prolog. Many different versions of Prolog are available for downloading free from various sites on the Internet. The examples used below use a version called SWI-Prolog, which can be downloaded from the site

http://www.swi.psy.uva.nl/projects/SWI-Prolog/download.html

When you install this version of Prolog, it will create a folder with a name of your choice, containing various subfolders. In the screenshot below, it has been installed into a folder named **prologswi**.

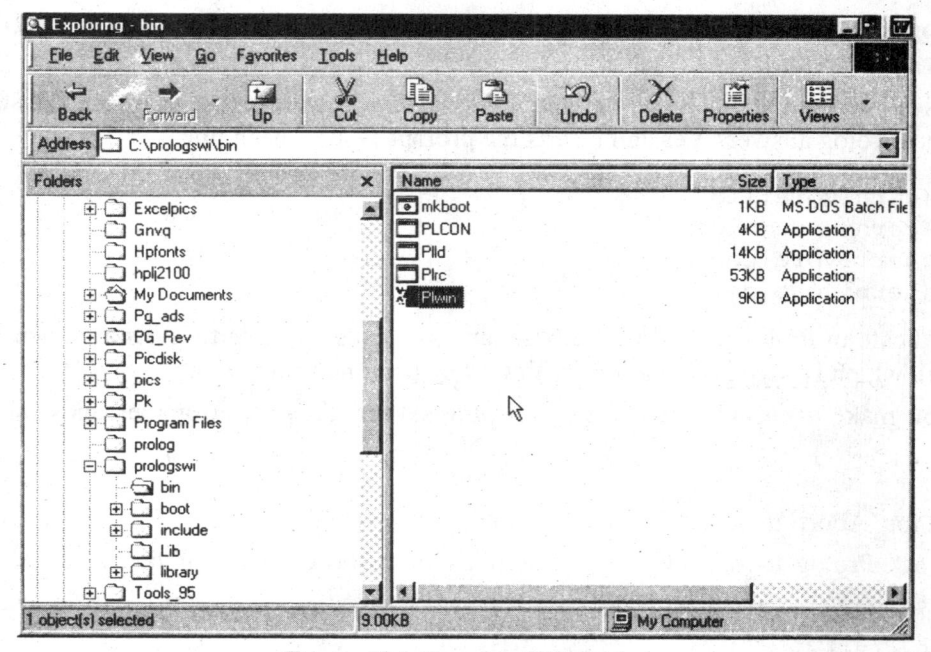

Figure 47.1: Running SWI-Prolog

To run Prolog, you can double-click **Plwin** in the **bin** subfolder.

Module 4 Processing and Programming Techniques

Using facts in Prolog

A Prolog program consists not of instructions but of a database of facts and rules. These facts and rules are then acted on by the Prolog interpreter in response to goals that you give it.

A fact consists of a predicate and zero, one or more arguments.

e.g.   carnivore(lion).
       isa (table, furniture).
       animal(reptile, large, crocodile).

Predicate names must be **atoms**, but arguments can consist of a variety of data types. Prolog recognises data types without you having to declare them at the top of the program. The most common data types are:

Integers	consist entirely of digits.
Reals	consist of digits and a decimal point.
Atoms	start with a lower case letter. They can contain numbers, letters and the underscore.
Strings	any characters enclosed in single quotes.
Variables	start with an uppercase letter.

Look at the sample program above. Note that each line has to end in a full-stop, and that the names *pam*, *bob* etc. have to be written with lower case letters because they are atoms, not variables.

Entering items in a Prolog database

You can enter facts and rules while Prolog is running, but they will all be deleted as soon as you close Prolog, so this is a not a very practical way of programming! Nevertheless it is a quick way to get started on your first Prolog program, and you can try it now.

- Start Prolog (by double-clicking **plwin** as described above, or however you are instructed to do it in your particular version).
- You will see the prompt ?-   Type the text shown below, remembering to type a full-stop at the end of each line. Prolog answers **Yes** and inserts the prompt ?- after each line.

```
assert(carnivore(lion)).
assert(carnivore(tiger).
assert(herbivore(cow).
assert(herbivore(deer)).
```

Assert is a predicate in Prolog's built-in database, and succeeds by 'asserting' its argument, for example **carnivore(lion)**, which is why Prolog answers **Yes** after each line is entered.

Note that if you make a mistake, Prolog may display several lines of error messages followed by the prompt

```
Action?
```

You can type **a** for 'Abort' to get back to the prompt.

You can now ask Prolog to answer simple questions from the database of facts. For example, at the prompt type

```
carnivore(lion).
```

Prolog finds this fact in the database and replies **Yes**.

To find all the carnivores in the database, type

    carnivore(X).

Prolog will respond **lion**. To get Prolog to continue searching, type a semi-colon. Prolog responds **tiger**. Type another semi-colon and Prolog responds **No**, since there are no more carnivores in the database.

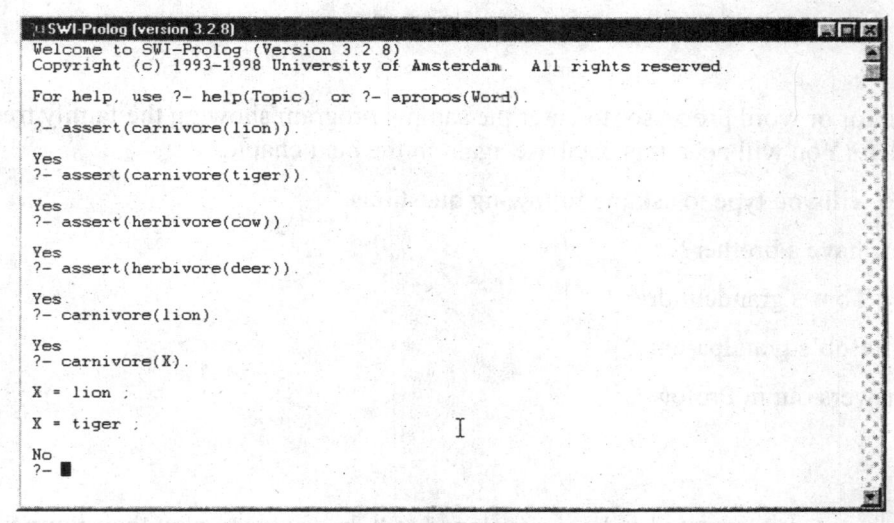

Figure 47.2: Inserting facts and making queries in Prolog

Entering rules

We can add a rule to say that X eats meat if X is a carnivore. Similarly Y eats grass if Y is a herbivore. (You could use the same variable X in both statements since the scope of a variable is only the rule it occurs in.) Type the following:

    assert(eats(X,meat):-carnivore(X)).
    assert(eats(Y,grass):-herbivore(Y)).

(Press Enter if you get a strange message such as X_ G303)

Now you can pose the question: *Which animals eat meat?* Type

    eats(X,meat).

Prolog will reply

    X = lion

Type a semi-colon, and Prolog continues

    X = tiger

Type a semi-colon, and Prolog says

    No

because it cannot find any more meat-eaters.

Exit from Prolog by typing **halt.** This will clear all the entries from the database.

Module 4 Processing and Programming Techniques

Creating a permanent Prolog database

Instead of entering facts and rules using the **assert** predicate, you will normally create a Prolog database using an editor (e.g. Notepad in Windows Accessories) or using a word processor. The file should be saved in the **bin** subfolder (if created in Word, as a **Text Only with Line Breaks** file) with an extension of **.pl** (that is PL, not p-one!). You can then load and run your program by doubling-clicking this file name.

Exercises

1. Use a text editor or word processor to enter the sample program showing the family tree given earlier in this chapter. (You will need this database again in the next chapter.)

   What queries will you type to ask the following questions:

   (i)   Does Liz have a brother?

   (ii) Who are Tom's grandchildren?

   (iii) Who are Bob's grandparents?

   Test your answers out in Prolog.

2. A route planning system system has been developed to help drivers to plan their journeys. A driver enters the locations of the starting point and destination of a journey. The system produces a route. A declarative high level programming language has been used for this expert system.

   Describe the essential features of such a declarative high level programming language.

3. (a) Analysts and programmers sometimes need to choose between programming languages.

      For instance, a programmer might have to choose between an *imperative* and a *declarative* language.

      (i) Explain what is meant by an *imperative* language, and state an example of an application which could sensibly use an *imperative* language.

      (ii) Explain what is meant by a *declarative* language, and state an example of an application which could sensibly use a *declarative* language.

   (b) A programmer is required to write a program to simulate the arrival of trains at a busy station. He/she has the choice of a *specialist simulation language* or a *general purpose* language.

      Describe **one** advantage of each type of language.

Chapter 48 – Prolog programming (2)

Tracing Prolog executions

You need to be able to trace through Prolog executions and show what facts and rules have been used in finding the answer to a question. The following exam question is written in a kind of pseudocode Prolog. You could turn the program into Prolog and type it in using a text editor or word processor.

Example:

A recruitment agency selects applicants based upon how well their experience matches the needs of an employer. The agency currently holds information about applicants in a database. Employers make requests to the agency in the form below:

> *Seeking a person with more than five years experience in high level language programming, with particular experience in Pascal.*

The recruitment agency would like to replace the applicant database with a knowledge-based system. This will hold employer requests and applicant details as a set of facts and rules, as shown below in clauses 1 to 18.

```
1. years_of_programming(charles 2)
2. years_of_programming(moira 5)
3. years_of_programming(derek 16)
4. years_of_programming(cynthia 12)

5. is_a_hll(pascal)
6. is_a_hll(comal)
7. is_a_hll(prolog)

8.  can_program_in(prolog charles)
9.  can_program_in(assembler charles)
10. can_program_in(prolog moira)
11. can_program_in(assembler derek)
12. can_program_in(comal derek)
13. can_program_in(prolog derek)
14. can_program_in(pascal cynthia)
15. can_program_in(assembler cynthia)
16. can_program_in(prolog cynthia)

17. hll_programmer(X Y)
    IF can_program_in (X Y)
    AND is_a_hll(X)

18. suitable_for_job(X,Y)
    IF hll_programmer(X,Y)
    AND years_of_programming (Y Z)
    AND Z > 5
```

Module 4 Processing and Programming Techniques

- (a) What solutions can be found to each of the following queries?
    - (i) `?hll_programmer(pascal Y)`
    - (ii) `?suitable_for_job(X derek)`
- (b) Trace the steps taken to evaluate the query in (a)(ii) as far as the first solution. You may use clause numbers in your answer.
- (c) The recruitment agency receives the new request below:

    Seeking a person to lead a team of high level programmers in a new development.

    Rule 18 will not handle this request as it holds no information about what it means to *lead a team*.
    - (i) Add a new rule that one person may lead another if person X has more years of experience than person Y and they have both programmed in the same high level language. Call this rule `can_lead(X,Y)`.
    - (ii) Identify the solutions to this new request.

SCE Computing Paper 2 Qu 17 1999

Discussion and method of solution:

(a) (i) To find the answer to the query `?hll_programmer(pascal Y)` Prolog traces through the program statements from the beginning looking for relevant statements. At Rule 14 it finds the first answer, **Cynthia**. There are no more facts or rules relevant to the query so that is the only answer.

(ii) To find the answer to the query `?suitable_for_job(X Derek)` Prolog first finds Rule 18. It then needs to establish whether Derek is a high-level language programmer, and finds rule 17. Now Prolog needs to look for clauses (X Derek) and it first finds clause 11, `can_program_in(assembler derek)`. Is assembler a hll? Prolog finds it is not, so moves to clause 12, `can_program_in(comal derek)`. Is comal a hll? Clause 6 says it is.
Returning now to clause 18, Prolog needs to look for clauses of the form `years_of_programming(derek Z)` and finds an answer at clause 3. As 16 is greater than 5, Prolog returns the first answer, **comal**.

Note that in SWI-Prolog, you can get a trace by typing **trace**. Then type the query, and you will get an output like the following. (Press Enter after each line is displayed.)

```
trace.
[trace]   ?- suitable_for_job(X,derek).
   Call:  (   5) rl_add_history([115, 117, 105, 116, 97, 98, 108, 101, 95, 102, 111, 114, 95, 106, 111, 98, 40, 88, 44, 100, 101, 114, 101, 107, 41, 46]) ? creep
   Exit:  (   5) rl_add_history([115, 117, 105, 116, 97, 98, 108, 101, 95, 102, 111, 114, 95, 106, 111, 98, 40, 88, 44, 100, 101, 114, 101, 107, 41, 46]) ? creep
   Call:  (   7) suitable_for_job(_G375, derek) ? creep
   Call:  (   8) hll_programmer(_G375, derek) ? creep
   Call:  (   9) can_program_in(_G375, derek) ? creep
   Exit:  (   9) can_program_in(assembler, derek) ? creep
   Call:  (   9) is_a_hll(assembler) ? creep
   Fail:  (   9) is_a_hll(assembler) ? creep
   Redo:  (   9) can_program_in(_G375, derek) ? creep
```

```
Exit:  ( 9) can_program_in(comal, derek) ? creep
Call:  ( 9) is_a_hll(comal) ? creep
Exit:  ( 9) is_a_hll(comal) ? creep
Exit:  ( 8) hll_programmer(comal, derek) ? creep
Call:  ( 8) years_of_programming(derek, _L146) ? creep
Exit:  ( 8) years_of_programming(derek, 16) ? creep
Call:  ( 8) 16>5 ? creep
Exit:  ( 8) 16>5 ? creep
Exit:  ( 7) suitable_for_job(comal, derek) ? creep

X = comal
```

(c) (i) The new rule will take the form
```
can_lead(X Y)
    IF   years_of_programming(X N)
    AND  years_of_programming(Y M)
    AND  N>M
    AND  can_program_in(L X)
    AND  can_program_in(L Y)
    AND  is_a_hll(L)
```

(ii) If you try adding this rule to the Prolog program and running it again, it will give the following solutions. See if you agree.

```
?- can_lead(X,Y).

X = moira
Y = charles ;

X = derek
Y = charles ;

X = derek
Y = moira ;

X = derek
Y = cynthia ;

X = cynthia
Y = charles ;

X = cynthia
Y = moira ;

No
```

Listing a Prolog program

You can get a listing of the current program by typing **listing**.

Exercises

1. The knowledge contained in the passage below is to be represented in a knowledge processing language.

    "Birds and mammals are air breathing creatures. Air breathing creatures have lungs. Birds have feathers and wings. Mammals have hair. Humans and apes are types of mammal. Chimpanzees and gorillas are types of ape. Bald and Golden are types of Eagle which is a type of bird."

    This information is represented as a set of facts and rules as shown below in clauses to 14. The numbers are for reference only.

    1. is_a (mammal, air_breathing)
    2. is_a (bird, air_breathing)
    3. is_a (human, mammal)
    4. is_a (ape, mammal)
    5. is_a (gorilla, ape)
    6. is_a (chimpanzee, ape)
    7. is_a (eagle, bird)
    8. is_a (bald, eagle)
    9. is_a (golden, eagle)

    10. has (bird, wings)
    11. has (bird, feathers)
    12. has (mammal, hair)
    13. has (air_breathing, lungs)

    14. has (A, B) IF is_a (A,C) AND has (C,B)

    In the above syntax:
        capital letters in a clause refer to variables;
        clause 1 has the meaning   "A mammal is an air-breathing creature";
        clause 10 has the meaning   "A bird has wings";
        clause 14 has the meaning   "A has B if it is true that A is a C and it is true C has B

    (a) What solution(s) would be found to each of the following queries?
        (i)   ? is_a (A, eagle)
        (ii)   ? has (mammal, B)

    (b) (i) What solution would be found to the following query?
                ? has (golden, wings)

        (ii) By tracing the steps in the search of the knowledge base, describe how you obtained your answer. You may use the clause numbers in your answer.

    (c) (i) It is required to extend the knowledge base to include the following knowledge.
                "Penguins and ostriches are types of bird"

    Devise suitable clauses that can be added to the knowledge base to represent this knowledge.

(ii) A new rule, with the meaning "a creature can fly if it has feathers", is to be added to the knowledge base. Devise a suitable rule and comment on its appropriateness. You should use the syntax used in clauses 1 to 14 above.

2. A simple logic programming language is used to represent, as a set of facts and rules, the *syntax* of sentences in a subset of English language. The set of facts and rules is shown below in clauses labelled 1 to 16.

   1. determiner(a).
   2. determiner(the).
   3. adjective(big).
   4. noun(monkey).
   5. noun(peanut).
   6. noun(cat).
   7. verb(ate).
   8. verb(chased).
   9. adverb(quickly).
   10. noun_phrase(X) IF noun(X).
   11. noun_phrase(X,Y) IF determiner(X) AND noun(Y).
   12. noun_phrase(X,Y,Z) IF determiner(X) AND adjective(Y) AND noun(Z).
   13. verb_phrase(X) IF verb(X).
   14. verb_phrase(X,Y) IF adverb(X) AND verb(Y).
   15. sentence(A,B,C) IF noun_phrase(A) AND verb_phrase(B) AND noun_phrase(C).
   16. sentence(A,B,C,D,E) IF noun_phrase(A,B) AND verb_phrase(C) AND noun_phrase(D,E).

   In the set of facts and rules above, variables are single letters in uppercase, e.g. A and B

   > Clause 3 has the meaning "big is an adjective"
   >
   > Clause 8 has the meaning "chased is a verb"
   >
   > Clause 11 has the meaning "X followed by Y is a noun phrase if X is a determiner and Y is a noun"

   (a) Explain the term *syntax*.

   (b) Using the given set of facts and rules (1-16 above), give one example of
      (i) a fact;
      (ii) a rule.

   (c) Using the given set of facts and rules (1-16 above), state whether or not the following sentences are valid indicating which rules have been applied in the process.
      (i) the monkey ate the peanut
      (ii) a peanut ate the monkey

   (d) The sentence "the monkey chased the big cat quickly" is not a valid sentence according to the given set of facts and rules. Write a rule or rules which make this sentence valid.
   (part of question)

3. The knowledge base below shows part of a family tree.

1	female(Catherine)	represents the fact that Catherine is a female
2	female(anne)	
3	female(sara)	
4	male(john)	represents the fact that John is a male
5	male(fred)	
6	male(andrew)	
7	male(peter)	
8	mother_of(catherine, fred)	
9	mother_of(catherine, anne)	
10	mother_of(catherine, andrew)	
11	mother_of(catherine, peter)	
12	mother_of(anne, sara)	

13 daughter_of(X,Y) if female(X) and   means X is the daughter of Y if X is female
                     mother_of(Y, X)   and Y is the mother of X

14 brother_of(X,Y) if male(X) and   means X is the brother of Y if X is male and
                     mother_of(Z, X) and   Z is the mother of X and
                     mother_of(Z, Y)   Z is the mother of Y

(a) What solution would be found to each of the following queries?
   (i) daughter_of(anne, W).
   (ii) NOT mother_of(anne, peter).   Explain your answer to this part.

(b) (i) Trace the steps taken to evaluate the query brother_of(A, B) as far as the first solution. You may use the numbering system to help you answer the question.
   (ii) Comment on your solution and amend rule 14 in light of your comments.

Chapter 49 – Recursion

Recursive procedures and stacks

Recursion is an important technique in many different types of programming language, including imperative languages such as Pascal and declarative languages such as Prolog. In this chapter we shall look at some recursive procedures written in Pascal.

The data structure called a **stack** is of crucial importance in understanding how recursion works. You may like to look back at Chapter 14 and remind yourself how stacks are used to store return addresses when a procedure is called. Q3 in that chapter has an example of how addresses are pushed onto a stack when a procedure is called, and popped when the end of a procedure is reached and the program needs to continue from where it left off.

The process is exactly similar to what you will do if you look up Chapter 14: you will remember the number of this page while you go off to Chapter 14, and when you have finished working through Q3, you will retrieve from your memory (the part of it that you are using as a stack) the page number to return to.

A procedure is **recursive** if it calls itself, and the process is called **recursion**. The short program below calls the recursive procedure **PrintList**.

```
program Recurs;
var abc:integer;

    procedure PrintList(num:integer);
    begin
        num := num-1;
        if num > 1 then PrintList(num);
        writeln(num)                      {LINE A}
    end; {procedure PrintList}

{***** main program *****}

begin
    abc := 4;
    PrintList(abc);
    writeln(abc)                          {LINE B}
end.
```

What happens when this program is run? The diagram of the stack in the margin shows the return address and the value of the parameter which will be displayed when a writeln statement is executed.

- First, the procedure PrintList is called with the parameter abc set to 4.
- The address of the instruction marked {LINE B} is stored on the return address stack, and execution will proceed from that line when the end statement in the procedure is reached.

| Line B | 4 |

- Now execution of PrintList begins; num is decremented by 1 and becomes 3. The procedure calls itself, and the address of the instruction marked {LINE A} is stored on the procedure stack, together with the information that num=3. When this line is eventually executed, the number 3 will be displayed.

| Line A | 3 |
| Line B | 4 |

235

Module 4 Processing and Programming Techniques

- PrintList now begins again, with the value of the actual parameter num set to 3. It is decremented to 2, the procedure is called again, the return address stored.

  | Line A 2 |
  | Line A 3 |
  | Line B 4 |

- PrintList begins again, num becomes 1 and the procedure call is not executed. At this point LINE A is executed for the first time and the number 1 is displayed.

  Output   1

  | Line A 2 |
  | Line A 3 |
  | Line B 4 |

- The end of the procedure has been reached, so the first return address is taken off the stack; this is also LINE A, with a parameter of 2, so the number 2 is displayed.

  Output   2

  | Line A 3 |
  | Line B 4 |

- The end of the procedure is reached again, so the next return address is taken off the stack; LINE A again, this time with a parameter of 3.

  Output   3

  | Line B 4 |

- Finally the end of the procedure is reached again and the address of the next instruction is LINE B, so the number 4 is written.

  Output   4

The above example illustrates three essential ingredients that must be present in any recursive process.

1. A stopping condition must be included which when met means that the routine will not call itself and will start to 'unwind'.
2. For input values other than the stopping condition, the routine must call itself.
3. The stopping condition must be reached after a finite number of calls.

Another example of recursion

Recursion is a useful technique for the programmer when the algorithm itself is essentially recursive. An example of this is the calculation of a factorial, where **n!** (read as **factorial n**) is defined as follows:

If $n = 0$ then $n! = 1$

otherwise $n! = n*(n-1)*(n-2)*........*3*2*1$

Thus for example $4! = 4 \times 3 \times 2 \times 1$, and $0! = 1$ (by definition).

This can be defined recursively as

If $n = 0$ then $n! = 1$

otherwise $n! = n*(n-1)!$ (For example $4! = 4 \times 3!$)

The pseudocode for a recursive function to calculate n! is as follows:

```
function factorial(n)
begin
    if   n = 0 or n = 1 then factorial = 1
    else factorial = n*factorial(n-1)
end
```

> Q1: Dry run the above function when it is called with the statement answer = factorial(4).
> Q2: What happens if the function is called with answer = factorial(-3)?
> Q3: Which of the 3 'essential ingredients' of a recursive function is not present?

Advantages and disadvantages of recursion

In general, a non-recursive solution is more efficient in terms of both computer time and space. This is because when using a recursive solution, the computer has to make multiple procedure or function calls, each time storing return addresses and copies of local or temporary variables, all of which takes time and space. Another point to consider is that if the recursion continues too long, the stack containing return addresses may overflow and the program will crash. If for example you try to calculate factorial 2000 using a recursive routine, 2000 return addresses have to be stored before the routine begins to unwind, and the computer may run out of memory while doing this.

For some problems, however, a recursive solution is more natural and easier for the programmer to write. (You will encounter a good example of this later when studying tree traversals).

Generally speaking, if the recursive solution is not much shorter than the non-recursive one, use the non-recursive one. Going by this rule, it would be better to use iteration rather than recursion to work out a factorial; it serves as a neat example of recursion but would be more efficiently and just as simply written iteratively, using a For..Next loop, for example. This is left as an exercise for the reader!

In the next chapter we will look at some recursive procedures in a logic programming language such as Prolog.

Exercises

1. (a) Distinguish between **iteration** and **recursion**, giving an example of each.

   (b) Give **two** advantages of using recursive routines and **two** disadvantages.

2. The following is a *recursively defined* function which calculates the result of multiplying together all the positive integers between n and 1, inclusively. For example, the factorial of 3 is the result of evaluating 3 * 2 * 1, i.e. 6.

   ```
   Define Factorial(n)
   if n = 1
       then Factorial := 1
       else Factorial := n * Factorial(n - 1)
   EndDefine
   ```

   (a) What is meant by *recursively defined*?

   (b) Trace the execution of this function for n = 4 showing carefully, for each re-entry into the factorial function, the value passed to the function and the results returned.

   (c) Why should this function not be used when n = 0?

   (d) (i) Describe the data structure known as a *stack*.

       (ii) Carefully explain the role of the stack in the execution of the factorial function.

   (e) Write a pseudocode non-recursive version of the factorial function.

   (f) (i) Give **one** reason why a non-recursive factorial function may be preferred to a recursive one.

       (ii) Give **one** reason why a recursive factorial function may be preferred to a non-recursive one.

Module 4 Processing and Programming Techniques

3. (a) Name and describe a data structure which could be used to store the values of variables from recursively called procedures.

   (b) Study the following procedure which includes a recursive call:
   PROCEDURE printout (word)
       Output word on a new line
       IF word contains more than one letter THEN
           delete the last letter from word
           call printout (word)
       ENDIF
       output word on a new line
   ENDPROCEDURE
   State the output which would be produced from the procedure call
           call printout (LONDON)

4. The following algorithm uses recursion.

   global integer n
   n:=5
   increase(n)
   stop

   procedure increase(n:**local integer**)
      if n < 30 then
         increase(n+8)
      endif
      display(n*2)
   endproc

   (a) Using the above algorithm as an example explain what is meant by recursion.

   (b) Using a trace table, or otherwise, demonstrate the effect of executing the program segment clearly showing the values produced by the **display** command.

Chapter 50 – Lists

Definition of a list in Prolog

In Prolog, a list is a collection of data items stored in some sequence, with the following properties:

- data items may be inserted or deleted at any point in the list;
- data items may be repeated in the list;
- lists may contain any type of object;
- a particular list may contain different object types.

The elements of a list are enclosed in square brackets and separated by commas. For example a list named Colours containing 6 items may be represented as follows:

Colours = [red,orange,yellow,green,indigo,violet]

A more complex list may contain items of different types, including a list:

Class = [2.15,14,12,[maths,physics,computing],jones]

Manipulating lists

Lists are manipulated by separating the head from the tail. The separator used is a vertical line, |.

e.g.   List = [Head|Tail]

Note that the tail of a list is itself a list.

e.g.   [focus|[fiesta,escort,mondeo]]
       [a|[b,c]]
       [a|[b]]

Note that [a|b] is not a valid list because the tail is an atom, not a list.

> Q1: Write the following as a list, with elements separated by commas.
>   anna bob claire damon emma
> Q2: Write the above list in Head|Tail form.
> Q3: Are the following valid lists?
>   (i)   [a|b,c]
>   (ii) [x]
>   (iii) [a|[c|[d,e]]]
>   (iv) a
>   (v)   [a,b,c]

Module 4 Processing and Programming Techniques

Writing out a list

Operations on lists are carried out by working through the list, successively removing the head from the tail.

A Prolog procedure to write out a list follows:

```
writelist([]).
writelist([Head|Tail]):-write(Head),nl,writelist(Tail).
```

Enter these statements into a Prolog program, either directly using the **assert** verb or by entering them into a text file. (**nl** stands for new line and makes the output move to the next line.)

You can then ask Prolog to write out the list [apple,banana,pear] by typing:

```
?- writelist[apple,banana,pear].
```

- The interpreter searches for writelist, passes over writelist[] since the list is not empty, and comes to the second rule.
- The list is split up into head and tail form as follows:
  writelist(apple|[banana,pear]):-write(apple),nl,writelist([banana,pear]).
- **apple** is written and the rule calls itself.
  writelist(banana|[pear]):-write(banana),nl,writelist([pear]).
- **Banana** is written out and the rule calls itself again:
  writelist(pear|[]):-write(pear),nl,writelist([]).
- **Pear** is written out and writelist is searched for again. This time the first writelist rule succeeds and stops the recursion.

Operations on a list

Lists can also be processed in a procedural language.

Several functions may be defined which take a list as their single argument and return a result which is either an element of a list, another list or a Boolean value.

Head(List)   returns the element at the head of the list if the list is non-empty, otherwise reports an error.

         e.g. Head[red,orange,yellow,green,indigo,violet] = red

Tail(List)   returns a new list containing all but the first element of the original list.

         e.g. Tail[red,orange,yellow,green,indigo,violet] = [orange,yellow,green,indigo,violet]

Empty(List)   returns TRUE if the list is empty or FALSE otherwise. The empty list is denoted by [ ].

Examples: What is the result returned by the following functions applied to the list Colours defined above?

      (a)   Head(Tail(Colours))   Answer: orange

      (b)   Empty(Colours)   Answer: FALSE

      (c)   Tail(Tail(Tail(Tail(Colours))))   Answer: [indigo,violet]

      (d)   Tail(Tail(Tail(Tail(Tail(Colours)))))   Answer: [violet]

A recursive procedure to print a list

Pseudocode for a recursive procedure to print a list is shown below:

```
Procedure T(List)
    If not Empty(List)
    Then
        T(Tail(List));
        Print(Head(List));
    Endif;
EndProc
```

The procedure keeps on recursively calling the procedure T(List), not executing the Print statement until the list is empty and the procedure runs to completion, when it begins to 'unwind'. It thus prints the list in reverse order.

Implementation of a list using an array

The elements of a list may be held in an array. The array needs to be large enough to hold the maximum number of elements that are likely to occur, and two additional variables are needed to hold the current size of the list and the size of the array. An example of a list is a display on a railway station that gives the arrival times of trains in order of arrival times, shown below with the two extra variables **size** and **max**.

e.g.

				time	starting_point
size	5	item	1	1450	Norwich
			2	1458	Colchester
			3	1520	Stowmarket
max	20		4	1545	Cambridge
			5	1555	Liverpool Street

The sequence may be **initialized** simply by setting **size** to 0.

Two other procedures can be performed on a linear list; **insertion** and **deletion**.

Inserting an item

Suppose we wish to insert an arrival, the 1455 from Liverpool Street. The best way of inserting an item into a list is to:

(a) include an extra item at the beginning of the list, with an index of 0 which is used to hold the item to be inserted, and

(b) search backwards instead of forwards through the list for the correct position of the new item.

The steps are given below:

```
Put the new item in item[0]
If the list is full, display a message 'list is full'.
Otherwise, start at the end of the list and examine each item.
While time of the current item is greater than time of the new item,
    move current item down one place.
Insert the new item.
```

Example: Show how the list of arrival times and starting points of trains can be held in a **table** (an array of records) in memory.

Write pseudocode for an algorithm to insert a new element in the list.

Answer: The table to hold the list can be declared as follows:

Module 4 *Processing and Programming Techniques*

```
type
   item_type = record
      time           : integer;
      starting_point : string;
   end;
var
   item           : array[0..20] of item_type;
```

Pseudocode for inserting a new element in the list is as follows:

```
Procedure Insert_Item
begin
   get new item
   item[0] = new item
   p = size
   if size = max then write 'list full'
   else
      while item[p].time > item[0].time
         item[p+1] = item[p]
         p = p-1
      endwhile
      size = size + 1
      item[p+1] = item[0]
   endif
end procedure
```

Retrieving and deleting an item from a list

To retrieve an item from a list, we again put the given item in item[0] and search backwards from the end of the list, for a time less than or equal to the time of the given item.

The pseudocode for a procedure to find an item is shown below. If the item is in the list, a flag called **found** will be set to **true**, and **p** will indicate its position, otherwise **found** will be set to **false**.

```
procedure Find_Item
begin
   item[0].time = given_time
   p = size                           ( set pointer to end of list )
   found = false
   while item[p].time > given_time
      p = p - 1                       ( continue searching )
   endwhile
   (if p = 0 on exit from the loop, then given_time is not in the list.
   If p is not = 0 then given_time may be present in the list)
   if p <> 0 then
      if item[p].time = given_time
         then found = true
      endif
   endif
end procedure
```

Example: Write an algorithm to delete an item from the list. (Use the above procedure FIND_ITEM).

```
procedure Delete_Item
begin
   get item to delete
   call Find_Item to see if item is in the list
   if found = false then write error message  (ie item is not in list)
```

```
        else                    (p gives the position of the item)
            while p < size      (if it's the last item, no need to move anything)
                item[p] = item[p+1]
                p = p + 1
            endwhile
            size = size - 1
        endif
    end procedure
```

Exercises

1. The list **Cities** contains the following names:

    [London Glasgow Belfast Cardiff].

    Table 1 shows some functions which take a list as their single argument and return a result which is either an element of a list, another list or a boolean value.

Head(list) – returns the element at the head of list (e.g. Head(Cities) → London) if list is non-empty otherwise reports an error.
Tail(list) – returns a new list containing all but the first element of the original list (e.g. Tail(Cities)→ [Glasgow Belfast Cardiff]) if list is non-empty otherwise reports an error.
Empty(list) – returns True if the list is the empty list or false otherwise. The empty list is denoted by [ ].

    Table 1

    (a) What is the final result returned when the following function calls are made?
    - (i) Empty(Cities)
    - (ii) Head(Tail(Cities))
    - (iii) Tail(Tail(Tail(Tail(Cities))))

    A recursively-defined procedure T, which takes a list as its single parameter, is defined below.

    ```
    Define Procedure T(list)
        If Not Empty(list)
            Then
                T(Tail(list))
                Print Head(list)
        EndIf
    EndDefine
    ```

    (b) What is meant by recursively defined?
    (c) Explain why a stack is necessary in order to execute procedure T recursively.
    (d) For the procedure call T(Cities), state the PRINTed output in the order in which it is produced.

    (e) A function MemberOf, which takes a list and an item as its two arguments, returns True if the item is a member of the list otherwise False. Write pseudocode which performs this function.

    (f) Draw a diagram to show the list **Cities** as a linked list.

Module 4 Processing and Programming Techniques

Chapter 51 – Linked Lists

Definition

A linked list is a dynamic data structure used to hold a sequence, as described below:

- The items which form the sequence are not necessarily held in contiguous data locations, or in the order in which they occur in the sequence.
- Each item in the list is called a **node** and contains an **information** field and a **next address** field called a **link** or **pointer** field. (The information field may consist of several subfields.)
- The information field holds the actual data associated with the list item, and the link field contains the address of the next item in the sequence.
- The link field in the last item indicates in some way that there are no further items (e.g. has a value of 0).
- Associated with the list is a **pointer variable** which points to (i.e. contains the address of) the first node in the list.

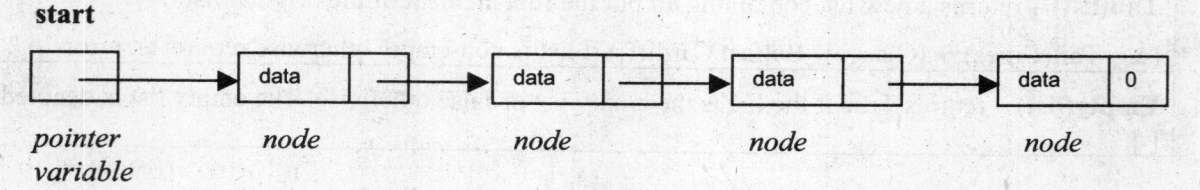

```
start
  □ → [data|→] → [data|→] → [data|→] → [data|0]
pointer      node        node        node        node
variable
```

Operations on linked lists

In the examples which follow we will assume that the linked list is held in a table in memory, and that each node consists of a person's name (the information field) and a pointer to the next item in the list. We will explore how to set up or initialise an empty list, insert new data in the correct place in the list, delete an unwanted item and print out all items in the list. We will also look at the problem of managing the free space in the list.

Imagine that the table holding the list has room for 6 entries, and 4 names have already been inserted into it in such a way that they can be retrieved in alphabetical order, so that it is currently in the following state.

Address	Name	Pointer
1	Browning	4
2	Turner	0
3	Johnson	2
4	Cray	3
5		
6		

start = 1

nextfree = 5

Figure 51.1

244

Notice that

- a pointer **start** points to the first item in the list;
- **nextfree** is a pointer to the next free location in the table;
- by following the links, names can be retrieved in alphabetical order.

To insert a new name, for example Mortimer, into the list, pointers will have to be changed so that it is linked into the correct place. At this stage we have not really decided how to manage the free space in the list, so we will simply add 1 to **nextfree**.

The table will now appear as in Figure 51.2.

Address	Name	Pointer
1	Browning	4
2	Turner	0
3	Johnson	5
4	Cray	3
5	Mortimer	2
6		

start = 1

nextfree = 6

Figure 51.2

> **Q1:** Show the state of the table and pointers after insertion of the name Allen. Write down the steps involved in inserting a new name to the list, so that alphabetical sequence is maintained.

Now we will delete a name. Return to the table as shown above in Figure 51.2 (before inserting Allen), and delete the name Johnson. After adjusting the pointers, the table looks like this:

Address	Name	Pointer
1	Browning	4
2	Turner	0
3	Johnson	2
4	Cray	5
5	Mortimer	2
6		

start = 1

nextfree = 6

Figure 51.3

Note that

- Johnson is still physically in the table, but not part of the list any more;
- **nextfree** hasn't altered, and we have come up against a problem; there is no way to reclaim the vacancy left by Johnson. If the table is not to become full of unwanted records with no room left in it to add new records, we will have to address this problem. (Note, however, that the so-called 'management of free space' adds a degree of complexity to algorithms which is not always required in answers to exam questions unless specifically asked for.)

Module 4 Processing and Programming Techniques

Management of free space

The solution is to keep **two** linked lists; one for the actual data, and one for the free space. When a new item is added, a node is grabbed from the free space list, and when a node is deleted, it is linked into the free space list.

When the table is first initialised prior to entering any names, it will consist of just one linked list of free space:

Address	Name	Pointer
1		2
2		3
3		4
4		5
5		6
6		0

start = 0

nextfree = 1

Figure 51.4

After the names Browning, Turner, Johnson and Cray have been added (don't worry about how they were inserted, we're coming to that) the table will look like this:

Address	Name	Pointer
1	Browning	4
2	Turner	0
3	Johnson	2
4	Cray	3
5		6
6		0

start = 1

nextfree = 5

Figure 51.5

Notice that we now have two linked lists going. We'll now work out an algorithm for inserting a name into the list. As an example, we'll insert Mortimer between Johnson and Turner.

Inserting an item

Here are the steps:

```
store the new name Mortimer in the node pointed to by nextfree
determine, by following the links, where the new item should be linked in
change nextfree to point to next free location
change Mortimer's pointer to point to Turner
change Johnson's pointer to point to Mortimer
```

Some extra steps would need to be inserted to cope with various special cases such as inserting a name at the very front of the list (e.g. Allen), or inserting the first name into an empty list, but we'll ignore these cases for now.

Diagrammatically, this is what we have done:

Before insertion:

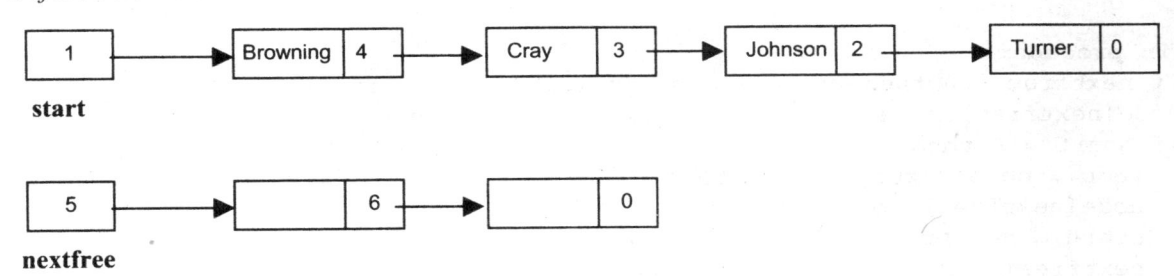

```
[ 1 ]→[ Browning | 4 ]→[ Cray | 3 ]→[ Johnson | 2 ]→[ Turner | 0 ]
 start
```

```
[ 5 ]→[       | 6 ]→[       | 0 ]
 nextfree
```

After insertion:

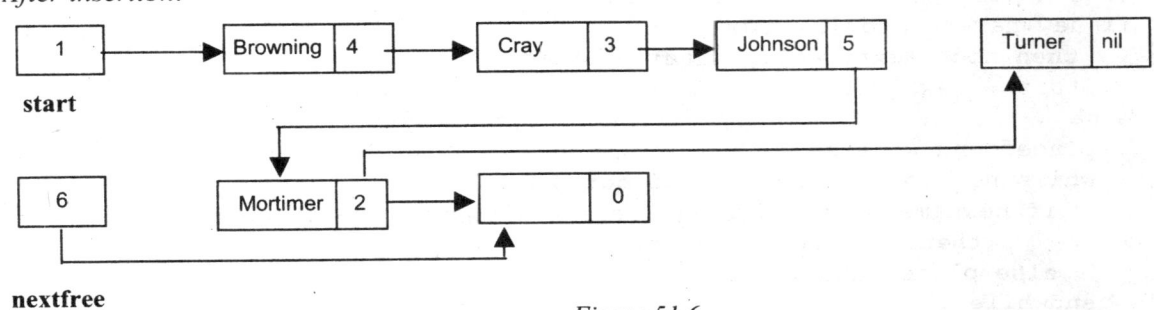

```
[ 1 ]→[ Browning | 4 ]→[ Cray | 3 ]→[ Johnson | 5 ]   [ Turner | nil ]
 start
[ 6 ]   [ Mortimer | 2 ]→[        | 0 ]
 nextfree
```

Figure 51.6

Before we go further and express this algorithm in more formal pseudocode, you need to make sure you clearly understand the notation used.

node[p].name holds the name in the node pointed to by p

node[p].pointer holds the value of the pointer in the node pointed to by p

> **Q2:** Looking at Figure 51.5, node[3].name = Johnson, and node[3].pointer = 2.
> What is the value of (i)   node[start].pointer?
> (ii) node[4].name?
> (iii) node[node[3].pointer].pointer?
> (iv) node[node[start].pointer].name?

Notice how we can 'peek ahead' using the pointers to see what name is in the next node, or even the node after that one, and so on. Here's a first attempt at the pseudocode for the algorithm to add a new name to the list.

```
begin procedure
    node[nextfree].name = new name      (store the new name in next free node)
    p = start
    follow pointers until node[p].pointer points to a name > new name
    temp = nextfree                                 (put 5 in temp)
    nextfree = node[nextfree].pointer               (put 6 in nextfree)
    node[temp].pointer = node[p].pointer  (put 2 in Mortimer's pointer field)
    node[p].pointer = temp                (put 5 in Johnson's pointer)
end procedure
```

Module 4 Processing and Programming Techniques

This algorithm is in enough detail to get you through most questions on how to insert a node into a linked list. However, to deal with the special cases (checking for a full list and inserting at the head of the list) and to specify how to follow the pointers until you reach the correct insertion point, you need the following:

```
begin procedure
  if nextfree = 0 then write ('List is full') and exit procedure.
  node[nextfree].name = new name    (store the new name in next free node)
  if start = 0 then                              (insert into empty list)
    temp = node[nextfree].pointer
    node[nextfree].pointer = 0
    start = nextfree
    nextfree = temp
  else
    p = start
    (check for special case inserting in front of list)
    if new name < node[p].name
        then node[nextfree].pointer = start
      start = nextfree
    else                                       (start general case)
      placefound = false
      while node[p].pointer<>0 and not placefound
        if newname >= node[node[p].pointer].name    (peek ahead)
            then p = node[p].pointer
        else placefound = true
      endwhile
      temp = nextfree
      nextfree = node[nextfree].pointer
      node[temp].pointer = node[p].pointer
      node[p].pointer = temp
    endif (general case)
end procedure
```

Deleting an item

Returning to the table as in Figure 51.1, we will delete Johnson. The steps are as follows:

```
follow the pointers until Johnson is found
change Cray's pointer to point to Turner
change Johnson's pointer to nextfree
change nextfree to point to Johnson
```

This is shown diagramatically on the next page.

Before deletion:

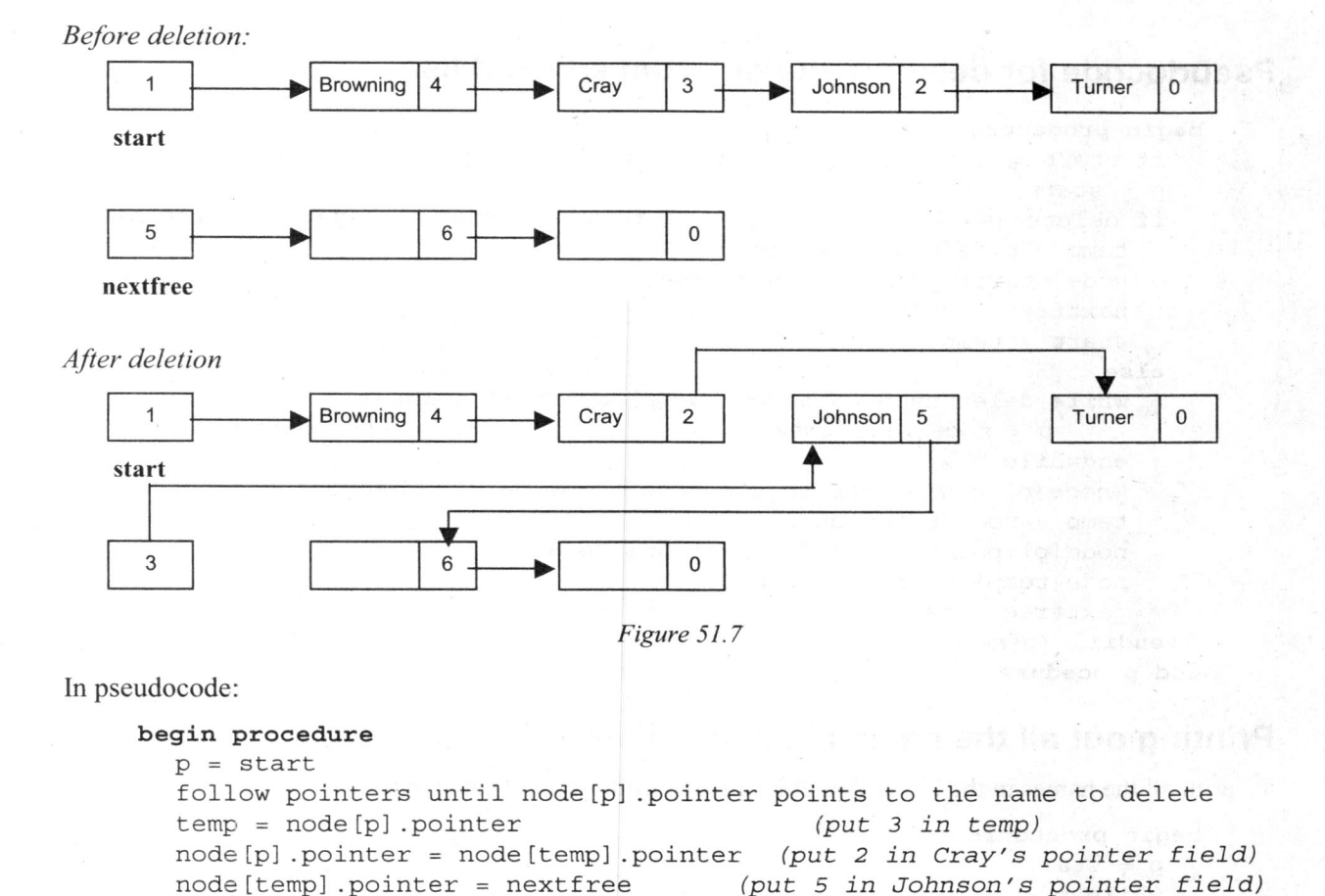

```
start: 1 → Browning|4 → Cray|3 → Johnson|2 → Turner|0
nextfree: 5 → _|6 → _|0
```

After deletion

```
start: 1 → Browning|4 → Cray|2 → Johnson|5 → Turner|0
         3 → _|6 → _|0
```

Figure 51.7

In pseudocode:

```
begin procedure
  p = start
  follow pointers until node[p].pointer points to the name to delete
  temp = node[p].pointer                    (put 3 in temp)
  node[p].pointer = node[temp].pointer      (put 2 in Cray's pointer field)
  node[temp].pointer = nextfree             (put 5 in Johnson's pointer field)
  nextfree = temp                           (put 3 in nextfree)
end procedure
```

This is enough level of detail to show the concept of deleting from a linked list and you may wish to skip the next couple of paragraphs. However, for those who wish to go deeper, a fuller discussion follows.

Once again, deleting the first node in the list is a special case because **start** has to be altered. In the general case, following the pointers until node[p].pointer points to the name to delete again involves 'peeking ahead' to see what is in the next node, because once we are at a node we can't get back to change the previous pointer. So we want to stop following pointers not when node[p].name = name to delete, but at the node before that; i.e. when node[node[p].pointer].name = name to delete.

Note that deleting the last node (or inserting onto the end of the list, in the case of insertion) causes no special problems; try it and you will see this is true.

The full pseudocode is given on the next page.

Pseudocode for deleting an item from a linked list

```
begin procedure
  if start = 0 then write 'List is empty' and exit procedure.
  p = start
  if deletename = node[start].name then     (special case for first node)
    temp = node[start].pointer
    node[start].pointer = nextfree
    nextfree = start
    start = temp
  else                                       (general case)
    while deletename <> node[node[p].pointer].pointer
      p = node[p].pointer                    (advance the pointer)
    endwhile
    (node[p] now points to the node to be deleted; adjust the pointers)
    temp = node[p].pointer
    node[p].pointer = node[temp].pointer
    node[temp].pointer = nextfree
    nextfree = temp
  endif    (general case)
end procedure
```

Printing out all the names in a linked list

To print all the names in the list, follow the pointers, printing each name in turn.

```
begin procedure
  p = start
  while p <> 0
    current = node[p]
    print current.name
    p = current.pointer
  endwhile
end procedure
```

Use of free memory, heap and pointers

So far, we have been using arrays to implement a linked list. Because the size of the array data structure has to be declared and is fixed prior to its application, it is **static**. Main memory is wasted if too many locations are reserved in advance. On the other hand, errors result if too few are reserved and an attempt is made to access locations outside the declared range.

Files are **dynamic structures**, in that the size of a file does not have to be declared in advance and is restricted only by how much data can be held on the storage medium, e.g. disk. A linked list is also a dynamic data structure but by implementing it using arrays this property is effectively lost. **Pointer data types** allow the creation of dynamic data structures in memory, using locations only when needed. No memory locations have to be reserved before they are referenced. When a location is needed, it is pulled from a pool of all the available locations in main memory called the **heap**. When it is no longer required, the locations can be returned to the heap for use by other applications.

Array and pointer variables differ in the manner in which they reference a main memory location. The name given to an array element represents the location in which a data item is stored.

The name given to a pointer represents the location that contains the address of the location you are using – you never know the address of the location being referenced; the pointer finds it for you from the heap.

Pointer variables

A pointer variable is one which is used for the sole purpose of pointing to another address in memory. The data type of a pointer depends on what it is pointing to. In Pascal, for example, you can use the following statements to define a pointer data type:

```
type
      pointertype = ^integer;
var
      p : pointertype;
```

start and **nextfree** may be defined as pointer variables in the linked list examples. In this case, the pointer points to a node in the linked list, and each node can be defined as a record data type. Thus:

```
type
      pointertype = ^nodetype;

      nodetype = record
            name      : string;
            pointer   : pointertype;
      end;
var
      p         : pointertype;
      start     : pointertype;
      current   : nodetype;
```

In this notation, if **start** is a pointer variable, **start^** is the variable to which **start** points.

Thus, looking at Figure 51.1, start^.name = Browning, and start^.pointer = 4

Using this notation, the pseudocode algorithm for printing out the names in the list becomes

```
begin procedure
    p=start
    while p <> 0
        current = p^
        print current.data
        p = current.pointer
    endwhile
end procedure
```

Getting and returning memory locations dynamically

When a new item is added to a linked list, a new location has to be taken from the heap. The **New** procedure in Pascal takes an available location and assigns a pointer variable to it.

    e.g.   New(p)

To return a variable to the heap, the procedure **Dispose** is used.

    e.g.   Dispose(p)

You will not be expected to write procedures using **New** and **Dispose**. A knowledge of the general principles is sufficient. You may be asked to trace through a given algorithm or write a simple procedure using pointer notation.

Module 4 Processing and Programming Techniques

Exercises

1. The text generated by a word processing package contains visible and embedded characters. This text is stored as a linked list of records. Each record consists of two fields. The first field contains a character and the second a link to the next record in the linked list.

   (a) List two types of embedded characters which would be stored within the text.

   (b) Give three advantages of storing the text as a linked list rather than a fixed length array of characters.

   (c) Produce an algorithm to delete the first occurrence of a given character within the text.

   (d) Produce an algorithm to insert a word into the text.

2. Tutor groups in a college are referred to by the initials of the tutor. Records of the students are stored on a computer system.

   The student records for each group are stored in a linked list in alphabetical order of student surname.

   Consequently, there are the same number of linked lists as there are tutor groups.

   To access a particular group, there is a table of tutor groups, again held in alphabetical order, which holds the location of the first student in that linked list.

   At one point the table of tutor groups is

	Tutor Group	Position of initial record
1	AD	F01C
2	CL	01AA
3	DW	1384
4	MT	2BC5
5	PL	3XD1
6	SM	2814
7	WB	19B4
8		
9		
10		

   Count = 7

   (a) Identify the error in the table.

   You may find it useful to use diagrams in your answers to the rest of this question.

   (b) Explain how an entry for a new linked list for the tutor NW with initial position 1111 can be inserted into the table.

   (c) Explain in outline how

   (i) a new student can be added to a tutor group,

   (ii) a student who has left the college can be removed from a tutor group,

   (iii) a linked list for a tutor without a tutor group can be represented?

   (d) Describe how a list of all female students, in alphabetical order, can be created from the information already stored, and kept prior to being printed out.

252

Chapter 52 – Queues and Stacks

Definition of a queue

A queue is a First In First Out (FIFO) data structure; new elements are added to the rear of the queue, and elements leave from the front of the queue. A queue can be implemented as an array with a pointer to the front of the queue and a pointer to the rear of the queue. An integer holding the size of the array (the maximum size of the queue) is needed, and it is useful to have an extra variable giving the number of items currently in the queue.

John	Catherine	Rob			

Front = 1   Rear = 3

MaxSize = 6   NumberInQueue = 3

After 2 people have left the queue and 3 more have joined, the queue will look like this:

		Rob	Max	Lisa	Anna

Front = 3   Rear = 6

MaxSize = 6   NumberInQueue = 4

Now what? Only 4 people are in the queue but the end of the array has been reached. To overcome this problem the queue may be implemented as a **circular queue**, so that when the next person joins they enter at the front of the array:

Ben		Rob	Max	Lisa	Anna

Rear = 1   Front = 3

MaxSize = 6   NumberInQueue = 5

Procedures to implement a circular queue

The above queue may be implemented by declaring variables as follows:

```
Q              : array [1..6] of string;
Front          : integer;
Rear           : integer;
NumberInQueue  : integer;
```

To initialise the queue:

```
Procedure Initialise
    Front := 1
    Rear  := 6      {or Rear = 0}
    NumberInQueue := 0
EndProc
```

Module 4 Processing and Programming Techniques

To add an element to the queue:

```
Procedure EnQueue
    If   NumberInQueue = 6
      Then Write ('Queue overflow')
      Else
        If   Rear = 6
          Then Rear := 1              } or Rear := (Rear Mod 6) + 1
          Else Add 1 to Rear
        EndIf
        Q[Rear] := NewItem
        Add 1 to NumberInQueue
    EndIf
EndProc
```

To remove an element from the queue:

```
Procedure DeQueue
    If   NumberInQueue = 0
      Then Write ('Queue empty')
      Else
        NewItem := Q[Front]
        Subtract 1 from NumberInQueue
        If   Front = 6
          Then Front := 1             } or Front := (Front Mod 6) + 1
          Else Add 1 to Front
        EndIf
    EndIf
EndProc
```

Implementing a queue as a linked list

A queue may be implemented as a special kind of linked list, with each element in the queue pointing to the next item. An external pointer points to the front of the queue, and items may only be removed from the front of the list and added to the end of the list.

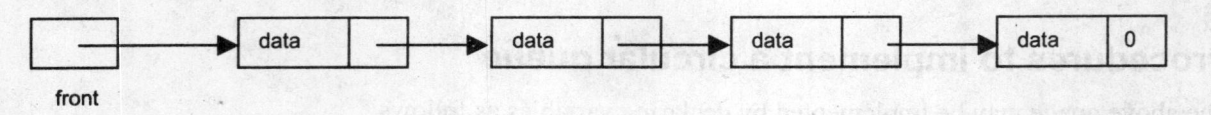

The front of the queue is accessed through the pointer **front**. To add an element to the queue, the pointers have to be followed until the node containing a pointer of 0 is reached, signifying the end of the queue, and this pointer is then changed to point to the new node. (In some implementations two pointers are kept; one to the front and one to the rear. This saves having to traverse the whole queue when a new element is to be added.)

Uses of Queues

Queues are used in a variety of applications such as:
- holding jobs waiting to be run by the computer;
- a keyboard buffer, to allow a whole line to be typed and edited while the processor is busy doing something else;
- spooling output onto a disk to await printing.

Stacks

A stack is a **Last In, First Out** data structure. Items can be added (pushed) on to the stack or removed (popped) from the stack. It is a dynamic data structure since the size of the stack varies according to the number of elements currently in the stack.

A stack may be implemented using an array and two additional variables, *MaxStackSize* holding the size of the array (i.e. the maximum size of the stack) and *Top* holding a pointer to the top of the stack. To initialise the stack the pointer (*Top*) will be set to zero, representing an empty stack.

The diagram below shows an array that can hold a maximum of 6 elements with 3 items currently in the stack.

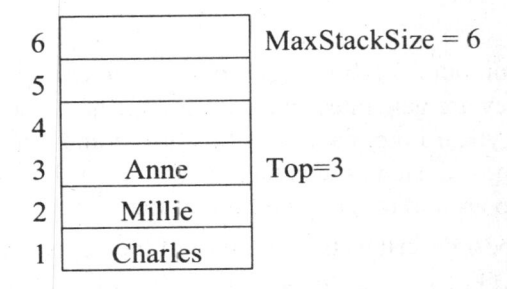

6		MaxStackSize = 6
5		
4		
3	Anne	Top=3
2	Millie	
1	Charles	

The following pseudocode procedure may be used to add ('push') an element onto a stack:

```
Procedure Push;
    If Top = MaxStackSize
        Then Write 'Stack is full'
        Else
            Add 1 to Top
            Stack[Top] := NewItem
    EndIf
EndProc
```

To remove ('pop') an element from a stack:

```
Procedure Pop
    If Top = 0
        Then Write 'Stack is empty'
        Else
            PoppedItem := Stack[Top]
            Subtract 1 from Top
    EndIf
EndProc
```

Uses of Stacks

Stacks are used in many different situations in computing, for example:

- To store return addresses, parameters and register contents when subroutines are called. When the subroutine ends, the address at the top of the stack is popped and the computer continues execution from that address.
- In evaluating mathematical expressions held in reverse Polish notation, i.e. a form of notation used by compilers as an intermediate step in translating expressions such as A:= (B*C) + D/E.

Module 4 Processing and Programming Techniques

Exercises

1. (a) Describe the essential features of the following data structures:
      (i) a queue,
      (ii) a stack.
   (b) Using a diagram, explain how a queue is implemented using an array.
   (c) Using pseudo-code, give the steps needed to add data to a queue which is held in an array. The queue cannot contain more than 10 items of data at any one time.

2. Keystrokes at a computer keyboard generate character codes which are temporarily stored in the order in which they are generated in a data storage area known as the *keyboard buffer*. A program which requires keyboard input accesses this buffer and removes one character code at a time. The code which is removed each time is the one which has been in the buffer the longest. New characters arriving may wrap around to the beginning of the buffer.
   (a) What name best describes the structure of the keyboard buffer?
   (b) The keyboard buffer is designed to hold up to 100 character codes at any one time but during the execution of the program several thousand character codes will enter and leave the keyboard buffer. Describe how the buffer can be best structured to make this possible. Use diagrams to illustrate your answer, clearly showing the full structure for:
      (i) an empty buffer;
      (ii) a full buffer before any characters have been removed;
      (iii) a full buffer after less than 100 character codes have been removed and some new characters have arrived.
   (c) Using pseudo code describe algorithms which:
      (i) initialise the buffer;
      (ii) add a character code to the buffer;
      (iii) remove a character code from the buffer.
   The algorithm should handle the error conditions generated when an attempt is made to add an item to an already full buffer and when an attempt is made to remove an item from an empty buffer.

3. (a) Describe the data structure known as a stack.
   (b) Describe how values are
      (i) added to a stack,
      (ii) removed from a stack.
   (c) Why is a stack used when a high level language program calls procedures?

Chapter 53 – Trees

Definition

A tree is a dynamic data structure which has zero or more nodes organised in a hierarchical way such that:

- except when the tree is empty, there is one node called the **root** at the beginning of the tree structure;
- lines connecting the nodes are called **branches** and every node except the root is joined to just one node at the next higher level (its parent);
- nodes that have no children are called **leaf nodes** or **terminal nodes**.

Note that every tree has only one root, but each node in the tree can be regarded as the root of a **subtree** of the tree. Thus a tree consists of a root and one or more subtrees, each of which is a tree. (This is an example of a **recursive** definition).

You first met trees in Chapter 15 and it would be a good idea to revise this chapter before proceeding.

In that chapter, the following names were entered into a binary tree so that they could be retrieved in alphabetical order:

Legg, Charlesworth, Illman, Hawthorne, Todd, Youngman, Jones, Ravage.

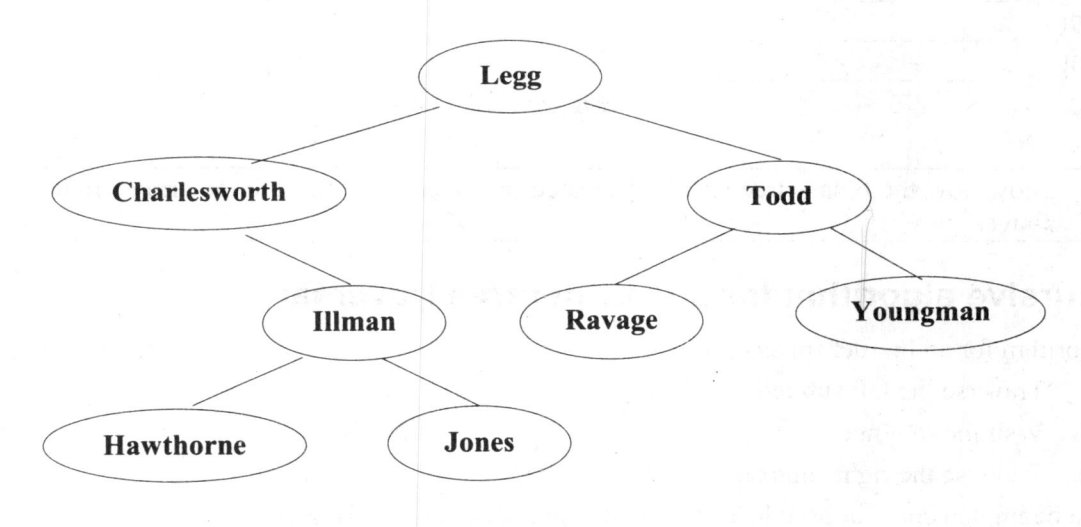

Figure 53.1: A binary tree

> **Q1:** Insert the following items into a binary tree for subsequent retrieval in alphabetical sequence: goldfinch, dove, robin, chaffinch, blackbird, wren, jay, sparrow, partridge.

Implementation of trees using arrays

Binary trees can be implemented using left and right pointers at each node. A node will consist of:
- a left pointer
- data item
- a right pointer.

	left	data	right
tree [1]	2	Legg	5
[2]	0	Charlesworth	3
[3]	4	Illman	7
[4]	0	Hawthorne	0
[5]	8	Todd	6
[6]	0	Youngman	0
[7]	0	Jones	0
[8]	0	Ravage	0
[9]			
[10]			

A pointer value of 0 indicates a 'nil' pointer
Note that, for example:
tree[1].left = 2
tree[tree[1].left].right = 3
tree[6].data = 'Youngman'

Figure 53.2

> **Q2:** Show how the binary tree structure created in Q1 may be stored in an array similar to the one above.

A recursive algorithm for an inorder tree traversal

The algorithm for an inorder traversal is:
1. Traverse the left subtree
2. Visit the root node
3. Traverse the right subtree.

This can be implemented in pseudocode as a recursive algorithm as follows:

```
Procedure traverse_from(p);
  if tree[p].left <> 0 then traverse_from(left);
  endif
  writeln (data);
  if tree[p].right <> 0 then traverse_from(right);
  endif
endproc
```

The procedure, when called with the statement **traverse_from(1)** will print out the contents of each node in sequence.

> **Q3:** What is a 'recursive algorithm'?

Preorder tree traversal

The algorithm for a preorder traversal is:
1. Visit the root node
2. Traverse the left subtree
3. Traverse the right subtree.

This can be implemented in Pascal as follows:

```
Procedure traverse_from(p);
  writeln (data);
  if tree[p].left <> 0 then traverse_from(left);
  endif
  if tree[p].right <> 0 then traverse_from(right);
  endif
endproc
```

The procedure, when called with the statement **traverse_from(1)** will print out the contents of the tree in Figure 53.1 in the sequence Legg, Charlesworth, Illman, Hawthorne, Jones, Todd, Ravage, Youngman.

Postorder tree traversal

The algorithm for a postorder traversal is:
1. Traverse the left subtree
2. Traverse the right subtree.
3. Visit the root node

This can be implemented in Pascal as follows:

```
Procedure traverse_from(p:integer);
  if tree[p].left <> 0 then traverse_from(left);
  endif
  if tree[p].right <> 0 then traverse_from(right);
  endif
  writeln (data);
endproc
```

The procedure, when called with the statement **traverse_from(1)** will print out the contents of the tree in Figure 53.1 in the sequence Hawthorne, Jones, Illman, Charlesworth, Ravage, Youngman, Todd, Legg

Recursion

The routine above illustrates just how useful recursion can be to the programmer. The code mirrors the high-level solution arrived at in thinking about the problem, and is far shorter and less complex than a non-recursive solution, which would involve having to store the addresses of nodes that had been visited in order to work back up each subtree.

Summary

A binary tree is an appropriate data structure when a large number of items need to be held in such a way that any item may be quickly accessed, or sequenced lists need to be produced. Additions are easily handled since they require only the adjustment of a single pointer. Different ways of traversing a tree mean that items can be stored in one sequence and retrieved in a different sequence.

Exercises

1. The following table is used to store the contents of an ordered tree which has its root at node 0:

Node	Left Pointer	Data	Right Pointer
0	1	Grimsby	6
1	10	Folkestone	5
2	-1	Manchester	-1
3	-1	Liverpool	-1
4	-1	Deal	-1
5	4	Derby	-1
6	11	Lincoln	9
7	-1	Burnley	-1
8	-1	Cosham	-1
9	3	London	2
10	7	Cleethorpes	8
11	12	Lancaster	-1
12	-1	Heysham	-1

   (a) Draw the tree using this data.
   (b) Show how the pointers in the table would change if:
      (i) Darlington were added to the tree at node 13;
      (ii) Lincoln were removed from the tree.

2. A binary tree is used to represent the following names in alphabetical order:

   Elizabeth, John, Mary, Abdul, Yacub

   (i) Draw a diagram of the binary tree with Elizabeth at the root node.
   (ii) Show how your binary tree might be represented using one or more arrays.

3. A tree is a data structure which consists of a number of nodes linked together. A binary tree can be traversed in a recursive manner.

   (a) Briefly explain the meaning of each of the **four** terms "node", "binary tree", "traversed" and "recursive".
   (b) Name and describe **one** method by which a tree can be traversed.

4. The algebraic expression

$$A * B + C * D$$

is stored as a *binary tree* in the three arrays: *term*, *leftpointer* and *rightpointer*, as shown in the table.

	Subscript						
	1	2	3	4	5	6	7
term	+	*	*	A	B	C	D
leftpointer	2	4	6	0	0	0	0
rightpointer	3	5	7	0	0	0	0

(a) What is a *binary tree*?

Draw a diagram of the binary tree represented by the three arrays: *term, leftpointer* and *rightpointer*.

A recursively-defined procedure P, which takes an integer as its single parameter, is defined below.

```
PROCEDURE P (subscript)
    IF leftpointer (subscript) > 0
        THEN P(leftpointer(subscript))
    ENDIF
    IF rightpointer(subscript) > 0
        THEN P(rightpointer(subscript))
    ENDIF
    PRINT term(subscript)
END of P
```

(b) What is meant by *recursively-defined*?

(c) Explain why a stack is necessary in order to execute procedure P recursively.

(d) Using a copy of the partially completed table shown below as an aid and given that the three arrays *term, leftpointer* and *rightpointer* are global, dry run the procedure call P(1) showing clearly the PRINTed output and the values of the parameter omitted from the table for the **seven** calls of P.

Call Number	Parameter
1	1
2	2
3	4
4	5
5	
6	
7	

(e) What tree traversal algorithm does procedure P describe?

Chapter 54 – Searching and Sorting

Linear search

Sometimes it is necessary to search for items in a file, a table or an array in memory. If the items are not in any particular sequence, the data items have to be searched one by one until the required one is found or the end of the list is reached. This is called a **linear search**. It is inefficient for all but a very small number of items.

Binary search

A binary search is used for searching an ordered array, and is much faster than a linear search for arrays of more than a few items.

The ordered array is divided into three parts; a middle item, the lower part of the array and the upper part. The middle item is examined to see if it is equal to the sought item. If it is not, then if it is greater than the sought item, the upper half of the array is of no further interest. The number of items being searched is therefore halved and the process repeated until the last item is examined, with either the upper half or lower half of the items searched being eliminated at each pass.

A pseudocode procedure for a binary search on an array of *n* items in an array A is given below.

ItemFound, SearchFailed are boolean variables, Top, Bottom and Midpoint are integer variables and A is an array of *n* items (could be any type). ItemSought is a variable of the same type as the items in the array A.

```
Procedure BinarySearch
   ItemFound := False
   SearchFailed := False
   Top := N
   Bottom := 1
   Repeat
      Midpoint := Integer part of ((Top + Bottom)/2)
      If A[Midpoint] = ItemSought
         Then Found := True
         Else
            If Bottom > Top
               Then  SearchFailed = true
               Else
                  If A[Midpoint] < ItemSought
                     Then Bottom := Midpoint + 1
                     Else Top := Midpoint - 1
                  EndIf
            EndIf
      EndIf
   Until ItemFound is True or SearchFailed is True
EndProc
```

The maximum number of comparisons that has to be made in a binary search of 2^n items is n + 1. Thus any item in a list of 1024 (2^{10}) items can be found in a maximum of 11 comparisons. Try it! By comparison, it will take an average 512 comparisons to find an item using a linear search.

Sorting

There are several methods of sorting items held in an array in memory into ascending (or descending) sequence. Both alphabetic and numeric items can be sorted in an identical manner; the sort algorithm is the same whether you are sorting integers or strings.

Bubble sort

This is a slow method but simple to understand and useful when there is a small number of items to be sorted. To sort an array of *n* items, a maximum of *n-1* 'passes' is made through the array, with each item being compared with the adjacent item and swapped if necessary. A 'flag' can be initialised at the beginning of each pass and set to a particular value (e.g. True) if a swap is made; at the end of the pass it is checked and if it has not been set, the values are already in sequence and no further passes need to be made.

The following pseudocode algorithm sorts an array of *n* items into ascending sequence.

Flag is a Boolean variable, Count is an integer variable and A is an array of N items (could be any type). Temp is a variable of the same type as the items in the array A.

```
Procedure BubbleSort
   Repeat
     Flag := False
     For Count := 1 To N - 1
       If A[Count] > A[Count + 1]
         Then
            Temp := A[Count]
            A[Count] := A[Count + 1]
            A[Count + 1] := Temp
            Flag := True
       EndIf
     EndFor
     Subtract 1 from N
   Until Flag = False Or N = 1
EndProc
```

A bubble sort is not a suitable algorithm to use when there are more than say, 50-100 items to be sorted. There are other much faster sort algorithms which may be used when there is a large number of items to be sorted. You will not be asked to reproduce the Insertion Sort or Quicksort algorithm for the AQA 'A' Level but you should be able to follow through an algorithm and state what the end result will be when it is applied to given data.

Quicksort

The quicksort is a very fast sort invented by C.Hoare, based on the general principle that exchanges should be made between items which are a large distance apart in the array holding them. It works by splitting the array into two sublists, and then quicksorting each sublist by splitting them into two sublists and .... remember **recursion**? The quicksort uses a complex recursive algorithm which starts by comparing the first and last elements in the array. For large arrays, it can be hundreds of times faster than the simple bubble sort.

Insertion sort

The easiest way to understand this sorting algorithm is to take say 5 cards or pieces of paper each with a number written on them and place them in a random sequence in a line on the table.

```
         □   5   3   8   6   2
POSITION 0   1   2   3   4   5
```

Starting with the second card, place it temporarily to the left of position 1, (in position 0) and compare the card to the left of the gap with the card in position 0, moving it right one place if it is greater. Repeat this until the card to the left of the gap is less than the card in position 0. Then replace the card from position 0 in the gap. Now place the third card temporarily in position 0, and so on.

```
         3   □   5   8   6   2   becomes   3   □   5   8   6   2
POSITION 0   1   2   3   4   5
                                 and then  □   3   5   8   6   2
```

On the next pass, nothing changes. On the third pass

```
         6   3   5   8   □   2   becomes   6   3   5   □   8   2

                                 and then  □   3   5   6   8   2
```

On the fourth and final pass,

```
         2   3   5   6   8   □   becomes   2   □   3   5   6   8

                                 and then  □   2   3   5   6   8
```

In the pseudocode algorithm for this sort shown below, the **n** values to be sorted are held in an array **card[0..n]**, with **card[0]** being used to hold the current card being looked at.

```
begin procedure
  for counter = 2 to n
    CurrentCard:= card[counter]      (start with the second card)
    card[0] = CurrentCard            (place it temporarily in position 0)
    ptr = counter - 1                (point to card just left of the gap)
    while card[ptr] > CurrentCard    (if it's greater than current card,
      card[ptr+1] = card[ptr]        move it along one space)
      ptr = ptr - 1;                 (ready to look at next card to left)
    endwhile
    card[ptr+1] = CurrentCard;       (put the card back in the gap)
  endfor
end procedure
```

The insertion sort is considerably faster than the bubble sort, but not nearly as fast as the quicksort, which with a given processor would take, say, about 3 seconds to sort an array of 2000 items, a minute using an insertion sort and 5 or 6 minutes using a bubble sort.

Choice of sorting method

The sort method chosen will depend on a number of factors such as the number of items to be sorted, whether they are already partially sorted and the length of the individual records to be sorted.

Exercises

1. The following algorithm is intended to sort an array **a** of integers into order. The algorithm has one error which will result in it not working in some cases.

   ```
   swap := TRUE;
   while swap = TRUE
       swap := FALSE;
       for i := 1 to n – 1
           if a[i] <= a[i + 1]
               temp := a[i + 1];
               a[i + 1] := a[i];
               a[i] := temp;
               swap := TRUE;
           endif;
       endfor;
   endwhile.
   ```

   (i) The algorithm is described using pseudocode. State **two** other methods of describing algorithms.

   (ii) Copy and complete the following table demonstrating the operation of the algorithm. Use the following data set:

   n = 4   a[1] = 7   a[2] = 8   a[3] = 4   a[4] = 3

swap	a[1]	a[2]	a[3]	a[4]	i	temp
	7	8	4	3		

   (iii) What difference does it make if the <= sign in the fifth line is replaced by >=?

   (iv) The algorithm fails when there are repeated numbers in the data set.

   I. What will happen in these circumstances?

   II. The error is in the fifth line of the algorithm:

   if a[i] <= a[i + 1]

   Write down a correct version of this line.

2. The following section of pseudo-code processes a one-dimensional integer array called *List*. The numbers in *List* are stored in ascending order, and *x*, *Low*, *High*, *Middle* are all integer variables. (The function Int returns the whole number part of its parameter.)

```
Proc Process(Low, High, x)
    Found ← False
    Repeat
        Middle ← Int((Low + High)/2)
        If List(Middle) = x
        Then Found ← True
        Else If List(Middle) > x
            Then High ← Middle – 1
            Else Low ← Middle +1      {List(Middle) < x}
    Until Found = True
```

(a) Complete the following dry-run table for Process (1, 10, 19), given that the integers in the list are:

2, 4, 6, 7, 11, 13, 19, 21, 27, 29

Low	High	Middle	Found
1	10		

(b) What type of routine does this pseudo-code define?

3. An array A[1] .. A[n] contains a list of random numbers.

(a) Produce a structured algorithm which will reverse the order of the values in the array.

(b) Briefly describe **one** method of sorting the array and comment on its efficiency if it is used when the elements of the array are already sorted.

Chapter 55 – Operating System Classification

The operating system

An operating system is a program or set of programs that manages the operation of the computer. The most frequently used instructions in the operating system must be stored in main memory and remain there whilst other programs such as application programs are being executed. This portion of the operating system is called by many different names such as **control program, nucleus, monitor, supervisor,** or **executive**.

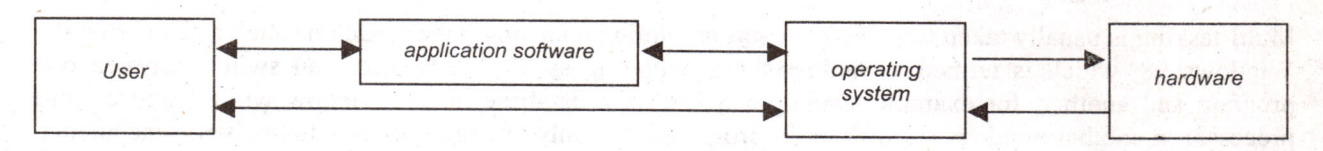

Figure 55.1

Loading an operating system

On all large computers and most micros, the operating system is held on disk and has to be loaded into main memory once the computer has been switched on, before any other programs can be run. The process of loading the operating system is called **booting** the system.

On a microcomputer system, the operating system is usually held on the hard disk. A small program held in ROM (the 'loader') will tell the computer where to look for the operating system, and give instructions for loading at least part of it into memory. Once part of the operating system has been loaded, more instructions can be executed to load the rest of the nucleus. This method of 'pulling itself up by its own bootstraps' is where the expression 'booting' comes from.

In smaller hand-held computers the control program is permanently held in ROM.

Modes of operation

Operating systems vary considerably in their capabilities, from relatively simple single-user microcomputer systems, to sophisticated mainframe computers. Various modes of operation are described below.

Single-user single-process

The operating system supervises the loading and running of one program at a time, and the input and output of data to and from peripheral devices.

Multi-programming

Multi-programming is defined as the **apparent simultaneous execution of two or more programs**.

A multi-programming operating system enables two or more programs to be held in memory at the same time, with each program being given a small amount of processor time before moving on to the next. This system makes efficient use of valuable processor time because when one program is held up waiting for input or output, the processor can be allocated to another program. It is the job of the operating system to maximise throughput while ensuring that all jobs are completed in a reasonable time.

Multi-user

By applying the concept of multi-programming to interactive processing it is possible to develop a multi-user operating system. A **multi-user** (multi-access) operating system is defined as one that **allows two or more users to communicate with the computer at any one time**, with each user interacting with the computer via a terminal (which must have, at the minimum, a keyboard and VDU). As with multi-programming, each program (or in this case, user) in turn is given a small amount of processor time. While some users are typing at the keyboard or using a disk or printer, the processor is working on other users' programs. So long as there are not too many users on the system, each user has the impression that they have sole use of the computer.

Multi-tasking

Multi-tasking is usually taken to mean multi-programming on a single-user machine such as a PC running Windows 98, which is termed a 'multi-tasking operating system'. The user can switch between one program and another, for example running a query on a database in one window while using a word processor in another window. As with multi-programming, only one program is actually being executed at any one moment, with the processor switching between tasks.

Batch

In a batch operating system, a job runs from beginning to end without intervention from the user. The running of batch jobs is normally controlled by a program written in Job Control Language (JCL), which specifies for example the job priority, maximum memory, print lines and execution time required. JCL is discussed in more detail in the next chapter.

Multi-programming systems were developed when all computers operated in batch mode. Thus several batch jobs may be running simultaneously in a multi-programming batch environment.

Multi-user and batch

Some operating systems provide for both multi-user and batch processing. In such systems batch processing jobs are run at times of low interactive demand, e.g., during the night when few users are active on the system. In this way expensive mainframe computers are kept productive twenty four hours a day.

Real-Time

Real-time operating systems can be of different types; process control, information storage and retrieval, and transaction processing. In any of these systems, the data input to the computer must be processed immediately, though in an information storage and retrieval system, or a transaction processing system, a delay of a few seconds is acceptable. Not so in the on-board computer controlling the 10.30 flight to Moscow!

Some systems are safety-critical meaning they must be **fault-tolerant** and guarantee a response within a specified time interval. Such systems have built-in redundancy – the processor may not be used at its full capacity for a large part of the time so that it can respond instantly when required. In addition many components may be duplicated. On airlines, three computers running programs developed by different programmers, but performing identical tasks, run concurrently to ensure that software or hardware errors will not result in disaster.

Chapter 55 – Operating System Classification

Any real-time system has to be able to respond to events happening at unpredictable times and which may happen in parallel.

Examples of real-time operating systems are:
- Booking systems for theatres, flights etc. The response time must be not more than a few seconds.
- On-board computers in an aircraft. The response time must be less than one thousandth of a second.

Client-server system

Most network operating systems operate a client-server system. Client-server computing splits processing between "clients" and "servers". Both are on the network, with the server machine usually being a more powerful machine holding the application programs and files. The clients are each loaded with an operating system which allows work to be carried out at the client computer, e.g., Windows 98, but in addition they contain an extension which intercepts requests to run application programs or to access files or other services which can only be met by the server.

The client-server approach is also used when printing work from an application running on a client computer. A **printer server** allows all the networked machines to have access to a variety of different printers. Printing jobs sent to the server from client computers are held in a queue on a disk (known as 'spooling') and sent to the printer when it is free.

Distributed computer systems [dedicated servers — mail server, printer server, web server.]

With the development of the personal computer (PC), the need arose for stand-alone PCs to be able to share expensive peripheral devices such as printers. This led, in the early 1980s, to PCs being organised in local-area networks (LANs) using interconnection technologies such as Ethernet. Allowing PCs access to the file system of another PC located somewhere else on the network became a requirement as well, especially as the cost of hard disk drives was still relatively high.

The file server and print server networks are examples of **distributed computer systems**. A distributed system is one **in which system resources, e.g. processors, disk storage, printers exist in separate nodes of a network with transparent access to these resources by users being possible.** For example, computer A can run a program on computer B, using a file located elsewhere on the network without the user being aware of where execution is taking place or where the files are physically located.

Exercises

1. A *multi-user*, *multi-tasking* operating system is installed in a microcomputer system. The operating system supports multi-programming. The microcomputer is used for both *batch* and *interactive* work. Explain the differences between:
    - (i)   multi-programming, multi-access and multitasking;
    - (ii) interactive and batch programs.

2. Computer controlled greenhouses and computer controlled nuclear power stations would both be run using *real-time* operating systems.
    - (a) Outline and explain one important difference in the requirements of these two examples of real-time systems.
    - (b) Suggest a suitable operating system for producing gas bills. State **two** characteristics of this operating system and **two** characteristics of the real-time control operating system, which distinguishes each from the other.

Module 4 Processing and Programming Techniques

Chapter 56 – Operating System Concepts

Overview of an operating system

The operating system is a large and complex program, and in this chapter we will be looking in more detail at some basic terms and concepts, and how the operating system works to make the most efficient use of processor time in a multi-programming environment. First of all the different types of user interface used by different operating systems are described.

User Interface

The user interface is the way in which a human user and the computer communicate. User interfaces may be classified as

- command-line;
- job-control language (JCL);
- graphical user interface or GUI.

Command line interface

In a command-line user interface, an interactive terminal allows the system to prompt and the user to type a command to initiate program execution or to perform housekeeping tasks, e.g.

> C:\>Copy Project.* a:

will cause all files named *Project* (with any extension) in the current folder to be copied to the current folder on the A drive. The command prompt is the > character and the **C:** is the pathname for the current folder. The user interface module contains a **command-line interpreter (CLI)** which performs the actual task of identifying and executing the command.

MS-DOS uses an interface of this type.

Job control language [process job in batch]

In a job control language interface a user has no direct interaction with the computer system. Instead a user prepares a series of instructions off-line using a JCL to describe to the system the requirements of his/her task. Eventually, when a user's job is executed the execution is guided by the JCL-prepared description and the results made available at a later time via some off-line medium, e.g., line printer paper.

Typically, Job Control statements will specify:

- who owns the job;
- job priority;
- the maximum processor time to allow the job;
- the maximum lines to be printed;
- the names of data files used;
- what action to take if one of the programs in the job fails to execute correctly.

Chapter 56 – Operating System Concepts

A sample JCL program to compile and execute a COBOL program might look something like the following:

```
$JOB USER123   G.MARRIOTT
$PRIORITY 2
$COBOL
$INPUT PROG1 (DISK 1)
$LIST LP
$IF ERROR THEN END
$RUN
$MEMORY 250K
$TIME 5
$FILES 'PAYFILE'
$IF ERROR THEN DUMP
$END
```

> Q1: What is the purpose of each of the statements in the above JCL program?

Graphical user interface [WIMP] – Windows, Icons, Menus, Pointers

A graphical user interface (GUI) allows the user to interact with the system using windows, icons, menus and a pointer to control the operating system. Icons represent programs, groups of programs, folders, devices and files. Figure 56.1 illustrates a typical GUI. Instead of typing a command or file name, selection is achieved by moving a pointer with a mouse and clicking a mouse button.

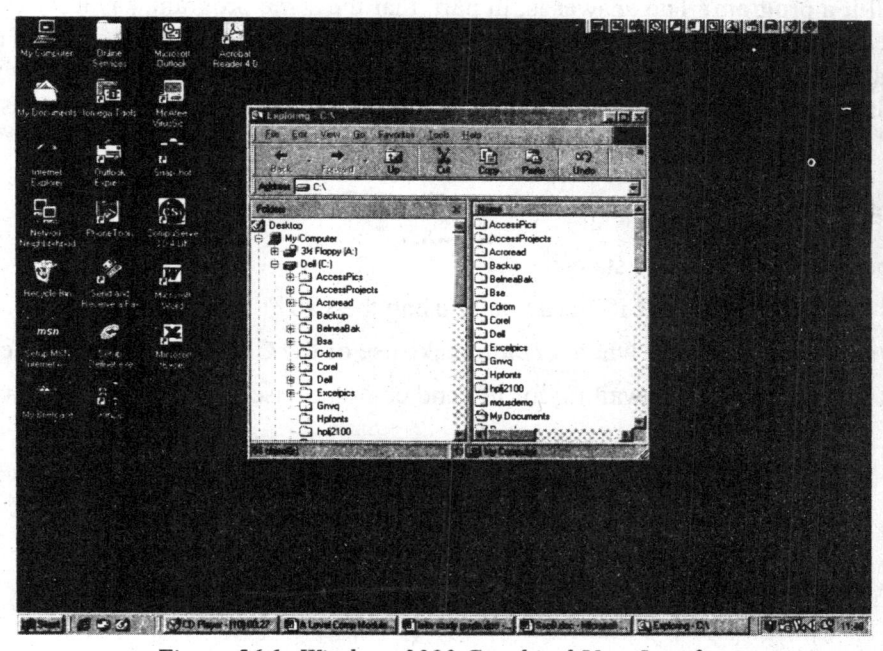

Figure 56.1: Windows 2000 Graphical User Interface

GUIs are easier for the novice to use because they are more intuitive. The screen is arranged as a metaphor of a desktop with graphical symbols to represent familiar objects. Only valid options are available and there is a consistency of layout and command representation in applications which can be launched into execution through operation of the GUI. Comprehensive on-line help is available.

Disadvantages of a GUI over a command-line interface are:
- they use more immediate access store and secondary store;
- they require a more powerful processor and a better graphics display;
- they are slower when executing a command because much more interpretation takes place;
- they can be irritating to use for simple tasks because a greater number of operations is required.

Operating system functions

The OS has four main functions:
- process management;
- memory management;
- I/O control;
- file management.

We will look at the first of these for the rest of this chapter.

The 'process' concept

The concept of a **process** is important in multi-programming operating systems. It is rather hard to define, and much of the time can be thought of as simply a program. One definition is:

*A **process** is a program actually running on the CPU, even though it might be waiting for I/O at a particular moment.*

Why not just call it a program? The answer is, in part, that the same program, say a Pascal compiler, may be being executed by several people simultaneously on a network. There will only be one copy in memory with different parts of it being executed as several people compile their programs, effectively sharing the same code. Each instance of the program running is a process, with separate data areas maintained for each 'execution'. A program working in this way is said to be **re-entrant**.

Process states

A process may be in any one of three states:
- a process is **running** or **current** if it is actually using the CPU;
- a process is **runnable** or **ready** when it *could* make use of the CPU if it was available;
- a process is **blocked** when it is waiting for I/O and could not use the CPU even if it were free.

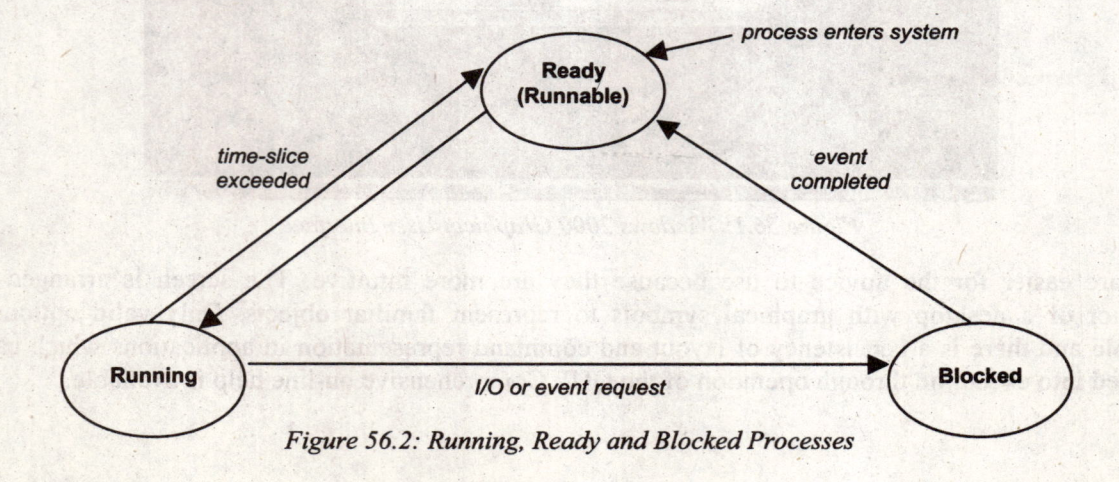

Figure 56.2: Running, Ready and Blocked Processes

The relationship between the three states for a particular process is shown above. For example, if a currently running process requests I/O, it relinquishes the processor and goes into the *blocked* state. If it uses up its time slice before completing then it is placed in a *ready* state while some other process gains the use of the processor.

The process control block (or process descriptor)

When a process gives up the processor, it is necessary to save the details of where the process was in its execution when it was interrupted so that it can resume from exactly the same place later on. In order to be able to do this, each process within the system has an associated **process control block.** This contains the following information:

- process ID
- job priority
- current state of the process
- register save area, where the current contents of all registers are saved before they are taken over by the next process
- a pointer to the processor's allocated memory area
- pointers to other allocated resources (disk, printer etc)
- estimated time to completion
- status (e.g. blocked, runnable)

Interrupt handling

All of the state changes described above are *interrupt-driven*. An **interrupt** is a signal generated by an event that alters the sequence in which a processor executes instructions. It is generated by the hardware of the computer system. When an interrupt occurs, the operating system saves the state of the interrupted process and passes control to the appropriate routine.

An interrupt may be initiated by the currently running process (perhaps it has some data to output, for example), or it may be caused by some event which may or may not be related to the currently running process.

Types of interrupt

The following different types of interrupt may occur:

- **Interrupts generated by the running process**. The process might need to perform I/O, obtain more storage or communicate with the operator.
- **I/O interrupts**. These are initiated by the I/O hardware and signal to the CPU that the status of a channel or device has changed. An I/O interrupt will occur when an I/O operation is complete, when an error occurs, or when a device is made ready.
- **External interrupts**. These could be caused by the interval timer on expiry of a time-slice, or the operator pressing an interrupt key, or the receipt of a signal from another processor on a multiprocessor system.
- **Restart interrupts**. These occur when the operator presses the restart button.
- **Program check interrupts**. These are caused by various types of error such as division by zero.
- **Machine check interrupts**. These are caused by malfunctioning hardware.

How the interrupt mechanism works

There is a special register in the CPU called the interrupt register. At the beginning of each fetch-execute cycle, the interrupt register is checked. Each bit of the register represents a different type of interrupt, and if a bit is set, the state of the current process is saved and the OS routes control to the appropriate interrupt handler.

Since more than one device may request an interrupt simultaneously, each device is assigned a priority. Slow-speed devices such as terminals and printers are given a high priority, since they are more liable to get behind with what they are doing, and so should be allowed to start as soon as possible so that they do not eventually hold up processing.

In some cases if an interrupt occurs during data transfer, some data could be lost, and so the OS will **disable** other interrupts until it completes its task.

In a large multi-user system there is a constant stream of interrupts directed at the processor, and it must respond as quickly as possible to these in order to provide an acceptable response time. Once an interrupt is received, the OS disables interrupts while it deals with the current interrupt. Since this could mean that interrupts are disabled for a large proportion of the time, the nucleus (i.e. the part of the OS that is always in main store) on large systems simply determines the cause of the interrupt and then passes the problem over to the specific interrupt handler, leaving itself free to deal with the next interrupt.

A special register called the PSW (program status word) indicates the types of interrupts currently **enabled** and those currently **disabled**. The CPU allows enabled interrupts to occur; disabled interrupts remain pending, or in some cases are ignored.

In smaller systems, the OS handles all interrupts itself, which means that the interrupts are disabled for a larger proportion of time.

Example:

> Program A is the currently running process. It needs to retrieve some data from disk, so an interrupt is generated. The interrupt handler changes the status of A to 'blocked', makes a request to the disk drive for data, and invokes a program called the **dispatcher** which selects Job B to run next. After a while, the disk drive has filled the buffer area and generates an interrupt to say it is ready. The interrupt handler is invoked, and changes the status of program A from 'blocked' to 'runnable', but B is left running. One millisecond later B's time up is called by the interrupting clock and the dispatcher hands the CPU back to A, leaving B's status as 'runnable'.

Allocating job priorities

In a multi-programming environment, users can allocate priorities to their jobs so that jobs with a high priority will gain processor time ahead of those with a low priority. Short program compilations, for example, may be given a higher priority than less urgent batch jobs.

The operating system also allocates priorities to jobs. Deciding which process to run next is the job of the **scheduler**, and will be done in accordance with a **scheduling policy**. This cannot be too complex or the computer will spend more time deciding whose turn it is than getting on with the job! It is not unknown for an operating system to occupy about 90% of the CPU's time, leaving 10% to be shared out among the users. Some compromise has to be reached.

Scheduling objectives

A scheduling policy should try to

- maximise throughput – try to process as many jobs as possible in as little time as possible;
- maximise the number of interactive users receiving acceptable response times (i.e. at most a few seconds);
- balance resource use – if for example a printer is idle, a high priority could be given to a job that uses the printer;
- avoid pushing the low priority jobs to the back of the queue indefinitely. This can be achieved by giving jobs a higher priority based on how long they have been in the queue;
- enforce priorities – in environments where users can assign priorities to jobs, the scheduler must favour the high priority jobs;
- achieve a balance between response time and utilisation of resources;

Some of these objectives may conflict with each other, making scheduling a complex process!

The scheduler will use a number of criteria such as:

- how much I/O a process needs;
- how much CPU time a process needs;
- whether the process is batch or interactive;
- the urgency of a fast response;
- process priority – high priority processes should be favoured;
- accumulated waiting time;
- how much more time the process needs to complete, though this is often not known.

Round robin scheduling

In round robin scheduling processes are dispatched on a first in first out (FIFO) basis, with each process in turn being given a limited amount of CPU time called a **time slice** or **quantum**. If it does not complete before its time expires (usually a few milliseconds) the dispatcher gives the CPU to the next process.

In order to do this the OS sets an interrupting clock or interval timer to generate interrupts at specific times. This method of scheduling helps to guarantee a reasonable response time to interactive users. In some systems users who have requested a high priority for their jobs may have more than one consecutive time slice each time their turn comes round.

Exercises

1. Distinguish between a command-driven user interface and a menu-driven user interface, stating one advantage of each.

2. Job Control Language is used to control how jobs are to be run in a batch processing system.
   (a) List two pieces of information which might be provided by the Job Control Language for a particular job.
   (b) Some Job Control Languages allow statements which specify to the Operating System the amount of Input and Output expected relative to the amount of CPU time required. What type of Batch Operating System would use this information, and how?

Module 4 Processing and Programming Techniques

3. (a) Briefly describe the main features of **each** of the following types of operating system:

   (i) Multi-user

   (ii) Multi-programming

   (iii) Real-time

   (b) Apart from the use of passwords, briefly describe **two** ways in which a multi-user operating system could control access to a file.

   (c) Explain how priorities are established by the scheduler in a multi-programming operating system.

   (d) A real-time operating system may use interrupts to monitor and control a security system.

   (i) State what is meant by an interrupt.

   (ii) Explain the role of interrupts in such a security system.

4. On a single processor machine the scheduler program for a particular multi-programming, multi-user operating system which supports both *interactive* and *batch processing*, maintains a *list of currently active jobs* and a *list of inactive jobs*.

   The *inactive list* consists solely of *batch jobs* whereas the *active list* contains a mixture of *interactive* and *batch*. New *batch jobs* are added to the *inactive list*. The scheduler transfers *batch jobs* from the *inactive list* to the *active list* when appropriate.

   A job on the *active list* may be running, runnable or suspended; if it is running it will be at the front of the list. When a job is completed it is removed from the *active list*.

   (a) Distinguish between *interactive* and *batch processing*.

   (b) State **three** items of control that will need to be specified by a job control language for **each** batch job.

   (c) Describe **two** situations that would lead to a job in the *active list* being suspended.

   (d) With the aid of a diagram/s describe appropriate data structure/s for storing the list of active jobs.

   (e) The operating system groups all information that it needs about a particular active job into a data structure called a process descriptor. Describe **three** distinct items of information of an active job that will need to be stored in this structure.

   (f) Give **three** factors on which the transition from the *inactive list* to the *active list* depends.

   (g) Describe **two** different events that lead to the scheduler being called upon.

   (h) With reference to the *active list*, briefly explain the method of round robin scheduling.

Chapter 57 – Memory, File and I/O Management

Memory management

The memory manager is primarily concerned with the allocation of the physical main memory to processes. No process may exist until a certain amount of main memory is allocated to it.

The objectives of memory management are:

- to allocate memory space to enable several processes to be executed at the same time;
- to protect processes from each other when executing concurrently;
- to enable sharing of memory space between processes when required;
- to provide a satisfactory level of performance;
- to make the addressing of memory space as transparent as possible to the programmer.

A process to be executed is loaded into main memory by a program called a **loader**, which may be one of two basic types:

- an **absolute loader**, which loads the program into a single fixed area of memory. All address references in the program are fixed at translation time (when the program is assembled or compiled) and it will only work properly when loaded into one specific position in main memory.
- a **relocating loader** which can load the program anywhere in main memory because the program has been translated in such a way that all addresses are relative to the start of the program. The start address of the program can be held in a special register called the **base register**. [offset]

For an object program to be relocatable it must have been prepared with a translator which has been designed for the purpose.

There are two basic forms in which a relocatable object program can be prepared. For the first form, **static relocation**, once the object program has been loaded into main memory relocatability is lost and the process cannot be moved again. For the second form, **dynamic relocation**, relocatability is retained and a process may be moved to a different memory area during its execution (essential in a multi-programming set-up where programs are constantly being swapped in and out of memory). This is made possible by not replacing any logical address references with physical addresses. The logical to physical mapping is done at run time using **base register addressing**.

Another register called the **limit register** holds the highest addressable location of the process, and this enables the memory manager to protect other program's memory space from being accidentally addressed by program error.

Virtual memory and paging

Virtual memory is a technique for making a computer appear to have more memory than it actually has. By holding processes in a special area on disk and only loading small portions of a process as and when they are needed, swapping them out when it is the turn of the next process to have processor time, many processes can effectively share the same memory space.

In a paging system, each process is divided into a number of fixed length blocks called 'pages', typically 4K bytes in length. Memory space is viewed as a series of 'page-frames' of the same size. When a process is to be executed, only the pages that are immediately required are loaded into memory. If necessary,

Module 4 Processing and Programming Techniques

pages of another process are 'swapped' out onto disk to make room for the new pages. Program pages are loaded when in demand and unloaded when not.

Each process has a corresponding **page management table (PMT)** which indicates whether a particular page of the process is loaded or not, and which page-frame it is occupying in memory.

An address of a location in a program takes the form

$$(p,d)$$

where   p is the number of the page-frame containing the location and

d is the displacement or offset of the location from the start of the page.

This allows processes to be **relocatable**; the displacement from the start of a page remains the same wherever the page is, and the page-frame address is obtained from the page-management table.

Dynamically linked libraries (routine)

DLLs can be loaded in any part of the memory :- relocating loader

A dynamic link library (DLL) is a collection of small executable programs which run in the presence of another program. They cannot run on their own, but can be called by another program to perform some task. For example, all the Microsoft Office programs require the Print function, and use it in the same way. It would be wasteful to include the code for printing in all the programs in the Office suite separately. Instead, this code is included in a DLL file, which can be called by any program requiring access to the printer.

Another advantage of the use of DLLs is that the code for printing does not need to be loaded into the computer memory when the main program is loaded. Instead, it can be loaded whilst the printing function is being executed and unloaded subsequently. This makes the operation of the program more efficient, as more of the resources are available for active processes more of the time.

Parameters may be required to be passed to or by the DLL according to the required function definition. If a call to a DLL is made incorrectly, for example by passing the wrong number of parameters, then a General Protection Fault (GPF) will occur.

Whilst some DLLs are used for common functions by several programs as described above, another use for a DLL is to reduce the amount of program code which needs to be loaded in the main memory at any one time. Thus, in a complex program, different modules can be coded in separate DLLs, and only need to be loaded into the memory of the computer when they are called.

File management

The file management part of an operating system has four basic functions:

- To allocate space on the storage device to hold each file stored, and to deallocate space when a file is deleted. Space is usually divided into fixed size *allocation units* (addressable blocks) of say 512 or 1024 bytes.
- To keep track of the allocation units occupied by each file. Files may be split over several allocation units, not necessarily contiguous (i.e. together). A file may initially occupy one unit of 512 bytes, and then when updated by a user, need extra space which may have to be found somewhere else on the disk.
- To control file access rights and permissions (see Chapter 33).
- To map logical file addresses to physical disk addresses. For example, a physical drive may be split into several logical drives C, D, E, F, G.

The file management system maintains a table called a File Allocation Table (FAT) which details the contents and status of each addressable block on the disk.

Blocks and buffers

Data is always transferred to and from disk in units of the physical block size of the disk – say 512 bytes. If the first 100 bytes of a file are requested by a program, the operating system reads the whole block of 512 bytes into a **buffer** in memory and the 100 bytes requested are extracted from the buffer. Similarly, when data is written, it is assembled in the memory buffer and written when a complete block is ready or when the file is closed. This process minimizes the number of disk transfers at the expense of a small amount of memory space and some extra processing complexity.

Input/Output management

The computer communicates with I/O devices by means of an I/O bus system. Each I/O device has an associated hardware controller unit attached to this bus system which can transmit data to, or receive data from, main memory. Each device attached to the bus has its own address which is used to identify it. A system of interrupts is used to enable each I/O device to transfer data independently of the processor. The device sends an interrupt signal to the processor when it has completed its task, and the processor then initiates a further data transfer if required.

The device controller provides a hardware interface between the computer and the I/O device. The controller connects to the computer bus and is designed for a particular computer system but conforms in interface terms with the requirements of the I/O device. If it were not for the controller, different I/O devices would be required for each different type of computer.

Device drivers

A device driver is a software module which manages the communication with a specific I/O device. The driver converts an I/O request from the user into specific commands to the device. For example, a request from the user to 'save a file' onto a disk will be translated by the device driver into a series of actions such as checking for the presence of the disk, locating the space for the file, positioning the read-write heads etc.

Exercises

1. (a) How could an operating system allow two files with the same name to be stored on the same floppy disk?

   (b) Immediately after formatting a new 720k floppy disk, the following message appears on the screen:

   Bytes free = 735232

   Give two reasons why all of the disk's capacity is not available to the user.

   (c) A computer has a *multi-tasking operating system* with a *command-line user interface*.

   (i) What is a multi-tasking operating system?

   (ii) What is a command-line user interface?

   (d) Describe the role of the following operating system modules when a command is entered, through the user interface, to load an executable file from disk. State **one** error that each module might have to deal with.

   (i) the command-line interpreter

   (ii) the file management subsystem

   (iii) the memory management subsystem

   (iv) the input/output system

Module 4 Processing and Programming Techniques

(e) When the command to load a file was entered the computer was executing several background tasks. Name **two** other operating system modules that are required for the successful management of multi-tasking. *Scheduler, dispatcher, loader, Kernel (nucleus)*

2. The figure below is a block diagram showing the architecture of a typical microcomputer. A device controller is a hardware unit which is attached to the bus system of the computer to provide a hardware interface between a computer and a device, e.g. a keyboard.

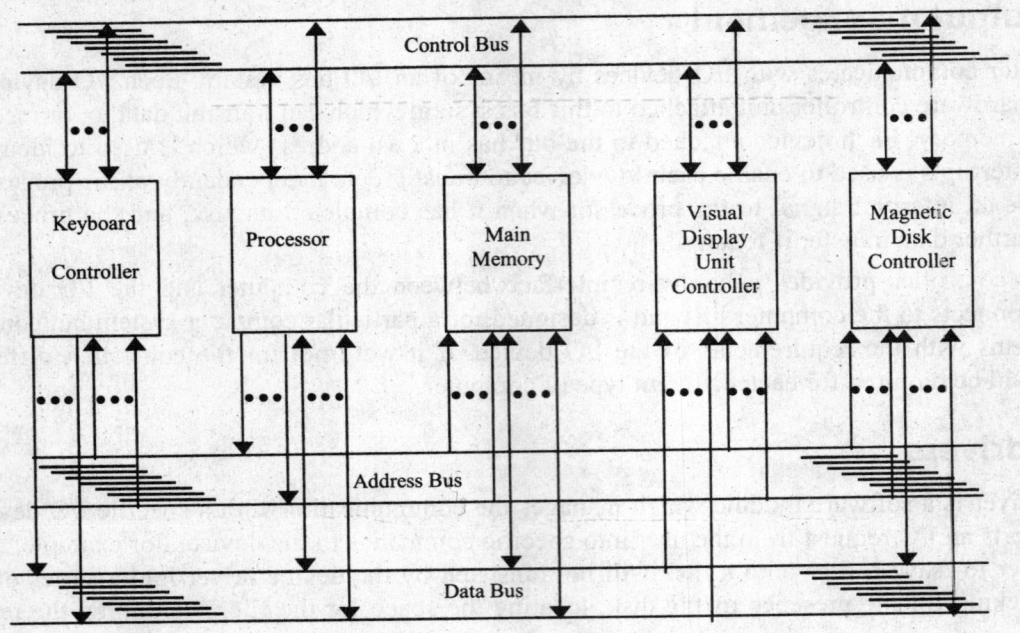

[Block diagram showing Keyboard Controller, Processor, Main Memory, Visual Display Unit Controller, and Magnetic Disk Controller connected via Control Bus, Address Bus, and Data Bus]

(a) Why are devices not connected directly to the processor?

(b) Name **two** other device controllers which may be found in a typical microcomputer.

(c) Name and describe the function of **two** signal lines that are usually present in a control bus.

(d) If every byte of main memory has a unique address, how many address lines does the address bus need for the processor to address all 16 Megabytes of main memory?

(e) If the processor is to address device controllers as well as main memory, how might the bus system do this?

(f) A device driver is a software module which manages the communication with, and control of, a specific device. In some operating systems, the device driver code is assembled and linked with the operating system's kernel object code, while in others, device drivers are loaded dynamically.

    (i) State **one** advantage and **one** disadvantage of each approach.

    (ii) Give **two** reasons why a device driver might need to be written in assembly language.

(g) State **two** advantages of writing other modules of an operating system in a high level language.

3. (i) What is meant by relocatable code?
   (ii) Give an advantage of using relocatable code.

Module 5

Advanced Systems Development

In this section:

Chapter 58 - Database Concepts
Chapter 59 - Database Design and Normalisation
Chapter 60 - Querying a Database
Chapter 61 - Database Management and Manipulation
Chapter 62 - Analysing a System
Chapter 63 - Systems Design, Development and Testing
Chapter 64 - System Implementation, Evaluation and Maintenance
Chapter 65 - Training and Documentation
Chapter 66 - Input and Output Methods
Chapter 67 - Networking
Chapter 68 - Local Area Networks
Chapter 69 - Wide Area Networks
Chapter 70 - The Internet
Chapter 71 - The World Wide Web
Chapter 72 - On-line Shopping and Banking
Chapter 73 - Internet Security and Other Issues
Chapter 74 - Artificial Intelligence and Expert Systems

Chapter 58 – Database Concepts

Traditional file approach

Most organisations began information processing on a small scale, buying a computer for perhaps one or two individual applications, and then computerising other departments one by one. Applications were developed independently, and files of information relevant to one particular department were created and processed by dozens or even hundreds of separate programs. This situation led to several problems.

- **Data redundancy**. The same data was duplicated in many different files. For example, details of a salesperson's name, address and pay rate might be held on a payroll file for calculating the payroll. The same data may be held on a file in the Personnel department along with a lot of other personal data, and in the Sales Department which has a program to keep track of each salesman's record and performance.

- **Data inconsistency**. When the same items of data are held in several different files, the data has to be updated in each separate file when it changes. The Payroll Department, for example, may change the commission rates paid to sales staff but the Sales Department file may fail to update its files and so be producing reports calculated with out-of-date figures.

- **Program-data dependence**. Every computer program in each department has to specify exactly what data fields constitute a record in the file being processed. Any change to the format of the data fields – for example, adding a new field or changing the length of a field – means that every program which uses that file has to be changed, since the file format is specified within each program.

- **Lack of flexibility**. In such a system, when information of a non-routine nature is needed, it can take weeks to assemble the data from the various files and write new programs to produce the required reports.

- **Data was not shareable**. If one department had data that was required by another department, it was awkward to obtain it. A second copy of the file could be made, but this would obviously soon lead to problems of inconsistency. If the same file was used, it would almost certainly be necessary to add extra fields for the new application, and that would mean the original programs would have to be changed to reflect the new file structure.

The database approach

In an attempt to solve these problems, the concept of a database was born.

A **database** is defined as a collection of non-redundant data shareable between different applications.

All the data belonging to the entire organisation would be centralised in a common pool of data, accessible by all applications. This solved the problems of redundancy and inconsistency, but two major problems remained to be addressed.

- **Unproductive maintenance**. Programs were still dependent on the structure of the data, so that when one department needed to add a new field to a particular file, all other programs accessing that file had to be changed.

- **Lack of security**. All the data in the database, even confidential or commercially sensitive data, was accessible by all applications.

Database Management Systems (DBMSs) are used to improve security and eliminate unproductive maintenance, as explained below.

The Database Management System (DBMS)

A DBMS is a layer of software inserted between the applications and the data, which attempts to solve these problems. Two essential features of the DBMS are:

- Program-data independence, whereby the storage structure of the data is hidden from each application/user;
- Restricted user access to the data – each user is given a limited view of the data according to need.

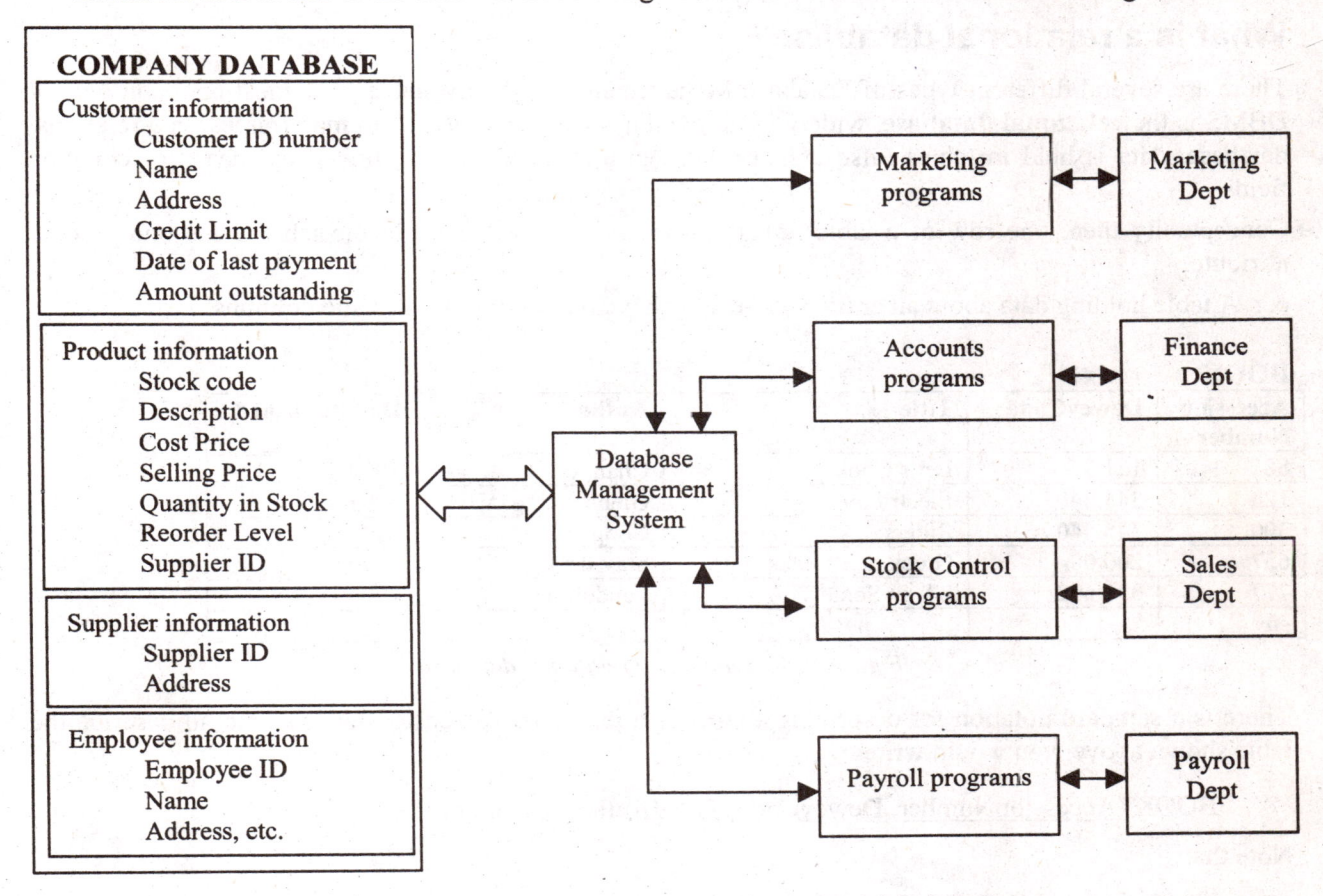

Figure 58.1: The DBMS acts as an interface between application programs and data

Entity-relationship modelling

Refer back to Chapter 31 for a discussion of entity-relationship modelling. This lays the foundation for the normalisation techniques covered in the next chapter. You should revise this before going on!

Exercises

1. What is meant by program-data independence in the context of a database management system?

2. A vet has a database to keep track of the animals seen at the surgery.
   (a) Name two entities in this database, and suggest an identifier for each one.
   (b) Name FOUR attributes for each of the entities.
   (c) What is the relationship between the two entities? (You may use a diagram).

Module 5 Advanced Systems Development

Chapter 59 – Database Design and Normalisation

What is a relational database?

There are several different types of Database Management System available. The most common type of DBMS is the **relational database**, widely used on all systems from micros to mainframes. In a relational database, data is held in tables (also called relations) and the tables are linked by means of common fields.

Conceptually then, one row of a table holds one record. Each column in the table holds one field or attribute.

e.g. A table holding data about an entity BOOK may have the following rows and columns:

BOOK

Accession Number	DeweyCode	Title	Author	DatePublished
88	121.9	Let's Cook!	Chan, C	1992
123	345.440	Electricity	Glendenning, V	1995
300	345.440	Riders	Cooper, J	1995
657	200.00	Greek in 3 weeks	Stavros, G	1990
777	001.602	I.T. in Society	Laudon, K	1994
etc				

Figure 59.1: A table in a relational database

There is a standard notation for describing a table in a relational database. For example, to describe the table shown above, you would write

>   BOOK (<u>AccessionNumber</u>, DeweyCode, Title, Author, DatePublished)

Note that:

- the entity name is shown in uppercase letters;
- the key field (unique identifier) is underlined;
- the attributes are shown in brackets, separated by commas.

Linking database tables

Tables may be linked through the use of a common field. This field must be a key field of one of the tables, and is known as a **foreign key** in the second table. An example best illustrates this.

In a library database, two entities named BOOK and BORROWER have been identified. An entity-relationship diagram may be used to describe the relationship between these two entities.

```
[BORROWER] ───borrows───<[BOOK]
```

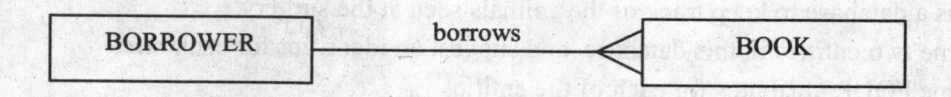

Figure 59.2: One-to-many relationship between BORROWER and BOOK

Chapter 59 – Database Design and Normalisation

The BORROWER table can be described using standard notation as follows:

BORROWER (<u>BorrowerID</u>, Name, Address)

In order to link the two entities, the key field Borrower ID needs to be added to the BOOK table as a *foreign key*. The BOOK table can be described as

BOOK (<u>AccessionNumber</u>, DeweyCode, Title, Author, DatePublished, *BorrowerID*, DateDue)

Note that a foreign key is shown in italics.

In practice, since only a very small proportion of books are on loan at any one time, it would be sensible to have a third table holding data about books on loan, who had borrowed them and when they were due back. The three tables would then look like this:

BORROWER (<u>BorrowerID</u>, Name, Address)
BOOK (<u>AccessionNumber</u>, DeweyCode, Title, Author, DatePublished)
LOAN (<u>AccessionNumber</u>, *BorrowerID*, DateDue)

The entity-relationship diagram would then look like this:

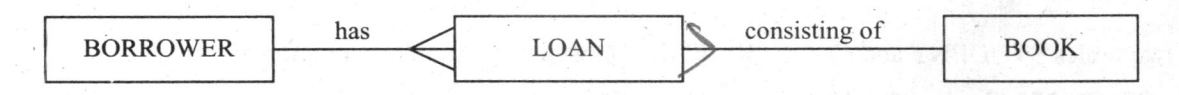

Figure 59.3: Entity-relationship diagram for a library database

> **Q1:** The model above assumes that the LOAN record will be deleted when a book is returned. If this is not going to be done, what adjustments will have to be made to the entity-relationship diagram and LOAN table?

Normalisation

Normalisation is a process used to <u>come up with the best possible design</u> for a relational database. Tables should be organised in such a way that:

- no data is unnecessarily duplicated (i.e. the same data held on more than one table); remove redundancy
- data is consistent throughout the database (e.g. Mr Bradley's address is not recorded as The White house, Sproughton on one table and as 32 Star Lane in another. Consistency should be an automatic consequence of not holding any duplicated data.);
- the structure of each table is flexible enough to allow you to enter as many or as few items (for example, books borrowed by a particular person) as required;
- the structure should enable a user to make all kinds of complex queries relating data from different tables.

We will look at three stages of normalisation known as first, second and third normal form.

First normal form

Definition: A table is in first normal form if it contains no repeating attributes [fields] or groups of attributes.

Module 5 Advanced Systems Development

Let's look at a simple example of two entities STUDENT and COURSE. A student can take several courses, and each course has several students attending. The relationship can be represented by the entity-relationship diagram shown below:

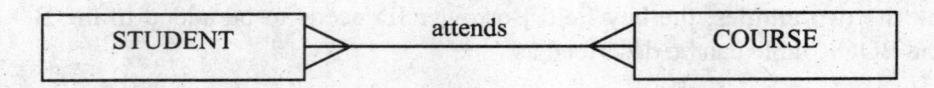

Figure 59.4: The many-to-many relationship between entities STUDENT and COURSE

Sample data to be held in the database is shown in the table below:

STUDENT

Student Number	Student Name	DateOf Birth	Sex	Course Number	CourseName	Lecturer Number	Lecturer Name
12345	Heathcote,R	20-08-83	M	EC6654	A-Level Computing	T345267	Glover,T
22433	Head,J	13-02-83	F	EC6654	A-Level Computing	T345267	Glover,T
				HM7756	A-Level Music	T773351	Reader,B
				AD1121	Pottery	T876541	Day,S
66688	Hargrave,R	13-09-54	M	BM3390	HNC Business	T666758	Newman,P
				HM7756	A-Level Music	T773351	Reader,B

The two tables STUDENT and COURSE will be represented in standard notation as

STUDENT (<u>StudentNumber</u>, StudentName, DateOfBirth, Sex)

COURSE (<u>CourseNumber</u>, CourseName, LecturerNumber, LecturerName)

The question now is, how can the relationship between these two tables be shown? How can we hold the information about which students are doing which courses?

The two tables need to be linked by means of a common field, but the problem is that because this is a many-to-many relationship, whichever table we put the link field into, there needs to be *more than one* field.

e.g. STUDENT (<u>StudentNumber</u>, StudentName, DateOfBirth, Sex, CourseNumber)

is no good because the student is doing several courses, so which one would be mentioned?

Similarly, COURSE (<u>CourseNumber</u>, CourseName, LectureNumber, LecturerName, StudentNumber)

is no good either because each course has a number of students taking it.

One obvious solution (and unfortunately a bad one) springs to mind. How about allowing space for 3 courses on each student record?

STUDENT (<u>StudentNumber</u>, StudentName, DateOfBirth, Sex, Course1, Course2, Course3)

> **Q2: Why is this not a good idea?**

What we have engineered is a repeating attribute – anathema in 1st normal form. In other words, the field CourseNumber is repeated 3 times. The table is therefore NOT in first normal form.

It would be represented in standard notation with a line over the repeating attribute:

STUDENT (<u>StudentNumber</u>, StudentName, DateOfBirth, Sex, CourseNumber)

To put the data into first normal form, the repeating attribute must be removed. In its place, the field CourseNumber becomes part of the primary key in the student table. The tables are now as follows:

STUDENT (<u>StudentNumber</u>, StudentName, DateOfBirth, Sex, <u>CourseNumber</u>)

COURSE (<u>CourseNumber</u>, CourseName, LecturerNumber, LecturerName)

> Q3: What is a primary key? Why does course number have to be part of the primary key?

The two tables STUDENT and COURSE now in first normal form, look like this:

STUDENT

Student Number	Student Name	DateOf Birth	Sex	Course Number
12345	Heathcote,R	20-08-83	M	EC6654
22433	Head,J	13-02-83	F	EC6654
22433	Head,J	13-02-83	F	HM7756
22433	Head,J	13-02-83	F	AD1121
66688	Hargrave,R	13-09-54	M	BM3390
66688	Hargrave,R	13-09-54	M	HM7756

COURSE

Course Number	CourseName	Lecturer Number	Lecturer Name
EC6654	A-Level Computing	T345267	Glover,T
HM7756	A-Level Music	T773351	Reader,B
AD1121	Pottery	T876541	Day,S
BM3390	HNC Business	T666758	Newman,P

> Q4: Why is this a better way of holding the data than having one table with the following structure?
> STUDENT (<u>StudentNumber</u>, StudentName, DateOfBirth, Sex, Course1, Course2, Course3)

> Q5: If student Head, J decides to take up A-Level Art, what changes need to be made to the table structure in Q4?

> Q6: How will we find the names of all students doing A-Level Computing?

> Q7: What are the weaknesses of the two-table structure illustrated above, with tables STUDENT and COURSE?

Second normal form - Partial key dependence test

Definition: A table is in second normal form (2NF) if it is in first normal form and no column that is **not part of a primary** key is dependent on only a portion of the primary key.

This is sometimes expressed by saying that *a table in second normal form contains <u>no partial dependencies</u>*.

The tables above are not in second normal form. For example, StudentName is dependent only on StudentNumber and not on Course number. To put the tables into second normal form, we need to introduce a third table (relation) that acts as a link between the entities Student and Course.

The tables are now as follows:

STUDENT (<u>StudentNumber</u>, StudentName, DateOfBirth, Sex)

STUDENT_TAKES(<u>StudentNumber</u>, <u>CourseNumber</u>)

COURSE (<u>CourseNumber</u>, CourseName, LecturerNumber, LecturerName)

Dealing with a Many-to-Many relationship

As you get more practice in database design, you will notice that *whenever* two entities have a many-to-many relationship, you will *always* need a link table 'in the middle'. Thus

[A]⟞⟝[B]

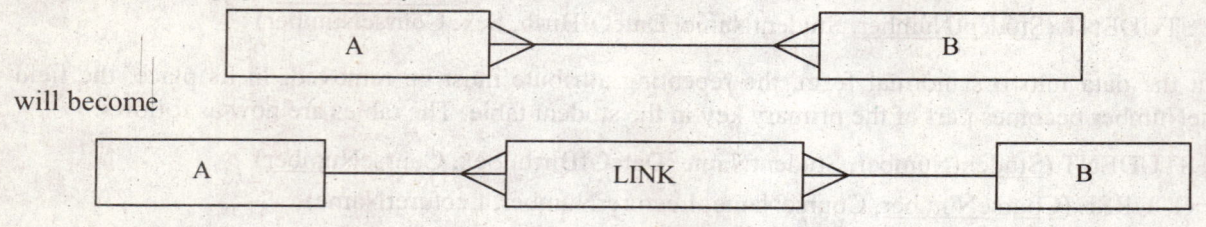

will become

[A]⟞⟝[LINK]⟞⟝[B]

Figure 59.5: A 'link' table is needed in a many-to-many relationship

Third normal form - Non-key dependence test

— all fields depend fully on the p/k and nothing else.

Definition: A table in third normal form contains no 'non-key dependencies'.

Looking at the COURSE table, the lecturer name is dependent on the lecturer number, not on the course number. It therefore needs to be removed from this relation and a new relation created:

LECTURER (<u>LecturerNumber</u>, LecturerName)

The database, now in third normal form, consists of the following tables:

STUDENT (<u>StudentNumber</u>, StudentName, DateOfBirth, Sex)
STUDENT_TAKES (<u>StudentNumber</u>, <u>CourseNumber</u>)
COURSE (<u>CourseNumber</u>, CourseName, LecturerNumber)
LECTURER (<u>LecturerNumber</u>, LecturerName)

Third normal form is as far as you need to go. **BCNF** (Boyce-Codd Normal Form) is, for practical purposes, equivalent to 3NF. It would be extremely rare to find a table that was in 3NF and not in BCNF, and you won't come across one on this course, so we'll stop there.

Foreign keys

Foreign keys are created in the process of creating a join between two tables. A foreign key is a field that is common to both tables; in one table it is the primary key and in the other it is the foreign key. It is usually shown in italics. If a table has two foreign keys, it is joined to two tables.

In the tables above, STUDENT_TAKES has two foreign keys, StudentNumber (the primary key of STUDENT) and CourseNumber (the primary key of COURSE). It may be written thus:

STUDENT_TAKES (*<u>StudentNumber</u>*, *<u>CourseNumber</u>*)

> **Q8:** Which other table has a foreign key? What is it?

Comparing a flat-file system with a relational database

From the example above you will have seen that a relational database is able to create **links** between tables representing different entities such as STUDENT and COURSE, through the use of **foreign keys**. *A flat-file system is not able to create links between tables* and is therefore only useful for very simple databases which contain information about just one entity. It is impossible to 'normalise' a database in a flat-file system, since this involves correctly establishing links between tables.

Flat-file systems do not have any of the sophisticated features of a full DBMS such as the ability to set individual user access rights, or allow several people to access the database at the same time.

Exercises

1. The data requirements for a league of cross-country running clubs are defined as follows.

   The league consists of a number of participating clubs whose runners race against each other in a series of races held throughout the season. The league secretary is responsible for recording data about clubs, races, race entries, race results and club league points.

   Each race has a race identification number, date, start time, distance covered and venue recorded. Runners from different clubs compete in each race. Each club has its name (unique) and the name, address and telephone number of its results secretary recorded. On receipt of a race entry form from a club, the league secretary assigns each listed runner a competitor identification number in the range one to one hundred and their name and club name are recorded. This competitor identification number applies to that particular race only. A competitor's race time and position are recorded after each race. The points a club scores for each race are computed from the positions of its runners and recorded.

   (a) Four entities for the league are Club, Race, ClubRacePoints and RaceCompetitor.
   Draw an entity-relationship diagram which shows four relationships involving the entities Club, Race, ClubRacePoints and RaceCompetitor that can be inferred from the given data requirements.

   (b) A relational database is to be used. Using the following format

   TableName(Attribute1, Attribute2, Attribute3, etc)

   describe tables, stating all attributes, for the following entities underlining the primary key in each case. **These are the only tables that are used.**

   (i) Race
   (ii) Club
   (iii) RaceCompetitor
   (iv) ClubRacePoints

   (c) It is required to print out in race position order the results for a given race. The results are to consist of the competitor's name, club name, race position and race time. Using a query language, show how the required data may be extracted from the relevant table(s) in (b).

Chapter 60 – Querying a Database

SQL

Although it is possible to extract a great deal of information from a database such as Access using Query by Example, there are occasions when complex queries cannot be formulated using this technique. This is when you need SQL, or Structured Query Language – pronounced either as S-Q-L or Sequel. SQL is not a programming language, but a data access language which deals only with the manipulation of tables of data. The major use of SQL is concerned with querying, but it is also possible to use SQL to perform other operations such as creating tables.

The part of the language concerned with asking questions of a database comprises the Data Manipulation Language (DML) statements of SQL. DML statements are conventionally written in UPPER-CASE.

The tables shown below will be used to demonstrate some SQL statements. The tables are part of a database used by a software company to keep track of customers who have bought various software packages that it produces. Each software package sold is uniquely identified by a software licence number. There is a one-to-many relationship between customers and software packages sold.

tblCustomer

CustomerID	CompanyName	Contact	Telephone
SEYMOUR	Seymour Glass	James Bolan	01354-543666
REDCABS	Red Cabs Ltd	Fred Gordon	0181-879965
SUPAG	Supa-Goods	Mavis Hunt	01202-888557
RENTA	Rent-A-Tool	Mark Wong	01473-212777
PRADESH	Pradesh & Co Ltd	Karl Pradesh	01763-396018

tblSoftware

LicenceNo	CustomerID	Package	Version	Price	ServiceAgreement	DateOfPurchase
1000	RENTA	Payroll	4.0	£550	Y	18/02/1999
1123	SEYMOUR	Accounts	6.1	£475	N	01/07/1999
2111	RENTA	Stock	2.0	£700	Y	13/07/1999
3456	SEYMOUR	Stock	2.0	£770	Y	06/11/1999
4870	REDCABS	Payroll	5.0	£620	Y	05/12/1999
5268	SUPAG	Stock	6.2	£900	N	14/02/2000
5381	REDCABS	Accounts	6.2	£520	Y	14/02/2000
6001	PRADESH	Payroll	5.0	£620	Y	
7114	RENTA	Accounts	6.2	£500	Y	17/03/2000

SELECT .. FROM .. WHERE

The SELECT statement is used to extract a collection of fields from a given table.

```
SELECT LicenceNo, CustomerID, Package, DateOfPurchase
FROM tblSoftware;
```

will produce the following Answer table:

Chapter 60 – Querying a Database

LicenceNo	CustomerID	Package	DateOfPurchase
1000	RENTA	Payroll	18/02/1999
1123	SEYMOUR	Accounts	01/07/1999
2111	RENTA	Stock	13/07/1999
3456	SEYMOUR	Stock	06/11/1999
4870	REDCABS	Payroll	05/12/1999
5268	SUPAG	Stock	14/02/2000
5381	REDCABS	Accounts	14/02/2000
6001	PRADESH	Payroll	
7114	RENTA	Accounts	17/03/2000

SQL does not eliminate duplicates by default, so for example

```
SELECT CustomerID, ServiceAgreement
FROM tblSoftware;
```

will produce:

CustomerID	ServiceAgreement
RENTA	Y
SEYMOUR	N
RENTA	Y
SEYMOUR	Y
REDCABS	Y
SUPAG	N
REDCABS	Y
PRADESH	Y
RENTA	Y

You can force SQL to remove the duplicates by using the statement DISTINCT, which only displays distinct rows. Thus

```
SELECT DISTINCT CustomerID, ServiceAgreement
FROM tblSoftware;
```

will produce:

CustomerID	ServiceAgreement
RENTA	Y
SEYMOUR	N
SEYMOUR	Y
REDCABS	Y
SUPAG	N
PRADESH	Y

Module 5 Advanced Systems Development

You can impose conditions on which records are found using the WHERE statement. Thus

```
SELECT LicenceNo, CustomerID, Package, ServiceAgreement
FROM tblSoftware
WHERE ServiceAgreement = "N";
```

will produce:

LicenceNo	CustomerID	Package	ServiceAgreement
1123	SEYMOUR	Accounts	N
5268	SUPAG	Stock	N

Conditions

Conditions in SQL are constructed from the following operators:

Symbol	Meaning	Example	Notes
=	Equal to	LicenceNo=1123	
>	Greater than	DateOfPurchase > #01/01/2000#	MS Access requires that the date is enclosed in # symbols.
<	Less than	DateOfPurchase < #01/01/2000#	
<>	Not equal to	Package <> "Payroll"	
>=	Greater than or equal to	DateOfPurchase >= #02/02/2000#	
<=	Less than or equal to	DateOfPurchase <= #31/12/1999#	
IN	Equal to a value within a set of values	Package IN ("Payroll", "Accounts")	
LIKE	Similar to	CustomerID LIKE "S*"	Finds SEYMOUR, SUPAG
BETWEEN…AND	Within a range, including the two values which define the limits	DateOfPurchase BETWEEN #01/01/2000# AND #31/12/2000#	
IS NULL	Field does not contain a value	DateOfPurchase is NULL	
AND	Both expressions must be true for the entire expression to be judged true	Package = "Accounts" and Version = 6.1	
OR	If either or both of the expressions are true, the entire expression is judged true.	Package = "Accounts" or Package = "Payroll"	Equivalent to Package IN ("Payroll", "Accounts")
NOT	Inverts truth	Package NOT IN ("Payroll", "Accounts")	

> **Q1:** SQL statements are written in the format
>
> ```
> SELECT *
> FROM tblSoftware
> WHERE condition
> ```
>
> Which records will be found from tblSoftware using each of the condition examples given above? (Note that the * means 'Display all fields in the record'.)

292

Specifying a sort order

ORDER BY gives you control over the order in which records appear in the Answer table. If for example you want the records in the Answer table to be displayed in ascending order of CustomerID and within that, ascending order of Package, you would write, for example:

```
SELECT *
FROM tblSoftware
WHERE DateOfPurchase BETWEEN #01/01/1999# AND #28/02/2000#
ORDER BY CustomerID, Package;
```

This would produce the following Answer table:

LicenceNo	CustomerID	Package	Version	Price	ServiceAgreement	DateOfPurchase
5381	REDCABS	Accounts	6.2	£520	Y	14/02/2000
4870	REDCABS	Payroll	5.0	£620	Y	05/12/1999
1000	RENTA	Payroll	4.0	£550	Y	18/02/1999
2111	RENTA	Stock	2.0	£700	Y	13/07/1999
1123	SEYMOUR	Accounts	6.1	£475	N	01/07/1999
3456	SEYMOUR	Stock	2.0	£770	Y	06/11/1999
5268	SUPAG	Stock	6.2	£900	N	14/02/2000

Ascending sequence is the default sort order. If you wanted Package to be displayed in Descending order rather than ascending order, you would write:

```
SELECT *
FROM tblSoftware
WHERE DateOfPurchase BETWEEN #01/01/1999# AND #28/02/2000#
ORDER BY CustomerID, Package DESC;
```

This would produce:

LicenceNo	CustomerID	Package	Version	Price	ServiceAgreement	DateOfPurchase
4870	REDCABS	Payroll	5.0	£620	Y	05/12/1999
5381	REDCABS	Accounts	6.2	£520	Y	14/02/2000
2111	RENTA	Stock	2.0	£700	Y	13/07/1999
1000	RENTA	Payroll	4.0	£550	Y	18/02/1999
3456	SEYMOUR	Stock	2.0	£770	Y	06/11/1999
1123	SEYMOUR	Accounts	6.1	£475	N	01/07/1999
5268	SUPAG	Stock	6.2	£900	N	14/02/2000

GROUP BY

The GROUP BY command is useful for finding sums and averages of values for one particular customer. For example, consider first the statement

```
SELECT SUM (Price) AS SumOfPrice
FROM tblSoftware
WHERE CustomerID = "REDCABS";
```

This would give the following table:

SumOfPrice
£1140

If you want to find the total amount spent by *each* customer, you can use the GROUP BY statement.

```
SELECT CustomerID, SUM(Price) AS SumOfPrice
FROM tblSoftware
Group by CustomerID;
```

This will give the following result:

CustomerID	SumOfPrice
PRADESH	£620
REDCABS	£1140
RENTA	£1750
SEYMOUR	£1245
SUPAG	£900

Extracting data from several tables

So far we have only taken data from one table. Using SQL you can easily combine data from two or more tables, by specifying which table the data is held in. For example, suppose you wanted to list the company name and contact, the licence number, name and date of purchase of each software package. You would write:

```
SELECT tblCustomer.CompanyName, tblCustomer.Contact, tblSoftware.LicenceNo,
       tblSoftware.Package, tblSoftware.DateOfPurchase
FROM tblCustomer, tblSoftware
WHERE tblCustomer.CustomerID = tblSoftware.CustomerID;
```

This will produce the following Answer table (sorted by default in the order in which the fields appear):

CompanyName	Contact	LicenceNo	Package	DateOfPurchase
Pradesh & Co Ltd	Karl Pradesh	6001	Payroll	
Red Cabs Ltd	Fred Gordon	4870	Payroll	05/12/1999
Red Cabs Ltd	Fred Gordon	5381	Accounts	14/02/2000
Rent-A-Tool	Mark Wong	1000	Payroll	18/02/1999
Rent-A-Tool	Mark Wong	2111	Stock	13/07/1999
Rent-A-Tool	Mark Wong	7114	Accounts	17/03/2000
Seymour Glass	James Bolan	1123	Accounts	01/07/1999
Seymour Glass	James Bolan	3456	Stock	06/11/1999
Supa-Goods	Mavis Hunt	5268	Stock	14/02/2000

Exercises

1. Write SQL statements to find from the tables in this chapter:

    (i) The Customer ID, software package, version number, date and price in descending order of price.

    (ii) The Company name, contact and software licence number for all software packages sold with a service agreement;

    (iii) The Company name and total amount spent on software for each company during 1999.

2. Explain the nature and purpose of a database query language.

Chapter 61 – Database Management and Manipulation

The three-level architecture of a DBMS

A database may be considered from several different levels or 'views' known as **schema**. The three levels of schema are:

1. **External** or **user schema**. This is the individual's view of the database – in a multi-user database, there will generally be several different external schema representing each user's view according to their needs and access rights.
2. **Conceptual** or **logical schema**. The overall view of the entire database, including entities, attributes and relationships, as designed by the database designer.
3. **Internal** or **storage schema**. This describes how the data will be stored and is concerned with file organisation and access methods. It is generally transparent to the user.

Data Definition Language (DDL)

The database schema, including aspects such as 'who has access to which data', may be modelled by the Database Administrator (i.e. the person in charge of the database design and maintenance) using a special programming language called a **Data Definition Language (DDL)**. Using this language the logical structure and the files within the database may be defined. Attributes such as record layouts, fields, key fields and validations can all be described using a DDL. This provides an alternative to the way in which tables, forms, reports etc are normally created in a database such as Access.

Example: A table named tblAuthor, with three fields Author-id (a compulsory integer field), Lastname (a compulsory variable length character field) and Firstname (an optional variable length character field) can be created with the DDL statements

```
CREATE TABLE tblAuthor
(Author-id int NOT NULL
lastname varchar(40) NOT NULL
firstname varchar(20) NULL)
```

Data Manipulation Language (DML)

The DML provides a comprehensive set of commands to allow modification of the data within a database. Some facilities of the language (such as SQL statements) enable users to execute queries, and in some systems the DML and the query language are the same thing. Other facilities of a DML allow advanced users to write programs to carry out sophisticated processing of the database.

Open systems and ODBC (Open Database Connectivity)

Open systems provide a standard to which applications may be written to allow portability to multiple systems. *Portability is the key.*

An ODBC interface provides a means of accessing data held in one type of database (such as Access, Oracle or SQL Server) from say, a Visual Basic or Delphi program or from another database or spreadsheet. The data source may be any file for which an ODBC driver is available – the ODBC driver translates ODBC requests into the correct format for a particular data source.

Module 5 Advanced Systems Development

This facility is extremely useful in many circumstances. For example, an Examination Board may use an Oracle database to store grades for all subjects taken by all students. Individual centres (schools or colleges) may not have the facility to access an Oracle database but using ODBC, the Exam Board can store the results for any centre in, say, an Excel spreadsheet which can then be electronically transmitted to the centre. The school or college administration can then manipulate this data in any way to produce a variety of reports and statistics relevant to their centre.

The Database Management System (DBMS)

The DBMS is an application program that provides an interface between the operating system and the user in order to make access to the data as simple as possible. It has several other functions as well, and these are described below.

1. **Data storage, retrieval and update.** The DBMS must allow users to store, retrieve and update information as easily as possible, without having to be aware of the internal structure of the database.
2. **Creation and maintenance of the data dictionary.**
3. **Managing the facilities for sharing the database.** The DBMS has to ensure that problems do not arise when two people simultaneously access a record and try to update it.
4. **Backup and recovery.** The DBMS must provide the ability to recover the database in the event of system failure.
5. **Security.** The DBMS must handle password allocation and checking, and the 'view' of the database that a given user is allowed.

We have looked in previous chapters at how the DBMS allows the storage, retrieval and update of data in the database. In the next few paragraphs we will look in more detail at the other functions of the DBMS.

The data dictionary

When you create a database, you design tables, populate the tables with fields, create joins, queries and macros. The information about which tables contain which fields, their names and data types, primary keys, indexes, how they are joined and so on has to be held somewhere, and it is stored in tables, just like the rest of the database.

The data dictionary is a 'database about the database'. It will contain information such as:

- what tables and columns are included in the present structure;
- the names of the current tables and columns;
- the characteristics of each item of data, such as its length and data type;
- any restrictions on the value of certain columns;
- the meaning of any data fields that are not self-evident; for example, a field such as 'coursetype';
- the relationships between items of data;
- which programs access which items of data, and whether they merely read the data or change it.

It is possible, though dangerous, to modify the database structure by manipulating directly data held in the data dictionary. There are separate tables in Access (identifiable by their names, which all start with *Msys*) for relationships, queries and macros, and these can be opened and viewed in the normal way. (Use **Tools, Options, View** and choose **Show System Objects**.)

The multi-access database

Many organisations have database software installed on a shared drive (file server) on a local area network. This means that:

- more than one person can use the actual **program (such as MS Access, Paradox, FoxPro** etc) at the same time;
- users can work with **databases (customised applications)** which are stored on the shared drive, as well as with tables stored on their local workstation hard drives.

If the database is appropriately configured, more than one person will be able to open it at the same time, and be able to view and update the same tables and other database objects **concurrently**. This is what is meant by the term **multi-access database**.

> Q1: Can you foresee any potential problems that may arise with a multi-access database?

Ensuring the integrity of a shared database

'Ensuring the integrity' means making sure that no data is accidentally lost or corrupted. For example, allowing multiple users to simultaneously update a database table may cause one of the updates to be lost unless measures are taken to prevent this.

When an item is updated, the entire record (indeed the whole **block** in which the record is physically held) will be copied into the user's own local memory area at the workstation. When the record is saved, the block is rewritten to the file server. Imagine the following situation:

User A accesses a customer record, thereby causing it to be copied into the memory at his/her workstation, and starts to type in a new address for the customer.

User B accesses the same customer record, and alters the credit limit and then saves the record and calls up the next record that needs updating.

User A completes the address change, and saves the record.

> Q2: What state will the record be in? (i.e. which address and credit limit will it hold?)

Locking

All multi-user database programs offer several ways of avoiding the type of conflict described above.

1. **Open the entire database in *exclusive* mode**, which prohibits all simultaneous access. This option is impractical when several users need to access the database, but it will give the fastest performance, because the software does not have to check for potential conflicts. It could be used, for example, on an overnight run to perform a time-consuming analysis and report, locking out the occasional stressed-out worker who has come in after hours to catch up on some work.

2. **Lock all records in the table being modified**. Once the first user opens the table, the software will prevent any other user from opening the same table in any view that would allow updating (but still allow it to be opened in *read-only* mode). This is usually unnecessarily restrictive and may prevent other users from getting on with routine tasks.

3. **Lock the record currently being edited**. The moment the first user begins typing changes, the record will be automatically locked by the database software so that no one else may update it. A user who attempts to do so will be presented with a warning message on screen.

4. **The user specifies *no locks***. It is then up to the software to ensure that the users are aware of the situation when a record is being simultaneously updated from two or more workstations, and it is up to the users to resolve the conflict.

5. **Open a table in Read Only mode.** If you do not need to update a table, but simply need to look up a record or print a report, you can avoid conflict by opening the table in Read Only mode.

Deadlock... or 'Deadly embrace'

If two users are attempting to update two related records in the same table, a situation can arise in which neither can proceed.

User1	User2
locks record1	locks record2
tries to access record2	tries to access record1
waits ..	waits ..

DEADLOCK!

The DBMS must recognise when this situation has occurred and take action. One of the two user's tasks must be aborted to allow the other to proceed. Another strategy would be to ensure that in a situation where two records are modified, the records are always updated in the same sequence so that no user calls up record 2 before record 1.

Software protection techniques

There are several ways in which a DBMS can control who has access to particular information. A typical security system will allow the Database Administrator to allocate individual users to named groups of one or more, and assign each group a set of **permissions** or **privileges**. The permissions determine whether a given user can view, modify, execute or update a particular object in a database.

Each user will be identified by a name (e.g. **K.Smith**, or **Accounts Group**), assigned by the Database Administrator. Each individual user will then have a password which he or she can and should change regularly. If an individual forgets their password, the Database Administrator can reset it. If the Administrator forgets **his/her** password, he/she will never again gain access to the database.

The database may be encrypted, for example in MS Access by selecting the **Encrypt** option from the File menu. All information regarding user groups and passwords is automatically encrypted and stored on a separate database to prevent anyone gaining information about user IDs or passwords.

Client-server database

Many modern databases management systems provide an option for **client-server** operation. Using a client-server DBMS, **DBMS server software** runs on the network server, and **DBMS client software** runs on individual workstations. The server software processes requests for data searches, sorts and reports that originate from individual workstations running DBMS client software. For example, a car dealer might want to search the manufacturer's database to find out whether there are any cars of a particular specification available. The DBMS client refers this request to the DBMS server, which searches for the information and sends it back to the client workstation. Once the information is at the workstation, the dealer can sort the list and produce a customised report. If the DBMS did not have client-server capability, the entire database would be copied to the workstation and software held on the workstation would search for the requested data – involving a large amount of time being spent on transmitting irrelevant data and probably a longer search using a less powerful machine.

The advantages of a client-server database are, therefore:

- an expensive resource (powerful computer and large database) can be made available to a large number of users;
- client stations can, if authorised, update the database rather than just view the data;

- the consistency of the database is maintained because only one copy of the data is held (on the server) rather than a copy at each workstation;
- the database processing is normally carried out by the server, with the query being sent by a client station to the server and the results assembled by the server and returned to the client station;
- communication time between client and server is minimised because only the results of a query, not the entire database, is transmitted between the server and client;
- relevant programs and report formats can be held on client workstations and customised for a particular department.

Sage Accounting software, for example, has a client-server version. The Server Network Installation procedure installs the software and data files on the server. The Client version of the software is then installed at each workstation. Report formats for Stock, Invoices, Customers etc. can be stored locally on the relevant client workstations where they can be customised and altered. Each client workstation is allocated access rights to particular files on the database; it may be possible for example to view stock levels, but not alter them from one workstation ('read-only access'), to make stock adjustments from another workstation ('read-write access'), or have no access at all to Customer account records from, say, a workstation in the warehouse.

Object-oriented databases

Conventional DBMSs were designed for homogeneous data that can be easily structured into predefined data fields and records. Many applications today, however, require databases that can store and retrieve not only structured numbers and characters but also drawings, images, photographs, voice and full-motion video. For example a patient database might need to store not only information on name, address, test results and diagnosis but also X-ray images. Conventional DBMSs are not well-suited to handling graphics-based or multimedia applications. An object-oriented database stores the data and methods as objects that can be automatically retrieved and shared.

Exercises

1. (i) What is meant by ODBC (Open Database Connectivity)?
   (ii) Describe one situation in which ODBC might be used.

2. A mail order company has a multi-user centralised database to allow its employees to process orders and deal with customer enquiries as they come in to the customer service department.
   (a) (i) Explain why different staff will have passwords allowing them different levels of access to the data stored.
       (ii) Give **two** other reasons why passwords would be used for this type of system.
   (b) A record within the main stock file is *locked* whenever one person is making changes to it.
       (i) Briefly explain what is meant by the term locked.
       (ii) Why is it necessary in this case to lock records?

3. (i) In the context of a relational database, what is a data dictionary?
   (ii) List 5 items that may be contained in a data dictionary.

Chapter 62 – Analysing a System

Systems investigation

The first stage in the Systems Life Cycle is the Problem Definition, followed by a feasibility study to determine whether a proposed solution is feasible, or achievable, given the organisation's resources and constraints.

Once the decision has been made to go ahead, a much more detailed investigation can take place. One of the most difficult tasks of the analyst is to define the specific information requirements that must be met by the new system. The aim is to gain a complete understanding of the existing system, and how it will change in the future. It will cover:

- the data – its origin, uses, volumes and characteristics;
- the procedures – what is done, where, when and how, and how errors and exceptions are handled;
- the future – development plans and expected growth rates;
- management reports – requirements for new reports and their contents and frequency;
- problems with the existing system.

Methods of fact finding

There are a number of ways of finding out about existing procedures and problems. These include:

- observation – spending some time in the department concerned, seeing at first hand the procedures used, workloads and bottlenecks;
- reading the documentation associated with the system;
- asking clerical staff to keep special counts during a trial period to establish where problems might lie;
- questionnaires – these can be useful when a lot of people will be affected by a new system;
- interviews – the most common and most useful way of fact finding. Interviews must be well planned and consideration given to such factors as:
  - whom to interview;
  - when to interview;
  - what to ask;
  - where to hold the interview.

Reporting techniques

The analyst may use different diagrammatic ways of reporting on the findings of the analysis. Data flow diagrams (DFDs) are a useful tool for showing:

- where the data originates;
- what processing is performed on it and by whom;
- who uses the data;
- what data is stored and where;
- what output is received and who uses it.

Data Flow Diagrams

The symbols used in DFDs are shown below:

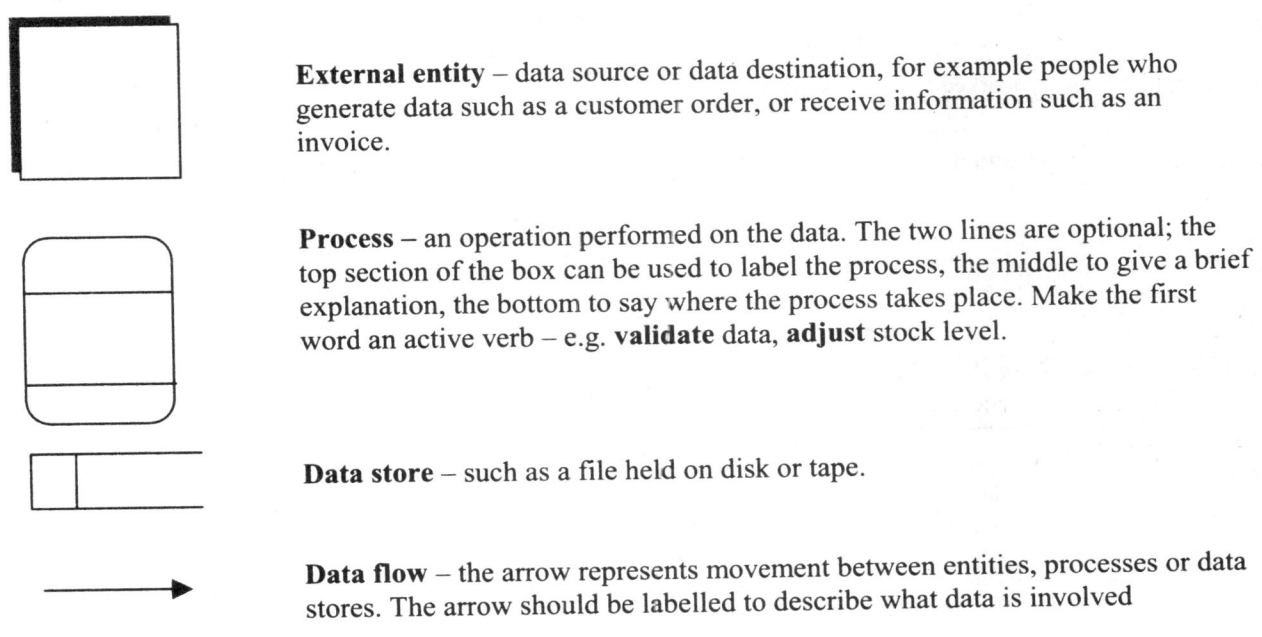

External entity – data source or data destination, for example people who generate data such as a customer order, or receive information such as an invoice.

Process – an operation performed on the data. The two lines are optional; the top section of the box can be used to label the process, the middle to give a brief explanation, the bottom to say where the process takes place. Make the first word an active verb – e.g. **validate** data, **adjust** stock level.

Data store – such as a file held on disk or tape.

Data flow – the arrow represents movement between entities, processes or data stores. The arrow should be labelled to describe what data is involved

Levelled DFDs

It is often impossible to represent a complete business system in a single diagram, so two or three levels of data flow diagrams may be used, each showing more detail.

Example 1:

The payroll system in a certain company may be described as follows:

At the end of each week, time sheets are collected and sent to the computer centre. There, the payroll data is entered via a key-to-disk system, verified and validated, producing a new file of valid transactions on disk and an error report. This file is used to update the employee master file, payslips are printed and funds are electronically transferred to employees' bank accounts.

Draw two levels of Data Flow Diagram, the top level showing a single process, and the second level showing the detailed system as described above.

Solution:

Top Level Diagram:

Module 5 Advanced Systems Development

Second Level Diagram:

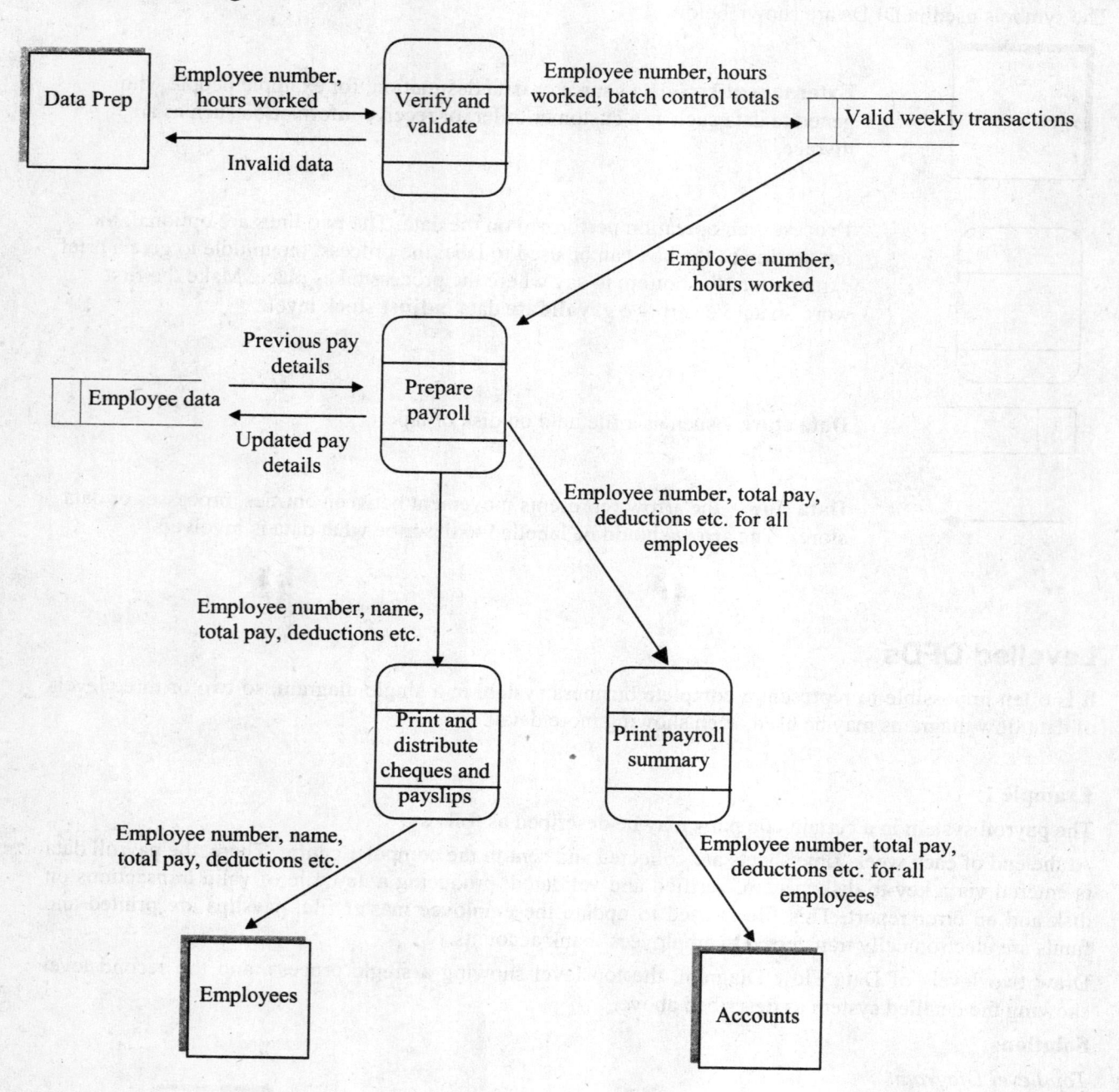

Figure 62.1: A data flow diagram

Example 2:

A student can register by mail for a college course by submitting a registration form with their name, ID number and the numbers of the courses they wish to take. The system verifies that the course is not full and enrolls the student on each course for which a place is still free. The course file and student master files are updated and a confirmation letter is sent to the student to notify them of their acceptance or rejection for each requested course.

Solution:

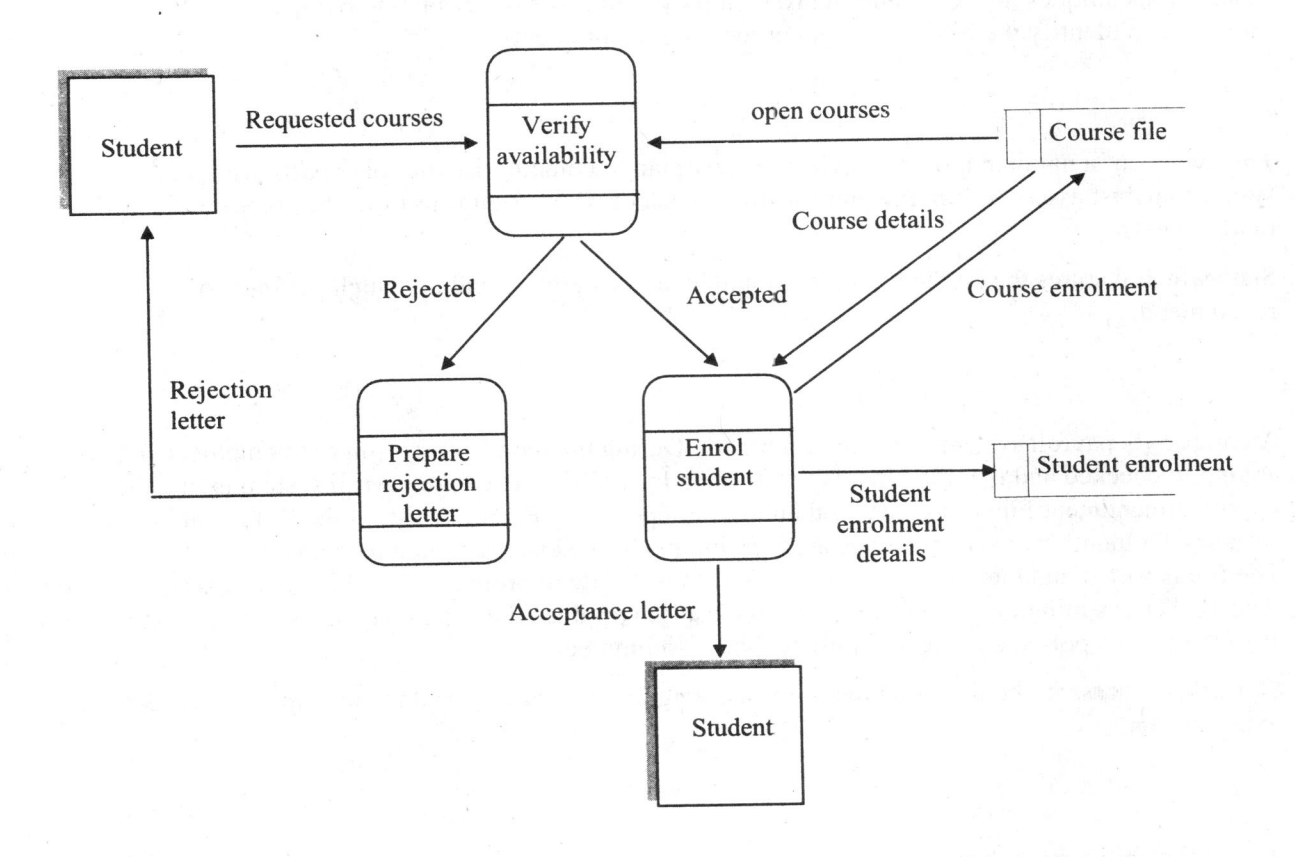

Figure 62.2: Data flow diagram for student registration

Entity Attribute Modelling (EAR)

The system designer may produce a conceptual design identifying the various entities and attributes, and showing how these entities are related. This may then be documented in an Entity-Relationship diagram. These diagrams are covered in Chapters 31 and 59.

Data dictionary

The data dictionary is a file that stores definitions of data elements and data characteristics such as usage, physical representation, ownership, authorisation and security. It will also show which programs and reports in the database system use the data. This is covered in Chapter 61.

Volumetrics

This refers to the volume of data to be processed and the characteristics of the users. The system will have to take into account, for example:
- the number of input documents or on-line requests to the system each day;
- the number of users and whether on-line or batch processing is required.

Exercises

1. State two techniques that a systems analyst, employed to investigate computerising a small business, might use to identify the business's data processing requirements.

2. The owners of a national motor-vehicle company plan to computerise the spare parts section. A systems analyst assesses four existing packages, each of which claims to fulfil the company's requirements.

   State which features the systems analyst should examine before deciding which package to recommend.

3. A company's payroll system is run once a month. During the month, any changes to employee details are input, checked and recorded in a Payroll Amendment File. When the payroll system is run, the Payroll Amendment File is sorted and then used to update the Payroll Master File. Details of hours worked that month by each employee are then input, checked and recorded in the Monthly Pay File. The file is sorted and then used with the Payroll Master File to produce a Pay File, payslips and reports. The resulting Pay File is then sent to a bank to produce the actual payments. At each stage, any errors are reported and the appropriate data re-submitted.

   Show this process in the form of a diagram, showing the flow of data and the information processing requirements.

4. After a feasibility study has been undertaken, a particular project is given the go-ahead. The systems analyst carries out a detailed analysis and investigation at the end of which a number of possible solutions is identified. The analyst evaluates these solutions with regard to how much each will cost and the time likely to be taken for implementation.
   (a) Identify **two** different fact-finding methods which might be used by a systems analyst.
   (b) Describe two criteria, other than cost and time, which could be used in evaluating the possible solutions.

Chapter 63 – Systems Design, Development and Testing

Systems design

The systems designer will consider

- output: content, format, sequence, frequency, medium (e.g. screen or hard copy) etc;
- input: volume, frequency, documents used, input methods;
- user interface: screens and dialogues, menus, special-purpose requirements;
- type of system: batch, on-line, real-time;
- files: contents, record layout, organisation and access methods;
- processing: the programs and procedures needed and their detailed design;
- security: how the data is to be kept secure from accidental corruption or deliberate tampering or hacking;
- testing strategies: how the system is to be thoroughly tested before going 'live';
- hardware: selection of an appropriate configuration.

Prototyping

Prototyping is a useful design tool. It involves building a working model of a system in order to evaluate it, test it or have it approved before building the final product. When applied to computer systems, this could involve, for example, using special software to quickly design input screens and running a program to input data. The user can then experience the 'look and feel' of the input process and suggest alterations before going any further.

Sometimes prototypes are simply discarded before the real system is started ('throwaway' prototyping), and in other cases the prototype may be developed into a working system ('evolutionary' prototyping).

The prototyping approach is supported by a different life cycle model which spirals towards a final solution, and hence is known as the **spiral** model, contrasting with the traditional **waterfall** model (see Chapter 37).

Systems flowcharts

When a systems analyst is developing a new computer system, his or her ideas need to be written down. Frequently a pictorial representation of how the system will work is easier to understand and take in than a lengthy text. A **systems flowchart** is a diagram showing an overview of a complete system. It will show:

- the tasks to be carried out in the new system, whether manual or by the computer;
- the devices (disk drives, tape drives, terminals etc.) that are to be used in the system;
- the media used for input, storage and output;
- the files used by the system.

You should be familiar with the standard symbols used in systems flowcharts.

Module 5 Advanced Systems Development

Systems flowchart symbols

The NCC (National Computing Centre) suggest using the following symbols in systems flowcharts:

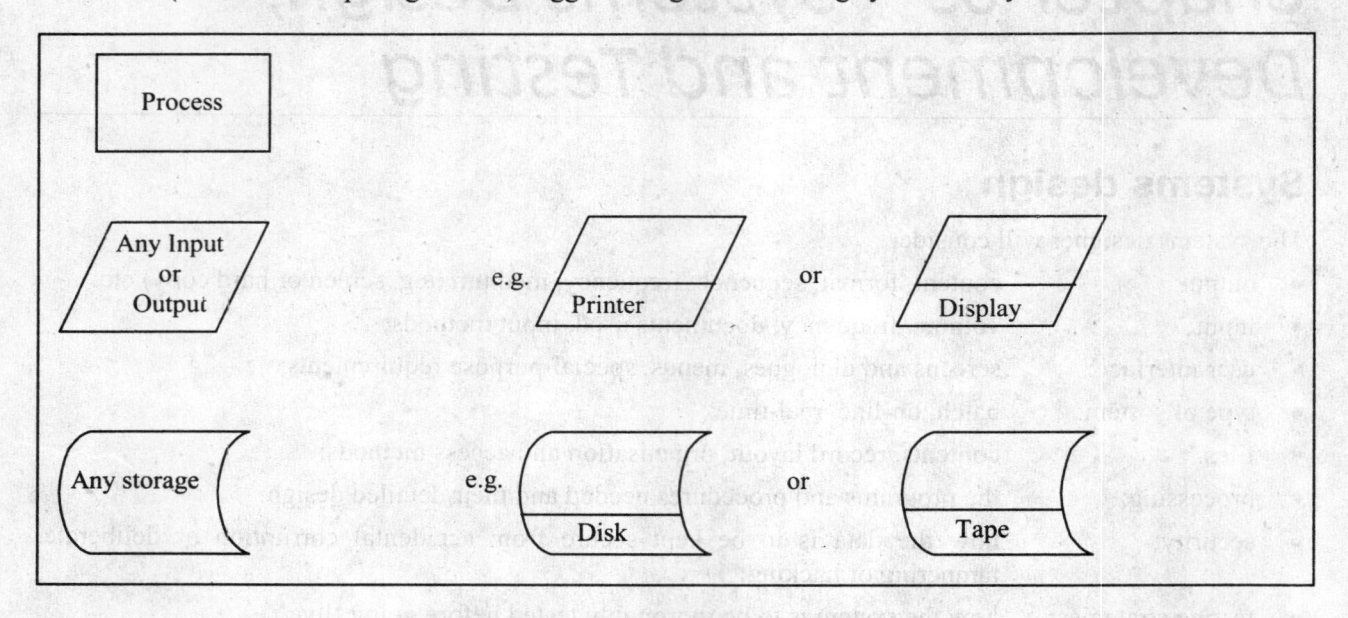

Figure 63.1: Systems Flowchart Symbols

Example: A customer file is held on tape. Receipts are held on a transaction file (also on tape) and are sorted and then used to update the master file, creating a new master file. Draw a systems flowchart to illustrate this process.

Notes: The system flowchart should show the files being used and the processes being carried out. The direction of the arrows on the flow lines indicates whether a file is being used for input, output or both.

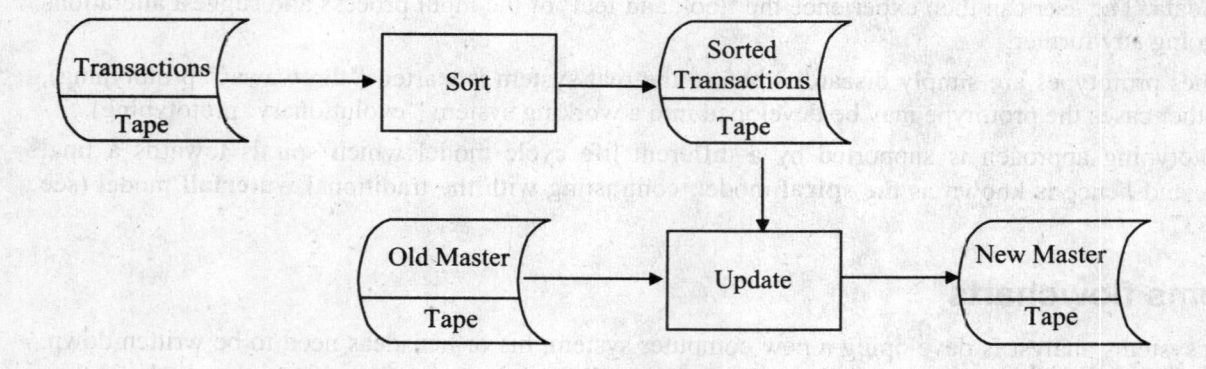

Example: A transaction file is used to update an indexed sequential master file held on disk.

Notes: This differs from the first example in that no new file is created; on an indexed-sequential file the updates will be done 'in situ'. Also, be careful to show the master file on disk, not tape, since it must be a direct access file if it is indexed.

Chapter 63 – Systems Design, Development and Testing

Example:

A stock master file stored in sequence order of a numeric key is updated by a transaction file using sequential file access. Transaction records, which represent additions and deletions to the stock levels, are collected in batches over a period of time and validated before being sorted into key order. Invalid data is corrected and entered into the next batch of transactions. The ordered transactions are used to update the master file. The update process produces a new master file and a file of all changes to records for audit purposes.

Draw a systems flowchart of the system described above.

(Note: Read the whole text through carefully first in order to work out what happens first; in this case, the second sentence is really the starting point of the whole process.)

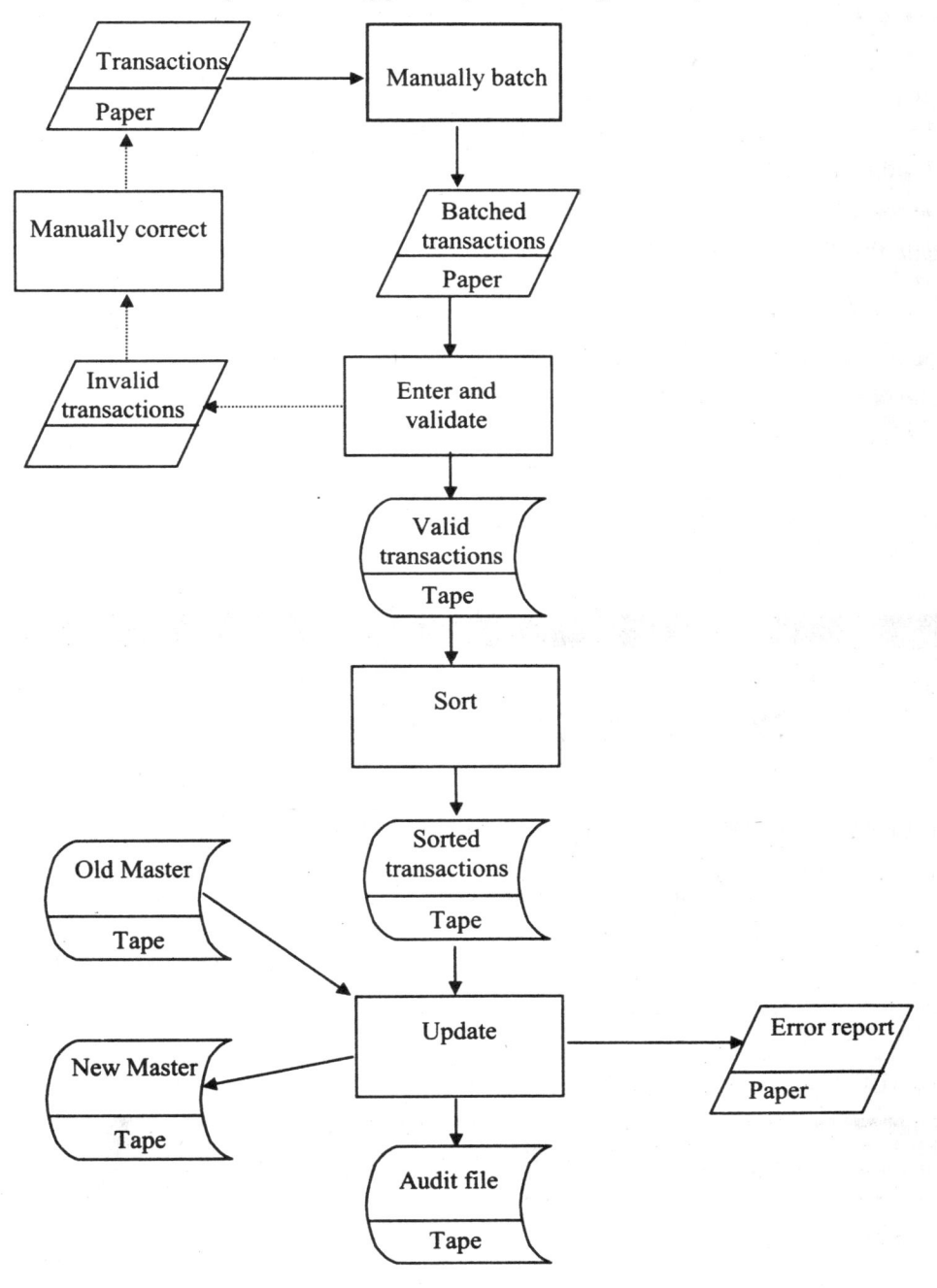

Module 5 Advanced Systems Development

User Interface

A good user interface design is an important aspect of a successful system. The design must take into consideration:

- **who** is going to use the system - members of the public, experienced computer users, young children, etc.;
- **what tasks** the computer is performing; repetitive tasks, life-critical tasks such as flying a plane or dispensing radioactive doses to cancer patients, or variable tasks such as switching between a word processor, spreadsheet and database;
- the **environment** in which the computer is used: hazardous, noisy, or comparatively calm and quiet
- what is **technologically feasible**.

In particular, careful **screen design** can make a huge difference to the usability of a system. When designing an input screen, the following points should be borne in mind:

- the display should be given a title to identify it;
- it should not be too cluttered. Spaces and blanks are important;
- it should indicate the size and format of data entry in each field; i.e. don't just put

    Date: _____

- items should be put into a logical sequence to assist the user;
- colour should be carefully used;
- default values should be written in where possible;
- help facilities should be provided where necessary;
- user should be able to go back and correct entries before they are accepted.

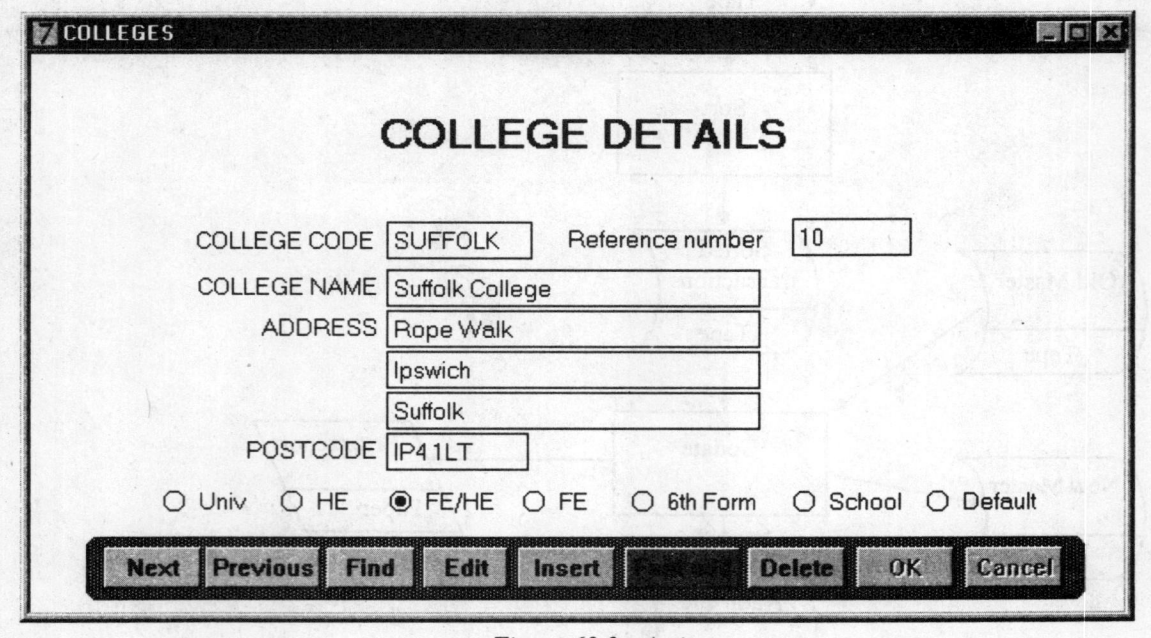

Figure 63.2: An input screen

Program design

This involves drawing structure charts and writing detailed program specifications.

Development

Development in this context refers to the coding and testing of the programs which make up the system, and the testing of the system as a whole. If a software package is being used it will probably involve tailoring the package, implementing screen designs and reports, writing macros etc.

Testing strategies

Obviously a system must be thoroughly tested before being installed to make sure that all errors are discovered and corrected before going 'live'. It is part of the designer's job to come up with a test strategy which will ensure that all parts of the system are properly tested.

Program testing

There are several possible strategies:

Bottom-up testing

1. Each individual module is tested as soon as it is written using pre-prepared test data. The data must include:
   - normal data which the procedure is designed to handle;
   - extreme values which test the behaviour of the module at the upper and lower limits of acceptability;
   - exceptional or invalid data which the procedure should reject rather than attempting to process it.

2. Each complete program in the system is tested. Data should be chosen which:
   - ensures that every route through the program is tested;
   - ensures that every statement in the program is executed at least once;
   - verifies the accuracy of the processing ;
   - verifies that the program operates according to the original specifications.

Top-down testing

The skeleton of the complete system is tested, with individual modules being replaced by 'stubs' which may, for example, display a message to say that a certain procedure has been executed. As individual modules are completed they are included in subsequent tests.

Testing each part of the system is sometimes referred to as **unit testing**.

Black box testing (functional testing)

Black box testing is carried out independently of the code used in the program. It involves looking at the program specification and creating a set of test data that covers all the inputs and outputs and program functions.

White box testing (structural testing)

White box testing is dependent on the code logic, and derives from the program structure rather than its function. The program code is studied and tests are devised which test each possible path at least once. The weakness of white box testing is that it will not detect missing functions – you cannot test what isn't there!

Integration testing

Integration testing takes place when all the modules have been individually tested, to ensure that they work together correctly.

Module 5 Advanced Systems Development

Exercises

1. In a data entry process, data is manually entered at the keyboard from documents, validated and then saved to disk if no errors are found. A printed report is generated if errors do occur during this validation process.

   Draw a *system flowchart* to show these processes.

2. (a) Imagine that you have been asked to produce a computer-based solution to a major problem, which is not currently computerised. Describe the steps that need to be taken to find the information requirements of the system.

   (b) A mail order business receives orders each morning by post. These orders are typed into the computer system by keyboard operators and are then stored on a hard disk.

   When the orders have all been typed into the system the following processing needs to take place.
   - checking that the goods are in stock
   - altering the stock file
   - sending a despatch note to the warehouse
   - send details of the goods despatched to the accounts department for invoicing
   - update the customer file

   Draw a systems flowchart which describes this system.

3. Describe **two** methods of testing which will be used during the development of a new software system.

4. Describe two different ways, other than during the testing stage, in which the end user can contribute to the development of a computer system.

Chapter 64 – Implementation, Evaluation and Maintenance

Implementation

This is the stage in the systems life cycle when people actually begin to use a new system. There are several tasks to be faced before the changeover is complete.

Installing the hardware

Before a new system can be put into operation, any new hardware will have to be installed. Even if it is only a matter of bringing in a couple of new PCs, this may mean changing office layouts, rewiring, acquiring new office furniture and moving personnel. In the case of a new mainframe, it will probably involve putting in a false floor in a specially designed computer room, laying cables and installing air-conditioning.

Training and education

Everyone involved with a new system will need to be given training in their new role, or in the use of new hardware and software. They will need to have hands-on practice with realistic test data before the system goes live.

Creation of master files

Data for all master files will have to be entered before the new system can be used. This usually takes place in two phases: the 'standing data' can be typed in over a few days or weeks, and the rest of the data immediately before the changeover takes place.

> Q1: In a new stock control system, what data could be entered in advance on the stock master file?
> Q2: What data will need to be entered immediately before the system goes live?

Methods of conversion

There are several choices when converting from an old system to a new one:

Direct changeover. The user stops using the old system one day and starts using the new system the next – usually over a weekend or during a slack period. The advantage of this system is that it is fast and efficient, with minimum duplication of work involved. The disadvantage is that normal operations could be seriously disrupted if the new system has errors in it or does not work quite as expected.

Parallel conversion. The old system continues alongside the new system for a few weeks or months. The advantage is that results from the new system can be checked against known results, and if any difficulties occur, operations can continue under the old system while the errors or omissions are sorted out. The disadvantage of parallel running is the duplication of effort required to keep both systems running, which may put a strain on personnel.

Phased conversion. This is used with larger systems that can be broken down into individual modules that can be implemented separately at different times. It could also be used where for example only a few customer accounts are processed using the new system, while the rest remain for a time on the old system. Phased conversion may be direct or parallel.

Module 5 Advanced Systems Development

Pilot conversion. This means that the new system will be used first by only a portion of the organization, for example at one branch or factory.

> Q3: For each of the following examples, state with reasons what type of conversion method would be suitable.
> (a) A bakery is introducing a system to input orders from each salesperson and use this data to calculate how much of each product to bake each day, and also to calculate the sales commission.
> (b) A chain store is introducing EPOS terminals connected to a mainframe computer which holds details of stock levels and prices.
> (c) A public library is introducing a computerised system for the lending and return of books.
> (d) A large hospital is introducing a computerised system for keeping patient records and appointments.
> (e) A college is introducing a computerised timetabling and room allocation system.
> (f) A company manufacturing electronic components is introducing an integrated system for production control, stock control and order processing.
> (g) A Local Authority is introducing a computerised system for the collection of a new type of tax.

Software testing

All software has to undergo a rigorous testing process before it can be released. When a new system is developed, the testing process may typically consist of five stages:

1. **Unit testing**. Each individual component (such as a subroutine or code for a particular function) of the new system is tested.
2. **Module testing**. A module is defined in this context as a collection of dependent components or subroutines.
3. **Subsystem testing.** This phase involves testing collections of modules which have been integrated into subsystems. (For example, the Purchase Order function may be one of the subsystems of an Accounting system.) Subsystems are often independently designed and programmed and problems can arise owing to interface mismatches. Therefore, these interfaces need to be thoroughly tested.
4. **System testing**. The subsystems are integrated to make up the entire system. The testing may reveal errors resulting from the interaction between different subsystems. This stage of testing is also concerned with ensuring that the system meets all the requirements of the original specification.
5. **Acceptance testing**. This is the final stage in the testing process before the system is accepted for operational use. It involves testing the system with data supplied by the system purchaser rather than with simulated data developed specially for testing purposes. It has the following objectives:
   - to confirm that the system delivered meets the original customer specifications;
   - to find out whether any major changes in operating procedures will be needed;
   - to test the system in the environment in which it will run, with realistic volumes of data.

Testing is an iterative process, with each stage in the test process being repeated when modifications have to be made owing to errors coming to light at a subsequent stage.

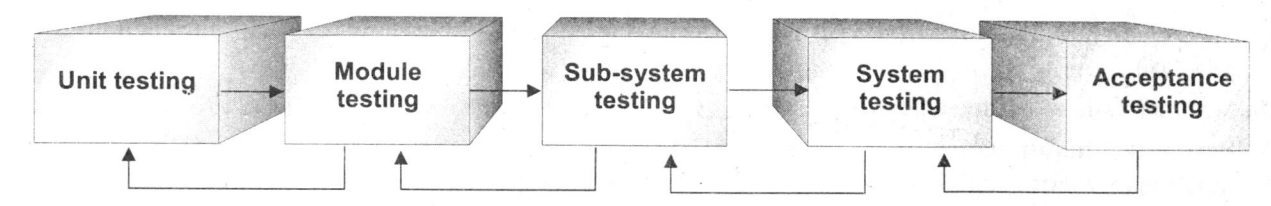

Figure 64.1: Stages in testing new software

Alpha testing

Acceptance testing is sometimes known as **alpha testing**. For specially commissioned software, this testing continues until agreement is reached between the developer and the system purchaser that the system works correctly and fulfils all the system requirements.

Alpha testing is essential because it often reveals both errors and omissions in the system requirements definition. The user may discover that the system does not in fact have the required functionality because the requirements were not specified carefully enough, or because the developer has overlooked or misunderstood something in the specification.

Beta testing

When a new package is being developed for release as a software package, **beta testing** is often used. This involves giving the package to a number of potential users who agree to use the system and report any problems to the developers. Microsoft, for example, delivers beta versions of its products to hundreds of sites for testing. This exposes the product to real use and detects problems and errors that may not have been anticipated by the developers. The product can then be modified and sent out for further beta testing until the developer is confident enough in the product to put it on the market.

Post implementation review (evaluation)

The post-implementation review is a critical examination of the system three to six months after it has been put into operation. This waiting period allows users and technical staff to learn how to use the system, get used to new ways of working and understand the new procedures required. It allows management a chance to evaluate the usefulness of the reports and on-line queries that they can make, and go through several 'month-end' periods when various routine reports will be produced. Shortcomings of the system, if there are any, will be becoming apparent at all levels of the organisation, and users will want a chance to air their views and discuss improvements.

The post-implementation review will focus on the following:

- a comparison of the system's actual performance with the anticipated performance objectives;
- an assessment of each aspect of the system against preset criteria;
- errors which were made during system development;
- unexpected benefits and problems.

Software maintenance

It is impossible to produce software which does not need to be maintained. Over the lifetime of any software system or package, maintenance will be required for a number of reasons:

- errors may be discovered in the software;
- the original requirements are modified to reflect changing needs;
- hardware developments may give scope for advances in software;

Module 5 Advanced Systems Development

- new legislation may be introduced which impacts upon software systems (e.g. the introduction of a new tax).

Maintenance falls into three categories.

- **Perfective maintenance**. The system can be made better in some way without changing its functionality. For example it could be made to run faster or produce reports in a clearer format.
- **Adaptive maintenance**. Changing needs in a company may mean systems need to be adapted – for example, a single-user system may be adapted to a multi-user system. A new operating system or new hardware may also necessitate adaptive maintenance.
- **Corrective maintenance**. This involves the correction of previously undetected errors. Systems may appear to work correctly for some time before errors are discovered. Many commercial software programs such as Windows, Word or Access have bugs in them and maintenance releases are regularly brought out.

Source: McKee 1984

Corrective maintenance 17%
Adaptive maintenance 18%
Perfective maintenance 65%

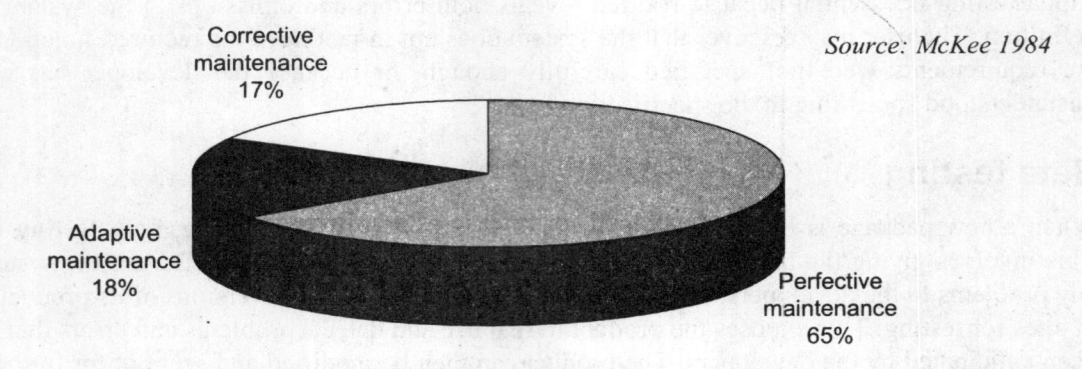

Figure 64.2: Maintenance effort distribution

Factors affecting maintainability

The maintenance process is generally triggered by requests for changes from system users or by management.

A study by Lehman and Belady carried out in 1985 resulted in a set of 'laws' of software maintenance.

1. **The law of continuing change**

    A program that is used in a real-world environment necessarily must change or become progressively less useful in that environment.

2. **The law of increasing complexity**

    As an evolving program changes, its structure tends to become more complex. Extra resources must be devoted to preserving and simplifying the structure.

3. **The law of large program evolution**

    Program evolution is a self-regulating process. System attributes such as size, time between releases and the number of reported errors are approximately invariant for each system release.

4. **The law of organisational stability**

    Over a program's lifetime, its rate of development is approximately constant and independent of the resources devoted to system development.

5. **The law of conservation of familiarity**

    Over the lifetime of a system, the incremental change in each release is approximately constant.

The third law above suggests that large systems have a dynamic of their own. Maintenance teams cannot simply make any changes they want to, because of structural and organisational factors. As changes are made to a system, new errors are introduced which then necessitate more changes. Major changes tend to be inhibited because these changes would be expensive and may result in a less reliable system. The number of changes which may be implemented at any one time is limited.

Maintenance is very expensive, being by far the greatest cost incurred in the overall systems life cycle. It is therefore cost-effective to put time and effort into developing systems which are as easy as possible to maintain. Factors affecting maintainability include:

- good program design;
- well-structured programs written in a modular fashion and following standards of best practice (comprehensible variable names, comments etc.);
- use of an appropriate high-level language;
- good system and program documentation;
- the availability of a record of all maintenance work carried out, when, why and by whom.

Exercises

1. Describe **three** ways in which a large system might be evaluated after installation and testing has been completed.

2. Give three tasks that would be performed in the *Maintenance Phase* of the system life cycle.

3. (a) Give three different techniques a software engineer might use to gather information during the analysis stage of the development cycle.
   (b) What are the advantages of using a top-down structured approach to program design?
   (c) Briefly describe two different methods of changeover from an old system to a new computerised system.
   (d) Why is maintenance documentation so important?

4. You have been requested to advise on the computerisation of a medium sized bookshop.
   (a) Describe briefly **two** significant costs which the shop will incur after the initial installation of the computer hardware and software.
   (b) Describe briefly two benefits that computerisation should bring.

5. A software system has been designed and is ready for implementation. Describe **four** factors which the systems analyst should consider in order to ensure a successful implementation.

6. Describe two ways in which each of the following should be involved in the system review:
   (a) the systems analyst;
   (b) the end user.

Chapter 65 – Training and Documentation

Introduction

Moving from an old system to a new one requires that end-users be trained to use the new system. Detailed documentation showing how the system works from both a technical and end-user standpoint is finalised during conversion time for use in training and everyday operations.

Installation manual

The installation manual will cover the following aspects:

- hardware requirements;
- operating system requirements, e.g. Windows 2000;
- details of how to install the software, folders used, etc.;
- how to customise the system by setting default values, etc.;
- special instructions for multi-user or networked versions;
- how to create new data files, set parameters for the first time,
- software registration instructions;
- upgrade instructions if upgrading from a previous version.

Operations manual

This document will be used by anyone concerned with the day-to-day operation of the computer system, including scheduled events such as generating summary reports for management and backups of the database and/or files. The operations manual will specify when and how these jobs are done. It may include:

- details of the procedure for starting the program;
- details of disks or tapes required;
- special stationery to be used;
- the number of copies of each report, and who is to receive them;
- backup procedures to be followed;
- recovery procedures in the event of hardware failure.

User manual

The user manual will be aimed at the various levels of end-user who will be using the system. End-users may include:

- senior managers who will be using the system to extract strategic information which they will be using for decision-making;
- middle managers who may want to produce extra reports or look up information on the latest sales figures, stock levels etc.

- clerical workers who are using the system for the daily input of data, and for answering queries such as 'When was the order despatched to Cardinal Newman College?'

The manual will therefore contain detailed instructions showing:

- the menu structure of the system;
- how to navigate around the package;
- how to enter data;
- the format of reports and how to print them;
- how to undo actions when an error has been made;
- how to get on-line help;
- a user support telephone number;
- possibly also a tutorial taking the user through the various facilities available.

Training in the use of information technology

Training staff in the use of new technology is crucial to the success of any computer system. Unless staff at all levels of an organisation know how to use the new technology effectively, investment in a computer system can be a waste of money.

Training for users

When a new software package is introduced into a company, users at different levels of the company may require different levels of training. At the lowest level, for example, a clerical worker may need to know how to enter the daily or weekly sales figures and print a report. A member of the sales staff in an electrical retailer's may need to know how to enter a customer's details to check their credit rating, and put through a sale.

Managers will also need to be trained to use the new computer system. They need to feel confident that they can show their staff how to perform certain tasks, and they need to be able to use the system effectively to extract information for decision-making.

Technical staff will need to be trained in correct backup procedures, customisation for specific user needs, trouble-shooting when things go wrong.

Training may be provided in a number of different ways, including:

- a training manual which includes a step-by-step guide on using the system;
- an on-line tutorial supplied with the software;
- a video training course;
- formal, instructor-led training courses.

Exercises

1. With a new computerised system, documentation needs to be provided. Name **two** types of documentation that would be included, and describe what each should contain.

2. Describe briefly **three** different ways in which training may be provided to the users of a recently installed computer system.

Module 5 Advanced Systems Development

Chapter 66 – Input and Output Methods

Input and output devices

I/O devices have been described in Chapters 34 and 35 and it would be a good idea to revise these chapters. In this chapter the principle of operation of some of the most common devices such as a scanner, touch screen and analogue input device will be briefly described.

How a scanner works

The scanner shines a bright light onto the image being scanned while the scan head moves from the top of the document to the bottom at a constant rate. As it moves over each 'line' of the image, the scan head collects data by measuring the intensity of the light that is reflected back from the document. Each scanned line therefore results in a stream of data which the scanner converts into digital information, with a certain number of bits representing each tiny area in the scanned picture. For line drawings or text which are only black and white, only 1 bit will be required; for 256 shades of grey, 8 bits will be required. This information is then stored in the computer's memory, and can be saved on disk.

The **resolution** of the scanner is measured in dots per inch (dpi) along the x and y axes, and this can be varied on more sophisticated scanners. The higher the resolution, the sharper the image, but the scanned image will take up more memory.

Three passes of the scan head, one each with a filter for red, green and blue, are required for colour scanning. Each filter eliminates all colours except the one that matches the filter, and the three resulting images are then combined into one complete full colour image.

Touch screens

A touch screen allows a user to touch an area of the screen in order to enter data, rather than having to type the data on a keyboard. They are widely used in industrial environments such as manufacturing, warehousing and security systems, and also in avionics and medicine. They are very suitable in situations where the operator is moving about and can quickly and easily enter commands by touching the screen. They are less suitable for everyday work in an office, because it is tiring to have to continually reach out to touch a screen.

Touch screens are now available in hand-held portable models and are used, for example, by airlines to record receipts for bar sales, by hospitals to collect information on maternity patients and by local authorities for door-to-door collection of taxes.

There are many different sensor technologies available for different applications. Some respond to pressure, and some use capacitive overlay screens which must be touched by the naked finger. These consist of two primary elements, a glass substrate covered with a tight fitting plastic sheet. Conductive coatings are applied to the inner surface of both elements. Separating the cover sheet from the glass substrate are separator dots, evenly distributed across the active area. Light finger pressure causes internal electrical contact at the point of touch, supplying the controller with the analogue voltage needed for digitisation.

A second type of touch screen uses accoustic wave technology. The screen is a single glass panel with electric transducers in the corners. An interfacing controller sends an elecrical signal to the transducers which convert the signal into surface accoustic waves. These waves are reflected across the active area of the glass by an array of reflector stripes located on the outer edges of the glass. When a finger or pen touches the screen, a portion of the wave is absorbed. The resulting change in the received signal is analysed by the microprocessor in the interfacing controller, and digitised coordinate pairs are transmitted to the computer.

Analogue to digital conversion

In many cases input devices generate signals which are analogue in nature rather than digital; that is they vary continuously between two values. Temperature, pressure, sound and movement are all analogue in nature, so that for example the movement of a **mouse** generates an analogue signal.

A computer cannot process analogue signals and therefore a special interface known as **an analogue-to-digital converter** is required to convert the continuously varying analogue signal to a digital form.

The basic process is as follows:

- The input signal range is divided up into a number of discrete levels, with the number of levels determining the resolution with which the analogue signal can be accurately reproduced.
- Samples of the analogue signals are taken at frequent intervals and converted in real time to digital values.

There are two fundamental ways in which such inputs may be detected. In an interrupt-driven system, the computer receives a signal as soon as data is collected, and can then decide what action, if any, to take. The cable that controls traffic lights is a familiar example of an interrupt-driven input to a processor; when a car drives over the cable (which is buried under the road), the processor that controls the lights is activated, increments a count and decides whether to change the lights or wait for another event, such as several more cars crossing the cable.

In a polled system, the computer periodically checks the input level from a device. One example is the device used on roads that automatically switches on speed limit signs when visibility is poor; the processor automatically checks a light meter in the device at fixed intervals.

Outputs from computers in automated processes can control other machines. They may switch devices on and off, or alter the level at which they operate. Computers in aircraft control the height, direction, state of wingflaps etc. In production control systems, the system often provides some output to machines and some to screens, and receives some input from sensors and some from keyboards. In some systems, such as the control of power stations, the computers propose a course of action and humans approve them for safety. In other systems, the humans may propose a course of action which the computers assess and either carry out or override.

In fly-by-wire aircraft, for example, the computer system checks the pilot's manipulation of the aircraft. The computer constructs a range of settings that it regards as safe, and within these settings, the pilot can decide whether to go faster or slower, higher or lower, etc. If the pilot moves outside these settings, the instructions are blocked.

Choice of input method

Methods of input will depend upon both the nature and volume of the data to be input and the characteristics of the user. In high-volume applications such as cheque processing by banks, the entry of details of gas and electricity consumption by customers, marking multiple choice examinations by a large examination board, input methods are used which cut out the manual process of keying in data. MICR (Magnetic Ink Character Recognition), OCR (Optical Character Recognition) and OMR (Optical Mark Recognition) respectively are suitable for the three applications mentioned. Mail-order systems often use key-to-disk data entry which is suitable for high volume batch applications. In some situations voice recognition may be ideal, for example when the operator needs both hands free or is disabled and unable to use a keyboard.

Module 5 Advanced Systems Development

Exercises

1. Speech recognition systems for Personal Computers are now becoming more affordable and useable.

   (a) State **two** advantages to a PC user of a speech recognition system.

   (b) Give **two** different tasks for which a PC user could take advantage of speech recognition.

   (c) Speech recognition systems sometimes fail to be 100% effective in practice. Give **three** reasons why this is so.

2. With the aid of examples, explain *on-line* and *off-line* methods of data collection.

3. "Firemen will be able to respond faster to emergency calls thanks to a system which relays data from the control room computer to the fire engine."

   Data that could be transmitted include maps or directions to give the best route to a fire and information on the hazardous chemicals that might be used at the site of the fire.

   Suggest and justify an appropriate device that could be used effectively in a fire engine cab for this system for:

   (i) input

   (ii) output.

4. Both stripe cards and smart cards are widely used in retailing. Describe the main differences between each of these types of card.

5. It would be possible for a computer system to be used to record the arrival of runners in a marathon at various stages along the route.

   (a) Briefly explain how competitors could be:

   (i) identified by;

   (ii) entered into;

   the computer system as they run past each stage point.

   (b) The Marathon Committee are concerned about the reliability of the system. Suggest **one** difficulty they might see in your method.

   (c) Give **two** validation checks for the data captured.

Chapter 67 – Networking

Wide area networks

When the devices in a network are close together, for example in the same building, they can be linked by means of cables, and this is what is meant by a Local Area Network. However, when devices are separated by more than a few hundred yards, data has to be sent over a communications link (e.g. telephone line) and extra equipment such as a modem is required.

A Wide Area Network is a collection of computers spread over a wide geographical area, possibly spanning several continents. Communication may be via microwave, satellite link or telephone line, or a combination of these. The use of global networks (including the Internet) has increased enormously over the past few years, owing to:

- changeover of telephone networks from old-style analogue to high-speed digital technology;
- reduction in the cost of connecting to and using networks;
- improved compression techniques which allow faster transmission of text and graphics.

Communications links

Communication may take place over a combination of different media:

- twisted pair (copper cable), used in much of the telephone network;
- coaxial cable – high quality, well insulated cable that can transmit data at higher speeds;
- fibre optic cable through which pulses of light, rather than electricity, are sent in digital form;
- microwave – similar to radio waves. Microwave stations cannot be much more than 30 miles apart because of the earth's curvature as microwaves travel in straight lines. Mobile telephones use microwave radio links;
- communications satellite, using one of the hundreds of satellites now in geosynchronous orbit about 22,000 miles above the earth. (Geosynchronous orbit means that they are orbiting at the same speed as the earth, and are therefore stationary relative to earth.)

Cabling systems

Type of cabling has a major bearing on a network's speed, performance, cost and practicality (a very thick cable being much harder to lay in or along walls). **Twisted pair**, like telephone wire, is the cheapest but has slow transmission rates and suffers from electronic interference. **Coaxial cable** is high quality, well insulated cable which can transmit data much faster and more accurately than twisted pair.

There are two types of coaxial cable:

- **baseband** carries one signal at a time. A bit value of 1 or 0 is sent by the presence or absence of a voltage in the cable. Baseband signals can travel very fast, but can only be sent over short distances. Over about 1000 feet special booster equipment is needed.
- **Broadband** can carry multiple signals on a fixed carrier wave, with the signals for 0 and 1 sent as variations on this wave. ISDN (Integrated Services Digital Network) is a broadband digital communications technology which offers faster transmission rates than with a modem and ordinary POTS (plain old telephone system) line and enables the transmission of voice, video and computer data simultaneously (e.g. for videoconferencing).

Synchronous data transmission

In **synchronous transmission mode**, timing signals synchronise the transmission at the sending and receiving end so there is no need for start and stop bits for each character, only at the beginning and end of the whole block. This makes it possible to achieve higher transfer rates, but there may be more errors. This mode of transmission is widely used in local area networks.

Time-division multiplexing

A **multiplexor** combines more than one input signal into a single stream of data that can be transmitted over a communication channel. This increases the efficiency of communication and saves on the cost of individual channels.

At the receiving end, the multiplexor (sometimes called the demultiplexor) separates the single stream of data into its separate components.

In time-division multiplexing, the transmission time is split up into tiny time-slices, and each user in turn is allowed to transmit a small amount of data. Because a high bandwidth is used for the line, thousands of users can have telephone conversations or transmit digital data, apparently simultaneously, down a single high-speed line.

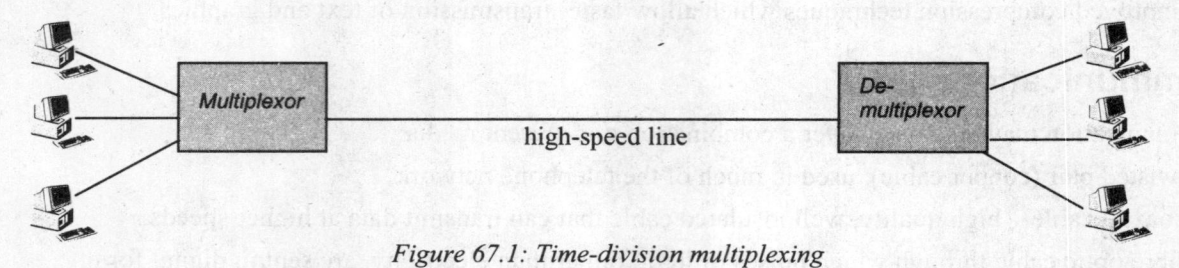

Figure 67.1: Time-division multiplexing

Circuit switching

The public telephone system is an example of a switched network using **circuit-switched** paths. When a caller dials a number, the path between the two telephones is set up by operating switches in all of the exchanges involved in the path. The circuit is set up and held for the whole duration of the call, even through periods of silence or heavy breathing. This permits the two people on the phone to hold a conversation with no waiting at either end for the message to arrive. However, because switches are used to connect and disconnect the circuits, electrical interference is produced, and although this is not a serious problem for speech, it may produce corrupt or lost data if the path is being used to transmit computer data. If this is likely to be a serious problem, a leased line may be used instead.

Packet switching

In a **packet switching system (PSS)** messages are divided into **packets** – fixed length blocks of data of say 128 bytes. As well as the data, each packet also carries:

- the source and destination address;
- a packet sequence number so that the whole message can be correctly reassembled;
- a checksum (longitudinal parity check) for the purposes of error checking.

In some protocols (e.g. TCP/IP, see below) a packet is known as a **datagram**.

The PSS (such as the one in Britain which is owned by British Telecom) takes the form of a computer network in which each computer redirects the packets it receives to the next computer along an appropriate route to its destination. The packets from different users to different destinations may be interleaved, and all the packets making up one transmission need not necessarily travel by the same route or arrive in the right order. The PSS ensures that they are all reassembled in the correct order at their destination.

The computers in the PSS are able to perform error checking and request retransmission of packets found to be in error. They are also able to perform error correction so that even if a transmission contained some errors, perhaps due to distortion on the line, it may be possible to correct these without having to retransmit.

In order to use the PSS, a user requires a network user identity, which is registered at his/her local packet switching exchange. The Internet is a prime example of a packet-switching network.

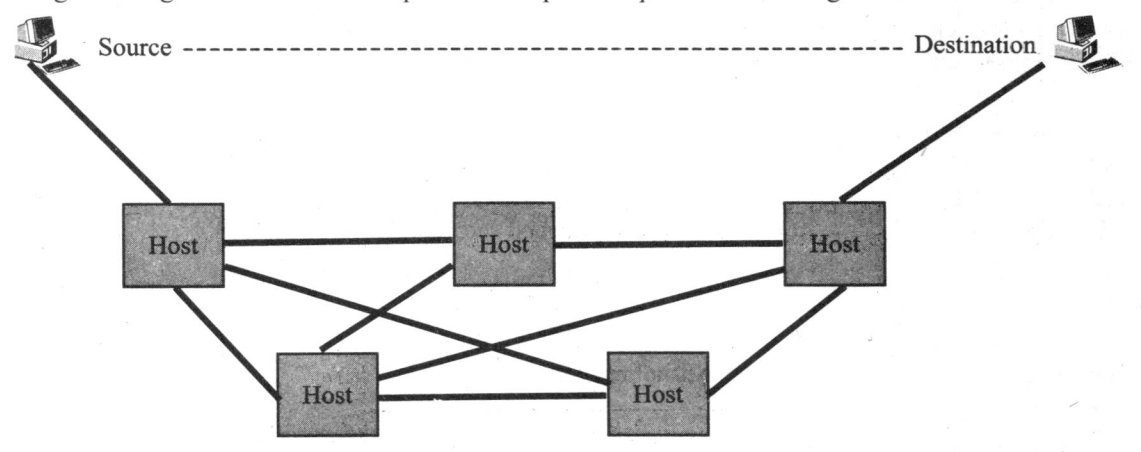

Figure 67.2: A packet-switching network

Virtual circuits

Many packet-switching networks employ **virtual circuits** to provide temporary 'dedicated' pathways between two points. There is no real cable between the two endpoints; rather, a virtual circuit consists of a logical sequence of connections where bandwidth is allocated for a specific transmission pathway. This pathway between sender and receiver is created once both computers agree on bandwidth requirements and request a pathway.

Advantages of packet switching

- more efficient use of lines;
- cost depends only on the number of packets sent, not on distance so all data can be transmitted at local call rates;
- less likely to be affected by network failure because of the multiple routes available to transmit data packets;
- better security; data is less likely to be intercepted because the packets may be sent along different routes or be interleaved with other unrelated packets.

Asynchronous Transfer Mode (ATM)

This is a type of packet-switching system which can support a wide range of different data types including computer data, voice, fax, CD-quality audio and real-time video. In the ATM system packets of data are referred to as cells: each ATM cell is 48 bytes of data plus 5 bytes of header information containing destination address and other information.

Digital lines are used to support ATM, and the resulting noise- and error-free communication enables ATM to deliver amazingly high transmission rates, typically 622Mbps.

Standard protocols

In order for two computers on a network to communicate successfully, they must share a common set of rules about how to communicate. At a minimum, such rules must include how to interpret signals, how to identify 'oneself' and other computers on a network, how to initiate and end networked communications, and how to manage information exchange across the network medium. These collections of rules are called **network protocols**.

Any computer that can access a network must have a **protocol stack**. This provides the software that enables computers to communicate across a network. The most common protocol stack is **Transmission Control Protocol/Internet Protocol (TCP/IP)**. The protocol follows the OSI (Open Systems Interconnection) guidelines that have been under development since 1977. Each layer in this seven-layer model has its own function:

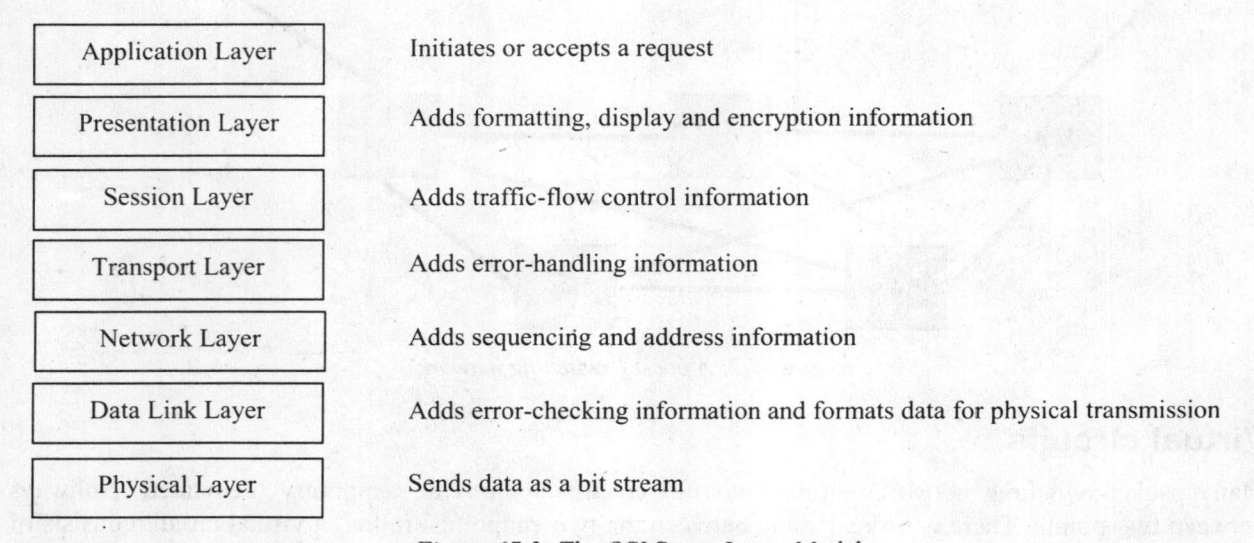

Application Layer	Initiates or accepts a request
Presentation Layer	Adds formatting, display and encryption information
Session Layer	Adds traffic-flow control information
Transport Layer	Adds error-handling information
Network Layer	Adds sequencing and address information
Data Link Layer	Adds error-checking information and formats data for physical transmission
Physical Layer	Sends data as a bit stream

Figure 67.3: The OSI Seven Layer Model

The TCP/IP protocol stack, although it predates the OSI model by nearly a decade, has similar protocols and functions. TCP is a Transport layer protocol, and IP is a network layer protocol which provides source and destination addressing and routing in the TCP/IP suite. IP is a connectionless datagram protocol that, like all connectionless protocols, is fast but unreliable. IP assumes that other protocols used by the computer ensure reliable delivery of data.

Exercises

1. Transmission of data over a wide area network may be carried out by circuit or packet switching.
    (a) Explain the difference between circuit and packet switching.
    (b) Give three advantages of packet switching compared with circuit switching.
    (c) Give one example of a packet switched network.
    (d) State **three** items that will be transmitted with a data packet in addition to the data itself.

2. (a) What is meant by a wide area network?
    (b) Explain the term protocol in the context of data transmission over a wide area network.
    (c) Why is a protocol needed for a wide area network?

Chapter 68 – Local Area Networks

Network topology

When a network is to be implemented a decision has to be made on how best to arrange the components in a **topology**. A network's topology refers not only to the physical layout of its computers, cables and other resources but also how these components communicate with each other. A network's topology has a significant effect on its performance as well as its potential for growth.

Networks are generally based on one of three basic topologies: **star**, **bus** and **ring**. These three topologies and their advantages and disadvantages were described in Chapter 18, which you should revise before proceeding. In this chapter we will cover the operation of each of these networks.

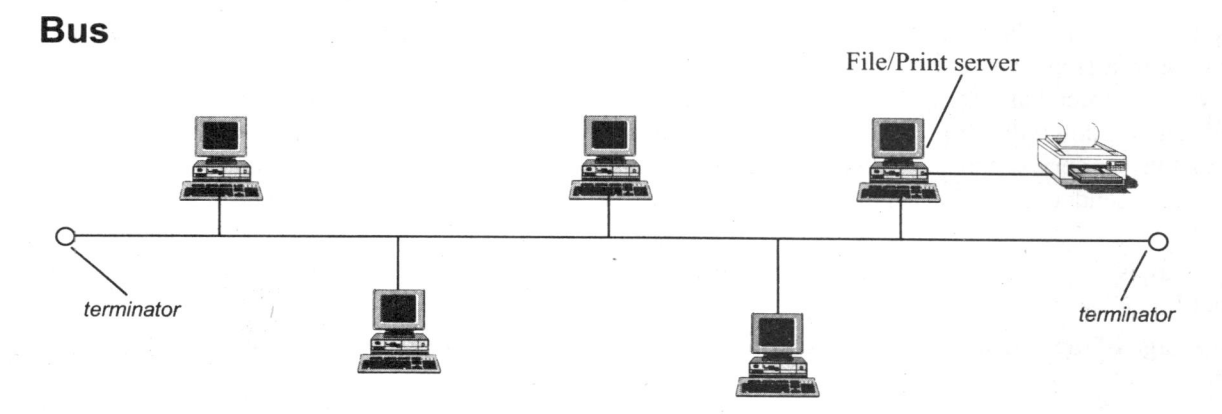

Bus

Figure 68.1: Bus network

In a bus network, all components are connected via a **backbone**, which is a single cable segment connecting all the computers in a line. The weakness of this arrangement is that the entire network will be brought down by a single cable break. At each end of the line there is a terminator which absorbs all the signals that reach it, thus clearing the network for new communication.

When a computer has data to send, the data is addressed, broken into packets and sent across the network as electronic signals. These signals are placed on the backbone and received by all connected computers; because of the address given to the packets, however, only one computer accepts the data.

In a bus environment, only one computer can send information at a time. The problem here is that several stations may want to transmit down the same line simultaneously, and there has to be some strategy for deciding who gets the line. A popular scheme called **Ethernet** uses a collision system known as '**carrier sense multiple access with collision detection**' (CSMA-CD). Before a station begins to transmit, it checks that the channel is not busy; if it is, it has to wait before transmission can begin. Once it begins transmission, it listens for other nodes also beginning transmission. If the transmitted message collides with another, both stations abort and wait a random period of time before trying again.

This system works well if the channels are not too heavily loaded. On the other hand if sixteen students sit down at sixteen computers all at once and all try to load software from the network's hard disk, the whole system more or less grinds to a halt!

Ring

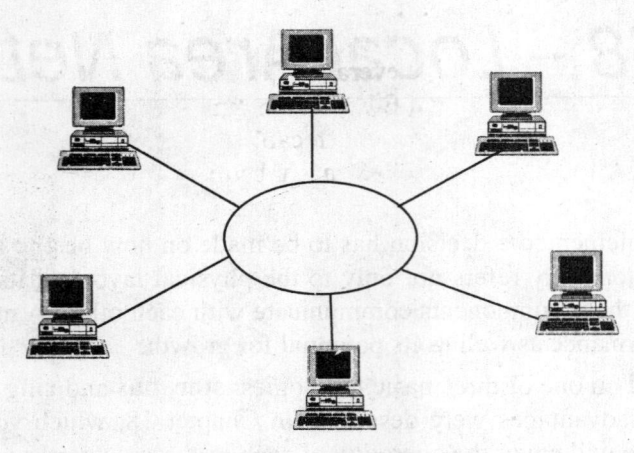

Figure 68.2: Ring network

In a ring network, signals travel in one direction only around the ring. **Token passing** is one method of sending data in a ring. A small packet, called the **token**, is passed around the ring to each computer in turn. If the computer has information to send, it modifies the token, adds address information and the data, and sends it down the ring. The information travels around the ring until it reaches the destination or returns to the sender. When a packet is received by the intended destination computer, it returns a message to the sender indicating its arrival. A new token is then created by the sender and sent down the ring.

This topology is surprisingly fast. A token can make a complete circuit of a 200-metre ring 10,000 times per second!

A disadvantage of the ring topology is that if one computer fails, the whole network will go down.

Star

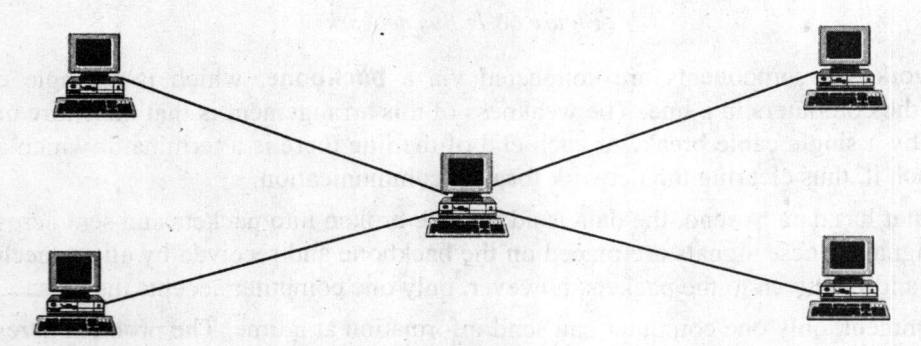

Figure 68.3: Star network

In a star topology, computers are connected by cable segments to a central **hub**. When a signal is sent from a computer, it is received by the hub and retransmitted down every other cable segment to all the other computers on the network. Again, only the computer the signal is addressed to acts upon the data.

If one computer fails in a star network, the others are unaffected, but if the hub goes down, the whole network goes down.

The hub regenerates the signals as they are received and sends them on.

Ethernet

Ethernet is a network architecture, available in several different implementations using different types of cable (coaxial, twisted-pair or fibre-optic). Each Ethernet has limitations on the total distance the network can cover. For example in 10Base5 Thick Ethernet each cable **segment** can be a maximum of 500 metres long. Up to five cable segments can be attached using hubs/repeaters, creating a network with a total length of 2,500 metres.

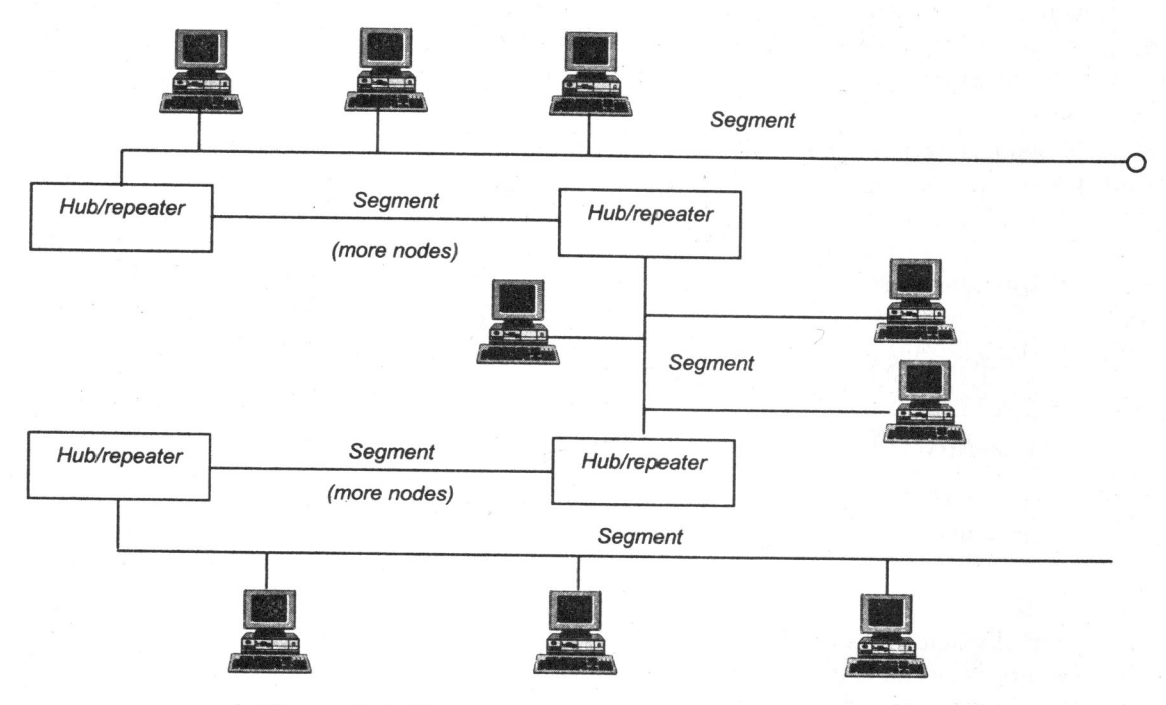

Figure 68.4: Ethernet network with 5 segments and 4 hubs

Segmentation

In most network implementations, having a large number of computers and heavy traffic can slow down the network unacceptably. One way to ease this problem is by segmenting the network into manageable segments by inserting a **bridge** or router between each network segment. Traffic is then reduced on each segment, giving better network performance.

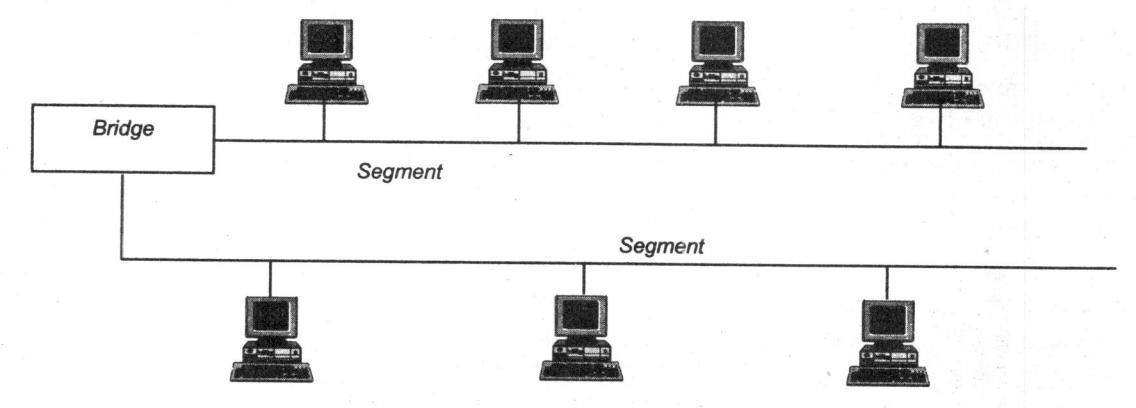

Figure 68.5: Bridge connecting network segments

Server-based vs peer-to-peer networks

There are two types of local area network: a **server-based** network is generally used when there are more than 3 or 4 computers on the network. A **peer-to-peer** network is suitable for a small company with a few computers in different offices because data can easily be accessed from any computer, and documents can be printed on any of the printers connected to any computer, for example.

In *client-server architecture*, different devices on the network are treated as clients or servers. The client devices send requests for service, such as printing or retrieval of data, to specific server devices that perform the requested processing. For example, the client devices might consist of twenty workstations in a room, and the server devices might be a laser printer and a computer dedicated to managing the network (the file server).

Peer-to-peer architecture is an alternative to client-server for small computer networks. In peer-to-peer, each workstation can communicate directly with every other workstation on the network without going through a server. Peer-to-peer is most appropriate when the network users mostly do their own work but occasionally need to share data or communicate with each other. One disadvantage of this arrangement is that if the workstation from which a user wishes to retrieve data is switched off, the data cannot be retrieved!

The differences between the client-server and peer-to-peer networks are summarised in the table below:

Server-based networks	*Peer-to-peer networks*
Example: Novell's NetWare	*Example: Microsoft Windows 98*
A central backing store is available to all users.	Storage facilities are distributed throughout the network. It can be difficult to remember which files are held on which computer.
Software is centrally held and shared. The server distributes the programs and data to the other microcomputers in the network (the 'clients') as they request them. Some processing tasks are performed by the desktop computer; others are handled by the file server. This is **termed 'client-server'** architecture. The use of servers provides the network with more speed and power, but adds expense and complication.	Copies of software may be held on individual machines. Peer-to-peer networks provide basic network services such as software, file and print sharing, and are less expensive and less difficult to administer than those set up with servers. They are most appropriate for smaller businesses that do not need the power and speed of client-server architecture.
User IDs, passwords and access levels are controlled by the central computer. Servers may be physically located in a secure office.	Security is not centrally controlled. Users may need to remember different passwords for each resource they wish to access.
Backup facilities are centralised; data and information held centrally are backed up regularly.	Backup is the responsibility of individual computer users.
All users are reliant on the service provided by the central facility. If the central computer goes down, all users are affected.	There is no central computer. Every time a shared resource such as a printer is used, the user at the machine where the resource resides will experience a drop in performance.
Can support hundreds or even thousands of users and grow to keep pace with an organisation's growth and expansion.	Works best with under 10 users, is easy and cheap to set up and requires no special network operating system.

Figure 68.6: Comparison of client-server and peer-to-peer networks

Exercises

1. An organisation is considering installing either a bus or a ring network to link together the computers within its head office. The computers are all situated on a single floor of the building.
   (a) Give **one** advantage of each method of linking the computers together.
   (b) To control the transmission of data, the bus network uses *collision detection* and the ring network uses *token passing*. Explain what is meant by the terms collision detection and token passing.

2. (a) Explain why performance degrades rapidly when large numbers of users log on to a bus network.
   (b) Suggest **two** ways this could be remedied.

3. Describe briefly the main features of a client-server network and a peer-to-peer network. Give **two** advantages and **two** disadvantages of using a peer-to-peer network.

4. (a) Describe, with the aid of a diagram, the main features of each of the following network types. Describe **one** drawback of each type.
   (i) bus network;
   (ii) token ring network.
   (b) Computer networks are very useful, but tend to be particularly prone to attack by computer hackers. Give **one** reason why this might be so.
   (c) State the name given to a simple network of personal computers where all the computers in the network have equal status.

Module 5 Advanced Systems Development

Chapter 69 – Wide Area Networks

Wide area network (WAN)

WANs span broad geographical distances, ranging from several miles to across the world. Carriers such as BT typically determine transmission rates and interconnection between lines. The communication links may consist of a variety of cable, satellite and microwave technologies. There are two options for communication over a WAN:

- Dial-up networking. The user pays for the amount of time spent using the telephone link.
- Dedicated or leased lines. The line is continuously available for transmission and the lessee typically pays a flat rate for total access to the line.

Dedicated lines are often set up to transmit data at higher speeds than public lines and are more appropriate for high-volume transmission. Public lines, on the other hand, are less expensive and more appropriate for low-volume applications requiring only occasional transmission.

> ➢ Q1: A bank has cashpoint machines in towns all over the UK, connected via a private wide area network to the bank's mainframe computer. What sort of line, public or leased, would you recommend? Why?

Value-added networks

Networks may be may be public, like the Internet, or privately-owned, as in the case of the bank mentioned above. An alternative to firms designing and managing their own private network is the **value-added network (VAN)**. A VAN is a private, multipath, data-only, third-party managed network that can provide economies in the cost of service and in network management because they are used by multiple organisations.

The VAN is set up by a firm that is in charge of managing the network. They then sell subscriptions to other firms wishing to use the network, and charge a subscription fee plus a charge for data transmission time. The network may use ISDN lines, satellite links or other communications channels.

The term 'value-added' refers to the extra value that subscribers get out of the arrangement by not having to invest in network equipment and software or perform their own error-checking, editing, routing and protocol conversion. Subscribers may achieve savings in line charges and transmission costs because the costs of using the network are shared among many users.

Electronic data interchange (EDI)

Electronic data interchange (EDI) is the electronic transmission of business data, such as purchase orders and invoices, from one firm's computerised information to that of another firm. Since EDI transmission is virtually instantaneous, the supplier's computer system can check for availability and respond quickly with a confirmation.

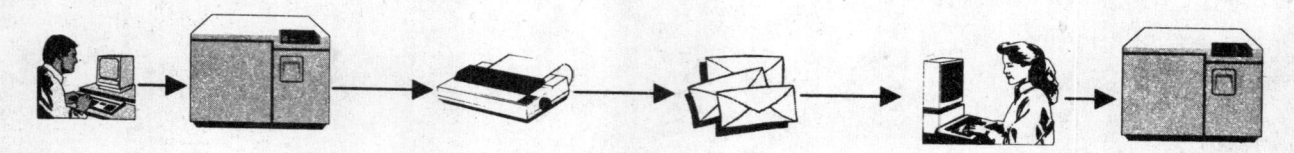

Figure 69.1 (a): Before EDI

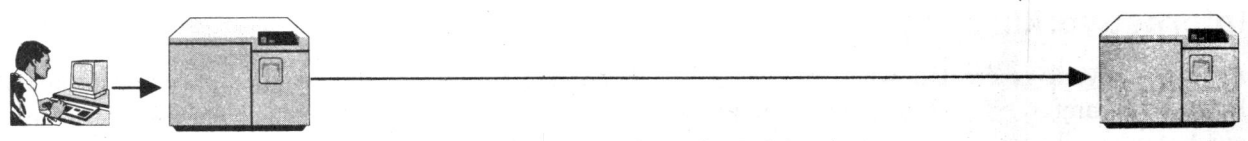

Figure 69.1 (b): After EDI

Speed and reliability are major advantages of EDI. It does away with re-keying data, increases accuracy and eliminates delays. Data such as 'A' Level results are now commonly transmitted direct to schools and colleges rather than being sent by mail. Using a service such as BT's CampusConnect, schools and colleges are able to download the results in encrypted form up to two days before their official release date; at one minute past midnight on results day, they are sent a password which allows them to decode the results. Having the results on computer also makes it far easier for the schools and colleges to collate exam results and produce the various statistics and performance indicators required by the DfEE for national league tables.

Connecting to a wide area network

The most common way to connect to a wide area network such as the Internet is to use a dial-up telephone line and a **modem**. A modem converts a digital signal received from a computer into an analogue signal that can be sent along ordinary telephone lines, and back to digital at the other end.

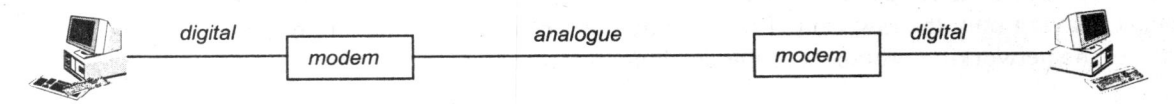

Figure 69.2: A modem (MOdulator/DEModulator)

Modem speed is measured in the number of bits per second (bps) that can be transmitted. A common speed in 2000 is 56K bps. When a modem is first installed, various parameters have to be specified, including:

- the telephone number of your ISP;
- The baud rate of your modem;
- Number of data bits per block;
- Number of stop bits;
- Whether odd or even parity is used.

When an ISDN line is used, a modem is not required as the line is itself digital. Instead, a **network termination device** and a **terminal adapter** are required. However, because most users are familiar with the term *modem*, the manufacturers of these devices often refer to them as **digital modems**.

Cable Television companies' desire to compete in the world of Internet access has driven the development of **cable modems**, which employ broadband transmission across regular cable television wires.

Another new development is the **Asymmetric Digital Subscriber Line (ADSL)**, a technology which turns traditional copper wires into 'fat data pipes'. This offers Internet connections up to 30 times faster than the fastest dial-up modem. ADSL and cable represent the claims of two separate and hostile industries to be the standard-bearers of the data revolution, thus offering the promise to the consumer of rapid investment and genuine price competition.

Internetworking

An internetwork is created when two or more independent networks are connected yet continue to function separately. The best known internetwork today is the Internet, which is, in essence, a large number of small networks connected to share information.

As networks grow and become a more integral part of an organisation, it is common to supply multiple paths through a network to provide fault tolerance. A bridge cannot handle multiple paths for data; instead, a **router** is used.

Routers and Gateways

Routers can be used like bridges to connect multiple network segments and filter traffic; also, unlike bridges, routers can be used to form complex networks with multiple paths between network segments as shown in Figure 69.3 below. Each network segment, also called a subnetwork (or subnet), is assigned a network address. Each node on a subnet is assigned an address as well. Using a combination of the network and node address, the router can route a packet from the source to a destination address somewhere else on the network.

Routers can route packets of the same protocol (such as TCP/IP) over networks with dissimilar architectures (such as Ethernet to token ring).

To connect two networks with different architectures and different protocols, a **gateway** is required. For example, a gateway can be used to allow network communication between a TCP/IP LAN and an IBM mainframe system. When packets arrive at a gateway, the software strips all networking information from the packet, leaving only the raw data. The gateway then translates the data into the new format and sends it on, using the networking protocols of the destination system.

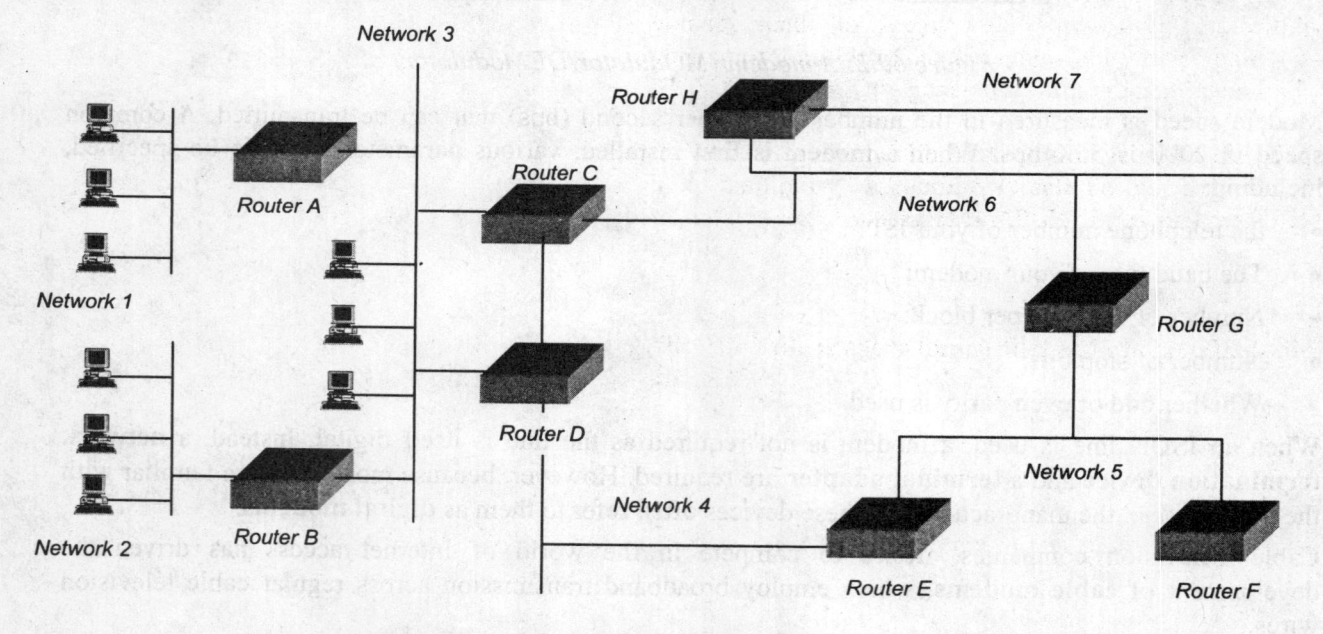

Figure 69.3: Routers provide alternative routes between networks

Exercises

1. A university is considering installing an Ethernet backbone to connect various departments' Local Area Networks to their mainframe computer. They also want to connect to external networks at other universities.
   (a) When would it be necessary to use a *gateway* rather than a *bridge* to join two networks?
   (b) Two methods of linking to the external networks are *public dialled lines* and *fixed leased lines*. Give **one** advantage and **one** disadvantage of each of these methods.

2. (a) What is the function of a *modem*?
   (b) Why does using an ISDN telephone line to connect a computer to a wide area network eliminate the need for a modem?
   (c) What is a *cable modem*?

3. A large international company wants to upgrade its network facilities. They are considering two options: a *private network*, or a *value-added network*. Give **two** advantages to the company of using a value-added network.

Chapter 70 – The Internet

Structure of the Internet

The Internet is a network of networks, connecting computers all over the globe. In 1969, the Internet started life as the ARPANET (Advanced Research Projects Agency Network) and consisted of just 4 computers. By the beginning of 1997, it included 1.7 million computers and it continues to grow exponentially. The cables, wires and satellites that carry Internet data form an interlinked communications network. Data travelling from one Internet computer to another is transmitted from one link in the network to another, along the best possible route. If some links are overloaded or out of service, the data can be routed through different links. The major Internet communications links are called the **Internet backbone**. A handful of network service providers (NSPs) such as BT each maintain a series of nationwide links. The links are like pipes – data flows through the pipes and large pipes can carry more data than smaller pipes. NSPs are continually adding new communications links to the backbone to accommodate increased Internet use.

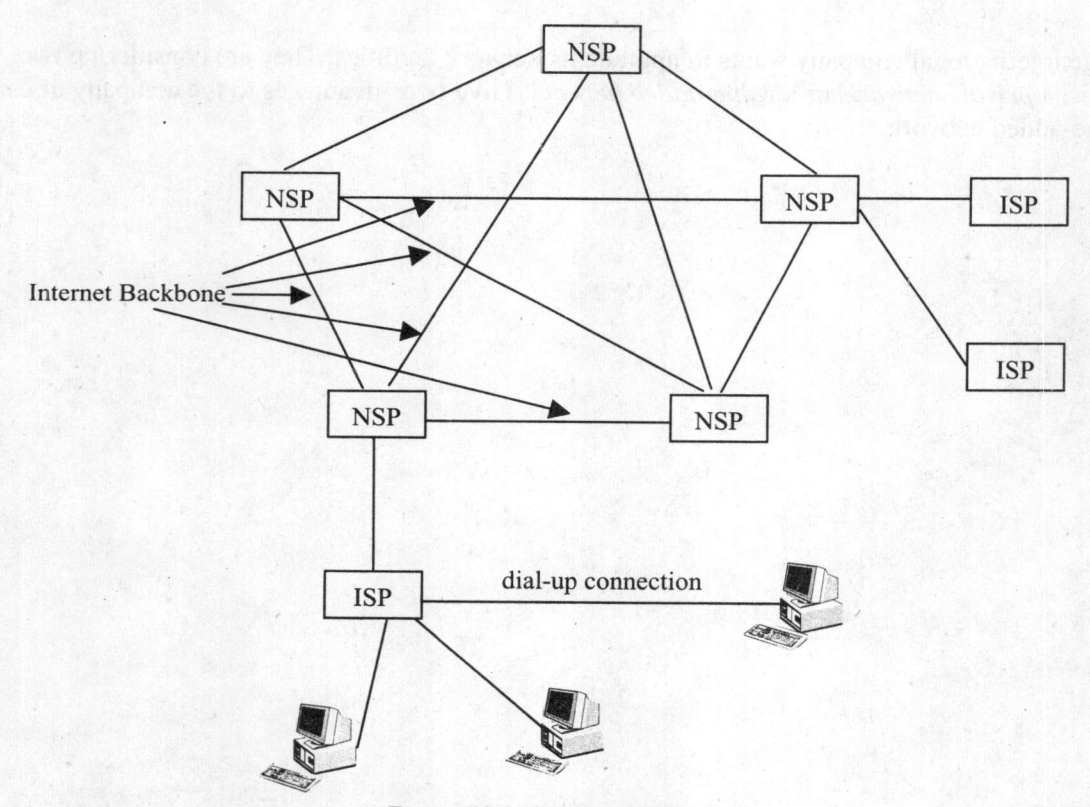

Figure 70.1: Structure of the Internet

When you connect your computer to the Internet, you do not connect directly to the backbone. Instead, you connect to an ISP (Internet Service Provider) which in turn connects to the backbone.

An ISP generally charges you a monthly fee for Internet access (though many such as Freeserve are free) and provides you with communications software and a user account. You need a computer with a modem to connect your computer to a phone line, and when you log on, your computer dials the ISP and establishes a connection over the phone line. Once you are connected, the ISP routes data between your computer and the Internet backbone. A phone line provides a very narrow pipe for transmitting data, having a typical capacity of 56K bits per second. Using a phone line, the time taken to transfer the contents of a 680Mb CD-ROM would be over 26 hours!

The World Wide Web

The World Wide Web is a special part of the Internet which allows people to view information stored on participating computers. It is an easy-to-use, graphical source of information which has opened the Internet to millions of people interested in finding out information. It consists of documents called pages that contain information on a particular topic, and links to other Web pages, which may be stored on other computers in different countries.

On-line Service Providers

To access the Internet you have a basic choice between **internet service providers** and **on-line services**. An ISP provides you with a connection to the net and the software you will need to navigate. An on-line service provider will give you access to the net and to their own private networks of services – databases of information, on-line editions of well-known magazines and newspapers, cinema listings, travel information, shopping, user forums, live chat rooms etc.

The difference between an on-line service and some ISPs is, like so much else in computing, often less than clear. Virgin Net, for example, sells itself as an ISP but when you sign up with them you get access to various members-only services. AOL (America On-Line) started out as an on-line service provider but is now the biggest ISP in the world.

Figure 70.2: An on-line service provider

Usenet newsgroups

Usenet was created in 1979 by a group of American Computer Science graduates who wanted to share their knowledge of the bugs and quirks of the Unix operating system with others and collectively make it better. Since then Usenet has grown to over 25,000 different newsgroups, most devoted to specific areas of interest. Usenet is one of the more controversial areas of the Internet, as it contains many undesirable groups such as paedophile groups and those wishing to exchange pornography. Newsgroups have also been hit by a plague of bulk junk mail messages (known as SPAM) which makes certain newsgroups unusable. Usenet II was set up, according to its creators, 'to create a structure where the traditional Usenet model of co-operation and trust can be made to work in the 21st century.' You can read about it on their Web site http://www.usenet2.org

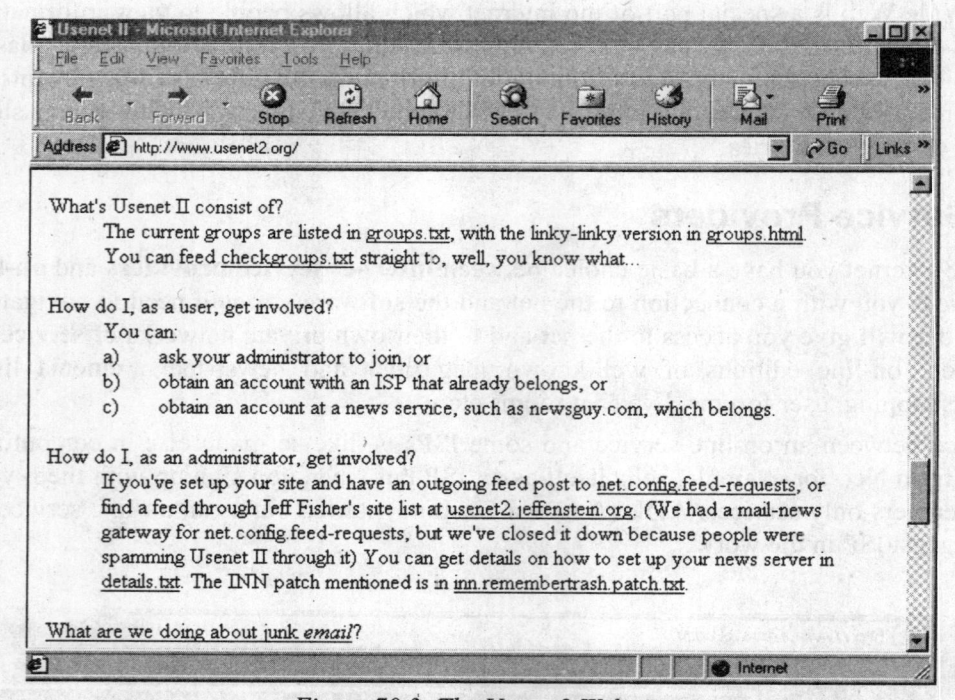

Figure 70.3: The Usenet2 Web site

Internet Relay Chat (IRC)

Unlike Usenet and e-mail, conversations on IRC are live. Whatever you say on the channel is instantly broadcast to everyone on the same channel, even if they are logged on to a server the other side of the world, and you can expect them to reply instantly.

Some channels are dedicated to particular topics, for example cricket, games or politics. To use IRC you need the right software: PC users can download mIRC from http://www.mirc.co.uk, and Mac users can download IRCLE from http://www.xs4all.nl/~ircle. For an interview with the Finnish programmer Jarkko Oikarinen who started IRC in 1988, in which he talks about the ideas behind IRC and how he thinks it will develop in the future, log on to http://www.mirc.co.uk/help/jarkko2.txt.

You can also chat on the on-line services such as AOL, by clicking on the CHAT button on the main screen. You should never give out personal details on a chat line like your real name, address, phone number, credit card number or details of your net account and password. For general tips on netiquette try http://www.albion.com .

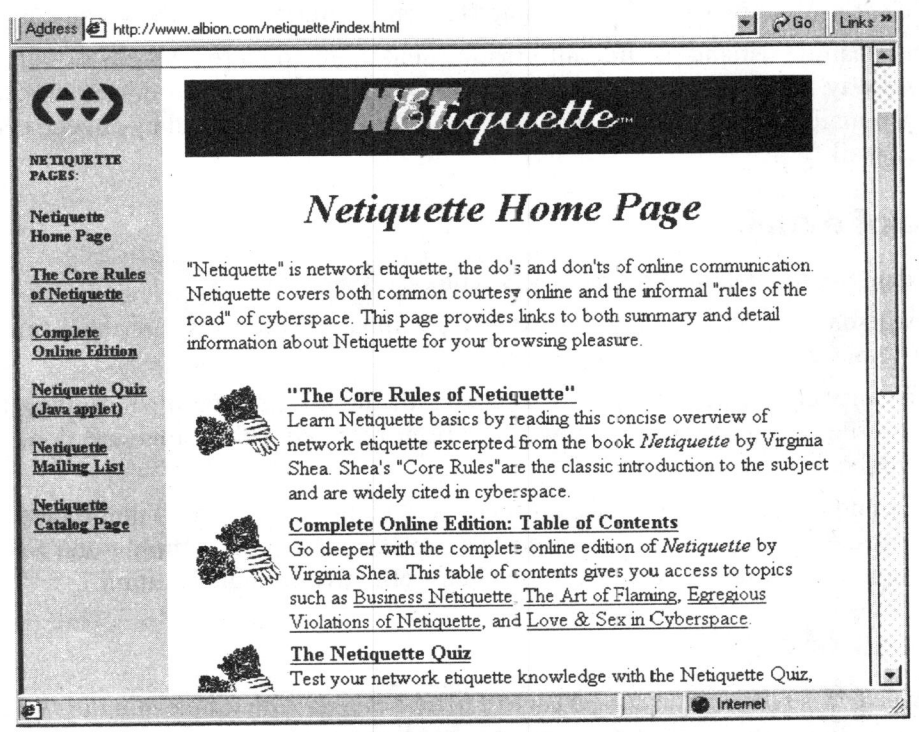

Figure 70.4: Tips for chat-line etiquette

Videoconferencing

It is possible, with appropriate hardware and an ISDN line, to try **videoconferencing**, which means that you can see the person at the other end of the line. With current technology it is more like seeing a series of stills than live video but if it means seeing your nearest and dearest while far from home maybe it's worth the effort.

E-mail

Writing your first e-mail to someone on the other side of the world and getting a reply within an hour or two is, no question, an exciting experience. Once you're hooked on e-mail you will probably never again use the regular mail service to post a letter to a friend. For both personal and business use, e-mail is a 'Killer App' that has significant advantages over snail mail, fax and phone. First of all, we will look at some of the facilities of e-mail:

- send a message anywhere in the world for the price of a local call;
- attach files such as documents, photographs, maps, executable programs;
- keep an address book of people you regularly e-mail;
- send the same letter to a group of people simultaneously;
- reply to an e-mail simply by clicking on the reply button, inserting text from the original message as required;
- forward a received message with comments on to an individual or group;
- with the right software or a Web-based e-mail address such as HotMail, you can pick up your mail from anywhere in the world, useful for example while travelling. **Telnet** is a software program which

Module 5 Advanced Systems Development

lets you connect to a remote computer via the Net and then use the programs on that computer. You can access Telnet in Windows 95/98 by opening **Run** on the **Start** menu and typing *telnet*.

- You can join a mailing list and get free information sent to you on a regular basis. Alternatively, you can join a two-way mailing list where you can send a message on a particular topic and it goes to everyone on the mailing list. Similarly, you receive all the messages posted by anyone else, which can lead to a lot of mail.

Advantages of e-mail

- It is cheaper than fax or telephone for messages sent over long distances.
- You can e-mail someone in Australia, for example, without having to worry about time-zones – the message will be picked up at a convenient time.
- You receive an answer much more quickly than by mail, and it is preferable to leaving a message on a telephone answering machine, as you know it has been received. (If the message does not reach the address you will be automatically notified.)
- It is easy to use and encourages friendly conversations and directness – you don't have to be formal in a business e-mail, and rules about the correct way to set out a letter simply don't apply. It breaks down barriers and cuts across hierarchies, which helps effective communication.

Disadvantages of e-mail

- Perhaps because it is so direct, it can be easy to offend people without meaning to. You can add little smiley faces :-) to show you are trying to be funny, but these can have limited appeal!
- Busy people may be overloaded with e-mail; it can be a bit depressing to get your mail at 9 a.m. and find you have 53 e-mails waiting to be answered. Junk mail can also be a problem.
- Viruses can be spread in e-mail attachments. You should always virus-check attached files before opening them, even if they are sent by a friend as they can be passed on unwittingly.

Exercises

1. Electronic mail (E-mail) is increasingly being used to supplement postal and telephone communications. Discuss, in an essay, the advantages, disadvantages and social implications of using E-mail.

2. Explain the difference between:

    (i) an *Internet Service Provider* and an *On-line Service Provider*.

    (ii) *Usenet* and *Internet Relay Chat*

3. A group of students has access to the Internet to carry out research as part of a coursework project. Describe **one** advantage and **one** disadvantage of using the Internet for this purpose.

4. A particular organisation has a number of divisions worldwide. A meeting is proposed between all divisional managers to be held at the company's headquarters. Outline the main features of E-mail which would assist the setting up of this meeting.

Chapter 71 – The World Wide Web

The World Wide Web

The World Wide Web is a collection of documents and other types of files that are stored on computers all over the world. These documents and files are called **pages**, and you can move from one page to another by clicking on **hypertext links** (usually shown in another colour and underlined). Links make use of URLs, the addresses used to find Web pages. You may need to look back at Chapter 20 to remind yourself of the relationship between URLs, domain names and IP addresses.

Web browsers

A Web browser is software used to view and download Web pages and various types of files such as text, graphics, sound and video.

If you know the URL of a Web page, you can view it by loading a Web browser such as Microsoft Internet Explorer or Netscape Navigator and typing in the URL (address) of the Web page. The screenshot below shows the default opening screen for Internet Explorer.

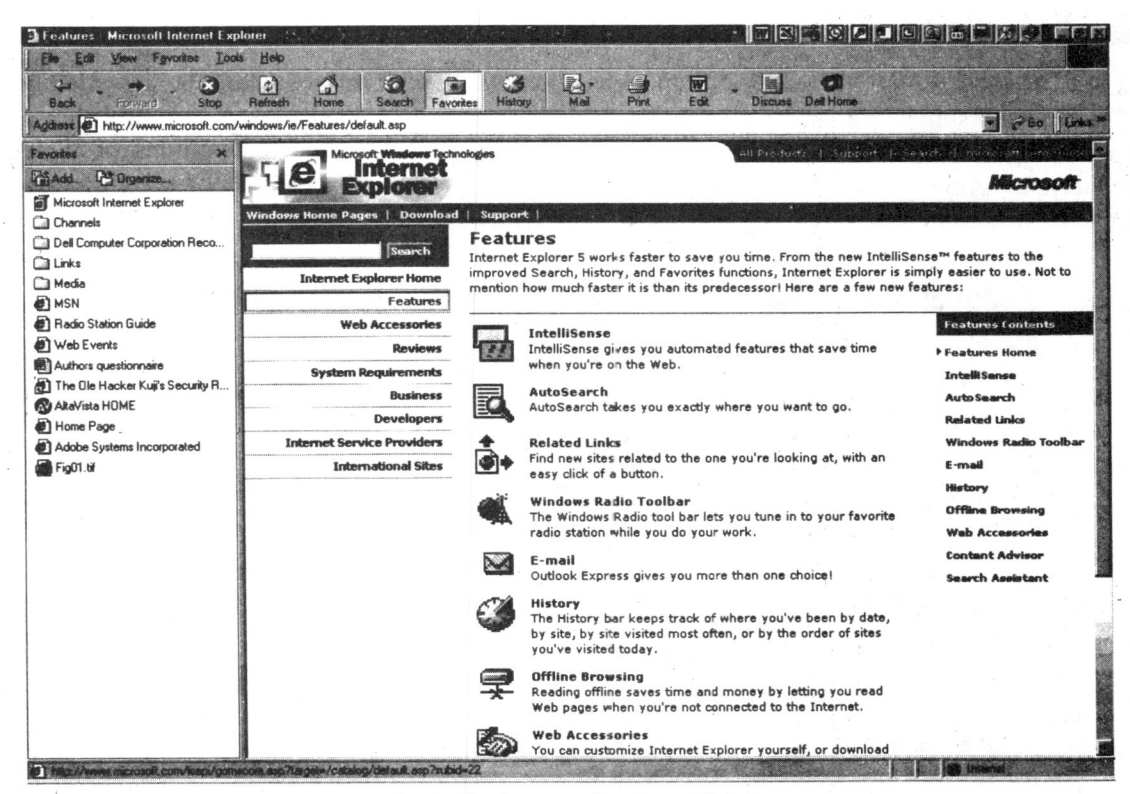

Figure 71.1: The Internet Explorer Web Browser

The other facilities offered by a typical Web browser allow you to:
- show a Web page for which you have either entered the address or URL (Uniform Resource Locator) or clicked on a 'hot' link;

Module 5 Advanced Systems Development

- browse back and forward through the most recently viewed pages;
- customise the basic options such as the opening page, content censorship, security levels and whether to download the page as text only to speed up transmission;
- 'bookmark' pages for quick reference later. This means that once you have entered a URL, and found the site worthwhile, you can click on the **Favorites** menu option and save the address for recalling at a later date.
- keep a 'History' list of pages visited within a specified period;
- save the most recently visited pages for viewing off-line;
- show animation sequences programmed in Java script;
- play back sound, video clips and multimedia if the appropriate 'plug-in' software (usually a Visual Basic ActiveX control) is installed, e.g. Shockwave;
- download files to a local hard disk;
- fill in an on-line form and submit it by e-mail;
- give links to search engines;
- access to some personal e-mail;
- have pages 'pushed' at you (Netcasting) rather than having to request them.

Internet Search Engines

The Web is massive – more than 500 million pages worldwide, with millions more being added daily. If you need to find out something specific on the Net, or research a particular topic, you probably need to use a **search engine**. A search engine enables you to search the contents of millions of Web pages simultaneously, by going to the search engine's Web page and typing key words or search terms into a simple form. Examples of search engines include Yahoo, HotBot and AltaVista.

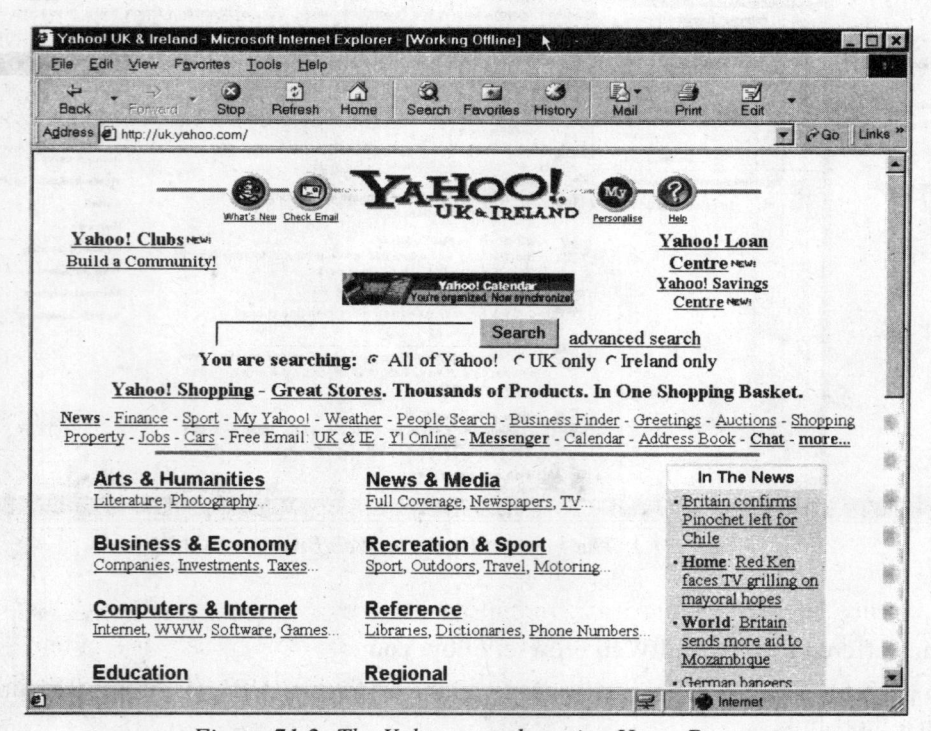

Figure 71.2: The Yahoo search engine Home Page

340

It is worth spending a little time learning how to use a search engine effectively otherwise it can be a very frustrating and time-wasting business. For example, if you want to look up information on the planet Pluto, typing the word **Pluto** will find you all the Web pages that include a reference to the planet but also pages to do with Walt Disney's character Pluto the dog.

Putting a + sign in front of a key word will list all pages containing the word. Putting a – sign in front will reject pages containing the word.

So typing in **Pluto +planet –dog –disney** is more likely to come up with useful information.

Typing in **Tower of London** will find all pages with the word **Tower**, and all pages with the word **London**. To get only pages containing the whole phrase, enclose it in quote marks, typing **"Tower of London"**.

Java applets

The Java programming language originated from the computer company Sun Microsystems, and is an object-oriented language based on C. Small Java programs or applications, called **applets**, can be executed through Web browsers. Applets have the suffix **.class**, for example **MyApp.class**. For useful information about Java applets, look at the Web site http://www.developer.com.

Applets are available to be downloaded from the Internet; the site http://www.Gamelan.com has hundreds of downloadable Java applets.

JavaScript is a cut-down, simplified version of Java which is easier to learn and use than Java, and allows fast creation of Web page events. Using a Java or JavaScript applet, you can create interaction between the user and your Web page. For example, if you have a form for the user to fill in, you can use an applet to check that the user has filled in the required fields and display a message prompt to do so if they have not. You can use a Java applet to make a button change appearance when the mouse hovers over it. The Web site http://www.javascripts.com contains over 5000 free Javascripts which can be downloaded, and JavaScript tutorials at this site will show you how to implement these items on your Web pages.

Figure 71.3: Web site to look for JavaScripts

Java applets can be called from an HTML program using the appropriate instruction. For example:
```
<APPLET CODE="appname.class"WIDTH="250"HEIGHT="22"></APPLET>
```

HTML

HTML (Hypertext Markup Language) is the programming language behind each and every Web page, controlling exactly how text and graphics are displayed. HTML enables anyone, anywhere to create a page of information and make it available to anyone else.

HTML files are commonly referred to as Web pages. Web browsers read HTML files and decide how they should be displayed in a graphical manner. Browsers take the HTML code and display pages that can include text, graphics, photographs, sound and video.

It is not necessary to know HTML to create a simple Web page. HTML editors such as Microsoft FrontPage or Claris Home Page enable you to create the page as you want it to look and then convert this into HTML ready to be loaded from your computer onto the Internet.

You can even create a document in Word and view the HTML code. Better still, use Internet Explorer's editor. An easy way of getting to grips with HTML is to go to the Web site http://www.webmonkey.com which has an excellent HTML tutorial.

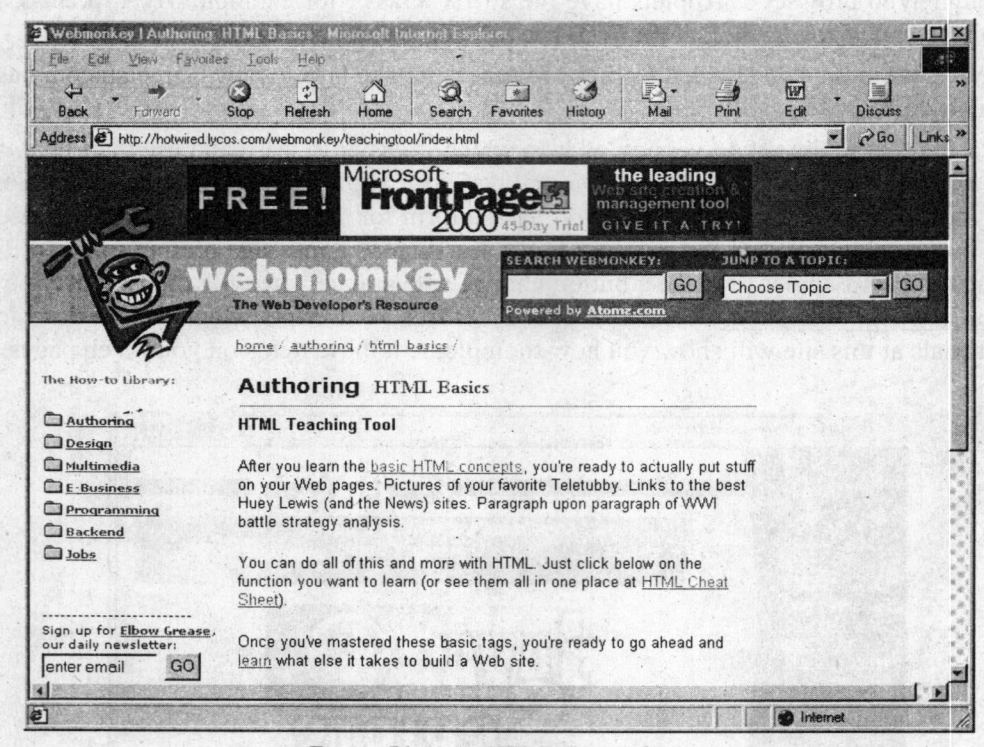

Figure 71.4: An HTML Tutorial site

Another way of learning new tricks in HTML is to load a Web page that you like the look of and select **View, Source** from the menu to display the HTML code in Notepad.

HTML structure

The basics of HTML are embodied in a few simple rules.

- HTML instructions or **tags**, are enclosed in angle brackets < and >. Tags always come in pairs. There are open tags i.e. <BODY> and close tags i.e. </BODY>.
- A standard page consists of two main sections – a head and a body. The <HEAD> contains any scripts or codes your page may require, and is not always present. Many pages will have a HEAD

- containing only the <TITLE>. The title is a simple line of text which appears in the coloured bar at the top of your browser.
- The head is followed by the body of the document which is contained within the <BODY> and </BODY> tags. The body makes up the bulk of an HTML page and contains all the text, images and other elements which are to appear.
- The <BODY> tag also contains a number of optional extras, or attributes, which allow for the setting up of colours, background images and other global settings for the page. For example:

  BGCOLOR – fills the background with a user defined colour expressed as either "blue", "green" etc. or as a six-digit hexadecimal number.

  BACKGROUND – can be used to fill the background with a picture, usually in GIF or JPG format.

  TEXT – using the same colour conventions as BGCOLOR, the TEXT attribute allows the text colour to be changed.

- Paragraphs should be enclosed within the <P> and </P> tags.
- The ALIGN command can be used within the open paragraph tag to specify left, centre or right alignment.
- <H1> to <H7> can be used to specify seven predefined heading sizes.
- <FONT FACE> and <FONT COLOR> can be used to select a particular font and colour.
- Graphics have their own tag <IMG>. The source file (SRC) of the graphic must be specified.
- The <A> tag is used to include hyperlinks within a page. This allows the user to navigate around a website or link to another site. e.g. To insert a hyperlink to jump to the Payne-Gallway site use the HREF attribute to specify the site:

  <A HREF="http://www.payne-gallway.co.uk">some text here</A>

A sample HTML program

You can type an HTML program using a text editor such as Notepad. For example, type in this program (insert your own name where it says "YOUR") and save it as **name.htm**. Save a picture of yourself as **myself.gif** in the same folder.

```
<HTML>
<HEAD>
<TITLE>My Home Page</TITLE>
</HEAD>
<BODY BGCOLOR = "WHITE" text ="BLUE">
<H1 ALIGN="CENTER">Your Home Page</FONT ></H1>
<P ALIGN="CENTER"><IMG SRC="myself.gif" width="100" height="100"></P>
<P><FONT FACE="MS Sans Serif"><FONT COLOR="RED"><FONT SIZE="7">WELCOME</P>
<P><FONT SIZE="3"><FONT COLOR="BLUE">This website provides lots of information
about me and my family. It is regularly updated so that our friends overseas can
easily keep up with our latest news</P>
</BODY>
</HTML>
```

Open your file in Internet Explorer and it will be displayed as shown below in Figure 71.5.

Module 5 Advanced Systems Development

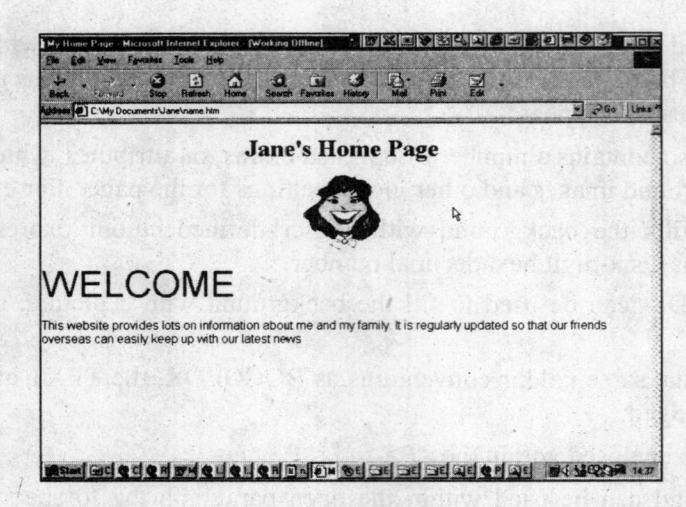

Figure 71.5: The Web page resulting from the HTML code

(Thanks to Rosemary Richards for HTML paragraphs and program.)

FTP (File Transfer Protocol)

Using FTP you can download files from the Web. Demo versions of games and software are often available to be downloaded. FTP files have ftp as the first part of the address instead of http.

You can also use FTP to upload pages onto a Web site, for example if you have created a new Web page offline and want to load it on to the Internet. Using software such as FrontPage you log on to your Web site and drag and drop the required filename from your local folder onto your Web site folder.

Exercises

1. (a) What is a Java applet?

   (b) How can a Java applet be executed?

2. A Web page was created using the following HTML code. Describe the appearance of the Web page when viewed through a Web browser.

   ```
   <HTML>
   <HEAD><TITLE>Sailing Page</TITLE></HEAD>
   <BODY>
   <H1 ALIGN="CENTER"><FONT COLOR="GREEN">Chuck's Chandlery</FONT></H1>
   <P ALIGN="CENTER"><IMG SRC="sailboat.gif"></P>
   <P ALIGN="CENTER"><FONT FACE="ARIAL">Provisions and Repairs</P>
   <P ALIGN="CENTER"><FONT FACE="ARIAL" FONT COLOR="RED">at all hours!</P>
   <P ALIGN="CENTER">Click here to see local
   <A HREF="http://www.nautical.com">Tide Tables</A></P>
   </BODY>
   </HTML>
   ```

Chapter 72 – On-line Shopping and Banking

E-commerce

An almost infinite variety of goods and services is available on the Internet. You can bid for a work of art at Sotheby's, swap a DVD, book your holiday, car hire, theatre tickets and restaurant meal, buy anything from groceries to a car. You can buy or sell stocks and shares on-line, do your banking, and apply for a job. In this chapter we'll look in detail at just a very few of these facilities.

On-line banking

One of the fastest growing areas of Internet usage is on-line banking. Banks and building societies are spending millions of pounds on developing their net-related services. Smile (http://www.smile.co.uk) is a genuine on-line bank with no branch network to support customers.

Once your bank account is running, it's as easy as logging on to the Internet. By accessing your account on-line using encrypted security codes, you can pay bills, set up, amend and cancel standing orders and direct debits, and transfer money to other Smile accounts or other accounts anywhere in the world. Cheques can be paid in via a post office or bank.

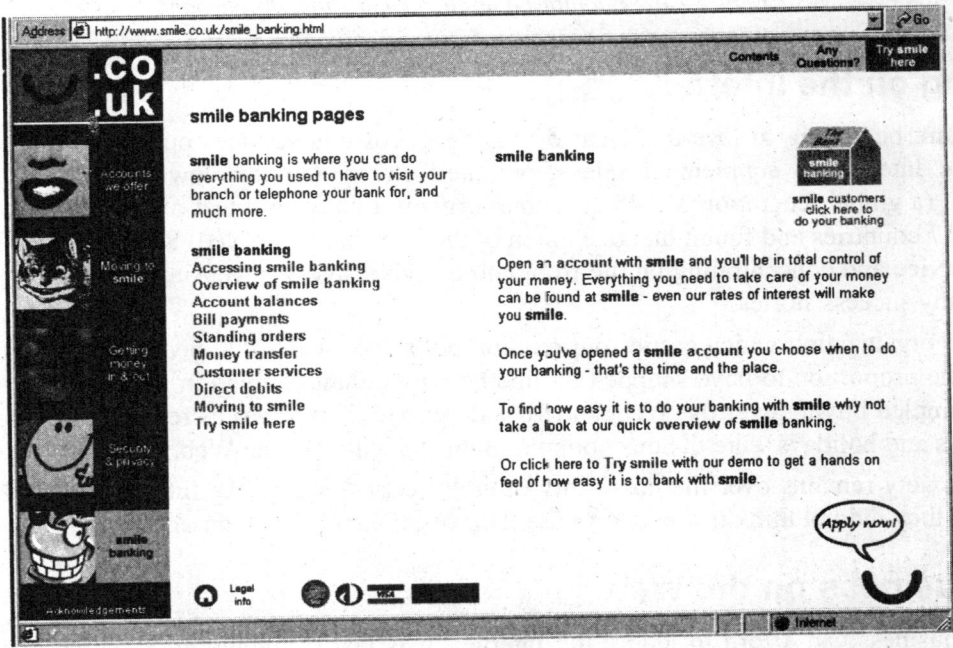

Figure 72.1: Logging on to Smile, the Internet bank

Internet banking is up to four times cheaper to operate than telephone banking and 10 times cheaper than high street banking. So what are the disadvantages? When you come to plead for a loan or overdraft, there will be little personal relationship to trade on, just your records. But how many of us have a personal relationship with the bank manager today?

You can log on to the Smile Web site and try a demo with no danger of setting up an unwanted account – it will show you exactly how on-line banking works.

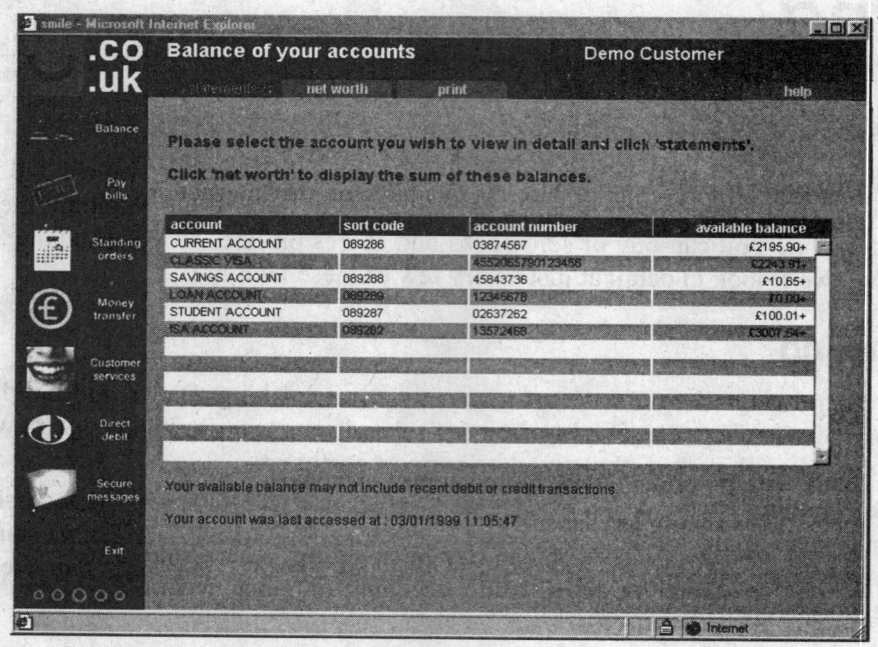

Figure 72.2: Facilities offered by Smile, the on-line bank

Shopping on the Internet

Consumers are beginning to lose their fear of buying goods and services on-line as traditional retailers move to the Internet to supplement sales from their stores. On the down side, in 1999 Consumer International (a global federation of 245 consumer organisations) ran a test of 'e-tailing' by ordering 151 items from 17 countries and found that one in ten of the items never arrived! Some e-tailers are neglecting customer service and concentrating on the front end of the business – websites and building volume. But there are many success stories.

MORI, is an organization which carries out opinion polls, sampled 2,000 people in September 1999 and found that the proportion to have shopped on-line had more than doubled in the past year. Some 40% of users had sampled buying over the Web, and 10% described themselves as regular Web shoppers. Cheap flights, books and holidays were the most popular items bought over the Web.

However, anxiety remains over the possibility of credit card fraud on the Internet, with 42% of Internet users saying they did not think it was safe to use their plastic in on-line transactions.

Doing business on the Web

Almost no business can afford to ignore the Internet. It is fast becoming an essential business tool for everyday correspondence, marketing, customer feedback and customer support. For businesses from a small country hotel to the world's largest airline, the Web can act as a shop front where customers can browse 24 hours a day, 365 days a year.

Amazon is an example of a company doing all its business over the Internet, selling books, music, videos and more. Log on by typing in the address www.amazon.co.uk and you will see the following screen:

Chapter 72 – On-line Shopping and Banking

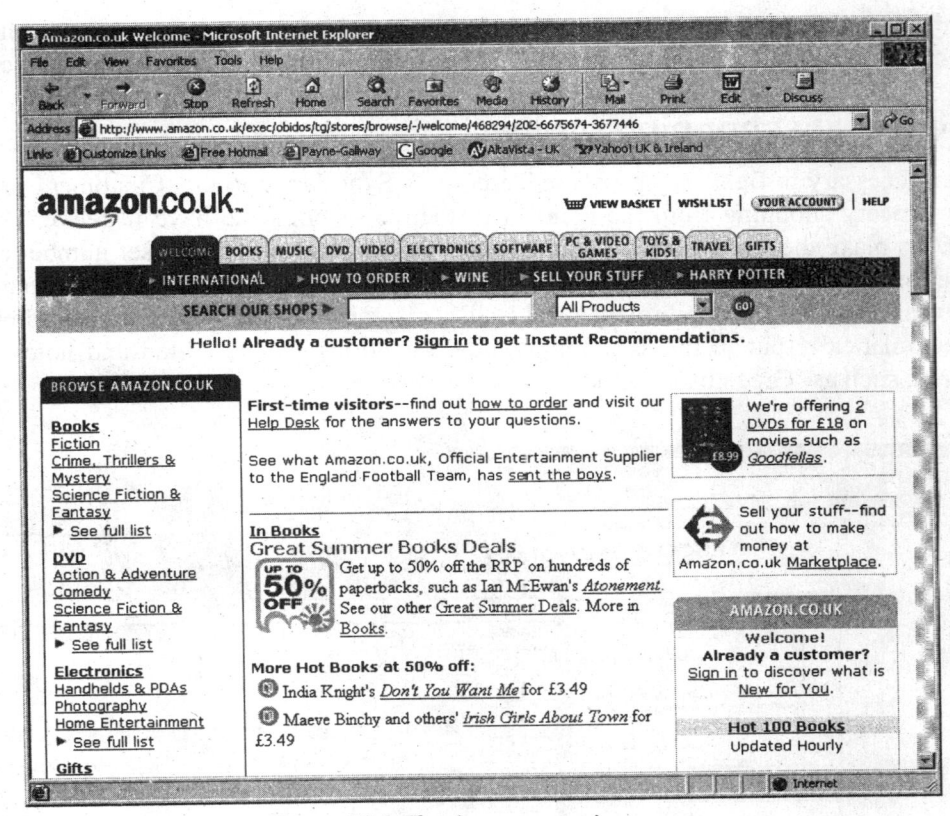

Figure 72.3 The Amazon opening screen

You can browse through new releases or search for a particular product. Once you have made your selection, added it to the shopping basket and proceeded to the secure checkout, your order details will be displayed on the screen. You'll receive an e-mail confirming your order the next day, and another when your goods have been despatched.

Couldn't be simpler!

Advantages to business

For a business such as Amazon, this way of doing business has numerous advantages.
- There is a huge saving on overheads: no costly warehouse space, rent, heating or employee facilities;
- The 'virtual shop' can stock every one of the 16,000 or so CDs produced in the last year whereas a conventional store would stock only between 5-10,000;
- The shop has arrangements for 'Just In Time' delivery from its suppliers, so does not get left with books and CDs which it cannot sell;
- It is a valuable market research tool – a list of customers' names and addresses, purchases, likes, dislikes and suggestions can be built up at absolutely no cost and used to improve the service provided.

Advantages to the customers

There are advantages to the customers, too. They can:
- Visit the shop without having to leave home, at any hour of the day;
- Hear snatches of a song before deciding to buy;
- Shop without being jostled by crowds, having to listen to music that is not to their taste.

Module 5 Advanced Systems Development

Amazon estimate that the proportion of visitors to their site who make a purchase is much higher than for those who respond to a direct mail shot. Many of their customers return to make further purchases.

Doing the weekly shopping on-line

It is no longer necessary to fight the crowds in Tesco on a Saturday morning. Customers can register and then do their grocery shopping from the comfort of their own home, to have it delivered for a modest £5.00 charge. To make the weekly order, the customer logs on, types in their user number and password, and has the latest up-to-date list of products and prices downloaded. The customer's shopping list is saved and can be recalled to help compile next week's list, a 'recipe for the week' can be downloaded and ingredients automatically put in the shopping trolley, quantities can be edited and notes added to any product ordered, such as 'Green bananas please'.

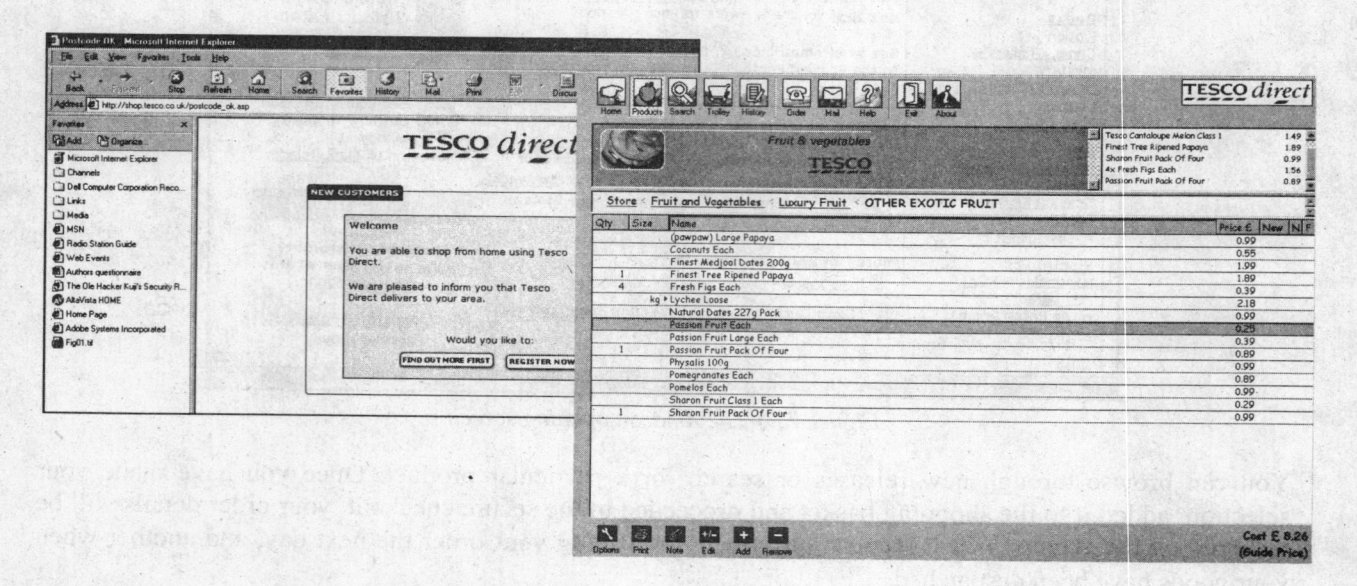

Figure 72.4: Registering and ordering from Tesco Direct

> Q1: What kind of people do you think are most likely to use the Internet for their grocery shopping? What do you think are the advantages and disadvantages?

Registering a domain name

If you want to set up in business on the Internet, or if you would like a snappy e-mail address, you need to register your chosen domain name and a few other details. You also need an Internet Service Provider (ISP). No one 'owns' domain names. The organisation responsible for registration of ".co.uk" and ".org.uk" names is Nominet (http://www.nic.co.uk) and this is a good place to check for the availability of your chosen domain name. If it is already taken, you can find out who by. You can register your domain name here for a fee (around £80.00 for the first two years) or you can find out how to get a free domain name by logging on to http://www.freename.co.uk. Nominet is an **Internet Registry**.

Cybersquatting

Many people try and speculate in domain names ("squatting") in order to try and earn a profit by selling the names they have registered. In 2000, Volkswagen successfully fought off an attempt by cybersquatters to hold the domain name VW.net for ransom. The name had been registered by Virtual Works, which attempted to sell the domain name to Volkswagen in December 1998. Virtual Works threatened that if Volkswagen did not buy the domain name, the company would sell it to the highest bidder.

A US Court saw differently, however, and ruled that Volkswagen was entitled to the Internet domain name VW.net. The Court ruled that under the recently enacted Anticybersquatting Consumer Protection Act, "Virtual Works has attempted to profit from the trafficking of a domain name of a previously trademarked name".

Exercises

1. Discuss in an essay the concept of a cashless society and the assertion that we will become one. You should refer to steps taken by banks and other financial institutions to move us towards a cashless society and explain why some people feel that it may never be possible to achieve such a goal.

2. The impact of computerisation on employment has been particularly significant in banking.
    (a) Briefly describe **one** way in which computerisation has led to a decrease in banking employment opportunities.
    (b) Briefly describe **one** way in which computerisation has led to an increase in banking employment opportunities.

3. Identify **three** additional costs necessary to enable a user to access the Internet from a typical standalone computer.

Module 5 Advanced Systems Development

Chapter 73 – Internet Security and Other Issues

Internet-based fraud

Internet-based fraud is the fastest growing criminal activity in the UK, according to crime figures published in 2000. Although Internet purchasing makes up only 2% of credit card transactions, the banking industry's research has shown that the net generates around 50% of all credit card complaints.

In 1999 more than £2 billion was spent in the UK on the Internet, and this figure is predicted to grow rapidly. But the public does not fully trust the security of Internet transactions, and many people do not feel comfortable giving their credit card numbers over the Internet. Traders, for their part, may have no way of knowing that the person placing an order is who they say they are.

Digital certificates

To prevent people from viewing incoming mail (e.g. an order containing a credit card number), an organisation or an individual can obtain a **digital certificate**, which comes with a public key and a private key. Anyone can know the public key – to enable someone to send you an encrypted message, you must send that person your public key, and the person must use the public key to send you the message. You can then decrypt the message using your private key, which should never be made known to anyone else. Using software such as Outlook Express you can have your e-mail program automatically send your public key whenever you send an e-mail.

When you send the message, a **digital signature** is generated by taking a mathematical summary of the document concerned (a hash code). Since the hash code is generated from the entire document, in the right sequence, it means that the slightest difference to the document will not generate the same code. This is appended to the document, transmitted with it, and checked by the receiver.

A digital signature thus authenticates the sender, proves that the message has not been tampered with, and prevents the sender from denying having sent it. This means, for example, that a person cannot later deny having made a purchase on a Web site, by claiming that it was made by someone else.

Digital signatures also offer some protection against viruses being downloaded in one of the thousands of Java applets or ActiveX controls that can be freely downloaded. A programmer in effect "signs" a program by attaching his or her digital signature. Theoretically, a programmer would not sign a program containing a virus, so all programs with a digital signature should be "safe". Your browser will warn you about programs that do not have a digital signature so you can decide whether or not to accept them.

The Web site http://www.itsecurity.com has a huge amount of information on every aspect of computer security and is well worth a visit. The site http://www.verisign.com belongs to VeriSign, a Certifying Authority, where a digital certificate can be obtained.

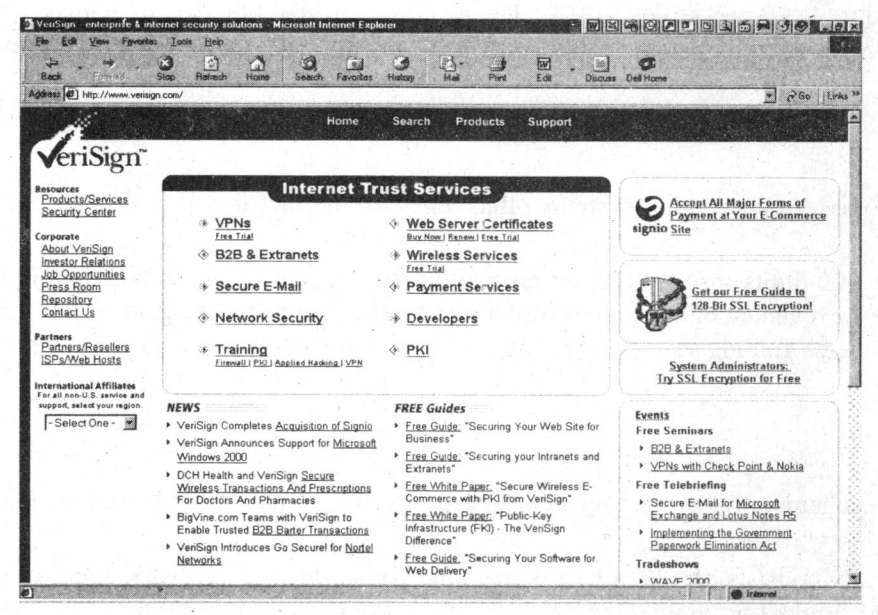

Figure 73.1: Obtaining a digital certificate

Encryption

Encryption is the scrambling of data so that it becomes very difficult to unscramble and interpret. Scrambled data is called ciphertext. Unscrambled data is called plaintext. Unscrambling ciphertext back to the original plaintext is called decryption.

Data encryption is performed by the use of a cryptographic algorithm and a key. The algorithm uses the key to scramble and unscramble the data. Ideally, the algorithm should be made public (so that it can be scrutinized and analyzed by the cryptographic community), while the key remains private.

Strong and weak encryption

The key is fundamental to the strength of the encryption. You need the one correct key before you can decrypt the ciphertext. It follows, then, that the longer the key, the greater the range of possible values it could have. The range of possible values is called the keyspace. The greater the keyspace, the more difficult it is for an unauthorized person to discover the correct key.

Encryption cannot make unauthorized decryption impossible; it can merely make it improbable. With unlimited processing capacity and unlimited time available, all cryptosystems could be broken. The purpose of encryption is to make it as unlikely as possible that a ciphertext could be broken within the period of time during which the contents should remain secret.

There is an arbitrary and subjective distinction between weak and strong encryption. Strong encryption implies that it would effectively be impossible to find the key within the effective lifetime of the secret. Weak encryption implies that the key could be found with a realistic amount of processing capacity and a reasonable amount of time. The difference between weak encryption and strong encryption is thus effectively a question of processing power. As computers become more powerful and less expensive, what is now 'strong' encryption will inevitably become 'weak' encryption. At the moment, any key length above 56 bits is generally considered to be 'strong' encryption.

Many governments around the world view strong encryption with concern. The argument is that the availability of strong encryption limits their ability to monitor the messages of suspected terrorists, drug traffickers and paedophiles. Some governments would like to ban the use of strong encryption unless either a back door is made available to Law Enforcement, or a decryption key is lodged with a Trusted

Third Party (TTP). This, needless to say, has led to considerable debate between government and government agencies on the one side, and academics, civil liberty groups and the greater part of industry on the other.

Factoring

The strength of modern encryption systems often relies on the fact that it is very difficult to factor large numbers.

If two large (say 200 digits) prime numbers are multiplied together, it would take many years of computer processing time to reverse-engineer the problem and deduce the two original prime numbers from the product. The process of doing so is known as factoring, i.e. attempting to find the two prime factors of the product.

Firewall

A firewall is a mechanism for protecting a corporate network from external communications systems such as the Internet.

A firewall typically consists of a PC or Unix machine containing two network interface cards (NICs) and running a special firewall program. One network card is connected to the company's private LAN, and the other is connected to the Internet. The machine acts as a barrier through which all information passing between the two networks must travel.

The firewall software analyses each packet of information passing between the two and rejects it if it does not conform to a preconfigured rule.

Virus spread and detection

When you download a file from the Internet, you can use virus detection software to make sure the file is virus-free before you run it. However, some Web sites automatically send a program to your Web site and run it before you get a chance to check it for viruses. Unfortunately, it is hard to protect against this. While you are connected to the Internet, you could be unaware that a program is busy deleting your most treasured files, making your browser hang up and scanning your hard disk for your IP address, user ID and password. Beware of e-mails saying "This document is very important and you've GOT to read this". Delete them immediately without opening any attachments!

In 1999 a macro virus called Melissa, once on a system using Outlook Express, took the first 50 entries from the Address Book and then mailed itself as an attachment to the e-mail addresses. The e-mail carried the message 'Here is that document you asked for ... don't show anyone else ;-)'. It rapidly spread to millions of computers worldwide, disrupting large systems by overloading servers and causing them to close down.

Security and the Law

Under the Data Protection Act (see Chapter 23), personal data must be kept secure. The reasons for this are fairly obvious.

> A spate of apparently random burglaries always took place when the home owners were away. A pattern emerged, however, when the police correlated the burglaries with a customer database on a stolen PC from a local newsagent. Customers cancelled their papers when away from home. This was duly noted on the customer database, and the thieves had a nice neat list of names, and addresses of empty houses.

You can check out other legislation pertaining to computers on the Web site http://www.itsecurity.com.

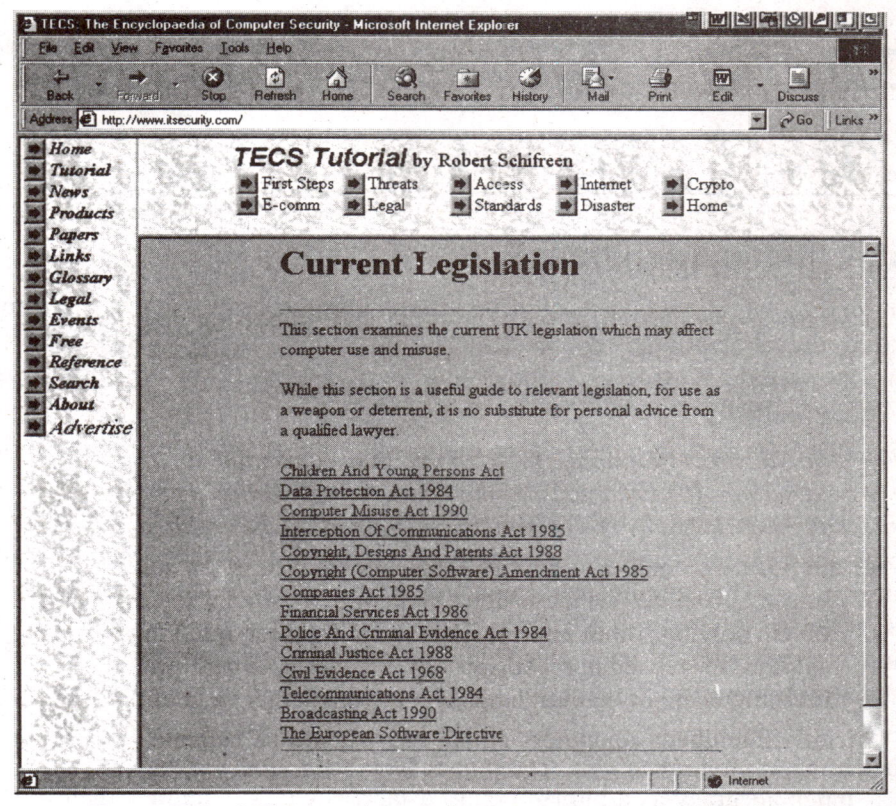

Figure 73.2: A Web site giving information about current legislation

Social and cultural issues

The Internet is used by millions and inevitably abused by a few. The net is not a totally risk-free environment and it is possible for unwanted pornographic material to find its way onto your screen via junk e-mail or a search on some perfectly innocent topic. There are racist Web sites put up by Nazi sympathisers, sites that feature information on making bombs, sites that feature accident and autopsy photographs. Stories circulate about paedophiles e-mailing schools and attempting to strike up relationships with children. To combat the dangers to children, blocking software can be installed which censors unacceptable material – among the best known are Net Nanny http://www.netnanny.com and Surf Watch http://www.surfwatch.com.

On the plus side, the ready availability of material suitable for all cultures is a real bonus. http://www.blink.org.uk is a site set up to promote good race relations from a black perspective. Sites for minority groups of all kinds – religious, ethnic or social groups, or groups brought together by a common bond of rare illness or disability – can be an invaluable source of information.

Exercises

1. Explain what is meant by *strong encryption* and *weak encryption*. Give **one** reason why strong encryption should be forbidden by law, and **one** reason why it should be allowed.

2. Explain the use of digital certificates and firewalls, giving an example of when each might be used.

Chapter 74 – Artificial Intelligence and Expert Systems

Definition of artificial intelligence

Conventional data processing is concerned with inputting and processing data in the form of facts and figures in order to produce operational or management information. **Artificial intelligence**, on the other hand, is based on **knowledge**. A widely accepted definition of artificial intelligence is based on a test devised by Alan Turing in 1950:

Suppose there are two identical terminals in a room, one connected to a computer, and the other operated remotely by a person. If someone using the two terminals is unable to tell which is connected to the computer and which is operated by the person, the computer can be credited with intelligence.

Following on from this idea we could say that artificial intelligence is the science of making machines perform tasks that would require intelligence if done by people. Artificial intelligence covers such fields as expert systems, problem solving, robot control, intelligent database querying and pattern recognition. Pattern recognition includes speech comprehension and synthesis, image processing and robot vision. Getting a computer to communicate in 'natural language' is yet another field of research.

One aspect of artificially intelligent computers is that they should be capable of learning, and therefore improving their performance at a given task. Computers have been successfully "trained", for example, to recognise (with as much accuracy as a human being) a face as either male or female, and to be able to recognise an Underground train station as being "crowded" or not.

Expert systems

Expert systems are computer programs that attempt to replicate the performance of a human expert on some specialised reasoning task. Also called **knowledge-based systems**, they are able to store and manipulate knowledge so that they can help a user to solve a problem or make a decision.

The main features of an expert system are:

- it is limited to a specific domain (area of expertise);
- it is typically rule based;
- it can reason with uncertain data (the user can respond "don't know" to a question);
- it delivers advice;
- it explains its reasoning to the user.

An expert system has the following constituents:

- 'the knowledge base' that contains the facts and rules provided by a human expert;
- some means of using the knowledge (an 'inference mechanism' or 'inference engine');
- a means of communicating with the user (the 'man-machine interface' or 'human-computer interface').

Programming the knowledge base

Computer languages such as PROLOG (PROgramming LOGic) have been developed for the creation of expert systems. Using PROLOG, the facts and rules are written down using the special syntax of the language, and the user can then type in a query which the program will attempt to answer.

The following is an example of part of a simple knowledge base which will deliver advice on whether a person may legally drive a certain class of vehicle.

```
1       age (edward  20)
2       age (robert  19)
3       age (flora  17)
4       age (emma 17)
5       age (andrew  16)
6       minimum_age (motor_cycle 16)
7       minimum_age (car  17)
8       minimum_age (heavy_goods_vehicle  20)
9       passed_test (edward  heavy_goods_vehicle)
10      passed_test (andrew  motor_cycle)
11      passed_test (emma  car)
12      has_provisional_licence (andrew)
13      has_provisional_licence (robert)
14      permitted_to_drive (X  V) If passed_test (X  V)
15      permitted_to_drive (X  V) If has_provisional_licence (X) And
            age (X  A) And
            minimum_age (V  L) And
            A >= L
```

In this syntax:

fact 1 means that Edward is 20 years old;

fact 6 means the minimum age for driving a motor-cycle is 16;

fact 10 means Andrew has passed the driving test for a motor-cycle;

fact 12 means that Andrew has a provisional driving licence;

rule 14 means that a person X may drive a vehicle V if person X has passed the test for a vehicle of class V;

rule 15 means that a person X may drive a vehicle V if person X has a provisional licence and is old enough to drive a vehicle of class V.

The query

```
?permitted_to_drive (flora car)
```
means "Is it true that Flora is permitted to drive a car?"

The program would first look at rule 14 and then scan the facts to see if Flora has passed the test. The answer is "no", so rule 15 is examined. The facts are scanned again to check if Flora has a provisional licence. No relevant fact is found so the program returns the answer "no".

The query

```
?permitted_to_drive (robert motor_cycle)
```

will return the answer "yes" using Rule 15 and facts 2, 6 and 13.

The query

```
?permitted_to_drive (emma V)
```

will return the answer "car" using rule 14 and fact 11.

Module 5 Advanced Systems Development

> ## Case study: ELSIE the expert system
>
> ELSIE is an expert system that was built in the 1980s for use in the construction industry, is still in widespread use today, and is continually being refined and improved. It is designed to take over many of the more mundane aspects of the job of a quantity surveyor. When a customer approaches a construction company to have, say, a new office block built, hundreds of questions first have to be answered with regard to the size of the building, the number of storeys, the type of central heating required, the number of lifts, the type of cladding (e.g. brick or stone), the state of the proposed building site (level or sloping, wet or dry, clay or rock etc.) The quantity surveyor then takes all these factors into consideration and comes up with an estimate.
>
> ELSIE is an expert system that runs on a PC and is organised in a simple menu-driven format with well-presented screen layouts. It can be used by people with no previous computer experience, and takes the form of a question-and-answer session. When the user has input the answers to all the questions, the system gives a total cost for the building, with a detailed breakdown. The user can then go back and change the answers to certain questions to see what the effects would be of selecting, for example, a less expensive form of heating, or having an extra storey and more car-parking space on the site. The knowledge base also contains current building regulations for all areas of the country to ensure that the proposed building stays within the law.
>
> ELSIE can perform calculations in a matter of seconds that would previously have taken days or even weeks of a quantity surveyor's time.

Expert system shells

An expert system shell is a special software program that allows a user to build an expert system without having to learn a programming language. It provides a straightforward user interface both for the expert to enter the facts and rules, and for the end-user to use the completed expert system to solve a problem.

A shell is basically an expert system without a knowledge base. It provides the developer with the inference engine, the user interface and the means of inputting the 'knowledge'. Many shells enable the developer to present examples with the correct conclusions and the system automatically builds the rules. Thus, for example, a medical team building an expert system could type in the symptoms of hundreds of patients with 'upper abdominal pain' with a known diagnosis of kidney stones, gallstones, stomach ulcers, cancer and so on for each one. The software will then calculate the significance of each symptom so that presented with a new case, it can give one or more diagnoses with an indication of the probability of each being correct.

Uses of expert systems

Expert systems have are used in a wide range of applications such as:

- **medical diagnosis**;
- **fault diagnosis** of all kinds – gas boilers, computers, power stations, railway locomotives. If your gas boiler breaks down, the service engineer may well arrive with a laptop computer and type in all the symptoms to arrive at a diagnosis, and then use the system to find out the exact part numbers of any replacement parts required for your particular model of boiler;
- **geological surveys** to find oil and mineral deposits;
- **financial services** to predict stock market movement or to recommend an investment strategy;
- **social services** to calculate the benefits due to claimants;
- **industrial uses** such as the expert system ELSIE described above.

> **Case study: Protecting endangered species**
>
> The annual turnover in live animals, skins and animal products of endangered species is astonishingly even greater than the money made from the illegal arms trade, amounting to £3 billion per year – second only to illegal drugs trading.
>
> At airports such as Heathrow, customs officers are often faced with the task of identifying the particular species of animal or reptile that, say, a handbag has been made from – not an easy task when there are over 35,000 different species of snake alone, each with a different level of protection. The item often has to be sent to a zoo or natural history museum, where an expert counts the number of scales and other features and cross checks this with reference material, a process which can take up to 3 weeks.
>
> Help is now at hand in the form of 'Nemesis', a computer system that can identify the species that a product is made from. A camera attached to a computer takes a photograph of the product, and the computer program compares the features with its database and displays the name of the species on the screen. The more skins it sees, the more accurate it becomes, a process known as 'training' the system.
>
> At the moment, it only stores information on the 15 most traded snake skins, but the developers hope that it will eventually be able to identify all species, and will also be used on furs.

And finally... applications of computers

Whole books have been devoted to the applications of computers and their effects on society and the individual. For this course, you will be expected to develop an awareness of the many different ways in which different types of computers, from an embedded computer in a washing machine, to a mainframe computer holding a giant corporate database, are used and how they affect our lives.

The best way of doing this is to look at relevant TV programmes, read relevant newspaper articles and magazines, and research some applications which interest you. The applications that you could be asked about in the examination include science, education, manufacturing industry, commercial data processing, publishing, leisure, design, communication, embedded systems, information systems, the Internet, artificial intelligence and expert systems.

You should look at the following aspects:

- consider the purpose of the application;
- discuss the application as an information system in the context chosen;
- examine specific user-interface needs;
- examine the communication requirements of the application;
- discuss the extent to which the given system satisfies both the organisation's and user's needs;
- discuss the economic, social, legal and ethical consequences of the application;
- discuss examples of software failure such as in safety critical systems, errors in commercial transactions and errors caused by poorly specified systems;
- discuss the possible effects of failure from a social, economic and legal point of view.

Good luck and goodbye!

Exercises

1. Expert systems are suitable for many different categories of application. Give **two** different categories and, for each category, **one** typical application.

2. One of the essential components of an expert system is a knowledge base.
   Using suitable examples, describe the nature and structure of the data held within a knowledge base.

3. (a) Briefly describe the three constituent parts of an expert system.
   (b) Users of expert systems claim that they are 'much more useful than a very large database'. Give two reasons to justify this claim.

4. State four reasons why the use of a robot would be preferred over the use of a human operator in a car assembly line.

5. Describe two ways in which the increasing use of telecommunications in computer systems has changed working patterns.

6. Explain the term *embedded system*. Give examples of devices which might incorporate an embedded system.

Appendix A

AQA Specification Summary

Computing

AS Module 1 – Computer Systems, Programming and Network Concepts

	Topic	Amplification	See Chapter
1.1	**Fundamentals of Computer Systems**		
	Hardware and Software	Candidates should understand the relationship between hardware and software and be able to define both.	1
	Classification of Software	Candidates should be aware of how software is classified. They should be able to explain what is meant by system software and application software.	2
	System Software	Operating system software Utility programs Library programs Compilers, assemblers, interpreters	2
	Application Software	Candidates should be able to describe the different types of application software.	2
		General purpose applications software. Special purpose applications software. Bespoke software	2
		Candidates should be able to explain what is meant by application package and integrated package.	2
	The generation of Bit Patterns in a Computer	Explain the different interpretations that may be associated with a pattern of bits. Bits, bytes. Concept of a word. Program and data.	3, 16 16
	Internal Components of a Computer	Processor, main memory, address bus, data bus, control bus, I/O port, secondary storage, their purpose and how they relate.	17
	Functional Characteristics of a Computer	Describe the stored program concept whereby machine code instructions stored in main memory are fetched and executed serially by a processor that performs arithmetic and logical operations.	17
1.2	**Fundamentals of Programming**		
	Generations of Programming Language		
	First generation – Machine code	Describe machine-code language and assembly language.	4
	Second generation – Assembly language	Some discussion of the development of programming languages and the limitations of both machine code and assembly-language programming would be useful.	4

361

Appendix   AQA Specification Summary

Third generation – imperative high level language	Explain the term 'imperative high level language' and its relationship to first and second generation languages	4
Types of Program Translator Assembler, compiler interpreter	Define each type of language translator and illustrate situations where each would be appropriate or inappropriate	4
Features of Imperative High Languages Data types Built - defined	Illustrate these features for a particular imperative, third generation language.	5, 6
Programming Statements Type definitions Variable declarations Constant definitions Procedure/ Function declarations		5 – 11
Assignment Iteration Selection	Describe the use of these statement types.	6 – 10
Procedure and function Calling	Explain the advantages of procedure/functions.	8
Constants and variables	Explain the advantages of named variables and constants.	7
Procedure and function parameters	Describe the use of parameters to pass data within programs.	11
Fundamentals of Structured Programming	Candidates should be familiar with the structured approach to program construction and should be able to construct and use structure charts when designing programs, use meaningful identifier names, procedures/functions with interfaces, use procedures that execute a single task, avoid the use of GoTo statements. Candidates should be able to explain the advantages of the structured approach.	8
Abstract Data Types **Binary tree** **Stack** **Linear queue**	Candidates should be able to recognise and use these in very simple ways. They will not be expected to have knowledge of how to implement these in a programming language. Uses of these should include a binary search tree and using a stack to reverse the elements of a linear queue.	14, 15
Data Structures **One and two dimensional arrays**	Candidates should be familiar with each of these and their uses.	10
Simple Algorithms	Candidates should understand the term algorithm and be able to hand trace simple algorithms.	7

1.3	**Fundamentals of Information and Data Representation** **Relationship between Data and Information**		
	Data. Sources of data	Explain the term data. Consider sources of data, both direct and indirect.	16
	Meaning of the term Information	Consider data as an encoded form of information and as any form of communication that provides understandable and useful knowledge to the recipient.	16
	Number Representation Systems Binary number system Pure binary representation of decimal integers	Describe the representation of unsigned decimal integers in binary. Perform translation from decimal to binary and vice-versa.	16
	Binary-coded decimal (BCD) representation	Describe the representation of unsigned decimal integers in binary-coded decimal. Perform translations from decimal to BCD and vice versa. Explain advantages of BCD.	16
	Information Coding Schemes ASCII EBCDIC Unicode	Describe standard coding systems for coding information expressed in character form and other text-based forms. Differentiate between the character code representation of a decimal integer and its pure binary representation.	3 16
	Representing Images, Sound and other Information Bit-mapped graphics Vector graphics Sampled Sound Sound Synthesis	Describe how bit patterns may also represent other forms of information including graphics and sound.	16
	Analogue and digital signals Analogue to digital converter (ADC)	Differentiate between analogue and digital signals. Describe the principles of operation of an analogue to digital converter.	16
1.4	**Communication and Networking**		
	Communication Methods Serial data communication Parallel data communication	Define both serial and parallel methods and illustrate where they are appropriate. Consider the effect of distance on the transmission of data. Define these terms.	18
	Baud rate, bit rate and Bandwidth	Differentiate between baud rate and bit rate. Consider the relationship between bit rate and bandwidth.	18

Appendix   AQA Specification Summary

Asynchronous data transmission	Define	18
Start and stop bits.	Describe the purpose of start and stop bits in asynchronous data transmission	
Odd and even parity	Explain the use of parity checks.	
Handshaking in parallel data transmission and meaning of the term protocol	Explain what is meant by a protocol in this context.	18
Modem	Describe the purpose and the method of operation of a modem.	18
Networking		
Network		
Local area network (LAN)		
Bus, Ring and Star LAN topologies	Define these networking terms. Candidates should be familiar with LAN topologies but will not be required to know details of their operation. Candidates should be aware of the advantages and disadvantages of each LAN topology. Candidates should be able to compare local area networking with standalone operation.	19
Wide area network (WAN) The Internet Intranet Network adapter Leased line networking Dial up networking		20
Uniform Resource Locator (URL)	Describe the term URL in the context of Internetworking.	20
Domain names and IP addresses	Explain the term domain name and IP address. Describe how domain names are organised	20

Appendix AQA Specification Summary

AS Module 2 – Principles of Hardware, Software and Applications

	Topic	Amplification	See Chapter
2.1	**A study of one Major Information Processing Application of Computing**	Consider the purpose of the application. Discuss the application as an information system in the context chosen. Examine specific user-interface needs. Examine the communication requirements of the application. Discuss the extent to which the given system satisfies both the organisation's and users' needs. Discuss the economic, social, legal and ethical consequences of the application.	
	General Purpose Packages Database, spreadsheet, word-processing, Desk-top publishing, presentation package, e-mail	Candidates should have experience in using a database and a spreadsheet package as part of their skills' development. In addition, they should be aware of how the listed packages facilitate the execution of particular tasks. Candidates should be able to assess the suitability of a given package for a particular task as well as its limitations.	25
	Social, Economic and Ethical Consequences of Current Uses of Computing	Discuss the social and economic implications for an individual in relation to employment, government, education and leisure.	21,24
		Discuss issues relating to privacy in the context of electronic mail and data.	23
		Consider the impact of encryption technology on the privacy of the individual, organisation and the state.	23
	Legal Implications of the Use of Computers	Discuss issues of ownership of information and programs, protection of data. Consider current legal controls on computerised data and programs and the implications of current legislation.	22, 23
2.2	**Files and Databases** File Types Text and non-text (binary files) files.	Define a file. Describe the meaning of the terms, text and non-text files.	26
	A file as a collection of Records. Records and fields (data items), primary and secondary key fields.	Illustrate how key fields are used to locate and index heterogeneous records.	26
	Fixed and variable length Records. File structure	Describe the use of fixed and variable length records. Consider the advantages and disadvantages of each. Define what is meant by the structure of a file.	26

Appendix   AQA Specification Summary

	File size	Calculate the size in bytes of a given file.	26
	File Organisation Serial Sequential Direct access	Describe the organisation of these files. Explain hashing.	27 27
	File Processing	Explain the principle of master and transaction files and methods used to retrieve, insert, edit and delete data.	27
	Security and Integrity of Data in a Data Processing Environment. The meaning of the terms Security Integrity	Define these terms.	29, 30
	File Security Methods Backing up strategies Encryption	Describe hardware and software protection of online files against unauthorised access and system failure.	29
	Data Processing Integrity `Methods`	Explain how corrupted data can be detected and prevented using techniques such as batch totals, control totals, hash totals, check digits, virus checking, parity checking, check sums.	30
	Database Concepts Data sharing Data consistency Primary key Alternate key/ Secondary key Indexing Secondary index Validation	Consider a database as an integrated collection of non-redundant, related data accessible from more than one application and stored in different record types together with a mechanism for linking related records. Consider how data inconsistency may arise in an application based on a separate file approach and how this is avoided in a database approach. Consider why indexing is used and how databases support multiple indexes. Describe typical built-in validation controls.	32
	Relational Databases	Explain the concept of a relational database. Define the term attribute.	32
	Querying a Database Querying by Example (QBE)	Illustrate the use of QBE to extract data from several tables of a relational database.	32

2.3	**Operating Systems**		
	Role of an Operating System Provision of a virtual machine	Candidates should understand that the role of the operating system is to hide the complexities of the hardware from the user.	33
	Resource management	In addition, it manages the hardware resources in order to provide for an orderly and controlled allocation of the processors, memories and I/O devices among the various processes competing for them.	33
	Operating System Classification Batch Interactive Real time Network	Define each type of operating system and explain their operational characteristics	33
	File Management File, Filename, Directory, Pathnames, Directory structure, Logical drives,	Define the term File, Filename and Directory. Describe the use of directories. Explain the relationship between the root directory and sub-directories and the use of pathnames.	33
	Access rights	Explain the term access rights in the context of file management.	33
	Backing-up, Archiving	Distinguish file backing-up from archiving.	33
2.4	**Hardware Devices**		
	Input and Output Devices	Consider how the application and needs of the user affect the choice of input and output devices. Candidates should be able to make appropriate selections based upon knowledge of the usage of contemporary devices. Principles of operation will not be required.	34,35
	Secondary Storage Devices	Explain the need for secondary storage within a computer system and discuss the difference between archived data and directly accessible data. Compare the capacity and speed of access of various media including magnetic disk and tape, optical media and CD-ROM storage. Give examples of how each might be used.	36

Appendix · AQA Specification Summary

AS Module 3 – System Development

	Topic	Amplification	See Chapter
3.1	System Development		
	The Classical Systems Life-cycle		
	Problem definition / Problem investigation / feasibility study, analysis, design, construction / implementation and maintenance	Describe the stages of development and maintenance of a hardware/software system including evaluating the operational, technical and financial feasibility of developing a new system. The importance of testing the specification, design and implementation.	37
	Evaluation	The importance of evaluating the effectiveness of the implemented solution in meeting the users' needs.	37
	Analysis Methods of gathering Information Data flow Diagrams	Describe methods of deriving the user and information requirements of a system and its environment. Evaluate the feasibility of a computer-based solution to a problem, specify and document the data flow and the processing requirements for a system to level one and identify possible needs for the development and maintenance of the system.	37
	Entity-Relationship Diagrams	Produce a data model from the given data requirement for a simple scenario involving two or three entities.	37
	Design Modular and top-down Design Pseudo-code Simple algorithm design	Specify and document a design that meets the requirements of the problem in terms of human computer interface (usability and appropriateness), hardware and software, using methods such as structure charts, hierarchy charts, pseudo-code, relations.	38
	Prototyping	Define prototyping.	
	Human Computer Interface	Examine and document specific user interface needs.	39
	Testing Strategies Construction / Implementation	Dry run testing. Unit testing. Integration testing. Identify suitable test data. Test solution. Make use of appropriate software tools and techniques to construct a solution to a real problem.	38
	Maintenance	Understand the need for and nature of maintenance. Understand how technical documentation aids the process of maintenance.	38
	Evaluation	Evaluate methods and solutions on the basis of effectiveness, usability, and maintainability.	38

A2 Module 4 – Processing and Programming Techniques

	Topic	Amplification	See Chapter
4.1	**Structure and Role of the Processor**		
	Arithmetic Logic Unit, Accumulator and Control Unit. Clock.	The role and operation of a processor and its major components should be explained. The effect of clock speed, word length and bus width on performance.	40
	General purpose and Dedicated registers.		40
	Machine code and processor instruction set The Fetch-Execute cycle and the role of registers within it.	Explain how the FE cycle is used to execute machine code programs and the stages in the process including details of registers used.	40
	Processing Concepts		
	Interrupts in the context of the FE cycle.	Define an interrupt, showing how it might be used within the computer system and its effects. Describe the vectored interrupt mechanism.	40
	Addressing modes including direct, indirect, immediate, indexed and base register addressing.	Describe the various modes of addressing memory and justify their use. Examples from actual machines might be useful.	44
	Assembly language Instructions and their relationship to machine code, memory addressing and use of the registers.	Describe the nature and format of assembly language statements. Illustrate their use for elementary machine operations.	43 43
4.2	**Programming Concepts**		
	High Level Languages The characteristics and Classification of high level languages.	Examine the characteristics and use of a number of high level languages, including both declarative and imperative for developing applications.	45
	Choice of programming languages to develop particular applications.	Discuss criteria for selecting programming languages for particular tasks.	45
	Programming Paradigms	Candidates should have practical experience of at least one programming paradigm and should have knowledge of and reasons for the range of paradigms references in section 4.2. Candidates should be aware of the application areas for which particular paradigms are best suited.	
	Imperative and declarative Languages	Distinguish between programming language types and generations.	45, 4

Appendix AQA Specification Summary

	Structured programming techniques		5–11
	Procedural-oriented Programming		
	Object-oriented Programming	Candidates should be familiar with the concept of an object, an object class, encapsulation, inheritance, polymorphism and containment, and event-driven programming.	46
	Logic programming	Candidates should be familiar with the concept of logic programming for declaring logical relationships.	47, 48
	Data Structures		
	Lists Trees Queues – linear and circular Stacks Pointers	Candidates should be familiar with the concept of a list, a tree, a queue, a stack, a pointer and be familiar with the methods (data structures) for representing these when a programming language does not support these as built-in types.	50 52 53
	Linked lists	Distinguish between static and dynamic structures and compare their uses. Use of free memory, heap and pointers.	51
	Standard Algorithms		
	Linear search Binary search Bubble sort	Describe, using algorithms or programming examples, the methods used by programmers when manipulating structured data. Discuss methods used in relation to efficiency criteria. Candidates should be aware of the link between choice of algorithms and volume of data to be processed.	54
	Tree traversal algorithms Stack, queue and list operations Creating and maintaining linked lists.	Describe the creation and maintenance of data within lists, trees, stacks, queues and linked lists.	51 - 53 51
	Recursive Techniques	Illustrate the use of recursive techniques in both procedural and logic programming languages.	49, 50
4.3	**Data Representation in Computers**		
	The concept of number bases Denary, binary and Hexadecimal	Describe the translation of a denary number to binary form and vice versa. Describe the translation of a denary number to hexadecimal form and vice versa. Describe the use of hex as shorthand for binary.	41
	Number Representation		
	Integer and real numbers	Draw a distinction between integers and reals in a computer context.	41
		Describe how an unsigned real number is represented in fixed-point form in binary.	41

Appendix   AQA Specification Summary

	Representation of negative Numbers by Two's Complement.	Describe the use of Two's Complement to perform subtraction.	41
	Floating point numbers.	Describe the format of floating point numbers including the concept of mantissa and exponent and the need for normalisation.	42
4.4	**Operating Systems**		
	Operating System Classification Batch Interactive Real time	Describe the role of Job Control Languages and systems that combine batch and interactive modes.	56
	Multi-programming, multi-user, multi-tasking systems	Describe the principles of multi-programming.	55
	Client-server systems, distributed file systems and network operating systems	Outline the principles of client-server operation. Explain the terms distributed file and network operating systems.	55
	Operating System Concepts		
	User-interface	Classify methods of user-interface including command-line, graphical and job-control.	56
	Memory Management	Outline how operating systems manage memory including the concepts of virtual memory and paging, code sharing (re-entrant code), dynamically linked libraries or DLLs.	57
	File Management	Outline how operating systems manage file space. Explain the concept of an addressable block and the use of the file buffer.	57
	I/O Management.	Outline the concepts of handlers and drivers and the use of interrupts	57
	Process / Task / Management	Explain the concept of a process, process states, and the need to schedule processes in a multi-programming operating system.	56

Appendix   AQA Specification Summary

A2 Module 5 – Advanced Systems Development

	Topic	Amplification	See Chapter
5.1	**Applications and Effects** **The applications of computing in a variety of contexts**	These could include science, education, manufacturing industry, commercial data processing, publishing, leisure, design, communication, embedded systems, information systems, the Internet, artificial intelligence and expert systems. Candidates should: consider the purpose of the application; discuss the application as an information system in the context chosen; examine specific user-interface needs; examine the communication requirements of the application; discuss the extent to which the given system satisfies both organisation's and user's needs; discuss the economic, social, legal and ethical consequences of the application.	
	Generic Packages Database, spreadsheet, word-processing, Desktop publishing, presentation packages,	As part of their skills development candidates should have sufficient experience of using a database to understand how a database management system controls access to the data via user views. In addition, they should be aware of how the listed packages facilitate the execution of particular tasks. Candidates should be able to assess the suitability of a given package for a particular task as well as its limitations. Candidates should also appreciate how these packages might be integrated or share common data and be customised by the use of macros.	74
	Expert system shells		
	Social, Economic and Legal Consequences of Computerisation	Discuss examples of software failure such as in safety critical systems, errors in commercial transactions and errors caused by poorly specified systems. Discuss the possible effects from a social, economic and legal point of view.	
5.2	**Databases** **Database Concepts** Three level architecture of a DBMS. External or user schema. Conceptual or logical schema. Internal or storage schema. Program / data independence. Concurrent access to data	Describe the structure of a Database Management System (DBMS). Distinguish between the use of a database and the use of a Database Management System (DBMS). Consider how a DBMS improves security and eliminates unproductive maintenance. Discuss how a DBMS overcomes problems that arise with multi-user access.	58 61

Appendix   AQA Specification Summary

	ODBC (Open Database Connectivity)	Explain the term and consider situations where it is used.	61
	Data Definition Language (DDL) Data Manipulation Language (DML)	Explain the terms DDL and DML. Candidates should be familiar with the use of a DDL to define a database.	61
	Database Design and the Relational Model		
	Entity-relationship modelling.	Illustrate the principles of database design using these techniques in the production of normalised tables that control redundant data, studied up to BCNF.	31
	Normalisation techniques		59
	Querying a Database		
	Structured Query Language (SQL)	Illustrate the use of a Structured Query Language using the constructs Select, From, Where, In, GroupBy and OrderBy to extract data from several tables of a relational database.	60
	Database Server	Define and explain the operation of a database server.	61
	Object-oriented Databases	Define and explain the need for object-oriented databases. Candidates need to understand that databases may need to store complex data types and their associated methods of access.	61
5.3	**Systems Development**		
	Analysing a System Fact finding techniques	Interview, observation, survey, examination of paperwork.	62
	Reporting techniques	Data flow diagrams, Entity Attribute Relationship Modelling (EAR)	62, 31
	Data dictionary	Explain a data dictionary.	61
	Volumetrics	Data volumes Characteristics of users	62
	Designing a System	System flowcharts, prototyping, user interface design.	63
	Testing Strategies for the Development of a System	Top down, Bottom up; Black-box testing, White-box testing. Unit testing, Integration testing.	63
	System Implementation Conversion	Consider the problems that may arise when converting from the old to the new system.	64
	Parallel, direct, pilot, phased	Describe the four main methods of converting from the old to the new.	64

Appendix   AQA Specification Summary

	System testing Acceptance testing Alpha and beta testing	Define the different types of testing that may be applied to the developed system.	64
	Training Installation manual, user Manual, operations manual, Training manual / Documentation.	Consider the training needs for the new system.	65
	Evaluation	Consider the purpose and timing of the evaluation.	64
	Maintaining a System	Explain the need for maintenance. Consider the factors that affect the maintainability of a solution and evaluate a solution for maintainability in terms of the ease with which a program / solution can be corrected if an error in encountered, adapted if its environment changes, or enhanced if customer changes requirements.	64
5.4	**Hardware Devices** **Input and output methods**	Examine the role of computer devices in relation to both the nature and volume of the data being input and the characteristics of the user. Consider how the application influences the input method. Discuss the choice of output method in relation to applications and user needs, including the issue of whether printed reports, visual display, sound or other outputs are most appropriate. Consider how computers may assist in situations where the user may be unable to utilise conventional methods of input and output. Discuss situations where output may control machinery. Candidates should be able to select appropriate hardware by making an informed choice, rather than by learning a list of devices. Comprehension questions, based on contemporary devices and the principles of their operation and use, would be most suitable for this area of the syllabus.	66
5.5	**Networking** **Methods** Baseband and broadband modes of network operation	Describe each method and illustrate where each is appropriate.	67
	Synchronous data transmission		67
	Time-division multiplexing		67

Circuit switching Packet-switching Datagram virtual circuit Asynchronous Transmission Mode (ATM)	Describe and contrast the operation of these three network types -circuit-switched, packet-switched, ATM	67
Standard Protocols TCP/IP protocol stack	Explain the concept and need for standard protocols both across a network and linking computers. Describe the layers of the TCP/IP protocol stack.	67
Local Area Networks Types of cable	Twisted pair, baseband coaxial cable, broadband coaxial cable, optical fibre.	68
Topology Bus Ring Star Switched Ethernet and Hubs	Define the term topology. Describe in general terms the operation of these networks. Compare the advantages and disadvantages of each.	68 68
Segment Bridge Peer-to-peer networking	Define the term and explain why local-area networks based on a bus topology are segmented. Define the term and explain why it is used. Explain what is peer-to-peer networking and compare with server-based networking.	68 68 68
Wide Area Networks Electronic Data Interchange (EDI)	Contrast wide area and local area networks Describe EDI.	69
Value-Added Network (VAN) Providers	Contrast private and public networks.	69
On-line service providers Internet Service Providers (ISP) Internet	What is meant by an on-line service? Explain why such services are provided.	70
Connecting to a wide area Network. Leased line ISDN. Cable modem, dial-up line and modem Asymmetric Digital Subscriber Line (ADSL)	Compare the various methods that may be used and consider where it would be appropriate to use each method.	69
Inter-networking	Explain the meaning of the term inter-networking.	69
Routers / Gateways	Define these terms and consider where and why they are used. In particular consider how routing is achieved across the Internet and how local area networks are connected to the Internet.	69

Appendix AQA Specification Summary

The Internet and its Uses		
World Wide Web (WWW) Internet registries and Internet registrars Client / server model of Internet.	Candidates should be familiar with the structure of the Internet and the facilities that it provides to users.	71
HTTP protocol Hyperlinks	Candidates should be familiar with elementary syntax and use of hypertext mark-up language.	71
Web site Web page construction The organisation of Web Pages on a Web site FTP	Candidates should have some experience of creating Web pages and be familiar with how Web pages can be organised on a Web site. Candidates should be familiar with the use of FTP to transfer files such as Web pages from a local machine to a Web server.	71
Telnet Role of URLs in retrieval of Web documents	Candidates should be familiar with how Telnet can be used to manage a remote Web site or to access a remote machine including retrieving e-mail.	70
Internet search engines	Candidates should have some experience of using a search engine and understand its purpose.	70
Web browser Java and applets	Candidates should be aware of how applications may be executed on a Web site and how Java applets allow programs to be executed through browsers.	71
E-mail Usenet Internet Relay Chat (IRC) Agents Video-conferencing	Candidates should be familiar with the use of these facilities, their advantages and disadvantages.	70
On-line shopping and banking		72
Moral, Ethical, Social and Cultural Issues	Candidates should be made aware of its use and misuse by individuals or groups. The World Wide Web as a force of empowerment.	73
Security and the Internet		
Firewalls Encryption Digital certificates	Describe and explain the need for these in the context of the Internet and understand the issues that surround them.	73

Index

1NF 285
2NF 287
3NF 288
Absolute loader 277
Acceptance testing 312
Access
    directory 138
    rights 138, 155, 156
Accumulator 193, 195
Ada 217
Adaptive maintenance 314
Address bus 80, 82
Addressing
    direct 212
    immediate 212
    indexed 213
    indirect 213
    modes 211
    relative 213
ADSL 331
Alpha testing 313
AltaVista 340
ALU .... *See* Arithmetic-logic unit
Analogue to digital
    converter 76, 319
AND 208
Anti-virus software 145
APPEND 60
Applets 341
Archive 158
Archiving 157
Argument 52, 226
Arithmetic
    logic unit 80, 192
    shift 208
ARPANET 334
Array 46
    two-dimensional 48
Artificial intelligence 354
ASCII 12, 56
Assembler 8, 16, 18
Assembly code 16
Assembly Language
    instructions 206
ASSIGN statement 59
Assignment statement 24
Asymmetric Digital Subscriber Line
    331
Asynchronous Transfer Mode .. 323
Asynchronous transmission 85
ATM 323

Atoms 226
Attribute 146
Auxiliary storage 4
Backup 139
    copy 157
    daily 157
    differential 157
    incremental 157
    normal 157
Bandwidth 86
Bar code reader 162
Base class 220
Base register addressing 277
Baseband 321
BASIC 17
Batch 268
    processing 143, 154, 160
Baud rate 84
BCD .... *See* Binary Coded Decimal
Bespoke software 10
Beta testing 313
Bidirectional 165
Binary
    Coded Decimal 75
    fixed point 203
    floating point 204
    number system 12, 13, 75, 199
    search 262
    tree 71
    tree traversal 72
Biometric security measures 139
Bit 12, 123
Bitmapped graphics 77
Black box testing 309
Block structure 50
Boolean 29
    function 47
    value 23, 76
Booting 267
Bootstrap loader 4
Branch instruction
    conditional 209
    unconditional 210
Breakpoint 32
Bridge 327
Broadband 321
Bubble sort 263
Buffer 279
Bus 79, 80, 325
    address 82
    control 81

    data 82
    network 89
    size 197
Business Software Alliance 103
Byte 3, 12, 23, 123
C 216, 217
Cable modems 331
Cabling systems 321
Cache memory 4
Carrier sense multiple access ... 325
Carry 207
CASE statement 41
CD-ROM 172
Cell 323
Central Processing Unit 79
Certifying Authority 350
Character 23
Check digit 144
Checksum 145
Child nodes 71
Chr 55
CIR 193
Circuit switching 322
Circular
    queue 253
    shift 208
Classes 218
Clearing the screen 26
Client-server
    architecture 328
    database 298
    system 269
Clock
    speed 197
    system 192
Coaxial cable 91, 321
COBOL 216
Collision 129
Command and control system .. 188
Command-line
    interface 185, 270
    interpreter 270
Comment 21
Communications
    links 91, 321
    media 91
    satellite 91, 321
    security 137
Compiler 8
Composite data types 67
Compound conditions 31

Index

Compound statements 26, 29
Computer
   abuse 101
   crime 101
   failure 99
Computer Misuse Act 103
Computers, and health............... 111
Conceptual
   data model 146, 283
   schema 295
Condition code 206
Conditional branches 209
Containment 222
Contents of documented system 182
Control
   bus 81
   program 267
   unit 80, 192
Conversion to new system 311
Copyright Designs and Patents Act
   103
Corrective maintenance 314
CPU ... *See* Central Processing Unit
Crime 101
CSMA-CD 325
Current instruction register 193
Cursor 26
Cybersquatting 348
Cylinder 171
Data
   bus 80, 82
   compression 86
   consistency 282
   Definition Language 295
   dictionary 296, 303
   direct collection of 74
   encryption 137
   flow 178, 301
   flow diagram 177, 301
   hierarchy 123
   indirect collection of 74
   integrity 141
   Manipulation Language 290, 295
   Protection Act 106
   Protection Registrar 107
   redundancy 282
   security 136
   shareable 282
   sources 74
   store 178, 301
   structure 46, 67
   subjects 107
   transmission rate 87
   type 23
   validation 143, 149
Data type

composite 67
   declaring 46
   elementary 67
   structured 67
Database 123, 282
   approach 149, 282
   client-server 298
   integrity 297
   locking 297
   Management System 283, 296
   privileges 298
   relational 150, 284
Datagram 322
   protocol 324
DBMS . *See* Database Management System
DDL *See* Data Definition Language
Deadlock 298
Deadly embrace 298
Debugging 27
Declarative language 216, 223
Decryption 351
Dedicated or leased lines 330
Degree of a relationship 146
Deliverable 175
Demultiplexor 322
Denary number system 14, 199
Design, top-down 35
Desktop publishing 116
Development of systems 309
Device driver 215, 279
DFD .... *See* Data flow diagram
Dialogue boxes 187
Dial-up networking 330
Digital
   certificate 350
   signature 350
Digitised sound 76
Digitiser 163
Direct
   addressing 212
   changeover 311
   file 129
Disaster planning 139
Disk
   cylinder 171
   floppy 4, 170
   hard 170
   magneto-optical 172
   sector 171
   storage 4
   track 171
   write-protecting 145
Dispose procedure 251
Distributed computer system 269
Div 24

DLL .... *See* Dynamic link library
DML .... *See* Data Manipulation Language
Documentation 316
Domain name system ... 93, 94, 348
Dot matrix printer 165
Dot notation 60
Drives 155
Dry run testing 181
Dummy value 28
Dynamic
   link library 278
   relocation 277
   structures 250
EBCDIC 12
E-commerce 345
EDI *See* Electronic data interchange
Electronic data interchange 330
Electronic mail 119
Elementary data types 67
ELF radiation 114
E-mail 119, 337
   and privacy issues 109
Embedded computers 6
Encapsulation 219
Encryption 137, 351
   strong 109
   weak 109
Entity 146
   Attribute Modelling 303
   Relationship Diagram 146
Eof 60
Eoln 47
Ergonomic environment 115
Error
   logic 25
   syntax 25
Ethernet 325, 327
Evaluation 182, 313
Evolutionary prototyping 181
Exclusive OR 208
Executive 267
Expert system 354
   shell 356
Exponent 204
External
   entity 177, 301
   schema 295
Extremely low frequency radiation
   114
Fact finding 300
Factorial 236
Factoring 352
FAT .... *See* File Allocation Table
Feasibility study 176
Fetch-execute cycle 193

Index

Fibre optic cable 91, 321
Field 123
File 123, 155
   access methods 133
   Allocation Table 278
   lookup check 143
   management 155, 278
   manager 155
   Pascal declaration 59
   random access 63
   Transfer Protocol 344
File organisation 126
   random 129
   relative 129
   sequential 127
   serial 127
Firewall 352
Firmware 6
First normal form 285
Fixed point binary numbers 203
Flag 130
Flat-file system 288
Floppy disk 170
Folders 155
FOR statement 42
Foreign key 151, 284, 288
Format check 143, 149
FORTRAN 216
Free memory 250
Free space 246
FTP ...... See File Transfer Protocol
Full-screen menu 185
Functional testing 309
Functions 50
   user-written 56
Gates, Bill 3
Gateway 332
Gb 3, 14
General purpose register .. 193, 195
Generations
   of files 133
   of programming language 16
Generic software 10
Geosynchronous orbit 91
Gigabyte 3
Global identifier 50
Grandfather, father, son 133
Graphical user interface 271
Graphics
   bitmapped 77
   tablet 163
GROUP BY 293
GUI .... 185. See Graphical User Interface
Hacking 101
Hand-held input devices 163

Handshaking 86
Hard disk 170
Hardware 2
Harvard Graphics 120
Hash file 129
Hashing algorithm 129
Health 111, 114
Health and Safety
   Executive 114
   Regulations 114
Heap 250
Hexadecimal number system 199
High level language 17, 215
Hit rate 134
HOLMES 105
Hot link 339
HotBot 340
HTML 342
Hub 326
Human computer interface 184
Hypertext links 339
Hypertext Markup Language 342
I/O controller 79, 82
I/O port 79
Icon 188, 271
Identifiers 21, 24, 50
   global 50
   local 50
IF..THEN..ELSE 31
Immediate addressing 212
Impact printer 165
Imperative high level language... 17
Imperative languages 216
Implementation 182
IN operator 29
In situ 133
Index 46
Indexed
   addressing 213
   sequential files 126, 130, 134
Indexing 150
Indirect addressing 213
Inference
   engine 354
   mechanism 354
Inheritance 220
   diagram 220
Ink jet printers 166
Inorder traversal 72, 258
Input/Output management 279
Insertion sort 264
Installation manual 316
Instruction
   format 211
   set 206
Integer 21, 23

Integrated packages 9, 121
Integration testing 181
Integrity of data 141
Interactive processing 154
Interface 82
   command line 270
   graphical 271
   windows 271
Internal schema 295
Internet 92, 334
   backbone 334
   Registry 348
   Relay Chat 336
   Service Provider 334, 335
Interpreter 8, 18
Interrogating files 131
Interrupt 193, 195
   enabled, disabled 274
   handling 153, 196, 273
   service routine 195, 196
Interviews 300
Intranet 94
IRC 336
ISDN line 86
ISP ... See Internet Service Provider
Iteration 28, 36
Jackson structure diagram 35
Java applets 341
JCL .... See Job control language
Job control language 270
Job priorities 274
Joystick 161
Kb 3, 14
Keyboard data entry 159
Key-to-disk system 160
Kilobyte 3
Knowledge base 355
Knowledge-based systems 354
LAN .... See Local Area Network
Language
   Data Definition 295
   Data Manipulation 290, 295
   declarative 216, 223
   for real-time 217
   high level 17, 215
   Hypertext Markup 342
   imperative 216
   job control 270
   low level 16, 215
   object-oriented 216
   portable 215
   procedural 223
   Structured Query 290
Laser printer 166
Last In First Out 68
Leaf nodes 71

Index

Leased lines 91
Length function 56
Library programs 8
LIFO 68
Light pen 161
Limit register 277
Linear search 262
Linked list 244
Linking database tables 151
List 239
Loader 267
   absolute 277
   relocating 277
Local Area Network 88
Local identifier 50
Locking 297
Logic bomb 102
Logic error 25
Logical instructions 208
Logical schema 295
Longint 23
Looping 28
Lotus Freelance 120
Low level language 16, 215
Magnetic
   Ink Character Recognition ... 161
   stripe 161
   tape 171
Magneto-optical disk 172
Main memory 3
Mainframe computers 3
Maintainability 314
Maintenance 314
   adaptive 183
   corrective 183
   perfective 182
Mantissa 204
Many-to-Many relationship 288
MAR *See* Memory Address Register
Master file 126, 131, 133
Mb 3, 14
MDR ... *See* Memory Data Register
Megabyte 3
Melissa 352
Memory 3, 14
   address register 193
   cache 4
   data register 193
   management 153, 277
   Read Only 4
Menu
   full-screen 185
   interface 185
   pop-up 186
   pull-down 186
Merging 128

MICR . *See* Magnetic Ink Character Recognition
Microprocessor 3
Microsoft Windows 188
Microwave 91, 321
MIDI 76
MOD 24
Modem 86, 331
Modes of operation 267
Modula-2 217
Modular programming 39
Module 35
   testing 312
Mondex 162
Monitor 267
Mouse 161
Movement files 131
Multi-access database 297
Multi-programming 153, 267
Multi-tasking 268
Multi-user 268
Natural language 186, 223
Near letter quality 165
Negative numbers 201
Net Nanny 353
Network
   protocols 324
   service providers 334
   termination device 331
   topology 88, 89, 325
New procedure 251
Newsgroups 335
NLQ .... *See* Near letter quality'
Node (in a linked list) 244
Normalisation
   of databases 285
   of floating point numbers 204
NOT 208
NSP 334
Nucleus 267
Object code 18
Object-oriented
   databases 299
   languages 216
   programming 218
Objects 218
Occam 217
OCR .... *See* Optical Character Recognition
ODBC .... *See* Open Database Connectivity
OMR *See* Optical Mark Recognition
One address instructions 211
On-line
   banking 345
   services 335

Open Database Connectivity ... 295
Open Systems 295
   Interconnection 324
Operating system 8, 153, 267
   batch 154
   client-server 269
   interactive 154
   multi-programming 267
   multi-tasking 268
   multi-user 268
   real-time 155, 268
   single-user single process 267
Operations manual 316
Optical Character Recognition 159
Optical Mark Recognition 162
OR 208
Ord 55
ORDER BY 293
OSI 324
Overflow 207
   error 70
Packet switching 322
Page
   management table 278
   of memory 153
Pages 339
Paging 277
Parallel
   conversion 311
   data transmission 84
Parameter 52
   actual 52
   formal 52
   passing by reference 53
   passing by value 52
   variable 53
Parent node 71
Parity 85
   bit 144
Partial dependency 287
Pascal 17, 20, 216
Passing parameters by value 52
Password 137
   protection 137
Pathnames 156
Peer-to-peer architecture 328
Perfective maintenance 314
Periodic backups 139
Peripherals 79
Permissions 298
Personal privacy 106
Phased conversion 311
Picture
   check 143
   element 77
Pilot conversion 312

Index

Pixel 77
Plaintext 351
Plotter 167
PMT ... *See* Page management table
Pointer 250
    variable 251
Polymorphism 221
Pop-up menu 186
Portable (language) 215
Postorder traversal 73, 259
Precision 204
Predicate 226
Preorder traversal 72, 259
Presence check 143, 149
Presentation graphics software. 120
Primary
    key 124, 150
    storage 169
Primitive data types 23
Printer
    dot matrix 165
    ink jet 166
    laser 166
    server 269
    thermal transfer 166
Priority (device) 274
Privacy 106
Private
    key 350
    lines 91
Procedural languages 216, 223
Procedure 30, 50
Process 177, 272
    control block 273
    descriptor 273
    states 272
Processing
    random 169
    sequential 169
Processor 3, 80
    performance 196
Program
    constants 32
    constructs 36
    counter 193
    design 35
    status word 274
    structure 35, 49
    testing 309
Program-data dependence 282
Programming
    aids 32
    modular 39
Prolog 216, 223, 224, 355
Protocol 86, 324
Prototyping 180, 305

evolutionary 181
    throw-away 181
Pseudocode 43
PSS .... *See* packet switching system
PSW .... *See* Program status word
Public
    key 350
    lines 91
Puck 163
Pull-down menu 186
QBE .... *See* Query by Example
Quantum 275
Query by Example 151
Querying a database 151
Queue 67, 253
Quicksort 263
Radiation, ELF 114
RAM *See* Random Access Memory
Random 56
    access file 63
    Access Memory 4
    files 129, 135
    numbers 44
    processing 169
Range check 143, 149
READ 25
Read Only Memory 4
READLN 25
Real 21, 23
Real-time 155, 268
Record 123
    Pascal declaration 59
Recovery procedures 139
Recursion 235, 259
Reference file 131
Register 192
Regulations
    Health and Safety 114
Relation 150, 284
Relational database 284
    design 150
Relationship 146
Relative
    addressing 213
    file 129
Relative file 129
Relocating loader 277
REPEAT..UNTIL statement ... 42
Repetition 28
Repetitive strain injury 112, 159
Requirements analysis 177
RESET 60
Resolution 167
Resource allocation 153
Review 313
REWRITE 60

Ring 326
    network 90
Rogue value 28
ROM .... 4. *See* Read Only Memory
Root 156
Rotate 208
Round 55
Round robin scheduling 275
Router 327, 332
RSI .... *See* Repetitive strain injury
Rule 227
Satellite 91, 321
Scanner 159, 162, 318
Scheduler 274
Scheduling methods
    Round robin 275
Scheduling objectives 275
Schema 295
Scope of identifiers 51
SCR . *See* sequence control register
Search
    binary 262
    engine 340
Second normal form 287
Secondary key 124, 150
Sector 170, 171
Security of data 136
Seek procedure 63
Segmentation 327
SELECT .. FROM .. WHERE . 290
Selecting programming language
    217
Selection 31, 36
Sentinel 28
Sequence 36
    control register 193
Sequential
    file 127, 134
    processing 169
Serial
    data transmission 84
    file 127, 134
Server-based network 328
Service providers 92
Seven-layer model 324
Shift instructions 208
Shopping on the Internet 346
Shortint 23
Simple data type 53
Simulation 67
Smart card 161
Software 2
    applications 9
    bespoke 9, 10
    copyright laws 103
    general purpose 9

Index

generic 10
   maintenance 313
   off-the-shelf 10
   special purpose 10
   suite 9
   systems 8
   testing 312
Sort 263
   bubble 263
   insertion 264
   quicksort 263
Sound 76
Source code 18
Special purpose software 10
Speech input 188
Speech synthesis system 189
Spiral model 305
Spreadsheet 118
SQL 290
Sqr 56
Sqrt 56
SR .... *See* Status Register
Stack 68, 255
Stack pointer 194
Standard
   functions 55
   protocols 324
Star network 88, 326
Static relocation 277
Status
   bit 206
   register 193
Storage
   auxiliary 4
   primary 169
   schema 295
   secondary 169
Stored program concept 80
Stress 111
String 23
Strong encryption 351
Structural testing 309
Structure diagram 35
Structured program 36
Subnetwork 332
Subscript 46
Subsystem testing 312
Supercomputers 3
Supervisor 267
Synchronous transmission .. 85, 322
Synonyms 129
Syntax
   diagram 29
   errors 25
System
   buses 80

clock 192
   design 180
   maintainability 181
   maintenance 182
   performance 181
   specification 180
   suitability 181
   testing 312
   usability 181
Systems
   expert 354
   flowchart 305
   investigation 300
   life cycle 174
   software 8
Tb 3
TCP/IP 324
Technical documentation 181
Teleworking 97
Telnet 337
Terabyte 3
Terminal adapter 331
Test
   data 181
   plan 181
Testing 312
   black box 309
   bottom-up 309
   dry run 181
   functional 309
   integration 181, 309
   program 309
   strategies 181, 309
   structural 309
   top-down 309
   unit 181
   white box 309
Text file 124
Third normal form 288
Three-level architecture of a DBMS 295
Throw-away prototyping 181
Time-division multiplexing 322
Time-slice 153, 275
Top-down design 35
Topology (of networks) 88
Touch screen 161, 318
Trace 27
   table 31
Track 170
Training 311, 317
   a computer 188
Transaction file 126, 131
Transcription errors 142, 159
Transmission
   asynchronous 85

errors 144
   rate 84, 87
   synchronous 85
Traversal 258
   of a binary tree 72
Tree 257
Trunc 55
Turing 80
   test 354
Twisted pair 91, 321
Two address instructions 211
Twos complement 201
TYPE statement 46
Unconditional branches 210
Underflow error 70
Unicode 74
Uniform Resource Locator 93
Unit testing 181, 312
Updating
   by copying 132
   by overlay 133
   files 132
   in place 133
   in situ 133
URL 93
Usenet newsgroups 335
User
   ID 137
   interface 308
   Interface 270
   manual 316
   schema 295
User-written functions 56
Utility programs 8
Validation checks 143, 149
Value-added networks 330
VAN 330
Variable 21
   length records 124
VDU 167
Vectored interrupt mechanism . 196
Verification 144
VeriSign 350
Videoconferencing 337
Virtual
   circuits 323
   machine 154
   memory 153, 277
Virus 102, 352
   detection 352
   protection 145
Visual display unit 167
Voice
   data entry 159
   recognition 188
Volatile 116

Volumetrics 304
von Neumann 80
   machine 80, 196
WAN .... *See* Wide Area Network
Waterfall model 175
Weak encryption 351
Web 346
   browsers 339
What If 118
WHILE..DO 29
White box testing 309
Wide Area Network 88, 91, 321, 330
WIMP 188
Windows 188, 271
WITH statement 60
Word 23
   size 82, 197
Word processing software 116
World Wide Web 335, 339
WORM disk 172
WRITE 25
WRITELN 25
Write-protecting 145
Writing to the printer 60
XOR 208
Yahoo 340
Zero address instructions 211

Other Titles of Interest from BPB/Payne-Gallway

Information Technology for Everybody - Vol. 1

This text covers all the essential theory needed by students preparing for one of the new information and Communication Technology specifications.

In particular it provides comprehensive coverage for the AQA short and long courses in Information and Communication Technology. The test is clear, concise and designed to be accessible to students of all abilities. Each chapter contains sufficient material for at least one lesson along with several standard questions. Links to relevant web sites are provided. Particular emphasis is placed throughout the text on problem areas of the syllabus that often cause candidates to lose marks unnecessarily.

ISBN : 81-7656-454-0 *Pages: 240* *Price: Rs. 99/-*

Information Technology for Everybody - Vol. 2

This book will be an indispensable class text for use by both non-IT specialists and IT teachers. It covers all the IT skills needed to achieve the information Technology at Levels 2 and 3, and explains exactly how the student can build a portfolio of evidence to achieve the qualification.

- It covers techniques in Windows, Word, Excel, Access, PowerPoint, Internet Explorer and Publisher.
- It covers the use of IT in society as required by the Key Skills Specifications.
- It demonstrates how to gather evidence and build a portfolio to gain the key skill qualification.
- It contains advice and examples of activities to demonstrate IT key skill competences.
- Sample text questions are included to give students practice for the externally set examination.
- Each chapter is cross-referenced to the relevant key skill specification

ISBN : 81-7656-455-9 *Pages: 224* *Price: Rs. 99/-*

Successful Projects in EXCEL

This book is designed to help students on an Advanced Level Technology course to complete a project using MS Excel 2000. It will also be useful to students on a wide range of other courses requiring an in-depth knowledge of spreadsheets. It assumes no previous knowledge of Excel and takes the reader from basics such as entering, editing and formatting text, numbers and formulae through to advanced features such as 'What if' scenarios, pivot tables, macros and customised toolbars. A wide range of examples is used to illustrate the different facilities of Excel, and a sample project shows students how to tackle and document each stage of project work.

What lecturers have said about this book:

"I am very impressed by the way you write your book in a clear and easy-to-follow layout."

"I have recommended this book for the Computer Applications in Business and Finance unit of the Association of Business Executives Diploma in Business Information Systems. Excellent book - my congratulations!

ISBN : 81-7656-454-0 *Pages: 240* *Price: Rs. 99/-*

Successful Projects in FrontPage 2000

This book is designed to help students on an 'AS' Level course to complete a project using MS FrontPage 2000. It will also be useful to students on a wide range of other courses requiring an in-depth knowledge of web page design and publishing. It assumes no previous knowledge of FrontPage and takes the reader from the basis such as entering, editing and formatting text and images on a web page through to creating hyperlinks, special effects and hot spots and using Java applets. It explain how to gather data using an online form and how to export this data to an Access database. A sample project shows students how to tackle and document each stage of project work.

ISBN : 81-7656-406-0 *Pages: 204* *Price: Rs. 99/-*

Other Titles of Interest from BPB/Payne-Gallway

Successful Projects in Visual Basic

This text will be useful for students on a wide range of courses such as 'A' Level Computing. It assumes no knowledge of programming and covers everything needed to write a large program.
- Part One goes through all the main programming concepts carefully.
- Part Two covers a variety of topics which students will find useful in their project work.
- Part Three goes through the design and coding of a sample project.
- All the material covered in Part One and the project in Part Three can be done using Version 4 or higher of Visual Basic. Some topics in Part Two need Version 5 or higher.

ISBN : 81-7656-401-X   *Pages: 256*   *Price: Rs. 99/-*

Successful Projects in ACCESS

This book is designed to help students on an Advanced Level and Communications Technology course to complete a project using MS Access 2000. It will also be useful to students on a wide range of other courses requiring an in-depth knowledge of databases. It covers database design, creating tables, forms and subforms, queries, importing and exporting data to other packages, analysing and processing data, reports and macros. It includes advice on choice of projects and a sample project.

What lecturers have said about this book:
"I've been all over the world and reviewed about 30 of the best-sounding books for Access, Word and Excel but yours are streets ahead. Doubled the price of your Projects books - they are worth it."
"We have found that these books are an absolutely excellent resource and have saved us so much work. We would like to convey our appreciation to the author."

ISBN : 81-7656-402-8   *Pages: 224*   *Price: Rs. 99/-*

Successful Computer Projects in Access with Visual Basic for Applications

Successful Computer Projects in Access with VBA provides students with a comprehensive and practical guide on how to tackle a computing project for an Advanced Level or Advanced computig course, using a software package and some programming in Visual Basic for Applications.

Features include:
- A wealth of ideas and advice for students on what constitutes as suitable project.
- Two specimen projects: the first project is a prototype system which is then developed into a full A Level project.
- Assessment guidelines and examiner's tips.
- Instructions throughout for development in Access 2000, 7 and 2.

Additional resources for teachers and studens are available form our website: www.payne-gallway.co.uk

ISBN : 81-7656-403-9   *Pages: 204*   *Price: Rs. 99/-*

Successful Projects in Word

This book is designed to help students in Information Technology to complete a project using the software package MS Word. It assumes very little previous knowledge of Word and covers the basics as well as the advanced features such as templates, fields, macros and customised toolbars. Full instructions are given for both Word 6 and Word 2000, with additional guidance for Word 7 and 97 users. All exercises can be completed on a school or college network which has no write access to certain files stored on a server.

Features include:
• Getting Started • Styles and Formatting • Graphics and Gridlines • Headers and Footers • Templates • Macros • Customising Menus and Toolbars • Tables, Formulae and Forms • Mail Merge • Designing the User Interface • Adding a Front End • Starting Your Project • Analysis and Design • Implementation and Testing • Evaluation

ISBN : 81-7656-399-4   *Pages: 208*   *Price: Rs. 99/-*

HOT SELLING
Titles from BPB/Payne-Gallway

INFORMATION TECHNOLOGY for Everybody - Vol. 1
This book provides all the essential theory in clear, concise, format need by IT and communication students. **99/-**

INFORMATION TECHNOLOGY for Everybody - Vol. 2
This book is an indispensable class text book for use by non-IT students and all the skills needed to achieve the key skills in Widows, Word-processig, Spread Sheets, Databases, PowerPoint, DTP and Web pages design. **99/-**

Successful Projects in ACCESS with VISUAL BASIC for Applications
It helps students to complete a project in MS Access and covers Database design, creating tables, forms and sub-forms, queries, importing and exporting data to other packages, analysing and processing data, reports and programming in VBA and advise on choice of projects and a sample projects. **99/-**

Successful Projects in COMPUTING : PowerPoint, Access Excel, Publisher
It includes complete documentation as well as implementation tips and explains, step by step, each of four different projects which are divided into the five stages of development; Identify, analysis, design, implement and evaluate. **99/-**

Successful Projects in ACCESS
This book is designed to help students to complete a project and assumes very little previous knowledge of Access and covers wide range and in depth knowledge of database design, creating tables, forms and sub-forms, queries, reports and charts, VBA importing and exporting data to other packages, analysing and processing data, reports and macros along with the sample project. **99/-**

INTERNET - Right from the start
A straightforward guide to the Internet and e-mail. **75/-**

COMPUTERS - Right from the start
This series is aimed at adults either at work, attending evening class or learning on a home PC. Starting from the very basic, with lots of screen shots and illustrations makes these books easy to follow. **75/-**

WORD 2002 - Right from the start
This book covers a wide range of word processing skills useful for school, work or home... .... **75/-**

Successful Projects in VISUAL BASIC
Extremely useful for students with no knowledge of programming and covers everythig needed to write a large programme with main programming concept, covers an variety of programme and includes each stage in designing and coding a full projects and includes a sample project. ... **99/-**

Successful Projects in WORD
This book is designed to help students to complete a project and assumes very little previous knowledge of Word and covers all the basics as well as advanced feaureas such as templates, fields, macros and customized toolbars with full instructions and additional guidance along with exercises, implementation, testing and evaluation of project. **99/-**

Successful Projects in FRONTPAGE
This book is designed to help student to design and implement a website using Frontpage alongwith the sample project **99/-**

Successful Projects in EXCEL
This book is design to help students to complete a project and assumes very little previous knowledge of Word and covers all the basics as well as advanced fearures such as entering, editing, and formatting text, numbers and formulae to advanced fetures such as macros, customize toolbars, pivot tables and 'What if' scenarios with full instructions and additional guidance alongh with exercises, implementation, testing and evaluation of a sample project. **99/-**

COMPUTING
This popular text book has been revised and updated edition containing computer systems, programming, network concepts, principles of Hardware, Software & Applications, System Development, Processing and Programming techniques, Advanced System Development, various types of Networking, WWW, Internet Security, E-Commerce, Artificial Intelligence and Expert Systems and College students will find this text book in an accessible and student-friendly way. **150/-**

EXCEL 2002 - Right from the start
Spreadsheets are made simple with this bok, which starts with the basics and gradually introduces more complex features. **75/-**

Notes

25 - 15 - 01

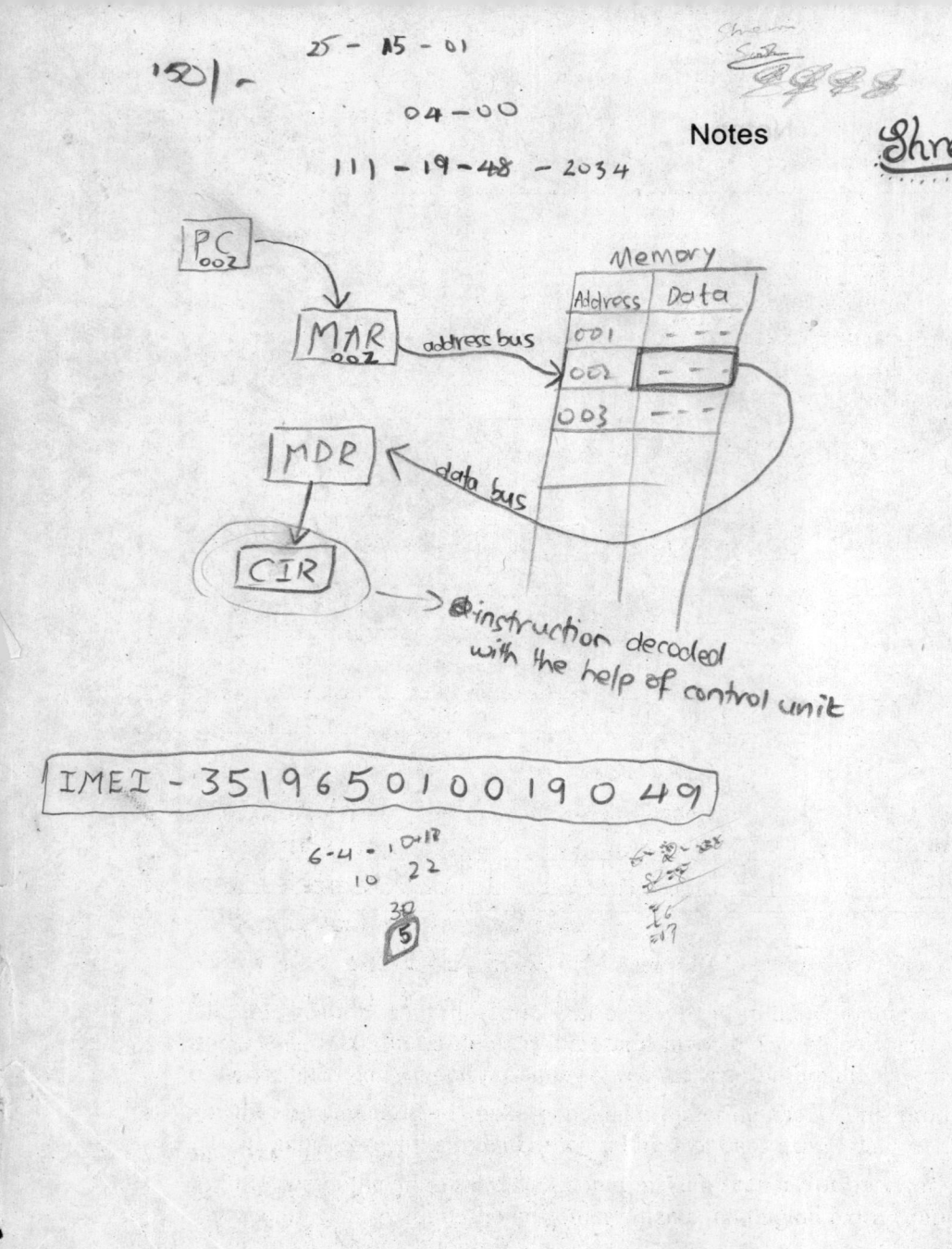

04 - 00

111 - 19 - 48 - 2034

Notes   *Shrevin*

| Object Oriented programs |
| Procedural and declarative languages |

```
PC
002
  ↓
MAR ──address bus──→ Memory
002                  ┌─────────┬──────┐
                     │ Address │ Data │
                     ├─────────┼──────┤
                     │  001    │ ---  │
                     │  002    │ ---  │
                     │  003    │ ---  │
                     └─────────┴──────┘
MDR ←──data bus──────────┘
  ↓
(CIR) → instruction decoded
        with the help of control unit
```

IMEI - 351965010019049

6-4 = 10+8
    10 22
       30
        5